* * *

The Compleat Politician

*Political Strategy
in Massachusetts*

Murray B. Levin

with George Blackwood

* * *

THE **BOBBS-MERRILL** COMPANY, INC.
A SUBSIDIARY OF HOWARD W. SAMS & CO., INC.
Publishers • INDIANAPOLIS • NEW YORK

To

Eight Dear Friends

Davela and Leon

Gladys and Jay

Lenore and Norman

Edith and Richard

Contents

Preface

Strange as it may seem, American political scientists know considerably less about the process by which candidates attempt to win
elections than they do about the political attitudes and behavior of
American voters during campaigns. There has, of course, been
much journalistic writing on the subject, but the ways in which candidates solicit campaign funds, gather public-opinion information,
bring pressures to bear on convention delegates, forge coalitions of
politically influential people, and resolve problems of political strategy have rarely been studied systematically. This book is concerned
largely with candidates, campaign managers, public-relations men,
pollsters, and fund raisers, and their attempts to elect a governor of
Massachusetts in 1960.

During the summer and autumn of 1960, the authors interviewed
the Democratic and Republican gubernatorial candidates or their
advisers in an attempt to discover how they formulated political
strategy for the primary and general election campaigns. Before the
primary and after the general election, the authors interviewed a
random sample of voters to determine the political attitudes of certain groups in the electorate and their reactions to the strategies designed by the politicians. By comparing these two sets of data, we
were able to appraise the accuracy of the candidates' assumptions
concerning public opinion and how it can be shaped.

The reader must regard our conclusions as tentative, for they are based on a study of only two campaigns in a state that has a fairly distinctive political culture. A study of other political campaigns in Massachusetts, or of campaigns in other states, might lead to different conclusions. Nevertheless, we believe that, as a model study, this book deals with representative problems of political campaigning as they are found in America today.

In Chapter 1 we describe and analyze the forces that shape politics in the Bay State, and in Chapter 2 we present the history of the 1960 Massachusetts gubernatorial primary and general election campaigns. This Part was written in collaboration with Professor George Blackwood, of Boston University. The public-opinion data that appear in Chapter 2 were collected and analyzed by Professor Philip Nogee, of Boston University, with the assistance of Miss Muriel Savitz. Professor Nogee was kind enough to read the entire manuscript and suggest several revisions.

The problem of winning the support of cynical and alienated voters who believe that all candidates are corrupt and all platforms mere verbiage is discussed in Chapter 3. The theoretical model for analyzing the behavior of alienated voters was designed in collaboration with Professor Murray Eden, of the Department of Electrical Engineering of the Massachusetts Institute of Technology. The techniques used by candidates to collect public-opinion data are described in Chapter 4. The process by which candidates gather and utilize the resources necessary to wage a successful campaign—money, favorable treatment by the press, and grass-roots organization—is described in Chapter 5. Several critical strategic decisions taken by candidates during the campaign are analyzed in Chapter 6. The morality of campaigners and the problem of "forcing" candidates to inform and educate the electorate during campaigns are discussed in the concluding chapter.

I am very grateful to four scholars—Professor Hubert Gibbs, of Boston University; Professor Robert Wood, of the Massachusetts Institute of Technology; Professor V. O. Key, Jr., and Mr. Richard Onorato, of Harvard University—who were always willing is discuss points of interpretation with me when I needed their aid. The book has, I believe, profited greatly from their sage counsel.

I would also like to thank Mrs. Gladys Topkis and Mr. Richard Onorato for a job of editing so rigorous that I was often compelled to consider intricacies of argument which I had perhaps implied if not consciously intended. My thanks are also due to Miss Alice Cooper, of Smith College, who read and criticized an early draft of this book.

I must mention here my gratitude to Miss Alice Straleau and Mrs. Helena Lothrop, who have typed many revisions of this book in manuscript, patiently deciphering the scrawled corrections with which I spoiled their neatest efforts.

The book could not have been written without the cooperation of the candidates and campaign advisers who graciously consented to be interviewed during the campaign and permitted me to quote from the transcribed interviews. I also wish to thank them for granting access to and permission to quote from their public-opinion polls and post-election analyses. It is our hope that this book will convey to the public some sense of the tremendous physical and emotional burdens that are placed upon those who seek public office in America.

Financial assistance for this research was provided by the Joint Center for Urban Studies of the Massachusetts Institute of Technology and Harvard University, the Citizenship Project of the Massachusetts Institute of Technology, and the Graduate Research Fund of Boston University. I wish to thank these institutions for their generous support.

MURRAY B. LEVIN

Boston, Massachusetts
March 1962

* * *

PART I

The Political History

GEORGE BLACKWOOD
and
MURRAY B. LEVIN

* * *

1.
Politics
in the Bay State

$* \quad * \quad *$

Boston was corrupt. So was Massachusetts. . . . Boston has carried the practice of hypocrisy to the nth degree of refinement, grace and failure. New England is dying of hypocrisy.

LINCOLN STEFFENS, 1931[1]

In his account of the 1960 presidential election, Theodore H. White points out the states of the union that have developed distinctive political patterns based on peculiarities of their historical inheritance. In classifying these patterns he writes:

If one were to choose as a proud grouping those American states whose politics are probably the most decent and worthy of respect, one would group Wisconsin, certainly, with Minnesota, California, and Connecticut. And if one were to choose those states whose politics (excluding the baroque courthouse states of the South) are the most squalid, corrupt and despicable, then one would add West Virginia to that Jukes family of American politics that includes Indiana, Massachusetts and Texas.[2]

White's judgment of Massachusetts politics is not idiosyncratic; it is shared by large numbers of citizens in the Bay State whose disgust

[1] Lincoln Steffens, *The Autobiography of Lincoln Steffens* (New York: Literary Guild, 1931), pp. 605, 607.
[2] Theodore H. White, *The Making of the President 1960* (New York: Atheneum Publishers, 1961), p. 97.

with Massachusetts politics and politicians, particularly with some Democratic politicians, is so great that they elected a Republican as governor in 1960 despite their devotion to John Fitzgerald Kennedy. The victory of the Republican gubernatorial candidate in a year when the Democratic party's nominee for the presidency was a native son, and an extremely popular one, is a remarkable, almost incredible, political fact. This fact, in and of itself, suggests that the politics of Massachusetts has some special, if not unique, historical circumstances.

Although Massachusetts, like many other New England states, had been a stronghold of the Republican party since the Civil War, in the last twenty years the Commonwealth has become a highly competitive two-party state. The number of voters who are not enrolled with any party (1,252,884 as of June 1961) is large enough to offset the advantage that registered Democrats (808,319) have over registered Republicans (657,774). This division of the electorate is one important cause of what is now a tradition of split-ticket voting, which often belies the predictions of the shrewdest professionals and makes the pollsters look quite amateurish. Massachusetts supported a Democratic presidential candidate, Al Smith, for the first time in 1928 and remained in the Democratic column until it favored Dwight Eisenhower in 1952 and again in 1956. Despite their allegiance to Franklin Delano Roosevelt, Harry Truman, and John Fitzgerald Kennedy, the voters of Massachusetts have kept at least one Republican in the United States Senate since 1936. In the thirty years since 1931, the Republicans have controlled the governorship for thirteen years and the lieutenant-governorship for eighteen. The Massachusetts congressional delegation went Democratic for the first time only in 1958, and in that year the Democrats also captured both branches of the state legislature for the first time, despite a gerrymander favoring the Republican party.

Despite the plurality of registered Democrats over Republicans and the fact that the Democrats now control both houses of the state legislature (the Democrats outnumber the Republicans in the Massachusetts House of Representatives 155 to 85 and in the Massachusetts Senate 26 to 14), the party lacks any semblance of centrality, organization, discipline, or loyalty at the grass-roots level. The party is led, if one may use that word, by a number of feudal lords, each of whom has a local following personally loyal to him rather than to the party. One such leader remarked, "We have a Kennedy faction, a McCormack faction, a McLaughlin faction, a Peabody faction, a Ward faction, a Thompson faction, a Furcolo faction . . . and they are always eyeing each other."[3] This feudalization of the Democratic party (the heraldic device of its leadership might be the Hydra rampant) leads, particularly during primary campaigns, to vicious internecine warfare, which often leaves the Democratic nominee at a disadvantage before the Republican in the general election. In comparison to the Democratic party, the Republican party is more or less unified, though the unity is that of a faithful minority, politically listless after years of slow and genteel decay and generally inhibited by principles and prejudices from adopting daring or imaginative ways of profiting maximally from the factionalism and disorder of the Democratic party.

The combined effect of a factionalized "majority" party and an opposition party of little force is that responsible party government in Massachusetts has all but disappeared. Massachusetts is governed not by organized or disciplined political parties but by shifting coalitions of prominent individuals for whom personal loyalties and commitments mean more than party unity and party platforms. A former United States Attorney in Massachusetts, who played a decisive role in the Goldfine case, has written:

The most striking feature of Massachusetts' political scene . . . is the subordination of programs and principles to personal relationships. Friendships and enmities, loyalties and feuds, courtesies and slights have an importance in determining political alignments that is exceeded only by the pocketbook. Amid the welter of personal conflict, the merits of issues are soon submerged.[4]

The pattern of close personal ties between a mass of low-income constituents who desperately need jobs and state legislators who will grant them in exchange for votes is reminiscent of the practice of politics in many American cities and states during the nineteenth century. Indeed, we will argue that Massachusetts politics has its particular characteristics because the Bay State has remained a nineteenth-century commonwealth in many ways. Personal politics

3 *Boston Traveler,* Sept. 11, 1961, p. 20.

4 Elliot Richardson, "Poisoned Politics, The Real Tragedy in Massachusetts," *Atlantic Monthly,* Vol. 208, No. 4 (Oct. 1961), p. 78.

with its corruptive influence is a fundamental fact of Massachusetts politics.

The feudalization of the Democratic party has resulted, in part, from the fact that its support comes from a loosely structured coalition of ethnic and religious groups—a coalition dominated, to be sure, by Irish Catholics. These groups often distrust one another and therefore tend to remain in a state of cultural and geographical isolation, not unlike that in which their grandfathers lived. The Irish, the Italians, the Anglo-Saxons, and the Jews tend, particularly in Boston, to live in distinct sections within the community. Each ethnic group has developed its own sphere of political influence. The greater unity of the Republican party is caused, in part, by the greater cultural homogeneity of its membership (Yankee and Yankee-oriented). Ethnic voting and ethnic hostility are also fundamental facts of Massachusetts politics.

The hostility and separatism caused by ethnicity, a problem within the Democratic party, has more consequential expression in the greater hostility and separatism that characterize relations between non-Yankees and Yankees—immigrant Americans and white Anglo-Saxon Protestants ("WASPS," as they are called by their detractors). This split corresponds roughly to the split between the Democratic and Republican parties. The exploitation and debasement of the immigrants by the Yankees, who still control many of the major financial institutions, manufacturing establishments, public utilities, and large insurance companies in Massachusetts, have left a legacy of fear and mistrust (some would say hatred) which fundamentally conditions Massachusetts politics and which often causes the Democrats to unite and pursue the politics of revenge. The low status of the immigrants and the bleakness of their prospects led the uprooted to seek careers in politics, the Church, sports, or crime, professions which require little capital and which place small premium on quality of birth. Indeed, what appears to be pervasive corruption in Massachusetts public life resulting from the style of personal politics must be understood in terms of the fact that, until recent years, opportunities in the professions and the big businesses were severely limited for immigrants. The signs that appeared so often in the nineteenth century in front of Yankee business establishments ("Irish need not apply") have vanished from the physical scene but not from the minds of many of the sons and grandsons of immigrants. And no newer, lesser minority flattered itself by supposing that only the Irish need not apply. One cannot escape the fact, repugnant though it may be, that ethnic and religious antagonism structures Massachusetts public life today and sets the limits within which political strategy is formulated.

The Uprooted: A Legacy of Economic Exploitation and Separatism

The modern history of politics in Massachusetts begins with the great Irish potato famine of 1845: hunger was the initial cause of the massive immigration of the Irish to the Bay State. By 1855, Boston, with a population of 310,000, had over 50,000 Irishmen, and only 47 per cent of her inhabitants in that year had been born in the United States. The subsequent waves of Irish and other immigrants swelled to such proportions that, by 1860, 61 per cent of the population of Boston was foreign born, as was 54 per cent of Lowell, 72 per cent of Lawrence, and 60 per cent of Fall River.[5] In the 1880's immigrants from Italy, Poland, Germany, Finland, Sweden, Lithuania, and Russia began to follow the Irish. By 1920, more than two thirds of the population of Massachusetts was either foreign born or born of foreign parents. The national average for this group was slightly more than one third.[6] By 1950, "Almost one half of the white population [of Massachusetts] was either foreign born or native born of foreign or mixed parentage."[7] Massachusetts today has the largest proportion of this group of any state in the union, with the possible exception of Rhode Island. The historical image of the Bay State as composed of Old English stock, of Puritans weathered into more worldly yet pious Yankees with Boston as the center of their genteel Brahmin culture, no longer fits the facts.

The saga of the early years in Boston of the Irish and those immi-

[5] See Earl Latham and George Goodwin, *Massachusetts Politics* (Medford, Mass.: Tufts Civic Education Center, 1960), p. 3.

[6] Duane Lockard, *New England State Politics* (Princeton, N. J.: Princeton University Press, 1959), p. 121.

[7] Latham & Goodwin, *op. cit.*, p. 3.

grants who followed them is a tale of horrors. Oscar Handlin, the distinguished historian of Boston's immigrants, points out:

An employed laborer could not earn enough to maintain a family of four. And as long as the head of the Irish household obtained nothing but sporadic employment, his dependents lived in jeopardy of exchanging poverty for starvation. Supplementary earnings—no matter how small—became crucial for subsistence. The sons were first pressed into service, though youngsters had to compete with adults willing to work for boys' wages. To keep the family fed, clothed, and sheltered the women also were recruited. In Ireland they had occupied a clearly defined and important position in the cottiers' economy. That place being gone, they went off to serve at the table of strangers and bring home the bitter bread of banishment.[8]

The Yankees of Boston could and did keep wages low because of the abundance of immigrant labor. In 1850 a typical unskilled worker in Boston—and most of the Irish were unskilled—earned approximately $4.50 to $5.50 per week, as opposed to his New York counterpart, who earned between $8.00 and $10.00 per week.[9] In the 1840's, women who worked an 80-hour week as domestics in the great Yankee homes earned as little as $1.75 per week, of which approximately 75 cents was taken for board.[10] Hemmed in by Yankee control and bigotry, the uprooted were shunted into the most degrading tasks and forced to live in the mudflats of the cities and the great waterfront slums. At the time that John Fitzgerald Kennedy's grandfather came to Boston, it was not uncommon to find five to fifteen persons living in a basement or cellar, often flooded by blocked sewers. One of Kennedy's biographers reports, "One sink might serve a house, one privy a neighborhood. Filth spread through courts and alleys, and with it tuberculosis, cholera, and smallpox, which thrived most in the poorest sections, where the Irish lived."[11]

The immigrant groups which followed the Irish were received in

[8] Oscar Handlin, *Boston's Immigrants: A Study in Acculturation* (Cambridge, Mass.: The Belknap Press of Harvard University Press, 1959), p. 60.

[9] However, average wage rates in Boston compared favorably with those in some other cities on the Eastern seaboard, such as Baltimore and Philadelphia.

[10] Albert B. Hart, ed., *The Commonwealth History of Massachusetts* (New York: States History Co., 1930), Vol. 4, p. 418.

[11] James MacGregor Burns, *John Kennedy, A Political Profile* (New York: Harcourt, Brace and Co., 1959), p. 6.

the same way. As the Irish improved their economic situation and moved to better neighborhoods, the slum vacancies were filled by Italians, Poles, Russians, and finally by Negroes. This process, which is still going on in Boston, can be observed in the poorest Irish and Jewish slum areas, which are now being taken over by Negroes and Puerto Ricans. It is perhaps tragic, but it is true, that the Irish proceeded to discriminate against the new immigrants just as the Yankees had discriminated against them. The experience of discrimination seems to be corrosive everywhere. The "foreign" languages of the new immigrants (some of them non-Irish Catholics) and the "foreign" religion of the Jews and of those who attended the Eastern Christian churches set the new immigrants off from both the Irish and the Yankees. Huthmacher traces this "new" discrimination to the fact that the

... brands of Catholicism imported by French-Canadians, Italians, Poles, and other groups differed in marked respects from the Irish Catholicism that had come to dominate the established Bay State Catholic community and its hierarchy. Appearance, manners, and mores also played a role, for if such considerations made Irishmen appear strange and inferior to old-stock people earlier, they now made New Immigrants seem strange to old-stock and Irish alike. Finally, strong attachments to various mother countries proved a copious source of hostility among the diverse newer nationality groups and served to differentiate them further from the bulk of the population whose nationality ties ran back to the British Empire or the Emerald Isle.[12]

The result of these successive waves of immigration and the consequent circumstances of poverty, fear, and prejudice was the growth of what Handlin refers to as "in-fellow feeling."[13] The ethnic and religious groups, partly as a reaction to discrimination and partly out of a natural desire to maintain the familiar, tended to perpetuate and justify the uniqueness of their cultural, religious, and linguistic inheritance. In the larger cities of Massachusetts, ethnic groups gathered in distinctive neighborhoods within which they could live a "normal" life. "By the beginning of the twentieth century," Huthmacher writes, "political alignment within Massachusetts was primarily a function of the ethnic and social structure. The Republican

[12] Joseph Huthmacher, *Massachusetts People and Politics 1919-1933* (Cambridge, Mass.: The Belknap Press of Harvard University Press, 1959), p. 10.
[13] Handlin, *op. cit.*

party . . . was controlled by the old-stock citizens and consequently
the Irish made the Democratic party the outlet for their growing
political consciousness."[14] The Republican party of Massachusetts
is still overwhelmingly suburban, rural, middle class, and Protestant,
while the Democratic party is predominantly urban, working class,
and Catholic.[15]

The Entry into Politics:
Self-expression and Social Security

In 1885, less than forty years after the great potato famine, Boston
for the first time elected an Irish-born man as mayor. The Irish had
so penetrated the Commonwealth by 1914 that David I. Walsh, an
Irish Catholic candidate and a moderate liberal, acceptable to Irishmen and to some Yankees, was elected as the first Irish Catholic
Democratic governor. In 1918 Walsh became the first Catholic to
represent Massachusetts in the United States Senate. He was re-
elected in 1926. As the Irish and the newer immigrants came to
control the great urban centers (around 1920), a predictable political
pattern emerged, with Democratic Boston opposing the predominantly Republican rural and small-town areas. To be sure, the
Boston Irish needed some support from the other major urban centers, and the rural Republicans had to get perhaps 35 to 40 per cent
of the Boston vote in order to carry the state, but the spheres of
influence were clearly delimited by the 1920's.

In 1928, the candidacy of Al Smith, the first Catholic nominated
for the presidency by the Democratic party, fundamentally altered
political alignments in Massachusetts. In 1920 and 1924, the Democratic presidential candidates received only 28.9 per cent and 28.5
per cent, respectively, of the Massachusetts vote. In 1928, for the
first time in the twentieth century, Massachusetts supported the
Democratic presidential nominee (50.5 per cent of the popular vote).
Significantly larger majorities were given to Franklin D. Roosevelt
and Harry Truman, while John F. Kennedy received a staggering

[14] Huthmacher, op. cit., p. 14.
[15] Duncan MacRae, Jr., "The Relation of Roll Call Votes and Constituencies in
the Massachusetts House of Representatives," American Political Science Review,
Vol. 46, No. 4 (Dec. 1945), p. 1047.

60.2 per cent of the popular vote. Only Dwight D. Eisenhower was able to break the Democratic allegiance of Massachusetts voters. Latham and Goodwin point out that 1928 was a critical year for Massachusetts politics:

The presidential campaign of Alfred E. Smith in 1928 probably laid the basis for the 20 years of uninterrupted Democratic successes in presidential elections which began in 1932. Smith, to be sure, was defeated in 1928, but his candidacy produced a shift in the alignment of parties, bringing out the immigrant and immigrant-derived votes in the great urban areas of the East as no candidacy before had done. Smith's candidacy also introduced class and religious cleavages into national politics that were not to be bridged and overcome until 1952.

The response to his candidacy in Massachusetts was tidal. As the archetype of the successful Irish politician, he symbolized a century of aspiration among the immigrant-derived population of the Massachusetts cities, especially Boston. The outpouring in Massachusetts was massive. Forty per cent more voters than in 1924 came to the polls. The increase in Boston alone was 44 per cent more than it had been in 1924.[16]

In a sense, the Yankees forced the Irish and all the new immigrants into politics and into the Democratic party. Prevented from entering the professions and unable to break the economic hegemony of the Yankees, the immigrants gradually became aware of the fact that politics opened up new opportunities for advancement. Although the immigrants had little or no political experience, they soon learned that politics in a democracy would work in their favor as their numbers grew. Under the tutelage of the precinct captains and ward leaders, they learned that political participation could have immediate advantages for them. The political boss, who had entry to City Hall if he could deliver the vote on election day, acted as a social worker and employment agency for the immigrants. In exchange for votes, the boss could and did supply jobs, food, licenses, and even, perhaps, a bed in the City Hospital. Above and beyond his employment and welfare functions, the boss served as an ethnic leader on whom group loyalty could focus.

Out of these needs and the highly personal network of relationships that was developed in response to them, there emerged in the late nineteenth century a distinctive immigrant attitude toward politics, which is still widespread in Massachusetts and which is in sharp

16 Latham & Goodwin, *op. cit.,* p. 6.

contrast to that held by the Yankee Protestants. Hofstadter has described these two conflicting systems of political ethics as they emerged during the era of the Progressive movement:

. . . Out of the clash between the needs of the immigrants and the sentiments of the natives there emerged two thoroughly different systems of political ethics. . . . One, founded upon the indigenous Yankee-Protestant political traditions, and upon middle-class life, assumed and demanded the constant, disinterested activity of the citizen in public affairs, argued that political life ought to be run, to a greater degree than it was, in accordance with general principles and abstract laws apart from and superior to personal needs, and expressed a common feeling that government should be in good part an effort to moralize the lives of individuals while economic life should be intimately related to the stimulation and development of individual character. The other system, founded upon the European backgrounds of the immigrants, upon their unfamiliarity with independent political action, their familiarity with hierarchy and authority, and upon the urgent needs that so often grew out of their migration, took for granted that the political life of the individual would arise out of family needs, interpreted political and civic relations chiefly in terms of personal obligations, and placed strong personal loyalties above allegiance to abstract codes of law or morals. It was chiefly upon this system of values that the political life of the immigrant, the boss, and the urban machine was based.[17]

One may argue that this description of the Yankee Protestant (Republican) system of political ethics in Massachusetts no longer fits the facts quite so well as it might have fifty years ago, but Hofstadter's description of the "immigrant" view of politics is still more or less accurate as far as many ethnic-group members in Massachusetts are concerned. Many of the Irish, Italian, French, Lithuanian, Jewish, etc. voters who comprise the Democratic party live with the memory of Yankee exploitation and remain lower middle class. Lawrence Fuchs, a student of Irish and Jewish political behavior in Boston, writes that "living conditions for the majority of the Boston Irish can still not be called middle class. In Wards 2, 6, 7, 8, 9, and 10, raggedly dressed children still play between wooden tenement buildings rotting with age and ill care."[18]

[17] Richard Hofstadter, *The Age of Reform* (New York: Alfred A. Knopf, 1955), pp. 8-9.
[18] Lawrence Fuchs, "Presidential Politics in Boston, The Irish Response to Stevenson," *New England Quarterly*, Vol. 30 (Dec. 1957), p. 439.

The constituents of these wards remain loyal to the local leader, not to that abstraction, the Democratic party. They need state jobs, bathhouses, business licenses, tax abatements, street lights, etc. In other words, they need personal contacts with politicians who can satisfy their needs. Many years ago, Martin Lomasny, one of the most powerful ward bosses in Boston, expressed his practical political philosophy unequivocally: "I think there's got to be in every ward a guy that any bloke can go to when he's in trouble and get help—not justice and the law, but help, no matter what's to be done." The immigrants agreed with him, and many of their children and grandchildren continue to do so.[19] The re-election to federal, state, and local office of several men who have served time in jail may be explained by the fact that they have personally taken care of the needs of hundreds, if not thousands, of constituents. James Michael Curley, who went to jail (not for the first time) during his term as mayor, is a case in point. A large segment of his supporters held the view that "He may steal from the rich, but he helps the poor and he gets things done."[20] A distinguished student of Massachusetts government, Robert C. Wood, has said of the Democratic party in Boston, "The 'in' group in politics here is still playing nineteenth-century politics. The problem is to divide the spoils, not how to manage society."[21] Fragmented parties, led by figures prominent locally in ethnic groups and concerned with spoils, are a product of the circumstances of cultural and geographical isolation from which lower-income ethnic-group members were forced into active politics. Their urgent needs and the willingness of self-interested public officials to

[19] William Shannon vividly describes this kind of relationship. Referring to a prominent state legislator, he writes:

"Outside his Statehouse office are two long benches always crowded with job seekers. In the Senate Reading Room, adjoining his office, he interviews two hundred applicants a day. Three secretaries handle the crowd as well as answer the hundreds of letters he receives. Usually when ———— goes down to breakfast in the morning, there are five or six people waiting for him in his living room. When he goes home in the evening, there are sixty to seventy more waiting for him.

" 'The number has been steadily increasing,' [he] says. 'They're all able people looking for jobs. I try to get them employment in private industry. There's just no State work, and most of what there is comes under Civil Service. I served in office during the WPA days and that was always a source of employment. Now we have to try outside' " (William V. Shannon, "Massachusetts, Prisoner of the Past," in Robert S. Allen, ed., *Our Sovereign State* [New York: Vanguard Press, 1949], p. 51).

[20] Quoted by Jerome S. Bruner and Sheldon Korchin, "The Boss and the Vote," *Public Opinion Quarterly*, Vol. 10, No. 1 (Spring 1946), pp. 18-21.

[21] Quoted in the *New York Times*, June 17, 1961, p. 1.

profit inordinately by serving them on a personal basis are characteristic of the political game as it was played in the nineteenth
century.

Liberalism in Moderation:
The "Al Smith Democrat"

Most immigrants in the nineteenth century were politically conservative. Many of their descendants in Massachusetts remain so today.
This accounts in part for the fact that the Democratic party in Massachusetts is far less liberal than its national counterpart, although
the New Frontier is led by Massachusetts' own native son. Referring
to the antipathetic attitude of the uprooted toward the Progressives
of the early twentieth century, Handlin writes:

. . . It was significant that the mass of immigrants should regard the
efforts of the various progressives with marked disfavor. In part this dis-
approval was based on the peasant's inherited distrust of radicalism but
it was strengthened by a lack of understanding among the radicals that
deprived them of all influence among the newcomers.

In the case of the Italians and other central Europeans, the revolutions
of the mid-nineteenth century had added fear of the pillaging reds to the
traditional suspicion of revolutionaries. All these old misgivings crossed
the ocean to the New World. Conservative enough at home, the peasants
had become more conservative still in the course of migration. They
dreaded political change because that might loosen the whole social order,
disrupt the family, pull God from His throne; the radicals themselves
talked that way and confirmed the worst such suspicions. Naturally the
influence of the churches on both sides of the Atlantic was thrown in
the balance on the side of stability and confirmed the unwillingness of the
immigrants to be involved in any insurgent movements.[22]

The platforms of the reformers (e.g., women's rights, temperance,
Sabbatarianism) and the Progressive attack on bosses and machines
were never very popular with the immigrants.

During the nineteenth century, a dichotomy existed between the
views of the Boston radicals, whose assumptions were "rational,"
progressive, and optimistic, and those of the immigrants, whose

[22] Oscar Handlin, *The Uprooted* (New York: Grosset and Dunlap, 1951), p. 217.

religion and historical experience had accustomed them to a conservative acceptance of the *status quo* and a pessimistic position on the possibility of changing the world.[23] Professor Handlin writes:

The mental set of tenement or seminary scarcely harmonized with the rational Bostonian's concept of reform as an infallible guide along the straight path of progress to ultimate perfectability. Indeed, the Irish were completely alien to the idea of progress and necessarily antagonistic to "the spirit of the age." Reform was a delusion inflating men's sense of importance, distorting the relative significance of earthly values, and obscuring the true goals of their endeavor—salvation of the *eternal* soul. Such movements were suspect because they exaggerated the province of reason, exalting it above faith, futile because they relied upon temporal rather than spiritual agencies, and dangerous because they undermined respect for established institutions.

The failure of the Irish to comprehend fully the democratic feeling basic to reform intensified their hostility. Generations of enforced obedience bred a deep respect for class distinctions. Irishmen could scarcely have a firm appreciation of the equality of man when their very school books taught them

Q. If the poor will not try to be good, what will follow?
A. That the rich will not help them.[24]

The Boston Irish opposed the spread of abolitionism,[25] while the Catholic press attacked the European revolutions of 1848. Catholic newspapers reminded their readers that

. . . Good Catholics must accept . . . the constitution of the State, when once established, whatever its form, [and] have no right to conspire to change the constitution, or to effect a revolution in the State. Consequently . . . our sympathies can never be with those who conspire against the law, or with the mad revolutionists and radicals, on the Continent of Europe, who are unsettling everything.[26]

The basically conservative ideology of the nineteenth-century immigrant, a consequence of his European peasant life, has its counterpart in the ideology of the so-called Al Smith Democrat, who has dominated the party in Massachusetts since the 1920's. The election of 1928, as we have pointed out, fundamentally altered political

[23] A few Irish leaders, however, notably John Boyle O'Reilly; were sympathetic toward the Boston radicals.
[24] Handlin, *Boston's Immigrants, op. cit.,* pp. 130-31.
[25] *Ibid.,* p. 132.
[26] *Boston Catholic Observer,* Dec. 6, 1848. Cited by Handlin, *ibid.,* pp. 139-40.

alignments in the Commonwealth. The "Al Smith Democrats" who elected Walsh in 1918 and 1926 and who carried Massachusetts for Smith in 1928 were not really liberals in the sense in which that term is used to describe New Dealers, and their descendants are not liberals today. Like his namesake, the Al Smith Democrat strongly identifies with the underdog. Unlike the "liberal," however, he sees himself as the underdog, even when he is victorious. Unlike the New Dealer and the New Frontiersman, he is profoundly suspicious of governmental power, except when it is used on behalf of the underdog and for very limited purposes. The Al Smith Democrat has very little ideological orientation of the traditional liberal sort, particularly when it relates to the planned use of governmental power for long-range goals. He must be persuaded first that planning will result in some immediate benefits to working men. Relying on personal and feudal politics, he finds that the abstract, impersonal concepts of a New Deal and a New Frontier (with their concern for the whole domestic and world scene) loom as somewhat vague and possibly inimical ideas, unless some local ethnic leader gives them local meaning. There is, finally, a peculiar dualism that characterizes much of the thinking of the Al Smith Democrat. Although he emphasizes "Americanism," he continues to stress the uniqueness of his cultural traditions and tends to remain separate. A sense of distinctiveness from both the traditional American brand of conservatism and traditional liberalism makes the Al Smith Democrat a unique political type. He is a Democrat without really being a Democrat. His ideas are often pre-New Deal and sometimes anti-New Deal.

Although he considers himself a member of the Democratic party, the Al Smith Democrat in Boston repudiated Stevenson in 1952 and 1956. He feels, Fuchs writes, "that the national Democratic leadership betrayed America either through communist sympathies or by letting the British ally fool us. The stress which the Republican orators gave to Yalta-type issues and the prominence of Senator Joseph McCarthy's crusade against twenty years of treason . . . helped to reinforce Irish suspicions."[27]

We have stressed the ethnic and religious complexion of Massachusetts because it is the fundamental factor that shapes politics in

[27] Fuchs, op. cit., p. 441.

the Bay State. Political leaders know this and attempt to exploit it, either by balancing state tickets or by giving the ethnic groups careful consideration when making appointments. The ethnic base of the parties reflects the fact that, as of 1960, approximately 32 per cent of the residents of Massachusetts are of Irish origin, 20 per cent of old-stock (Yankee) origin, and 9 per cent of Italian origin. Groups whose origins are Polish, French Canadian, and non-French Canadian each comprise approximately 3 per cent of the population, while Jews, primarily of Russian and Lithuanian descent, make up about 5 per cent.[28] The close link between ethnic divisions and politics is illustrated by Table 1, which shows the national origin of members of the state legislature in 1959.

TABLE 1
Ethnic Composition of the Great and General Court,
by Parties (1959)*

Republican		Democratic	
Old-stock Yankee	86	Irish	109
Irish	5	Italian	22
Swedish	4	Polish	9
Italian	3	French	7
German	2	Portuguese	6
Polish	2	Negro	2
French	2	Lebanese	1
Armenian	1	Lithuanian	1
Greek	1	Armenian	1
Unclassified	5	Unclassified	11
	111		169

* From *Public Officers of the Commonwealth of Massachusetts, 1959-1960*, compiled by Irving N. Hayden, Clerk of the Senate, and Lawrence R. Grove, Clerk of the House (Boston, 1959). Newspaper accounts of candidates were also used as a source.

The feudalization of the Democratic party, we have suggested, is a reflection of the ethnic diversity of its membership. The relative solidarity of the Republican party reflects the homogeneity of its constituents and the prestige of its Brahmin candidates. It is obvious that

28 See p. 31. The remainder of the population is of indeterminate background. Negroes comprise 2 per cent of the state's population.

a serious defection of Italo-American or Jewish voters from the Democratic party (certainly a possibility, given their opposition to an "all green" Democratic ticket, provided that these groups were represented on the Republican ticket) could swing the balance of power to the Republicans. This, we shall argue, accounts in part for John Volpe's gubernatorial victory in 1960.

We have emphasized the fact that many ethnic-group members, particularly the Irish, are at most moderate liberals and truly conservative on some issues. This, we shall see, is reflected in the politics of Democratic legislators, although many of them tend to be more "New Deal" than their constituents. This bizarre configuration of ethnic loyalties and pseudo-liberal attitudes, which developed out of quite unique historical circumstances, has structured the political behavior of the Irish, other ethnic-group members, and, in general, the Democratic party in Massachusetts. The identification with the underdog, which is still part of the Irish psychology despite a change in the circumstances of many citizens of Irish origin, has led to an aggressive political rhetoric with a strong revenge motif. The suspicion of governmental power and the acceptance of personal rather than party government make the Irish only nominal supporters of the party to which their numbers contribute so heavily. It is interesting to note that President Kennedy had to transcend this parochialism before emerging as a national leader of the party, but it is questionable, certainly, whether his success in his home state had much to do with his platform.

Religion and Politics

Some citizens of Massachusetts, particularly non-Catholics, firmly believe that His Eminence Richard Cardinal Cushing, Roman Catholic Archbishop of Boston, is the most powerful social and political figure in the Commonwealth, except for John Fitzgerald Kennedy. This belief does not take into account certain facts evident to those familiar with Massachusetts politics. The Cardinal and other Catholic leaders evince a strong interest in only a limited range of issues. Cardinal Cushing, like his predecessor, Cardinal O'Connell, usually speaks of political matters in vague generalizations and frequently remains silent on the most controversial issues. The Cardinal takes a strong position only on matters that openly and directly affect the Church. Moreover, there is in Massachusetts an undercurrent of resentment among some politicians against "men of the cloth" who involve themselves in political issues. A few state legislators have been known to assert privately that the clergy are naïve about politics and government and, realizing this fact, do not attempt to exert much political influence. The only basis for the belief in the power of the Cardinal and other members of the Catholic hierarchy is the fact that roughly half of the residents of Massachusetts are Roman Catholics. The *Roman Catholic Official Directory* for 1960 states that there are 2,560,493 Catholics in Massachusetts (49.7% of the population).

Although half of the population is Catholic, roughly one quarter is Protestant or affiliated with Protestantism. As of November 18, 1960, there were 553,505 members of churches affiliated with the Massachusetts Council of Churches.[29] This is about 18 per cent of the adult population; however, there are numerous Protestant churches, mostly small ones, which are not members of the Council. If one takes account of these and includes a segment of the citizenry who have Protestant backgrounds but who are not church members, the percentage may run as high as one third of the total population. The remaining constituents of the population are either unchurched, Jewish, or of other persuasions (such as Greek or Armenian Orthodox).

Estimates of the Jewish population vary widely. The *American Jewish Year Book* for 1960 counts 222,000 Jews in Massachusetts, or 4.58 per cent of the state population. Of this number, 150,000 reside in Boston. These figures are too conservative, however, since such communities as Newton, Natick, Sharon, and Brookline, which have significant Jewish populations, are (unaccountably) omitted from the compilation. According to a more realistic estimate, there are 270,000 to 300,000 Jews in Massachusetts, perhaps 5 to 6 per cent of the state population.[30]

The religious composition of the state, like the ethnic, contributes

[29] Information obtained from Rev. Eugene Carper, Director of Research and Statistics for the Massachusetts Council of Churches.

[30] See Albert S. Gordon, *Jews in Suburbia* (Boston: Beacon Press, 1959), pp. 248-49.

to the peculiar character of Massachusetts politics. In those matters in which the churches are interested, they are indeed a formidable force; but the fairest judgment is that they take a special interest in a quite limited number of matters. This is true of the churches as *organizations;* but the effect of religion on political life in Massachusetts depends on the religious backgrounds of *individuals,* which means that shared personal preferences or prejudices can have force quite apart from any official church position. The very fact that in some areas there is a heavy predominance of Catholics, and in others a smaller majority of Protestants or Jews, shapes the thinking and voting of the people in those areas. For example, in many of the wards of Boston and other cities in Massachusetts, elections for such offices as state senator and state representative are decided in Democratic primaries; comparisons of ethnic and religious distribution and election results in particular wards indicate that in most of these elections the strongly Irish areas return Irish Catholics, Jewish wards elect Jews, and Italian districts return Italians. A fair number of legislators build their local reputation by demonstrating administrative ability in the Knights of Columbus, the Holy Name Society, or the Sons of Italy. Voting for one's "own kind" is a major aspect of political behavior in Massachusetts, particularly on the local level.

As in the case of ethnicity, the religious composition of the Great and General Court reflects the religious division of the population. Table 2, which shows the religious affiliation of state legislators in 1959, illustrates this point.

TABLE 2
Religious Composition of the Great and General Court,
by Parties (1959)*

Republican		Democratic	
Protestant	58	Catholic	134
Catholic	11	Jewish	9
Jewish	2	Unclassified	26†
Unclassified	40		169
	111		

* Compiled from *Public Officers of the Commonwealth, op. cit.,* and newspaper accounts about some of the members of the General Court.
† Two members of this group may be affiliated with Protestant churches.

The Democratic party is overwhelmingly Catholic; the Republican party is predominantly Protestant.[31] It should be noted that John A. Volpe is the first Catholic Republican to be elected governor of Massachusetts. During the last forty years, especially in the 1950's, Republican leaders have attempted to develop tickets balanced not only ethnically but religiously. The sudden death of George Fingold (the first Jew to be nominated for statewide office by the Republicans) on the eve of the 1958 primary was a severe blow to the Republicans, who hoped that his candidacy would attract Jews and other minority elements to the party. Given the prevalence of voting along ethnic and religious lines in Massachusetts, it makes political sense for the Republican party to nominate some Catholic candidates.

The impact of particular religious factors on political issues is substantial at times. When attempts were made in 1942 and 1948 to repeal or amend the 1879 law forbidding the dissemination of birth-control information, the Catholic hierarchy was the major defender of the law. In 1942, the law was upheld by 58 per cent of the voters; in 1948, by 57 per cent. There is also little doubt that the opposition of the late Cardinal O'Connell and of Cardinal Cushing has played a major role in the refusal of the General Court to institute a state lottery, although the Protestant clergy have also vehemently attacked the lottery proposal. Cardinal O'Connell single-handedly defeated one lottery bill overnight, by granting a newspaper interview in which he attacked the proposal as "an out-and-out gambling machine" and "a source of corruption."[32] When the House reconvened the next morning, 68 legislators switched their vote and the bill was defeated. Such outspoken protests by church leaders are unusual. The Massachusetts Council of Churches (Protestant) has shown its influence by successfully opposing the legitimization of "games of chance" and the repeal of laws forbidding certain activities on Sundays (the so-called Blue Laws). If the churches were to espouse different positions, this could conceivably coincide with Republican-

[31] Professor George Goodwin, of the University of Massachusetts, has shown that the correlation of religious affiliation and party identification is high for students attending the state university. See George Goodwin, Jr., "The Last Hurrahs: George Apley and Frank Skeffington," *Massachusetts Review*, Vol. 1 (Spring 1960), pp. 467-68. This is also true of students at Boston University. See Philip Nogee and Murray B. Levin, "Some Determinants of Political Attitudes Among College Voters," *Public Opinion Quarterly*, Vol. 22, No. 4 (Winter 1958-59), p. 462.

[32] Lockard, *op. cit.*, p. 164.

Democratic differences on issues, but they are more likely to act individually or jointly to restrain excessive worldliness in legislation.

The Geography of Massachusetts Politics: Boston and "Outstate"

Boston is the largest state capital in the country, a fact that has implications for Massachusetts politics that sometimes pass unnoticed. Plagued by enormous problems of urban renewal and mass transportation, faced with a declining population and a shrinking tax base, Boston has distinctive social and political features that divide her from the rest of the state. The tension between the Hub and "outstate" is of long standing and relates to more than party differences, for the non-Boston Democrats, who have developed a quarrel of their own with Boston, have been unwilling to help.

For all practical purposes, Boston has been restrained firmly by the state legislature for many years. "Home rule" does not exist. The legislature requires the city to shoulder a large portion of the deficit of the Metropolitan Transit Authority and to pay the entire cost of administering the county in which Boston is located. The hapless position of the city is in part the result of the strong hold of the past upon the present. After the first Irish mayor of Boston was elected in 1885, the state legislature, fearing "infiltration" of the Boston police by the Irish, took the power to appoint the city police commissioner away from the mayor and gave it to the governor. This power remained with the governor until 1962, when it was given to the mayor once again. Meanwhile the legislature, dominated by Republicans (until recent years), sought other measures to check the Democrats who controlled Boston, many of whom were stereotyped as crooked.[33] The conflict deepened as the ethnic divisions in the state became more prominent. As the years passed and Boston's difficulties grew, the legislature did little to alleviate the city's problems.

At the same time, a rift developed between Boston Democrats and "outstate" Democrats. As Democrats ousted Republicans in various areas of the state, the Boston Democrats expected more sympathy

[33] Murray B. Levin, *The Alienated Voter: Politics in Boston* (New York: Holt, Rinehart and Winston, 1960), Chap. 4.

in the General Court; however, the "outstaters," resenting what they regarded as the domination of the party by Boston Democrats, did not supply it. Mutual suspicion deepened. The result has been a hidden struggle for control, a struggle which Lockard feels is so profound that "In truth, the Democratic party seems to be two parties— a Boston party and a western Massachusetts party."[34] The friction between "the parties" is based in part on the belief of many outstaters that the Boston Democrats are stained with corruption and have generally low political standards.

V. O. Key, Jr., has shown that, while the split of the Democratic vote between the Boston area and the rest of the state has "remained fairly constant," the candidates on the state ticket have tended to come more and more from Boston and its suburbs. This fact, he feels, is closely related to Boston dominance in party primaries.[35] A Democratic candidate who is very popular in Boston can often win a plurality that is large enough to ensure his nomination. Since the adoption of a pre-primary-convention law in 1954, the situation has changed slightly. The law was passed partly because outstate Democrats objected to Boston's control of places on the party slate. It is notable that none of the candidates for governor from 1954 to 1960—Furcolo, Murphy, and Ward—was from the city. The pre-primary convention, however, did not shake the hold of Boston Democrats on nominations for minor offices. During the four elections from 1954 through 1960, 16 of the 27 candidates were from Boston or Chelsea (a nearby city). Thus, Boston candidates continued to dominate the state ticket, although not so strongly as before. In fact, in the 1960 convention, although the men endorsed for the offices of governor and United States senator were outstaters, the other five nominees were all from the Hub. The fact that many citizens tend to stereotype the Boston politician as corrupt may seriously hamper the efforts of the state organization to win general elections.

The Pre-primary Convention

Underrepresented on the state ticket because of the geographic and ethnic factors inherent in Massachusetts politics, non-Irish and out-

[34] Lockard, *op. cit.,* pp. 125-26.
[35] V. O. Key, Jr., *American State Politics: An Introduction* (New York: Alfred A. Knopf, 1956), pp. 154-57.

state Democrats complained about the "all green" slates of the 1920's and 1930's. In the early 1930's, the chairmen of both parties endorsed a bill setting up pre-primary nominating conventions, claiming that such conventions would serve as a "guide to the voters in the nominating primary and . . . would give the stamp of party regularity to the candidates so designated."[36] The law was passed in 1932, and candidates were endorsed by conventions in 1934 and 1936. Delegates to these conventions were selected by town and city committees in proportion to local population.

The Democratic convention of 1934 endorsed a Yankee Protestant, General Charles H. Cole, for governor and an Italo-American for secretary of state on an otherwise Irish ticket, while the Republicans included on their predominantly Yankee slate a French-American candidate for state treasurer. In a hard-fought primary, James M. Curley defeated Cole to win the Democratic nomination. The Italo-American Democrat and the French-American Republican survived their primaries, but both were defeated in the general election. The experience of 1936 was comparable; many of the convention endorsees were challenged in the primary. That year there were rumors of votes bought on a wholesale basis, and the legislature repealed the law in 1937. By the late 1940's, there was again a good deal of unrest in the parties, the Yankee blue and the Irish green tending to dominate the respective tickets. After some bitter primary fights in 1950, the GOP decided to propose the restoration of the pre-primary convention. With the aid of Democratic ethnic groups who stood to gain (Italians primarily), the bill passed the legislature in 1951, only to be vetoed by the Irish Democratic governor. In 1953, the same coalition was formed again, and this time Republican Governor Christian A. Herter signed the bill into law. Since 1954 both parties have held pre-primary conventions.

In addition to providing "guidance" to voters and increasing the probability of balanced slates, pre-primary conventions are meant to serve two other purposes: to write platforms, and to activate ward and town committees. Little attention, however, is paid to the platforms; one critical newsman observed that the Democratic documents present "forthright, imaginative, socially conscious and specific programs" that are not carried out, while the Republicans "can't

[36] Michael E. Hennessy, *Four Decades of Massachusetts Politics* (Norwood, Mass.: Norwood Press, 1935), p. 505.

seem to muster up enough ideas or thought to deliver a sermon."[37]

The real object of the convention, other than the nomination of candidates, is to activate the "grass roots" organization (the ward and city committees). Under Massachusetts law, these committees are the official agencies of the parties, although they were largely inactive or nonexistent when the law was passed. One political columnist estimated that not more than 10 per cent of the ward and town committees had more than a shadowy existence in either party.[38] Although in theory they were supposed to carry on the campaign on the local level, in fact they failed to do so. Almost immediately after the law setting up conventions was enacted, many local politicians who had ignored the committees previously became active in order to become delegates to the convention.

The law was carefully constructed so that only those who are most interested in politics vote in the elections for town and ward committees. The election is held at the time of the presidential-preference primary every four years. At this primary the voters write in their choice for the next president of the United States and vote for their selections for delegates to the national party conventions and members of the state party committees. In most cases, there are no real contests over delegates to the national convention; the state committee chairmen, in consultation with party leaders, set up lists of delegates, and they are usually elected without opposition. Voter interest in this particular primary, however, is incredibly low; only hard-core "regulars" in both parties, who are interested in seeing that the "right people" are elected to town and ward committees, remember to appear at the polls. In 1956 and 1960, only 7 or 8 per cent of the electorate voted in these elections.

The control of these elections by the regulars is extremely significant. For all intents and purposes, the bulk of the party membership (Schattschneider calls them "innocent bystanders")[39] has abdicated control over convention delegates, leaving it to the regulars, who have, therefore, far more power in party affairs than their numbers warrant. Massachusetts is not unique in this respect. The control of the state party by the professionals and a small core of activists

[37] A. A. Michelson, "The Image of the Governor: One Man's View," Tufts Assembly on Massachusetts State Government (working paper), April 1961.

[38] W. T. Mullins, *Boston Herald,* March 11, 1953, p. 8.

[39] E. E. Schattschneider, *Party Government* (New York: Farrar and Rinehart, Inc., 1942).

results in a peculiar form of inbreeding that has created a distinct political class whose private will is ultimately translated into public law. This political class is quite free to pursue its own purposes because it knows that the electorate, with rare exceptions, is apathetic and can be counted on to do nothing. This makes for irresponsible political parties; it is the electorate's contribution.

Democrats and Republicans:
The Atrophy of Party Organization

As we have mentioned, the ethnic, religious, and geographical factors in Massachusetts politics account, in part, for the feudalization of the Democratic party and the moderate liberalism (and at times conservatism) of its supporters. The ecological basis of Massachusetts politics also accounts, in part, for the relatively greater stability and centralization of the minority Republican party. The feudalization of the Democratic party is also a result of the ideological divergence of the several blocs that compose the party. Setting aside President Kennedy and the peculiar blend of Harvard, New Deal, and "lace-curtain Irish" heritage he represents, the Democratic party of Massachusetts is split into five major groups, whose political ideologies vary widely. They are:

1. A small group of ardent New Dealers who wish to expand state services in the fields of education, mental health, and public welfare, and who recognize that these programs require increased taxation. The New Dealers' leadership is drawn from a small but articulate community of intellectuals, professional men, and a very few labor leaders. Their strength is limited by the fact that many who share their views (people associated with universities, a fair number of the skilled engineers and technical personnel in such industries as electronics, and a group of small businessmen) vote Republican on the state level and Democratic on the national level.

2. A small group of moderate liberals who favor expansion of state services and vigorously defend civil rights. They hesitate, however, to endorse significant tax increases, preferring moderate gains in public services commensurate with the expansion of the economy.

3. A larger group of "job-conscious" Democrats. Although

vaguely committed to the goals laid down in the party platform, this group is interested in government chiefly as a source of income or prestige for themselves or their friends. Its members tend to think in terms of jobs, low-number license plates, and other favors of various kinds. Their activities are not necessarily corrupt (patronage and corruption may be distinct). The bulk of these job-conscious Democrats are lawyers or insurance men who use political influence to make business contacts and secure positions on the state payroll. A few regard politics as an opportunity to work with and for people they like, regardless of political issues.

4. A very large group of "Al Smith Democrats," who form the broad base of the party. These Democrats are essentially what James MacGregor Burns calls "bread-and-butter liberals"; that is, they are concerned with immediate economic gains for the working class. John Fitzgerald Kennedy was one for much of his congressional career.[40] The Al Smith Democrats often believe that the national party is too "leftish." Many of them deserted Adlai Stevenson in 1952 and 1956[41] and were not unfavorably disposed to Senator Joseph McCarthy. They also look with disfavor on the "internationalism" of the party and its "friendly" relations with Great Britain.[42] They usually oppose increased taxation on the state level, unless party leaders can demonstrate some urgent need.

5. A small group of strongly conservative Democrats who identify with the party simply by the historical accident of birth, rather than by ideological conviction. Their views on governmental matters are dramatically similar to those of the conservative segments of the Republican state party.

In contrast to the Democratic party, conflicts among the Republicans tend to center on problems of political strategy rather than political philosophy. The Bay State Republicans are a microcosm of the national party. That is, they fall into three categories, exemplified by such national figures as Nelson Rockefeller, Richard Nixon, and Barry Goldwater, as follows:

1. A small group of liberals who look to Rockefeller as their national leader. They are represented by a few outspoken and articulate leaders in the state legislature who argue that if the party is to

[40] Burns, *op. cit.*, Chap. 5.
[41] Fuchs, *op. cit.*, p. 1.
[42] *Ibid.*

regain its strength it should be friendly to labor, advocate the expansion of some important state services, and stoutly champion civil liberties. This group is strongly opposed by the "Old Guard."

2. A very large group, the party core, that accepts the moderate conservatism typified by President Eisenhower but whose state heroes are such "blue bloods" as Saltonstall, Lodge, and Herter. This group accepts Nixon, respects Rockefeller, and is somewhat dubious about Goldwater. Although its members venerate prestigious Brahmins, the leading Republicans in the state legislature and most of the "working politicians" in the party are what are called "swamp Yankees"—that is, white Anglo-Saxon Protestants who have money or professional prestige but not "blue blood." The party core consists largely of middle-class Protestant suburbanites who are cautious about spending but who nevertheless believe that some of the programs suggested by liberal Republicans warrant investigation and possibly endorsement (if they do not result in heavier taxes).

3. A small group of ultra-conservatives who find Goldwater's views congenial and who stress the need for a very distinctive stand in opposition to the Democrats, especially on economy in government. They favor minimal governmental "interference" and a "return" to the "virtues" of laissez faire, thrift, and individual initiative.

There are, in addition to these ideologically distinctive groups, a number of ethnic-oriented revisionists within the GOP (equivalent to the "job-conscious" and "Al Smith Democrats") who are more concerned with the "image" of the party than with its policy. The ethnic-oriented Republicans argue that the party must broaden its ethnic and religious base by endorsing some candidates who are not Protestant and Anglo-Saxon. This group supported George Fingold and promoted the candidacy of John Volpe for the governorship in 1960. Ethnic-oriented Republicans can be found in all the major groups within the party. Unlike the Democrats, who resolve their group differences, often noisily, in public during primary campaigns, the Republicans manage to "harmonize" their differences within the party caucus and are thus able to present a "united" front to the voters.

Before analyzing the manner in which the parties operate in the state legislature, it is necessary to examine in greater detail the feudalization of the Democratic organization and the relative unity of the Republican organization.

In his distinguished work *American State Politics,* V. O. Key, Jr., notes, "Over a period of a half century party organizations have seriously deteriorated. Their decay has been associated with the rise of the direct primary system of nomination."[43] The fact that the Democratic party organization in Massachusetts has disintegrated more than its Republican counterpart although both must operate with the same pre-primary convention system suggests that factors other than the direct primary contribute to the atrophy of party organization. We can appraise the viability of a party organization on the basis of three criteria: (1) its ability to prevent primary fights, (2) its ability to control finances and patronage, and (3) its ability to develop a working base at the grass-roots level.

TABLE 3

Number of Candidates in Primary Contests for Statewide
Offices, by Parties (1950-60)*

Office	DEMOCRATS						REPUBLICANS					
	1950	1952	1954	1956	1958	1960	1950	1952	1954	1956	1958	1960
Governor	1†	1†	2	2	1†	7	6	1	1†	1	3	1
Lt. Governor	5†	6†	1	3	1†	2	5	1	1†	1	1	1
Sec. of State	8†	1†	1†	2†	1†	3	7	1	1	1	1	1
Treasurer	1†	7†	3	5†	2†	6	2	2	1	1	1	2
Auditor	1†	1†	1†	1†	1†	2†	2	1	1	1	1	1
Attorney General	4†	4†	1	2	2	1†	5	1	1†	1†	1	1
U. S. Senator	—	1	3	—	—	3	—	1†	1†	—	—	1†

* Duane Lockard compiled this table for the years 1950-56. The authors "completed" the table for the period 1958-60. We wish to thank Mr. Lockard and his publishers, the Princeton University Press, for their kind permission to reproduce this table from Lockard, *New England Politics* (Princeton, N. J.: Princeton University Press, 1959), p. 133.
† Indicates races in which incumbents were involved.

A party organization that is highly centralized and disciplined should be able to prevent, or at least minimize, challenges to convention endorsees during the primaries. The Republicans have been far more successful than the Democrats in protecting their endorsees from such challenges. Table 3 shows the number of candidates in the Republican and Democratic primaries who competed for statewide offices from 1950 to 1960.

43 Key, *op. cit.,* p. 267.

Since 1950, 100 Democrats have competed for their party's nominations while only 64 Republicans have competed for Republican nominations. The Democratic organization often has been unable to force the various party leaders to accept the decision of the convention. Since 1952, when the Republican party resorted to the pre-primary convention, only two Republicans have opposed the endorsee.[44] Since 1954, when the Democratic party endorsed candidates in pre-primary conventions, 33 individuals have opposed endorsees.

One of the reasons that the Democratic party has had so much difficulty in preventing challenges to the convention endorsee is that many endorsed candidates have very common Irish names. In several instances, individuals who happened to have the same last name (and sometimes the same first name and middle initial) as an endorsee have been tempted to run, and have in fact run, on the theory that massive confusion of the voters might result in their election. The classic case of what is commonly known in Massachusetts as "the name's the same" is that of one John Francis Kennedy, who ran against the Democratic party endorsee for state treasurer in 1952, 1956, and 1958, winning each time. In the 1960 gubernatorial contest, Kennedy ran against the convention endorsee, Joseph Ward, who remarked, when estimating Kennedy's chances, "He has a magic name, and believe me, a name in politics is like Ivory Soap in business, or like Coca Cola. Once the American people have accepted it, it is pretty difficult to have them accept something else." One of Ward's advisers who was worried by Kennedy's "appeal" stated to the authors:

It's tough enough for them [the voters] to find out who the candidates for governor and president and senator may be, and so at that level the name becomes terribly important, just the familiarity of the name, the reaction to the name. It doesn't even have to be "Kennedy."

V. O. Key, Jr., has compiled "the saga of the Hurleys in Massachusetts," which illustrates the tribulations of the Democratic party leaders and "the name's the same":

In 1930 Francis X. Hurley won the Democratic nomination for auditor and Charles F. Hurley won the Democratic nomination for treasurer.

[44] The 1958 Republican gubernatorial primary is a special situation. George Fingold, the convention endorsee, died before election day, and "stickers" for two candidates were placed on the ballot.

Both went on to victory and in 1932 were renominated and re-elected. Four years of publicity for the Hurley name gave it a political potency. In 1934, as Charles F. Hurley, unsuccessful in his bid for convention endorsement for governor, had to be content with a renomination for treasurer, one Joseph L. Hurley turned up on the scene and won the nomination for lieutenant-governor. Elected as lieutenant-governor, he shared the stage with Treasurer Hurley for a couple of years and the name of Hurley became more and more of a household word. The two Hurleys, Charles F. and Joseph L., vied in 1936 for the convention endorsement for governor. Charles F. won the nod and Joseph L. disappeared from the limelight. The magic of the name Hurley seeped over into the Republican ranks and, also in 1936, the Republicans endorsed and nominated a William E. Hurley for treasurer, the post held by the Democrat, Charles F. Hurley, now running for governor. Simultaneously, the Democratic convention proposed J. C. Scanlon for the treasury post, but one James M. Hurley won the primary nomination for the place that had been so adequately filled by Charles F. Hurley. Mr. Charles F. Hurley went on to win the governorship but his colleague Mr. James M. Hurley, of Marlborough, fell before the campaign of Mr. William E. Hurley, the Boston Republican.[45]

The fact that so many candidates challenge the Democratic convention endorsee leads to bitter primary fights characterized by mutual character assassination, and the bitterness of the primary fight causes some followers of losing Democratic candidates to abstain from voting or support a Republican in the general election. The ethnic diversity of the Democratic constituency and the "infellow" feeling of the ethnic-group members undoubtedly heighten the bitterness of Democratic primaries, particularly when Italo-American oppose Irish-American candidates. The primary election that we shall analyze is a classic example of this type, in which the convention endorsee, Joseph Ward, an "outstate" American of Irish descent, was opposed by three other Irish Americans, two Italo-Americans, and one Yankee Protestant. The successful Republican candidate in the general election, John Volpe, an Italo-American, won partly because of the support of many non-Irish Democrats who objected to the "all green" ticket endorsed by their party. In contrast to the Democrats with their hotly contested primaries, the Republicans, whose convention endorsee is customarily unopposed, enter the general election "unsmeared," at least by each other.

[45] Key, *op. cit.*, pp. 163-64.

It is also possible to evaluate the strength of a party organization on the basis of its ability to control its funds. Strong party organizaions are able to centralize fund-raising efforts and control the disbursements for expenses. Here too, the Republican organization is far more successful than its opposition. Lockard points out that in the bitter campaign of 1954 "most of the Republican money was spent by the state committee and little by the organizations directly associated with the leading candidates. The reverse was true with the Democrats. . . . Roughly the same situation prevailed in 1952."[46] This was also true in the 1960 elections. The Republican party customarily collects money through the central organization, which then proceeds to distribute it to local organizations as it sees fit. This control of the purse is, of course, an awesome device for enforcing party discipline in the hands of the state committee. Most of the money spent by Democratic organizations in local communities is collected in the local communities by the local organizations. Each Democratic candidate raises his own funds in whatever way he can and with little or no direction or control from the state committee. Quite often the Democratic candidate who survives a bitter primary fight has exhausted his resources. Republicans, who are uncontested in the primary, are able to preserve their financial strength for the general election.

The ultimate test of a vigorous and centralized party organization is its ability to sustain working organizations at the ward and precinct level and "force" them to support the convention endorsee. In this respect too, the Republicans are far more successful than the Democrats. We have already pointed out that the Democratic organization has not been very successful in preventing challenges in the primary and that it is divided regionally and ethnically. Lockard writes:

The Democratic organization in fact seems at times to be nothing at all. . . . Personal organizations are numerous and various strong men often go their own way without regard for other candidates in a campaign. In a good many areas, particularly in the small Republican towns, there is no Democratic organization of any kind. In some smaller urban centers where there are Democratic majorities, the party organization may practically give way to labor groups who do most of the work of campaigning. The lack of constant contact between the central party and the local units has tended to result in the atrophy of some local units, and

[46] Lockard, op. cit., pp. 137-38.

if the central organization has not atrophied it has certainly suffered badly from weakness born of internal division.[47]

On the local level, the Republicans are frequently better organized than the Democrats. This does not mean that Republican organization in the smaller cities and towns is adequate; it means simply that what leadership there is tends to think in terms of its relationship to the state organization more than do the Democrats, who, with locally loyal followings, think in terms of "every man for himself." In most of the larger cities, Republican organizations are weak or nonexistent. In Boston, for example, the GOP as an organization is impotent in all but two or three of the city's 22 wards. Until recent years, prestigious party leaders were able to determine the Republican ticket with little opposition.

The feudalization of the Democratic party organization and the relative unity of the Republicans also result from the belief held by many Republicans that they have little chance of winning statewide contests. The Republicans can maintain some semblance of unity because their minority status discourages challengers to the convention endorsee and forces the party to unite. The Democrats, on the other hand, believe that they are likely to win most of the contests for statewide office. This whets the appetite of potential candidates, who are willing to defy the convention and develop organizations of their own. The degree of internal cleavage within a state party organization is related to the party's strength in the electorate.

During the period 1916-30, Democrats in Massachusetts believed (and correctly so) that they had little chance of winning many statewide contests. For this reason, relatively few notables within the party attempted to establish rival organizations. If we measure party unity during these years using the same criteria we used above, the Democratic party is unified, the Republican party is feudalized.

Despite the relatively superior Republican organization, there is little doubt that a majority (perhaps 55%) of the voters in Massachusetts identify in some way with the Democratic party. The overwhelming victories of the Democratic party in recent years in the state legislature indicate this. If the Democrats could overcome the mutual hostility of ethnic groups and so unite them, the Republicans

[47] *Ibid.,* p. 125.

would be able to maintain their current position only in their safest districts. The natural advantages of the Democratic party, however, are dissipated by continuous primary warfare, a plethora of candidates with the "right" name, the Boston-*vs.*-outstate antagonism, and the taint of corruption—all serious problems which can be dealt with only after some awakening of interest in responsible party organization.

Because it is not the nominal "majority" party, the Republican party is forced to pursue a strategy of divide-and-conquer; the party stands to do best if it nominates ethnically balanced slates, continues to force investigations of corrupt practices by the incumbent Democrats, and maintains its superior organization. The gubernatorial elections of 1960, with which we are concerned, illustrate the interplay of these forces so far as election strategy is concerned. Before turning to the 1960 elections, however, it is necessary to examine briefly the operation of parties in the state legislature and the incidence of corruption in Massachusetts public life, because the legislative record of the incumbents and corruption in public life were the prime issues of the 1960 elections.

Party Influence in the General Court

We have been using the concept "political party" in two senses. At times we have used it to refer to that group of voters who consider themselves party members. The vast majority of voters who make up the Democratic and the Republican "parties" in Massachusetts (and other states) are politically active only on election day, although many view political issues during the intervals between elections in a predictably partisan fashion. This group can be called the "party-in-the-electorate."[48] As we have said, the Democratic "party-in-the-electorate" is a loose coalition of ethnic groups which are, at best, moderately liberal; the Republican "party-in-the-electorate," is predominantly Anglo-Saxon, Protestant, and moderately conservative. We have also used the term "political party" to refer to the relatively

[48] We are indebted for this differentiation of the concept "political party" to V. O. Key, Jr. See his *Politics, Parties, and Pressure Groups* (4th ed.; New York: Thomas Y. Crowell Co., 1958), pp. 181-82. The phrase "party-in-the-electorate" is Ralph M. Goldman's. See his *Party Chairmen and Party Factions—1789-1900* (Chicago: University of Chicago, Ph.D. dissertation, 1951), Chap. 17.

small group of active, professional political workers who maintain the party organization (i.e., the members of the state central committee, the members of the ward and town committees, and the active workers at the grass roots). The Democratic "party-organization" is feudalized and relatively ineffectual. The Republican "party-organization," in comparison, is relatively centralized and disciplined. The "party-in-the-electorate" includes the apathetic and the active.

The term "political party," however, may also refer to groups within the government (Democratic and Republican state legislators, governors, senators, and congressmen). The "party-in-the-government" may be quite distinct from the "party-organization" and may espouse an ideology that is somewhat different from that held by the amorphous blocs that make up the "party-in-the-electorate." Such, as we shall see, is the case in Massachusetts.

Despite the feudal character of the Democratic "party-organization" and the ethnic diversity of the Democratic "party-in-the-electorate," the Democratic "party-in-the-government" is relatively solid, unified, and disciplined with respect to such issues as labor-management relations; health, welfare, and education; taxation; governmental operations; and the regulation of the economy. Democratic legislators tend to unite in support of the so-called liberal position; Republican legislators tend to unite in favor of the "conservative" position. The national party "philosophy" and the expressed wishes of national party leaders tend to be reference points for large numbers of state legislators. Massachusetts, in fact, ranks near the top of the American states with respect to the level of party cohesion in the state legislature.[49] It is not unusual, for example, for the majorities of the two parties to take opposite sides on approximately 80 to 85 per cent of all roll-call votes in a given legislative session.[50]

One state legislator summarized the conflict between the "parties-in-the-government" by remarking that "an issue supported by labor is a Democratic party issue, and an issue supported by management is a Republican party issue."[51] A close relationship exists between

[49] Malcolm E. Jewell, "Party Voting in American State Legislatures," *American Political Science Review*, Vol. 49 (1955), pp. 773-91.

[50] See Lockard, *op. cit.*, p. 153.

[51] Quoted in Corinne Silverman, "The Legislator's View of the Legislative Process," *Public Opinion Quarterly*, Vol. 18 (Summer 1954), p. 184.

the Massachusetts AFL-CIO and the Massachusetts Democratic party. In some districts, the local labor unions are the major source of funds for Democratic legislators and for aspirants seeking to unseat Republicans "unfriendly to labor." Only two or three Republicans are regarded as "friendly" by the AFL-CIO, which publishes an "Official Labor Record of the Massachusetts Legislature" for each session. Republicans consistently score "wrong" on labor-management bills from the viewpoint of labor. The major bills on which interparty divisions have occurred in recent years are those concerning increases in workmen's compensation, maximum unemployment-insurance benefits, provisions of the minimum-wage law, and state action in labor disputes; all these bills were supported by Democrats and opposed by Republicans. Business organizations, such as the Associated Industries of Massachusetts and the Greater Boston Chamber of Commerce, usually oppose increases in workers' compensation and unemployment insurance, and most Republican legislators agree with them.

As Democratic strength in the legislature has grown, however, labor has had more trouble with its ally. The unions have never lobbied successfully for a "cash sickness" bill (i.e., one that would provide a state insurance fund to cover unemployment due to illness). The insurance companies (perhaps the most powerful lobby in Massachusetts) have consistently opposed the bill. The united Republicans, combined with a significant number of Democratic "defectors," have managed to block the bill. The political alignments of the labor-industry battle remain, therefore, less than certain. In the 1960 session, for example, a bill requiring registration of imported strikebreakers was passed with strong Democratic support (a distinct victory for labor). Another AFL-CIO-sponsored bill (to provide unemployment compensation to strikers after six weeks) was defeated when half the Democratic legislators responded to industry's argument that employers would be financing strikes against themselves. Seventy-six Republicans voted against the bill and only three for it; 66 Democrats were against the proposal while 62 favored it.

In addition to supporting most pro-labor bills, the Democrats tend to unite in favor of welfare legislation, particularly increased old-age assistance, aid for retarded children, and the expansion of state facilities for the mentally disturbed. The Republicans split occasionally in their response to these measures, but their position over the years has been basically "conservative."[52] The division between the two parties on problems of taxation is much less sharp than on labor-management or welfare problems. The GOP has consistently opposed tax increases, particularly taxes on income. The Republicans feel that the revenue from increased taxes on income or a sales tax (if passed) ought to be used to relieve property taxes rather than to expand "state bureaucracy." They also oppose the graduation of the income tax, while the Democrats and organized labor favor it. The position of the Democrats on other aspects of the tax problem is less unified. Traditionally, the party has opposed a sales tax; in 1957-60, it split down the middle on Governor Furcolo's proposed limited sales tax. On the key vote in 1957, a small majority of Democrats voted with the Governor; the margin of defeat was provided by the Republicans. This occurred despite the fact that most Republican businessmen and newspapers were strongly in favor of the bill.[53]

Since the 1940's, the Democrats have strongly advocated extensions of civil rights, including fair-employment laws and laws forbidding discrimination in college admissions and in housing. A sizable minority of Republicans has usually voted with the Democrats. The Republicans, however, are more favorably disposed toward the extension and protection of civil liberties. With some help from a small band of vocal Democrats, the Republicans generally lead the fight for the enactment of most bills advocated by the Civil Liberties Union of Massachusetts, such as those providing for curbing of police wire-tapping and the protection of the individual from sweeping investigations by committees seeking out Communists. In recent years, some of the Democratic leaders have shown a growing concern for civil liberties.

Local issues, which often cut across party lines, cause more defections within the parties than any other area of legislation. For example, outstate Republicans vote as a body to retain curbs on Boston's city government, while the few Republicans from Boston vote for

[52] Duncan MacRae, Jr., "Roll Call Votes and Leadership," *Public Opinion Quarterly,* Vol. 20 (Fall 1956), pp. 553-54.

[53] See John P. Mallan and George Blackwood, "The Tax That Beat a Governor: The Ordeal of Massachusetts," in Alan Westin, ed., *The Uses of Power* (New York: Harcourt, Brace & World, 1961).

TABLE 4

The Party Division of the Massachusetts House of Representatives,
1943-62 (Total Seats: 240)

	Republicans	Democrats
1943-44	143	97
1945-46	138	102
1947-48	144	96
1949-50	118	122
1951-52	116	124
1953-54	124	116
1955-56	112	128
1957-58	108	132
1959-60	95	145
1961-62	85	155

greater "home rule." The same alignment characterizes the Democratic vote on this issue. The high degree of "independent" voting
on local issues reflects the fact that his constituency is often a more
significant reference point for a state representative than is his party.

The cohesion of the parties in the state legislature is remarkable
given the amorphous character of the Democratic "party-in-the-
electorate," the atrophy of the Democratic organization, and the
absence of a unified political philosophy among Democratic ethnic
groups, on the one hand, and the Rockefeller-Nixon-Goldwater division that exists among Republican voters, on the other. Several factors, which are themselves interrelated, must be considered in attempting to account for the cohesiveness of the parties in the legislature. These include the closeness of party competition, the differences between typical Republican and Democratic constituencies,
differences in the occupational backgrounds of Republican and
Democratic legislators, and differences among the types of lobby
allied with each party. In addition to these factors, the enormous
power and prestige of the speaker of the Massachusetts House of
Representatives and the president of the Massachusetts Senate must
be taken into account.

For the 15 years preceding the 1958 state elections, the party
division in the legislature was often highly competitive, as is shown
in Tables 4 and 5.

TABLE 5

The Party Division of the Massachusetts Senate,
1943-62 (Total Seats: 40)

	Republicans	*Democrats*
1943-44	26	14
1945-46	23	17
1947-48	24	16
1949-50	20	20
1951-52	22	18
1953-54	25	15
1955-56	21	19
1957-58	21	19
1959-60	16	24
1961-62	14	26

Close competition of parties induces legislators to stay with their party, for a relatively small number of "defections" in such a situation may seriously affect the strength of the party and hence an individual legislator's prospects for patronage and personal promotion. To desert one's party when the party balance is extremely close is to risk castigation as unreliable or denunciation as a traitor. Lockard has pointed out that the re-election of an individual legislator in a close district ". . . may be tied in closely with the chances of the gubernatorial candidate, who must in part run on his party's legislative record. To the extent that the record of the party is an issue in campaigns, the party must concentrate on making at least a reasonable record of legislative action."[54] This fact often compels the legislator to support his party. But the impact of close party competition on party regularity is also shown by the fact that since 1958, when the Democrats took a commanding lead in the House of Representatives, the number of Democratic "defectors" has greatly increased.

The closeness of party competition, however, does not fully explain the case; the party division in the United States Congress is often close, but there is less cohesion among party members in Congress than in the Massachusetts state legislature. Perhaps the most important factor leading to party cohesion is the similarity among the several constituencies from which each party draws most of its

[54] Lockard, *op. cit.*, p. 155.

support. "Like-minded legislators," Lockard suggests, "will come from similar districts and if the party's legislators are drawn from widely differing constituencies the degree of cohesion will accordingly be less."[55] State legislators, like United States congressmen, must cater to local constituencies, regardless of the party position on an issue. If, then, most of the Democrats in the state legislature represent relatively similar constituencies, one would expect a high degree of cohesion in the Democratic party. And such is, in fact, the case—for both parties in Massachusetts. As we have said, the majority of the Democrats represent constituencies which are urban, Catholic, and lower-middle to middle class. The majority of the Republicans represent districts which are suburban or rural, Protestant, and middle to upper-middle class. A "typical" Republican constituency has a much greater proportion of owner-occupied dwelling units than does a "typical" Democratic constituency.[56] MacRae has pointed out that "those representatives who come from districts that are most typical of their parties tend to show the highest 'party loyalty' on roll calls."[57] He has also shown that

The extent of party deviation in each party is greatest in districts that are atypical of one's own party, and are most like those of the opposing party. The Democrats from high owner-occupancy districts tend on the average to vote more like Republicans, and the Republicans from low owner-occupancy districts tend to vote more like Democrats.[58]

Party cohesion may also result from the fact that Republican and Democratic representatives tend to be drawn from quite different occupations. V. O. Key, Jr., has shown, for example, that the "typical Republican" background is "business-managerial" whereas the "typical Democratic" background is "sales-clerical."[59] The greater concern of the Republicans with ideological aims (conservatism)[60] is explained by Lockard, who suggests that "a greater number of Republicans who go to the legislature have a very definite 'stake' in the community, which makes their conservatism a natural position."[61]

[55] Ibid.
[56] MacRae, "The Relation of Roll Call Votes and Constituencies . . . ," op. cit., p. 1047.
[57] Ibid., p. 1055.
[58] Ibid., p. 1051.
[59] Key, American State Politics, op. cit., p. 262.
[60] MacRae, "Roll Call Votes and Leadership," op. cit., p. 588.
[61] Lockard, op. cit., p. 158.

It is this "stake" in business and property of Republican legislators and many of their constituents that makes the Republican party the party of conservatism. The labor orientation of Democratic representatives and their constituents obviously adds motive power to the "liberalism" of the party. Except when the local needs of constituencies divide intraparty interests on specific issues, this general differentiation of the parties makes for cohesion within each party.

The separatism and cohesion of the parties in the state legislature may also be explained as both cause and consequence of the types of lobby that finance and pressure the parties. According to Lockard, the most significant groups supporting the Democratic party are labor and such reform organizations as Americans for Democratic Action (ADA). The most significant lobbies supporting the Republican party are "the public utility interests, the real estate lobby, the Associated Industries of Massachusetts (the local version of the NAM), the Chamber of Commerce, the insurance companies, and the Massachusetts Federation of Taxpayers' Associations. All these groups have easy access to the leaders of the Republican party."[62] The lobbyists for these groups, however, work closely with the more conservative Democrats when it is advantageous for them to do so. This formidable alignment not only indicates that a conservative-liberal split does exist in the General Court but accounts, in part, for its continued existence.[63]

The high degree of party discipline in the state legislature is also a consequence of the power and prestige of the speaker of the House and the president of the Senate. The speaker and the president have the power to designate the chairmen of all committees and to appoint all members, thus determining the party composition of every committee. They also have the power to depose any chairman or remove any committee member at any time without showing cause. All investigations undertaken by either body must be approved by its Committee on Rules. The speaker of the House and the president of the Senate serve as chairmen of their respective Committees on Rules. They also have the power to "seat" any member at any time

[62] *Ibid.*, pp. 163-66.

[63] This split is not unrecognized by voters in Massachusetts. The public-opinion poll taken by the authors before the primary indicates that the stereotype of the Democratic party as the party favorable to the working man had wide currency in Massachusetts.

with cause. It is obvious that their power is considerable. The speaker of the House and the president of the Senate can and do use their power to enforce party discipline and maintain control over the legislature.

Despite the existence of fairly distinctive orientations for the "parties-in-the-government," the major issue in recent elections so far as the voters are concerned has been the apparently massive and pervasive corruption in public life at all levels of Massachusetts government. For political commentators in this country and abroad, Boston and Massachusetts politics have become prime examples of the kinds of corruption and conflict of interest that too frequently degrade American local and state government.[64] Any analysis of politics in the Bay State is naïve, incomplete, and highly inaccurate if it does not include an examination of forms and causes of corruption in Massachusetts public life.

Corruption and Conflicts of Interest, 1919-50

Prior to World War I, corruption was probably no more prevalent in Massachusetts public life than in America generally. Flagrant instances of payoffs to public officials and conflicts of interest were rare, although petty graft was common on the state and local levels.

[64] See, for example:

Anthony Lewis, "Massachusetts Is Aroused by Corruption Scandals," *New York Times,* June 19, 1961; "Massachusetts Turnpike Chief Criticized in Rising Scandals," *ibid.,* June 20, 1961.

Louis M. Lyons, "Boston: Study in Inertia," in Robert S. Allen, ed., *Our Fair City* (New York: Vanguard Press, 1947), pp. 21-24.

Levin, *op. cit.*

U.S. *v.* Worcester, 190 Federal Supplement 548.

Charles L. Whipple, "Dirty Money in Boston," *Atlantic Monthly,* Vol. 207, No. 3 (March 1961).

William H. Wells, "Conflict of Interest in Massachusetts," *Boston Globe,* March 19, 20, 21, 23, 24, 26, 28, 30, April 2, 3, 4, 6 (1961).

Emile Tavel, "Is Massachusetts Worst? Bookies, Kickbacks, Payoffs," *Christian Science Monitor,* August 9, 1961, p. 1; "Public Aroused," *ibid.,* August 10, 1961, p. 2; "Massachusetts Issue: Ex-Convicts in Office," *ibid.,* August 11, 1961, p. 2.

"A Birthday Letter from Home," *Boston Globe,* May 29, 1961, p. 1.

Richardson, *op. cit.*

"Battle for Boston," *The Economist* (London), Vol. 198 (March 11, 1961), pp. 952-53.

Hearings of the U.S. House of Representatives Committee on Public Works (Subcommittee), March 1962.

However, the incidence of corruption among public officials (as measured by investigations, indictments, and convictions) increased noticeably during the 1920's, and there was a corresponding decline among the electorate in respect for officials and sense of "civic duty." During the nineteenth century and in the early twentieth century, the governors of Massachusetts had been able to recruit large numbers of public-spirited citizens outside the party fold who were willing to donate their time and abilities for public service without compensation. By the 1930's, as a result of widespread disillusionment with politics and politicians, there were few volunteers for public service.[65]

The increase in corrupt practices that began after the war coincided with an expansion in state services and state expenditures. In 1920, State Treasurer Fred J. Burrell (a Republican) was accused of forcing bankers who wished him to deposit state funds in their banks to advertise through an agency of which Burrell was part-owner. When Governor Coolidge indicated that he would remove Burrell if the evidence warranted it, the Treasurer resigned. On several subsequent occasions, Burrell ran for his old position. The lesson learned from his victory in the 1950 primary and subsequent defeat in the general election was one of the reasons for Republican leaders' support of a pre-primary convention.

In 1928, another Republican official, Attorney General Arthur K. Reading, resigned after admitting that he had taken a "legal fee" of $25,000 from a fraternal organization which his office had previously investigated and absolved. But graft, then as now, was not confined to one party; it was bipartisan. An especially notable case occurred early in the 1920's, when three well-known political figures, one Republican and two Democrats, were indicted. The Republican, Nathaniel Tufts (District Attorney of Middlesex County), and one of the Democrats, Joseph Pelletier (District Attorney of Suffolk County), were disbarred after it was revealed that they had been involved in "a lucrative perversion of justice involving frame-ups, blackmail and suppressed prosecutions."[66] They were charged primarily with using women to lure wealthy men to hotel rooms and arranging police raids to trap them there. Daniel Coakley, the other

[65] Robert C. Wood and Bradbury Seasholes, "The Disintegration of an Image: Reflections of Five Governors," Tufts Assembly on Massachusetts State Government, working paper, April 1961, pp. 5-6.
[66] Huthmacher, *op. cit.,* p. 55.

Democrat involved, gradually returned to the practice of law and re-entered politics. One newspaper referred to him as "an uncrowned boss of the state during the 1930's."[67] In 1941, while he was a Governor's Councilor, Coakley was accused of using "deceit, fraud and improper conduct" in obtaining releases from prison for three convicts. The 76-year-old Coakley was impeached and charged with having written and submitted pious statements from nonexistent priests in order to secure pardons. It was broadly hinted that bribes had changed hands. After a sensational trial, he was removed from office and barred from public life.[68]

In the 1930's, the practice of bribing public officials for licenses and contracts became widespread in Boston. Many Boston businessmen report that it was standard procedure when doing business with the city to pay 10 per cent of the total involved in the purchase to a so-called bagman. The payoffs, presumably, ultimately went from the "bagmen" to influential city officials. The scandals in which James M. Curley was involved, for example, were so well known that Curley offered his own interpretation of them, vigorously defending himself in his autobiography, I'd Do It Again. In one case, "the Mayor of the Poor," as many called him, was found guilty of defrauding the city of Boston of $30,000 and forced to repay it. After his conviction, thousands of his loyal supporters, whom he had aided at one time or another, surrounded his house for several days to contribute to his cause. Curley received more than enough to pay the fine.[69] With Curley as their example, several of his associates became notorious in their own right for the imaginative ways in which they took graft. One of the most adept was John F. Dowd (Democrat), the Sheriff of Suffolk County in the 1930's. The jail that Dowd ran was known as "Hospitality Hall" to the underworld; for a suitable fee, any inmate could obtain privileges ranging from liquor to outside holidays, and the jail was actually used as a sanctuary by criminals fleeing from the police.[70] Dowd's lucrative operation, which included the large-scale selling of jobs, was exposed by

[67] Christian Science Monitor, editorial, Oct. 3, 1941, p. 16.
[68] Accounts of the trial in the Senate appeared in the Boston press, Aug. 25-Oct. 3, 1941.
[69] Joseph Dineen, The Purple Shamrock (New York: W. W. Norton & Co., 1949), pp. 276-79.
[70] Ibid., pp. 259-74.

accident, as a result of an investigation of the selling of a job by the County Clerk, John Patrick Connolly.[71]

By the end of World War II, corruption was taken for granted as a facet of public life in Massachusetts. In a report filed in 1945, the Boston Finance Commission, which had been set up to check public expenditures, exposed the practice of large-scale payroll padding. The report stated, for example, that firemen who were absent from duty over long periods of time nevertheless received their paychecks at regular intervals. It indicated not only widespread cheating on city contracts but also what appeared to be intimate relationships between bookies, politicians, and police officials. When Attorney General Robert Bushnell (a Republican) began to probe into these relationships, the Democrats and members of Bushnell's own party curbed the investigation.[72]

These relationships evidently still exist. Lockard writes, for example,

. . . Where horses and dogs race there is a lucrative opportunity for extra-legal betting, which does not flow through the pari-mutuel machines and which makes no returns to the state treasury. In short, the bookies move in, and move in they have in Massachusetts. Although the Kefauver Crime Investigating Committee never made an invasion of New England, more recently the Massachusetts Crime Commission submitted a 1,307-page report in which it was charged that a $2-billion business in gambling flourished in the state. A minority report claimed that the total amounted to only $1 billion. The difference is unimportant in one sense: the lucrative nature of the "business" is clear whichever figure is correct. The report charged that there were ties between the gambling interests and other crime, such as prostitution, narcotics, and theft. The police, according to the investigators, know the situation and make no move to stop it. No sooner had the report hit the headlines than there were vigorous denials and challenges to show where action could be taken. Even allowing for some exaggeration, the political influence of the gambling fraternity seems a fact. The original reluctance to pass the laws necessary to establish the investigation and to continue it at later intervals suggests that there are ties between the political world and the underworld. It is not a very pretty picture, to say the least, but whoever tries to unravel the

[71] Connolly was subsequently elected a Boston City Councilor and was defeated for re-election in November 1961.

[72] Lyons, *op. cit.*, pp. 21-24.

mysteries of the state's politics without considering these influences is bound to end up with only part of the answer.[73]

We will argue that the electorate today is dissatisfied with the partial explanations offered by candidates during campaigns.

Corruption and Conflicts of Interest, 1950-61

The postwar era brought new opportunities for those who shared the philosophy of George Washington Plunkett, the Tammany ward-heeler who explained his political career simply: "I seen my opportunities and I took 'em."[74] As governmental activities expanded, so did the opportunities for graft and corruption. The major locus of corruption in Massachusetts has been state contracts for the building of roads. In the past decade, Massachusetts has been constructing an extensive network of throughways. More than one billion dollars' worth of bonds has been issued since 1949 to pay for the Common-wealth's road-construction program. Although officials argue that corruption in the awarding of highway contracts involves only a few men, the public apparently believes that it pervades the political structure. This suspicion arises in part from a belief (essentially correct) that a very substantial portion of the campaign funds of candidates for major public office comes from those who furnish the state with goods or services, particularly the contractors.

Some idea of the nature and extent of corruption and conflicts of interest in Massachusetts public life was provided by William H. Wells, a reporter for the *Boston Globe*, in a series of 12 articles analyzing the problem in Massachusetts. In his final article, Wells summarized his findings:

The corrupt and questionable activities that permeate the common-wealth's political life are, like the iceberg, largely submerged and difficult to disclose.

While the guilty escape punishment, the honest majority of legislators and government employees are tarnished by suspicion and rumor.

Only fact-finders armed with the power of subpoena can hope to break

[73] Lockard, *op. cit.,* pp. 169-70.
[74] William L. Riordan, *Plunkett of Tammany Hall* (New York: Alfred A. Knopf, 1948), p. 4.

the pattern that stretches from towns and cities through the executive departments into the Legislature and into the courts. Conflict-of-interest legislation that would provide such power to an enforcement team is now in the General Court under study.

Meanwhile these things have happened:

—Engineers and consultants have paid off legislators and highway officials to obtain contracts.

—Governor's councilors have done business with the state and traded votes for promises of future jobs.

—Government employees quit state service to work for firms with whom they did business on behalf of the state.

—Probate judges awarded trustee positions to relatives and friends.

—Lawyer-legislators voted on bills to raise the pay of judges before whom they practice.

—Officials with regulatory powers received cash benefits from testimonial dinners attended by those whose affairs they regulate.

—Legislators and state employees received commissions for selling performance bonds on state contracts.

—Lawyer-legislators practiced before state agencies.

—Legislators who are insurance brokers sold insurance to the state.

—Government employees and legislators profited through landtakings for state highways.

—Town employees dominated representative town meetings and voted their own pay raises.

—Community road superintendents rented equipment to the communities they served.

—Friends and relatives of politicians and the politicians themselves were on the payrolls of state agencies and public authorities.

—They were also on the payrolls of firms doing business with these agencies and authorities.

—An attorney general and assistant attorneys general represented clients in cases against the state.

—City councilmen intervened to secure performance bonds and insurance from contractors dealing with their cities.

—Assessors fixed valuations on properties of firms in which they had an interest or for which they worked—or as realtors owned property which they assessed.

—Labor officials sat on boards negotiating with the unions for which they worked or which they represented.

—Legislators fought for legislation benefitting their own businesses.

—Attempts to uncover such activities encounter a maze of interlocking conflict situations.

—A legislator does business with a state agency but the agency head is a party to the wrong-doing and conceals any record of the transaction.

—A governor's councilor does business with an agency head who owes his appointment to the councilor's vote.

—Private business officials, lawyers, judges, legislators, executive department heads will all be parties to the same act of wrong-doing and owe their income to each other's goodwill.[75]

According to Wells, conflicts of interest are common in local as well as state government.

Town and city governments are as infested with unethical activities as the state government—in some cases more so.

Real estate men double as assessors; contractors who are highway superintendents do public business with their own firms; town counsel represent private clients against their communities; city councilmen have interests in firms doing business with the city; individuals and families dominate communities by holding most of the public jobs. . . .

One way in which local police chiefs and captains help their "friends" is through the ticket fix—making certain these friends are not brought to court for minor law infractions.

The protection given illegal activities by some police officers has been demonstrated in revelations of establishments selling liquor after hours within sight of patrolmen—of state and Federal police forced to conduct vice raids that should have been conducted by local police.

Even school systems are not immune. The placing of contracts for school equipment, for school construction and for school bus service has been carried out in some communities with private profit motivating school officials and committeemen.

Policemen and firemen maintaining a construction business on the side and using their contacts made at work to obtain company contracts.

Town officials selling insurance to the community.

City councilmen and highway superintendents leasing trucks and other equipment to the community.

The varieties of civic corruption are known to every resident of a suburban or rural town or city. The hard-fisted rule of the urban boss has given way to the more sophisticated maneuvering of city employees who know the angles.[76]

These examples of conflict of interest are relatively trivial compared to the wrong-doing in the Metropolitan District Commission,

[75] William H. Wells, "Conflict of Interest: How Bad Did It Get?" *Boston Globe*, April 6, 1961, p. 4.

[76] William H. Wells, "Same Game Played in Town, City Halls," *Boston Globe*, April 4, 1961, p. 1.

which is in charge of parks and parkways, water, and sewage-disposal in and around Boston. An inquiry by the State Senate has resulted in the conviction, on criminal charges, of the MDC Chairman, an associate MDC Commissioner, and a state representative. Anthony Lewis, of the *New York Times,* gave the following examples of the inquiry's findings:

[The MDC] paid a swimming coach $5,000 for a report on the "desirable characteristics of a pool" it was going to build. The Senate inquiry said the need for such advice was "obscure, because MDC has already built several pools."

Another consultant on a different swimming pool was paid $17,000. All he did, according to the investigators, was to use specifications that had been given to him free by a pool manufacturer and, in suggesting a bathhouse design, to copy the plan of another commission bathhouse.

The investigating committee found that the commission had ordered items from contractors that it did not need, apparently to make the contracts more profitable. One contract required the contractor to supply a $1,000 calculating machine "for which there was no use at the site," according to the committee.

A constant practice of the district commission was to break its projects into contracts of less than $1,000 each. The Senate committee suggested that the reason was that state law requires competitive bidding on all contracts of more than $1,000.

Contractors, the investigating committee said, "billed the MDC without regard to the fair value of the work done or a fair profit to themselves. Each took as a yardstick the starting point of $1,000 [and] picked some figure as close to $1,000 as their courage permitted."

The committee found that on some jobs the contractors had done no work, and on most jobs only part of the contracted project. In "an overwhelming majority" of instances, the committee said, the work done "was sloppy, shoddy, unworkmanlike and an outright public disgrace."

The head of the agency, Commissioner John E. Maloney, was also the 40 per cent owner of an insurance agency that received many commissions on the agency's performance bonds.

Charles J. McCarty, an associate commissioner, was the local distributor for one kind of highway guard rail. The MDC bought large quantities of this kind of rail, producing net profits of about 60 per cent for the distributing company on each sale.[77]

Activities of the Massachusetts Department of Public Works have also been investigated (1960) by a committee of the State Senate.

[77] Lewis, *op. cit.*

A report of the investigating committee ("which was widely de-nounced as a whitewash")[78] indicated that it was a common practice for the Department to split up contracts in pieces of less than $1,000 so that it could award them without competitive bidding.[79] The report also noted that surveyors had received payment for working on the day of a blizzard. It criticized J. L. Hayden, a consulting engineer, because he was unable to show how he had arrived at the figure of $84,000, which he had charged the state for one job. Firms in which Hayden had an interest received nearly $2,500,000 from the state in consulting fees over a three-year period. Prior to this investigation, the federal government had begun to investigate prices paid by the Department of Public Works for "rights of way" on highways that are partially financed by federal funds. In 1960, the Federal Bureau of Public Roads froze all federal monies assigned to Massachusetts for landtakings.[80] A subcommittee of the United States House of Representatives has investigated landtakings in Massachusetts, and three individuals (including a prominent Demo-cratic politician) have been convicted on charges of conspiring to defraud the federal government of more than $30,000.

Perhaps the shabbiest aspect of Massachusetts public life has to do with public servants who have served or are now serving time in federal or state penal institutions or who have been convicted of various crimes. During the early stages of his career, James M. Cur-ley successfully campaigned from jail for re-election as a Boston alderman. In 1945 Curley ran for mayor of Boston while under indictment for mail fraud and won the largest plurality any candidate had received for that office. Curley was ultimately convicted and served time in a federal penitentiary. In 1956 Massachusetts had the unique distinction of becoming the first state in the union to elect to Congress an individual who had served a term in a federal peni-tentiary while in office. Thomas J. Lane, a Democrat from Law-rence, Massachusetts, was found guilty in 1956 of willfully evading payment of $38,543 in federal income taxes over a three-year period. He served four months in the Federal Correctional Institu-tion in Danbury, Connecticut. Fifteen days after his release from prison Lane was returned to his old seat in the House of Represen-

[78] *Ibid.*

[79] State Auditor Thomas J. Buckley cited 52 cases of such contract splitting.

[80] As of September 1961, the Federal Bureau of Public Roads released $6,000,000 to Massachusetts.

tatives by a margin of 87,332 to 48,154 votes. He was re-elected in 1958 and 1960. Currently serving in the Massachusetts House of Representatives is Charles Iannello, a Democrat of Boston, who has been tried, convicted, and sentenced to one year in the house of correction on charges of larceny from the state in connection with work performed for the Metropolitan District Commission by a firm owned by Iannello and members of his family. Representative Iannello's case is now on appeal. He was re-elected in November 1960 (while under indictment) by a margin of more than two to one. Former United States Attorney Elliot Richardson reports that "Boston radio and television station WBZ . . . made random phone calls to residents of . . . Iannello's district in Boston's South End after he had been sentenced to a year of jail. . . . Of twenty voters called, eighteen said they would vote for Iannello again."[81]

We have cited some examples of conflict of interest, bribery, and larceny involving public officials in Massachusetts.[82] The individuals involved and the nature of the "business" transacted between them suggest that there is a fairly well-established pattern of corrupt practices in Massachusetts. This pattern consistently involves public officials who are in a position to grant some kind of favorable treatment, businessmen who seek their favors, and influence peddlers who often act as intermediaries; but examples with precise details from start to finish (the kind of detail prosecution would supply) are rarely available for analysis. Much was revealed, however, in the dramatic case of Thomas Worcester, a prominent engineer who was indicted and convicted by a federal grand jury for income-tax evasion (United States *v.* Worcester, 190 Federal Supplement 1960). The testimony in the Worcester case is extremely important because it shows in detail the operation of this pattern of extortion, bribery, and conflict of interest.[83]

---

[81] Richardson, *op. cit.,* pp. 80-81.

[82] "Extensive as these disclosures have been, no citizen of Massachusetts would be likely to assume that all the dirty money has been brought to light. As a former United States Attorney, who, while in office . . . brought the federal aid highway investigation to the point of indictments, I know full well that it has not been. However, both a fair regard for the responsibility of my successor and the restrictions against disclosing grand jury proceedings or Internal Revenue Service information combine to prevent me from discussing facts that are not a matter of public record" (*Ibid.,* pp. 77-78).

[83] For an incisive analysis of the proceedings in the Worcester case see Whipple, *op. cit.*

Thomas Worcester, a graduate of Harvard College, was the head of a reputable engineering firm that had done 100 million dollars' worth of consultation and construction for the Army and Navy during World War II and considerable work for various agencies of the Massachusetts state government. In September 1960, Federal Judge Charles E. Wyzanski, Jr., offered to suspend Worcester's sentence if he would name in court the man or men whom he or his agent had bribed. Worcester agreed and proceeded to reveal his "business" dealings with various state officials. He reported that in 1948 he was approached by the late Francis Norton, who said that he was certain he could get jobs for Worcester because he (Norton) knew William F. Callahan (former Commissioner of Public Works, 1934-39, 1949-53). Worcester hired Norton, who had cards printed identifying him as "Assistant to the President." Worcester received $2,750,000 in state contracts between 1948 and 1952 and testified that he had given Norton 10 per cent of the total, charging this sum off as a business expense on his income-tax returns. Norton evidently did not tell Worcester how the money was spent.

During the course of his testimony, according to Judge Wyzanski, Worcester identified, under oath, "former members of the state legislature, a former candidate for the Republican nomination for Governor, and a present member of Congress as recipients of what may, with euphemism, be called 'the Worcester bounty.' " A former Democratic mayor of Brockton, Massachusetts, C. Gerald Lucey, who was a state representative at the time of the "Worcester bounty," testified that the Republican chairman of the House Ways and Means Committee, who was probably in a position to influence state expenditures affecting the Worcester firm, suggested that he see Worcester. Lucey said the chairman "knew I was not representing any company there and he thought I should become associated. . . . He was a fine, honorable gentleman, even though he was a Republican."

While testifying that he had contributed to the late Governor Dever's campaign fund in 1952, Worcester remarked, "Of course, the thing always has been to try to play both ends against the middle, if you could—contribute to both sides—but Mr. Dever, of course, had the strong argument that we had received all this work and there was more in the offing. He was dangling something quite attractive." Governor Dever, who evidently had some influence on the officials who granted highway contracts, "suggested" not only that Worcester contribute to his campaign but also that he hire a Democrat, who later became a state representative. The man testified that he was hired, had received $75 per week from Worcester, and had done no work. Worcester also hired an attorney, Henry M. Santosuousso, who was paid $11,000 in a ten-month period for "legal consultations" that never took place. Charles Whipple, who covered the Worcester case for the *Boston Globe,* reports that "when the tax agents caught up to [Santosuousso], he hurriedly phoned the firm's counsel, whom he had never seen, and asked what jobs the company had worked on so he could have 'something to hang my hat on.' "[84] Worcester also employed other people "referred" to him by the governor. One of these was William A. Beale, president of *Public Relations, Inc.,* who received $29,000 from Worcester for "standing by."[85]

Whipple suggests that "phony jobs were but a small part of the story." Larger sums of money and more flagrant instances of conflict of interest may be involved in the matter of contractors' performance bonds. Building contractors who are employed by the state are required by law to file bonds that insure against any losses resulting from the contractor's failure to fulfill the terms of the contract. These bonds may be placed with any licensed insurance broker in the state. In theory, the contractor is free to select the broker. In practice, however, the public official who grants the contract often "suggests" that a particular broker be given the business. In many cases, the broker turns out to be a friend or relative of the public official or a state legislator himself. The commissions paid to insurance brokers in Massachusetts are lucrative. Whipple estimates that commissions on performance bonds for contractors employed by the Massachusetts Turnpike Authority alone have totalled $300,000 in a two-year period.[86]

The subject of contractors' performance bonds was raised during the Worcester trial. Percy G. Cliff, an insurance broker who was a friend of Norton and is a friend of Callahan, testified that he had handled performance bonds for the Massachusetts Turnpike Authority. Cliff also admitted that he had been "associated since 1953 with John M. ("Moon") Shea, Callahan's personnel manager and job dis-

84 *Ibid.,* p. 44.
85 *Ibid.,* p. 46.
86 *Ibid.*

penser.[87] Callahan testified that "Shea had received a share of the commissions on Turnpike performance bonds. . . ."[88] Callahan also admitted that his nephew, Francis R. Murphy, Jr., had been associated in business with Cliff and that state legislators had also received a share of the commissions paid to Cliff.

Charles Whipple also suggests that many of the activities of those state legislators who are insurance brokers may involve them in serious conflict of interest: "The conclusion seems inescapable that some legislators who voted for the Turnpike Authority and its huge bond issues were involved with at least one of these men, and it was naturally to their advantage to support the legislative proposals of a person or persons who would see to it that they received their share of the commission."[89]

The pattern in the Worcester case is fairly clear. It extends from the influence peddler to those who know influential people or to the influential people themselves and their associates and relatives. Connections exist between heads of state agencies, insurance brokers, governors, congressmen, state legislators, job seekers, and high party officials, most of whom know one another. Worcester, whose profits were large enough to permit him to pay a 10-per-cent fee for bribes, was evidently afraid not to contribute to the campaign funds of certain candidates and afraid not to hire several individuals "referred" to him by those in a position to affect the granting of state contracts. Most of the men involved had come to know one another in obvious ways: state legislators know governors, heads of commissions know contractors, job seekers know legislators, etc. The Worcester case is a classic example of what Elliot Richardson has referred to as "poisoned politics"—that is, the politics of personal relationship, of *quid pro quo*.

In his opinion in the Worcester case, Judge Wyzanski raised several questions about this pattern of corruption and conflict of interest that had been revealed under oath.

Upon what basis was Worcester singled out for prosecution? Can it be true that of the successful bidders for contracts with the state, Worcester *alone* paid bribes and took them as deductions from federal income tax?

May it be that the report on Worcester came from a bank which was

[87] *Ibid.,* p. 45.
[88] *Ibid.*
[89] *Ibid.*

properly dismayed to find that Worcester was reassigning to another an account heretofore assigned to it?

Could it be that the bank knew no other contractors equally guilty of income-tax evasion? Doesn't the landlord almost always know when the tenant runs a gambling casino?

And once informed of Worcester's subjection to extortion, and Worcester's improper deductions of bribes, why did the Internal Revenue Service stop its scrutiny, if it did stop, before checking all reputable firms of engineers?

What sort of responsibility have the press and other media of communication displayed in reporting this case? Can it truly be said that with a high standard of detachment they have told the public all the court evidence that was discreditable, no matter whose ox was gored?

Did they report the testimony that in their own press contractors inserted advertisements which served no legitimate purpose of contractors but, so far as appears, could have had as their objects only the glorification of state officials of something less than perfect purity and the increase of advertising revenues of media which might thereafter be friendly to such officials?

Did they recite that Beale and his firm, Public Relations, Inc., both allegedly engaged in public relations, or in "putting out fires if fires occurred" (an eventuality which seems never to have occurred), apparently received money not only from Worcester but from a public utility?

Was the press aware that a news report of that extraordinary expenditure by a company having its own normal public relations staff and its own regular advertising agencies might force the Department of Utilities to slough off its indifference and start an inquiry about some friends and patrons of the press?

On the whole, except for a commendable uncovering of the details of how many state legislators are currently serving as agents for fidelity, bonding, and other insurance companies, how much has the press thought of itself as the protector of civic integrity?

... How far has the bar initiated reform based upon its daily experience with the sufferings its clients have undergone at the hands of a network of corruption? Were sophisticated lawyers unaware, until this case began, that to secure certain types of public business a contractor had to get his performance bond, or his materialman's bond, or his bond for wages, or his trustee's bond from a relative of a judge, or of a public official, or of a legislator?

Has there been no way to expose this system, whereby the favored insurance agent receives cash for nothing more than a telephone call and a few details passed on to the fidelity or insurance company?

Is the only method by which this venal system will be supplanted a
public insurance system modeled on other governmental insurance
systems?

Have the private interests which professedly care about the capitalist
system no awareness of what kind of free enterprise they have been
fostering?

Do they not realize that the people will smite them when they see what
this corruption costs in taxes, and, more important, in trustworthiness of
judges, legislators, and executives?[90]

The questions raised by Judge Wyzanski were on the minds of many
citizens who went to the polls in 1960.

Since most of the investigations, indictments, and convictions we
have described here took place during the administrations of Governor Foster Furcolo (1956-60), a Democrat, Furcolo and his party
became the focus of much of the public cynicism toward and disillusionment with politics.

Personal Politics and the
Structure of Massachusetts Government

We have suggested that politicians in Massachusetts play the political game as it was played in the nineteenth century because the
structure of government in the Commonwealth has in many respects
remained unchanged since that time. The abuses of the present have
evolved from and continue to deal with peculiarities of the past.
Current party programs, party principles, and party discipline are
matters of secondary importance. Issues in the state legislature are
very often resolved, not in terms of party positions or on the merits
of cases, but rather in terms of a complex network of friendships,
opportunities, enmities, courtesies, slights, etc. One state representative, who has served four terms in the Great and General Court,
described the operation of the House of Representatives to the authors as follows:

. . . The legislature is a different world, and it is a club. It's an area, and
the longer you're there the more you get used to being there and you

[90] U.S. v. Worcester, 190 Federal Supplement 548.

become alienated in a sense from the outside world. You begin to talk a language of your own. You begin to discuss constituents in a more or less impersonal manner. The talk is in a large measure about "how many summer jobs did you get?" You're there a long time and you begin to observe the personalities of the other people that are there and it's almost like being in the army. You live with your buddies here and this becomes your world and there's a certain feeling and obligation that we're all there to help each other and protect each other. I suppose much like the medical societies exist to take care of their own first, and there's this feeling which we have among ourselves, that we work very hard, and that we're entitled to some satisfaction for what we do and . . . we don't feel any qualms about a legislator being given a job and that sort of thing. But the world outside is not something that we're really alerted to. . . . Very often I think we're way behind the feelings of our constituents—you know the old saying that politicians are fifty years behind their times—I think there's something to that because we feel we got in by a certain method and we've taken our course and we might as well stick on that course and why look for change and why fight for change. . . .

I think there are a certain amount of pressures [upon legislators]. Well, of course, if there are no skeletons in the closet I don't suppose there can be much in the way of pressure, but there's some other informal pressures. Many times somebody will say, "Well, why get involved in that —why look into that—you know you're not going to make yourself very popular around here by doing it," and very often people succumb to that kind of talk. You want to be a good fellow and you want the others to say hello and joke and sit . . . next to you and have a feeling of comradeship— . . . you want to be part of the gang, you want to participate and contribute to the *esprit de corps*. You can't do that if you're going to strike out on your own and yell for things which . . . in the minds of many legislators—not only legislators but politicians, in the minds of political people who have influence over legislators—may be a very unpopular thing to do. So the pressure is really one of being accused of being a nonconformist within the legislature. I suppose the legislator is in many instances a greater example of conformity than in any other body. You talk about the conformity on the outside but you have it in the legislature.

He went on to describe the policy of *quid pro quo* that characterizes the relationships of legislators:

. . . The fact . . . that the whole legislature is run on a personal basis leaves a lot of room for back-scratching and for "put this man on and I'll see that this man gets in that department," or "I know so-and-so up in this department that's looking for a job and maybe we can work him into an-

other job but at the same time, if I do that for you or for your cousin up
there, why don't you do something for my friend down here?" I think
there's a good deal of that. I think really this is one of the problems that
the legislature faces and which prevents the legislature from doing the
best possible job it could do in the way of legislation. If we had a strong
party government outside the legislature, this wouldn't have to happen. . . .

The system of personal exchanges of favors results in weakening
of the parties, which in turn makes it difficult for the voter to fix responsibility for party action or to perceive the real reason a particular
representative voted with or against his party. Fragmentation of the
parties tends to make legislators easy prey for powerful groups in
search of political favors. The result in many instances is a government of men, not of laws. But the exchange of personal favors does
not necessarily result in corruption and conflict of interest. Barter-
ing of favors on a personal basis characterizes the actions of many
representatives in many state legislatures in this country; indeed, it
appears to be part of the democratic process. In Massachusetts,
however, the evidence indicates that the exchange of personal favors
between influential individuals has all but replaced government by
parties. Consequently, party responsibility has decreased and corruption increased.

Disciplined, responsible government is possible only if public officials have the political power necessary to execute their duties. Political power in Massachusetts, however, is fragmented—indeed, it is
atomized. The governor is hamstrung by a plethora of archaic checks
and balances which often prevent him from controlling key officials
in his own branch of government. Indeed, he must often work with
department heads who, appointed by a previous governor, may be
members of the opposition party. The governor's council, established in the eighteenth century to check and advise the governor, is
a vestigial organ which performs no useful service to the community.
The bureaucracy, an anarchic collection of 177 separate units, is a
model of administrative chaos. Many boards, commissions, and
public authorities, which are beyond the effective control of the
governor or the legislature, operate as independent (and thus irresponsible) centers of power. This fragmentation of political power
makes for irresponsible parties and personal politics—an atmosphere
conducive to *quid pro quo* and corruption.

* * *

In 1960, the voters of Massachusetts, in response to the personalization of politics and the scandals that had occurred during the Furcolo administrations, elected John Volpe, a Republican, Governor of Massachusetts. In Chapter 2, we shall describe the 1960 Democratic gubernatorial primary campaign, undoubtedly one of the most vicious and vindictive ever held in Massachusetts. We shall also describe the final campaign, which equalled the primary in innuendo and vilification.

2.
Massachusetts Elects a Governor

$*$ $*$ $*$

A primary fight, at any level, is America's most original contribution to the "art of democracy"—and, at any level, it is that form of the art most profanely reviled and intensely hated by every professional who practices politics as a trade.

THEODORE H. WHITE[1]

The nomination of John Fitzgerald Kennedy for the presidency of the United States was received with great enthusiasm by the leaders of the Democratic party in Massachusetts. They felt quite certain that Kennedy's plurality in the Bay State would be large enough to ensure the victory of every Democrat on the state ticket, with the possible exception of Governor Foster Furcolo, who, it was assumed, would oppose the prestigious and popular Leverett Saltonstall for his seat in the United States Senate. Although the Republicans were fully aware of the tremendous pulling power of Kennedy's coattails, they were encouraged by a Massachusetts tradition of split-ticket voting and by the large number of so-called independents, who are not affiliated with either party. Republican leaders were also hopeful that public indignation over the scandals of the Furcolo administra-

---

[1] Theodore H. White, *The Making of the President 1960* (New York: Atheneum Publishers, 1961), p. 78.

tion would work to their advantage. From their point of view, the outcome of the state elections would depend upon the decisions of hundreds of thousands of cross-pressured independents and Democrats, who would be attracted to a native son in the national election but repelled by what they believed to be the corruption, ineptitude, and vulgarities of Democrats in the State House.

The likelihood of a Kennedy and Democratic sweep in Massachusetts raised the political ambitions of several local Democratic lords, who began to rally their followers during the late spring of 1960. However, the leading contender for the Democratic pre-primary-convention endorsement for governor, Secretary of State Joseph Ward, had been developing a grass-roots organization and seeking the support of convention delegates for several months prior to the convention, which was held on June 18. At this point, Ward's only serious opponent was Lieutenant Governor Robert F. Murphy, a former majority floor leader in the Massachusetts House of Representatives. Murphy, like Ward, had been touring the state for several months in an effort to win the support of convention delegates. When Ward received the convention endorsement—on the first ballot—Murphy defied the party organization and decided to run in the primary.

Five other Democrats ultimately announced their intention to oppose the convention endorsee. Two of these men were Italo-Americans—Gabriel Piemonte, a former Boston city councilor and a prominent citizen in local Italian circles, and Alfred Magaletta, a real-estate developer who was a friend of Furcolo but politically unknown to the general public. Two were Irish—Francis E. Kelly, former state attorney general, who had run for statewide office 13 times before, and John Francis Kennedy, the state treasurer, who, according to his opponents, was the master of that popular Massachusetts political tactic known as "the name's the same." Adding to the ethnic variety was the fifth candidate, Endicott Peabody III, scion of a distinguished Yankee family and a former governor's councilor.

The Republicans, of course, were delighted by the prospect of a seven-man Democratic primary contest. Experience had taught them that a vicious struggle was likely to occur, in which party funds would be exhausted and ethnic antagonisms heightened. They hoped that the bitterness and vilification characteristic of such intraparty contests in Massachusetts would lead many supporters of the six losing gubernatorial candidates to desert the Democratic party in the November general election. Their hopes, as we shall see, were fully realized.

The Republican party was faced with four men actively seeking the party's convention endorsement. Three of these—Frank Giles, Philip A. Graham, and Howard Whitmore—were Yankee Protestants, and one—John A. Volpe—was an Italo-American Catholic. Giles was minority floor leader in the Massachusetts House of Representatives. Graham, a state senator from Hamilton, a small town in northeastern Massachusetts, was noted for his forthright, colorful, and bombastic speeches on the senate floor, many of them attacking corruption in Massachusetts. Whitmore, the choice of the "old-stock" Yankees, was a former mayor of Newton (a large and prosperous suburb of Boston) and had once held the strategically important position of chairman of the Ways and Means Committee of the Massachusetts House of Representatives. Volpe, whose life story is in the Horatio Alger tradition, had risen from extreme poverty to become president of one of the largest construction firms in Massachusetts. Although he had never been elected to public office, Volpe had served as public-works commissioner of Massachusetts from 1953 to 1956 and as federal roads administrator during part of the Eisenhower administration.

During the 1950's, Republican-party leaders had come to realize that their success depended, to some degree, upon slates that were ethnically balanced. Their strategy was therefore based on the theory that their nomination of Irish, Jewish, French, and Italian candidates would cause many Democrats who were disgusted with the "all green" Democratic ticket to vote along ethnic rather than party lines. The major source of tension within the party during the 'fifties was the question of the extent to which the ticket should be ethnically balanced. Many Republicans argued in the summer of 1960 that a massive defection of Italo-American Democrats could elect John Volpe, provided that Yankee Republicans did not abstain from voting.

The views of ethnically oriented Republicans prevailed at the state convention, which met on June 11, 1960. Giles's chances for the endorsement never materialized because many Republican members of the Massachusetts House of Representatives were converted to the ethnic strategy. Graham, whose followers marched around the floor of the convention carrying signs reading "Alienated Voters for Graham," never had more than a small core of loyal supporters; his outspoken manner and gruffness had alienated the more genteel members of the party. The Yankee choice, Whitmore, who is widely respected within the party as an able administrator, was considered a poor candidate by many because they thought his personality colorless. Volpe ultimately prevailed as the endorsee, not only because of ethnic considerations, but also because of the well-founded conviction that he could attract considerable financial support. After endorsing Leverett Saltonstall for the United States Senate (without opposition) and John Volpe for governor, the convention proceeded to endorse a "United Nations ticket" for the other offices: Augustus Means, a Yankee Brahmin, for lieutenant governor; George Michaels, a Jew, for attorney general; Edward Brooke, a Negro, for secretary of state; and Walter Trybulski, a Polish American, for state treasurer. For state auditor, an office which the Republicans knew they could not possibly win,[2] the convention endorsed Gardner Wardwell, an accountant who was unknown to the general public.

Faced with the challenge of a Republican ticket that was purposely and skillfully designed to appeal to ethnic groups, the Democratic party assembled in convention one week after the Republican conclave. In contrast to the Republican meeting, the Democratic convention was a spectacle of mismanagement and disorder, which seems to be a Democratic tradition in Massachusetts. The convention was held in the Boston Arena, a poorly ventilated and shabby hall which is often used for circuses and prize fights. The faulty loudspeaker system and the raucousness of the delegates made it impossible to hear speakers beyond the first twenty or thirty rows of seats. The main events were, of course, the contest for the endorsement for the United States Senate and for the governorship. Despite the scandals that had occurred during the Furcolo administration and the ethnic antagonism that exists between Irish Americans, who dominate the party, and Italo-Americans, who can wield the balance of power, Governor Furcolo was endorsed for the senatorial contest. Token opposition to Furcolo at the convention was voiced by the

[2] The incumbent state auditor, Thomas J. Buckley (Democrat), had been elected to that position for 10 consecutive terms. His popularity was based on the fact that his audits had led to several investigations of wrong-doing in both Republican and Democratic administrations. On November 7, 1961, Buckley received more votes in Massachusetts than John Fitzgerald Kennedy.

followers of Thomas J. O'Connor, the 34-year-old mayor of Springfield, who had served two terms in the state legislature. The party
leaders supported Furcolo, in part, because they assumed that the
usual resentment of an "all green" ticket was gaining strength within
the party.

The contest for the gubernatorial endorsement, however, attracted
more interest. Joseph Ward and Robert Murphy, as we have noted,
were the only party leaders who had been contacting convention
delegates prior to the convention. Shortly after the balloting began
it became obvious that Ward had done his fieldwork thoroughly. He
received the endorsement on the first ballot. Murphy, who was bit-
terly disappointed, mounted the podium, congratulated the endorsee,
and then stated that he would have to re-evaluate his political plans.
A few days later he announced his intention to oppose Ward, and
the intraparty war was under way. Murphy declared to the press
that John Thompson, Democratic speaker of the House, had used
his political power in Ward's behalf and had "bullied and bludg-
eoned" delegates into line. He described the convention as "power
politics at its worst," quoting newspaper accounts which stated that
Ward had spent large sums of money to provide hotel rooms for 160
delegates from western Massachusetts and had paid for a breakfast
attended by 900 delegates.[3] He charged: "Ward-heelers traded with
those higher up and those higher up, in turn, manipulated the ward-
heelers . . . , each seeking to enrich himself at the expense of the
public. The leadership was power-drunk, the ward-heelers hungry
for votes. Votes went to the highest bidder with total disregard of
the consequences and cost to the taxpayer."[4] From the viewpoint of
Republican public-relations men, Murphy's description of the convention was perfectly designed to alienate Democrats and independents.

The Candidates in the Democratic Primary

With seven candidates seeking the Democratic gubernatorial nomination, the outcome of the primary was likely to depend more upon

[3] *Berkshire Eagle,* June 20, 1961, p. 18 (editorial).
[4] *Boston Globe,* June 23, 1961, p. 1.

the personalities, ethnic origins, and religions of the candidates than on their programs or the "issues." For this reason we present profiles of each candidate.

Joseph D. Ward

Joseph Ward's endorsement by the pre-primary convention entitled him to first place on the ballot and the support of what may euphemistically be called "the Democratic organization." In the opinion of local professional politicians, these two factors made Ward the leading contender for the nomination. A graduate of the College of the Holy Cross and the Boston University Law School, Ward was elected to the Massachusetts House of Representatives in 1948 from Fitchburg, a small industrial town 47 miles west of Boston. A highly articulate speaker, who indulges in florid political rhetoric, Ward became known on Beacon Hill as a vigorous spokesman for bread-and-butter liberalism and anti-Communism. During his eight years in the House of Representatives (1948-56), Ward consistently supported the major Democratic bills favoring workmen's compensation, maximum unemployment-insurance benefits, and a minimum wage.

Like many other Al Smith Democrats, however, Ward was vociferous in his demand for a thorough investigation of Communism in Massachusetts. In 1953, he antagonized civil libertarians by introducing a resolution urging the United States Senate to send an investigating committee to Harvard University to "see what is going on behind those red brick walls over there." He also demanded an investigation of Harvard President James Bryant Conant,[5] who was appointed United States High Commissioner to Germany by President Eisenhower in 1953.

During a debate in the House of Representatives on a resolve to continue the term of the Special Commission to Study and Investigate Communism and Subversive Activities, Ward introduced the following amendment relating to the report of the commission:

Such report shall include the name and all other identifying data available to the commission of any individual presently a member or believed to be

[5] *Worcester Telegram*, Feb. 1, 1953, p. 2A.

a member of the Communist party, or concerning whom the commission has evidence that such individual is in any respect a subversive or security risk by reason of disloyalty.[6]

Before his election to the House of Representatives, Ward had been the legal counsel for the Massachusetts Retail Liquor Dealers' Board of Trade. Ward's father-in-law is a former president of this organization. After he won the primary nomination, Ward was attacked by some Volpe supporters on the ground that he had introduced 15 bills which would benefit his former client. During the campaign, a handbill was widely circulated in Massachusetts[7] which was attributed to the "Beverage Dealers for Joseph D. Ward." The handbill described Ward as "the best friend our industry ever had" and urged liquor dealers to

Protect your business by taking positive action to assure the election of Joe Ward. This may well be the most important political action of your business career. Please go to your local Democratic chairman and volunteer to work—there are many things you can do to help out. The Ward campaign is seriously short of funds. The opposition have unlimited funds with which to campaign. Send us a substantial contribution or whatever you can afford immediately. Make your check payable to the Beverage Dealers for Ward. You'll never make a better investment in your business . . . and the future of Massachusetts.

In 1956 Ward was endorsed by the Democratic pre-primary convention for the office of attorney general. He was defeated, however, in a bitter primary contest by Edward McCormack, nephew of the present majority floor leader of the United States House of Representatives. In 1958 Ward was elected secretary of state by the state legislature when the incumbent died. It was from this position that he launched his campaign for the governorship in 1960. In response to a query concerning his hobby, the Secretary replied, "My hobby? It's politics. That's what I do in my spare time and all the time."[8] As secretary of state during this election, he was responsible for preparing the primary ballot, a responsibility he carried out with some dramatic and embarrassing effects.

[6] *Journal of the House*, 1954, p. 1808.
[7] The authors do not know who distributed this literature, but only that it was distributed.
[8] *Boston Globe*, June 19, 1960, p. 18.

Robert F. Murphy

Ward's opponent for the convention endorsement, Robert F. Murphy, has never been a controversial figure in the Massachusetts Democratic party. A rather quiet and modest man, who has been hailed by his followers as "the greatest living Democrat in Massachusetts,"[9] Murphy was elected to the Massachusetts House of Representatives in 1942 from Malden, one of the less prosperous suburbs of Boston. In 1948, when the Democratic party won a majority in the House of Representatives for the first time in this century, Murphy was chosen majority leader by his colleagues. He gradually developed a loyal following in the legislature and received the party's endorsement for the governorship in 1954, when he defeated Francis E. Kelley in the primary. He was defeated in the general election, however, by Christian Herter. In 1956, Murphy, who campaigned as "Mr. Integrity," won the lieutenant governorship. Two years later he was re-elected by a greater margin than his running mate, gubernatorial candidate Foster Furcolo.

As a leading Democratic legislator, Murphy, in combination with other party leaders, was responsible for the passage of an ambitious program of road-building and of legislation that greatly expanded the mental-health facilities of the Commonwealth. He also played a leading role in the enactment of bills increasing appropriations for state teachers' colleges and expanding the facilities of the University of Massachusetts. During his career, Murphy has advocated legislation forbidding discrimination in the issuance of insurance and has favored an increase in the budget of the Massachusetts Commission Against Discrimination, so that the Commission could undertake a far-reaching program of education and research.

Murphy's reputation as "Mr. Integrity" developed out of his insistence that honest public officials and socially progressive legislation were necessary for the welfare of Massachusetts. He saw to it, during his term as majority floor leader, that his colleagues exercised moderation and circumspection in their attacks on Republican policies. On several occasions he curbed the tendency of some Democratic and Republican legislators to engage in vituperative and irresponsible debate. As floor leader and as lieutenant governor, Murphy contended that careful reorganization of the state administration would

[9] *Boston Herald,* June 22, 1960, p. 6.

save millions of dollars. He advocated an increase in the power of the governor that would permit the chief executive to institute such reforms. His basic campaign promise in the 1960 primary was that he could "hold the line" on new taxes and still increase state services.

During the campaign, Murphy issued four "Messages to Democrats," outlining proposals for a party platform based on "Democratic" principles, a stronger party organization, an expanded program of civil rights, and more efficient state administration. In public-opinion polls taken by the authors during the two weeks before the primary election, the overwhelming majority of those interviewed demonstrated no knowledge of or interest in Murphy's program. The only "issue" that many citizens were aware of, or had strong feelings about, was the proposal of Francis E. Kelly that Massachusetts establish a state lottery.

Francis E. Kelly

Since 1929, when he was elected to the Boston City Council at the age of 21, Francis E. Kelly has run for statewide office 13 times. In the poorer sections of Boston, where he has concentrated his political efforts, his name, which one opponent described as "a wonderful name for politics," has become a household word. Although Kelly has been defeated on nine occasions (1932, 1934, 1938, 1940, 1942, 1944, 1946, 1952, 1954), he is the only man who has ever defeated Leverett Saltonstall for public office. Kelly accomplished this in 1936, when he was elected lieutenant governor of the Commonwealth. (The Democratic governor at that time, Charles Hurley, was reportedly so antagonistic to Kelly that he ordered painters and repairmen to come in to redecorate his office while he was to be away in order to prevent Kelly from even occupying the governor's chair in Hurley's absence. Kelly, however, was not to be denied this privilege. He moved into the governor's office and transacted the affairs of the Bay State "at a desk covered with painter's canvas and flanked by buckets and stepladders."[10]) During one election Kelly campaigned on the slogan: "A free light bulb for every housewife in the state."

Kelly was elected attorney general in 1948, re-elected in 1950,

[10] William A. Shannon, "Massachusetts: Prisoner of the Past," in Robert S. Allen, ed., *Our Sovereign State* (New York: Vanguard Press, 1949), p. 31.

and defeated for that office by George Fingold in 1952. Since the late 'forties, Kelly had been advocating a statewide lottery as a solution to the tax problems of Massachusetts. The lottery became Kelly's major campaign plank in the 1960 gubernatorial primary. According to his proposal, he believed that $600,000,000 worth of lottery tickets would be sold annually. Half of the receipts would go to ticket holders as prizes; the rest would be devoted to alleviating the financial problems of the state. Kelly's $600,000,000 estimate was based on an assertion of the Massachusetts Crime Commission in 1955 that $2,000,000,000 is spent annually in the Bay State on illegal gambling. Kelly argued that approximately one third of this sum would be channelled into a legal lottery. Tickets were to be sold throughout the year in state-chartered banks in Massachusetts and by the treasurers of the 39 cities and 312 towns of the Commonwealth, who were to be bonded. An unlimited number of tickets, at three dollars apiece, could be purchased by any individual. According to Kelly's plan, tickets would also be sold to residents of other states and foreign countries. He failed to mention to the voters of Massachusetts, however, that federal law prohibits the mailing of lottery tickets.

Despite the opposition of Catholic and Protestant clergymen, who let it be known that they or their respective churches disapproved of a "Massachusetts sweepstakes," the overwhelming majority of the citizens of Massachusetts who were given an opportunity to vote on this issue in 1958 favored it.[11] Kelly, therefore, knew that he was advocating a position that was strongly preferred by a significant bloc of voters. No other candidate could make this claim. Although the number of voters who favor such a position may be a relatively small proportion of those who vote in a general election, the fact remains that it may be large enough to decide a primary election in which the turnout is small and the vote is likely to be split among several candidates.

Although most of Kelly's opponents argued that the lottery proposal was politically irresponsible, demagogic, immoral, and financially unsound, they recognized and were troubled by its potential political appeal. One campaign manager suggested during the campaign, "The closest thing to a real issue has been the sweepstakes.

[11] Massachusetts has 160 election districts. The "public-policy" question appeared on the ballot in 60 of these and was favored in 56 of them.

I think many observers may be underestimating Kelly's appeal to the voters."[12]

John Francis Kennedy

In 1952, an inventory clerk employed by the Gillette Safety Razor Company in Boston decided that he would like to become treasurer of the Commonwealth of Massachusetts. Although this clerk had never run for public office and was totally unknown to the voters of the Bay State, he collected a sufficient number of signatures to entitle his name to be placed on the primary ballot and succeeded in finishing a strong second in a field of seven candidates. In 1954, this clerk, whose name happens to be John F. Kennedy, defeated the Democratic endorsee and won the nomination. The Democratic state committee, forced to support him in the general election, pointed out to the voters of Massachusetts that Kennedy's success was "typically American" and that he had obviously captured the "imagination and interest" of the public. The Committee also argued that Kennedy's election would be "proof that in Massachusetts democracy works and that Americans invariably draw their best talent for leadership from the rank and file of the people."[13]

Democracy (Democratic-state-committee style) evidently does work in Massachusetts, for Kennedy defeated his Republican opponent in 1954 by 174,000 votes. Despite their view that Kennedy had captured the "imagination and interest" of the public, the party leaders refused to endorse him in 1956. This did not prevent the treasurer from being re-elected by 152,814 votes, a feat which he repeated in 1958, with a plurality of 455,811 votes. Some sources, evidently not close enough to the Democratic state committee to hear its interpretation of the phenomenon, suggest that the treasurer's success has something to do with the fact that many voters confuse him with another John F. Kennedy. The treasurer, however, reported to the authors in 1960 that in his opinion "not more than 5 per cent" of the voters mistake him for his younger and more popular namesake.

[12] The authors' pre-primary public-opinion poll indicates that Kelly received the bulk of his support from the least educated and lowest income groups in the state. Most of Kelly's supporters specifically mentioned the lottery when asked why they were planning to vote for him.

[13] Quoted in V. O. Key, Jr., *American State Politics: An Introduction* (New York: Alfred A. Knopf, 1956), p. 216.

Kennedy's appeal to the voters of Massachusetts, however, may be based on more than his name. In his campaigns since 1952, Kennedy has ignored the party organization and has refused to purchase television or radio time or newspaper space on his own. In fact, he claims not to have spent more than $200 in any single campaign. He attributes his success to the fact that the voters of Massachusetts are profoundly cynical and distrust politicians who spend large sums of money because they "know" that opulent campaigns mean that the candidate is "owned" by the contributors. He argues that the voters "know" he is not a corrupt politician because he spends no money and has no formal organization. A few days before the 1960 gubernatorial primary, he stated to the authors:

People have been fooled for years. They throw out one rascal and perhaps the fellow they put in is worse than he is. That's kind of disillusioning to them. They don't like it but they haven't been able to see any logical alternative to voting the way they do. I figure in this particular campaign I'll give them the alternative. If they don't want my type of government, then they're entitled to the type of government they want.

It is interesting to speculate on the embarrassment John Fitzgerald Kennedy might have experienced had John Francis Kennedy won the Democratic primary contest for governor of Massachusetts.[14]

Endicott Peabody III

One week after the Democratic convention endorsed Joseph Ward, Endicott ("Chub") Peabody III, grandson of a former master of the Groton School, son of an Episcopal bishop, and a graduate of Harvard College and Harvard Law School, announced his intention to run for the governorship. Peabody is a Democrat with a difference. He is not of Irish or Italian extraction. He is not Roman Catholic, and he was not "born" a Democrat. In fact, his political opponents often reminded the voters of Massachusetts that Peabody's "first entry" into politics was in behalf of a Republican and also a Yankee, Robert Bradford, who was elected governor in 1946. Unlike some of his opponents and many Al Smith Democrats, however, Peabody entered the Democratic party because he shared the liberal political and intellectual convictions of the New Dealers.

[14] Two of the six Democratic candidates for State Treasurer were also named John Kennedy.

Upon entering law practice in Boston after World War II, Peabody became well known for his advocacy of anti-discrimination and civil-liberties legislation. He often spoke out publicly against "McCarthyism" and became one of the leaders within the American Bar Association who attempted to persuade the Association to oppose the Bricker Amendment. During the early 1950's, he frequently acted as a spokesman on legislative matters that interested the Civil Liberties Union of Massachusetts, the Americans for Democratic Action, and the American Veterans Committee.

In 1954, Peabody, a Democrat, was elected to the governor's council from a traditionally Republican district. His victory, which came as a surprise to the professionals of the Democratic party, was attributable largely to his tremendous energy as a campaigner. Peabody was willing and able to meet thousands of constituents in an endless round of handshaking and conversation. He was aided in this campaign by a small but enthusiastic group of amateurs who found his liberalism appealing. His success, however, was also due to the fact that the Republican incumbent did not run and to the fact that the Republican party supported a relatively unknown candidate, who became ill during the campaign.

The governor's council, an ancient institution originally established to check and approve certain actions of the governor, has become a stepping stone to higher appointive office in Massachusetts. Because of their power to approve gubernatorial appointments, paroles, and some state contracts, the councilors are in a position, if they choose to make use of it, to exchange favors with politicians and businessmen and thereby create the basis of a campaign organization.

In 1956, Peabody sought and failed to win the Democratic convention endorsement for attorney general. The convention endorsed Ward, who was defeated in the primary election by Edward McCormack. In 1958, the convention endorsed McCormack, who defeated Peabody in the primary because Peabody did not have adequate strength outside Boston to offset McCormack's pluralities in the low-income, industrialized Irish sections of the Hub. Peabody ran well only in his old councilor district (Middlesex County). Nevertheless, he received the majority of the votes cast in Boston's ward 1 (primarily Italo-American), ward 14 (approximately 70-75% Jewish), ward 22 (primarily middle-income Irish), and ward 21 (middle-income Jewish and Irish). It is clear that his strength in 1958 lay in those areas where resentment against the "all green" ticket was great.[15] All his opponents in the 1960 gubernatorial primary assumed that Peabody, as the only Protestant candidate, would do well if the Irish vote were split among the four Irish candidates. This assumption was also made by Peabody's supporters.

According to his supporters, Peabody had substantial assets in his own right. They argued that he alone would be perceived by disenchanted Democrats and by independents as a non-politician and a non-grafter. Peabody could also claim—and did, during the campaign—that he was the only candidate who had been asked by John Fitzgerald Kennedy to help him in the bitter West Virginia presidential primary. (Kennedy may have believed that a Yankee liberal Democrat from Massachusetts could be an asset in Fundamentalist mining areas.) Peabody, however, was not the only candidate who expected to benefit from the anticipated split in the Irish vote.

Gabriel F. Piemonte

Gabriel F. Piemonte is probably the best-known Italo-American in the Massachusetts Democratic party, with the exception of Foster Furcolo. Piemonte had served three terms in the Massachusetts House of Representatives from a district composed predominantly of Italo-Americans. He also served as a member of the Boston City Council from 1951 to 1959. As a state representative, Piemonte consistently voted as a bread-and-butter liberal; as a city councilor, he developed a reputation as an opponent of what he calls "tax chiselers." Campaigning as "Honest Gabe" in the 1959 Boston mayorality primary, Piemonte finished a strong third in a five-man race, drawing the bulk of his support from Italo-American and Yankee precincts. Before the 1960 gubernatorial primary, Piemonte predicted that he would receive the overwhelming majority of votes from constituents of Italian descent, "because I'm qualified."[16] In the 1960 gubernatorial primary Piemonte campaigned on the slogan: "Let the Sun Shine All Over Massachusetts." Piemonte was

[15] Middle- and upper-middle-income Irish apparently do not have the same loyalties to the "all green" ticket that low-income Irish do, perhaps because they do not have the same needs or expectations.

[16] *Boston Herald,* Aug. 24, 1960, p. 11.

opposed in the primary by another American of Italian descent, one
Alfred Magaletta.

Alfred Magaletta

Alfred Magaletta, a businessman and real-estate developer, had
served one term as a selectman in his home town of Westwood, Massachusetts, a suburb of Boston. Although Magaletta had been
appointed to two minor positions by Governor Furcolo, he was unknown to the general public. During the campaign, he was the
only candidate who supported Furcolo's proposal for a limited sales
tax. Professional politicians in the Democratic party and newspapers
in Massachusetts believed that Magaletta had no chance of winning
the primary. Some of his opponents suggested that he had entered
the race at the behest of Furcolo, who wanted to ensure a large
turnout of Italo-Americans. Others argued that Ward had played
some part in Magaletta's candidacy, on the assumption that Magaletta would deprive Piemonte of some Italo-American votes.

The Democratic Primary

The Rhetoric of the Campaign

Following the Democratic state convention, most professional
politicians and inside dopesters believed, and for good reason, that
Joseph Ward was the frontrunner. Ward had several advantages,
which he exploited with considerable skill, while his opponents were
at a disadvantage, each in a different way. In primary elections,
party organization at the grass-roots level usually pays off. Ward
knew this and had carefully developed the nucleus of a statewide
organization in the months before the primary. The endorsement by
the pre-primary convention gave Ward the support of the Democratic
party organization (such as it is) and presumably the votes of most
of the hard-core regulars, who remain with the party's endorsee
regardless of who he may be. The endorsement also gave Ward
the favored first-place position on the primary ballot, an advantage
probably worth an extra 5 per cent of the votes cast.

The fact that Ward, who is not from Boston, was running against
four men who were from the metropolitan area—Piemonte, Peabody,

Kelly, and Murphy—may also have been an advantage. Boston voters traditionally support Boston candidates while outstate voters tend to vote "anti-Boston." If voters maintained this tradition, it would be likely that the Boston vote would be split four ways, while Ward would receive the bulk of the outstate votes, having only Treasurer Kennedy to worry about there. (Magaletta, who was from a suburb of Boston, was not regarded as a contender by any of the other candidates.) And Ward, as convention endorsee, could count on some of the Boston vote, too. Ward could and did stress these "advantages" when seeking financial support. It is customary for candidates to argue that those who want to be with a winner would be wise to contribute to their campaigns.

Ward's advantages were enhanced by the inability of his opponents to draw on organizational support or sources of funds or both. Magaletta and Piemonte had neither of these essentials. Murphy, who also had great difficulty in raising money, was forced to revive the defunct organization that had supported him in previous elections. Although he was modestly successful in this, his organization was pitifully small in contrast to Ward's. Only Peabody succeeded in developing anything that resembled a large-scale organization, and it failed to reach throughout the state and was ineffectual in many parts of the Commonwealth. Peabody, however, was able to raise enough money to compete with Ward for voter attention until the last few days of the campaign, when lack of funds forced him to cancel several television and radio programs and many newspaper ads.[17] Kelly's lottery proposal and Kennedy's confusing name were at first discounted as assets by the Ward brain trust—the lottery because Kelly lacked funds for full publicity, the Kennedy name because John Fitzgerald Kennedy was running for the presidency this time, which made it seem less likely that people would confuse him with John Francis Kennedy, who was running for state office.[18]

Although intraparty primary elections on the state level are often

[17] Peabody's campaign manager stated to the authors, "If we had the money Ward is spending in this campaign, we would win this thing quite handily."

[18] An open question, this. Lyndon B. Johnson was running for both vice president and senator from Texas at the same time. In fact, there would have been more reason than ever to believe that the same J.F.K. was running for two offices, president and governor, among those likely to be confused in the first place. This kind of confusion stems from unfamiliarity with the facts that regular newspaper readers might be assumed to have. We will argue that Treasurer Kennedy failed to campaign at the level necessary to make enough people aware of his candidacy at all, much less to confuse a large enough number.

"issueless," most of the candidates did present programs to the voters, some of them highly detailed and thoughtfully constructed. Although Ward, for example, relied heavily throughout the campaign on the "fact" that he was the "official Democratic nominee" (he was the official Democratic *endorsee,* not nominee), he also presented to the voters a 23-point program, parts of which he discussed at various times on television and radio. Seven of his 23 points were designed to appeal to those who place a high value on family life and "togetherness." Thousands, perhaps hundred of thousands, of multicolored postcards were mailed to voters, imprinted with a photograph of Ward, his wife, and their seven daughters. Ward's key campaign slogan was printed on the other side: "The family unit is the heart of Joseph D. Ward's program. Will you help him to help all our families by electing the Democratic Nominee for Governor?" Ward's wife appeared on television several times and proudly announced, "Joe Ward has been a good father to his children, he will be a good father to you."

In addition to playing up the family, Ward advocated (1) the creation of a state youth council to coordinate private efforts in the field of juvenile problems; (2) the establishment of a "code of ethics" for public officials; (3) the expansion of the University of Massachusetts and increased support for state and community colleges; (4) the creation of special educational programs for gifted children; (5) the creation of an economic development commission to attract new industries to Massachusetts; (6) the enactment of a constitutional amendment to permit low-interest loans to encourage private development of middle-class housing; (7) the passage of bills providing increased housing for the aged; (8) the passage of bills increasing participation by the state in urban renewal; (9) the assumption by the state of all local welfare costs; (10) the creation of new facilities for aiding retarded children and providing improved recreation programs, day nurseries, and halfway houses; and (11) the passage of a bill calling a convention to revise the state constitution. No other candidate had a program so comprehensive or liberal as Ward's. The pre-primary public-opinion poll taken by the authors indicates that only a tiny fraction of those interviewed knew of, or were interested in, Ward's program. Kelly's proposal for a Massachusetts sweepstakes was the only programmatic issue that excited much interest or support.

Throughout the campaign Ward stressed the importance of party loyalty. This strategy was designed to win the support of rank-and-file Democrats, who traditionally support the convention endorsee. He also attempted to attract the votes of working men by citing his legislative record in favor of unemployment compensation for employees involved in lengthy strikes, of "cash sickness" insurance, and of a more liberal workmen's-compensation and unemployment-compensation law. Ward was in fact supported by several trade unions whose presidents are closely affiliated with the key leaders of the Democratic party in Massachusetts.

During the primary campaign Ward appears to have spent more money than any other candidate. He purchased more television and radio time and more newspaper space than any other candidate. He also advertised on more billboards and sent out larger mailings than his opponents. The day before the primary election Kelly charged that Ward had spent $900,000.[19] Most of the other candidates, campaign managers, and fund raisers involved in the campaign estimated that Ward had spent between $300,000 and $500,000. A Boston political columnist reported that Ward supporters had openly admitted to him that they had "no financial problems."[20] Ward's financial support, combined with his convention endorsement and his organization (during the final week of the campaign Ward had 2,000 supporters in Boston conducting a massive door-to-door canvass), made him the candidate to beat, in the opinion of most of his opponents.

While Ward toured the state stressing his program and the need for loyalty to the Democratic party, Murphy hammered away at the charge that the convention had been "rigged." He lost no opportunity to remind the voters that Ward's actions "have only added to the deep distrust in the minds of people throughout the state of politics and politicians."[21] On occasion Murphy stressed his program, which was almost as liberal as Ward's but not so comprehensive. Murphy, however, had no single issue which he could use to dramatize his candidacy. His advocacy of "No New Taxes" smacked of the traditional campaign vocabulary; such a promise is interpreted as mere verbiage by many voters and ignored by those who

19 *Boston Herald*, Sept. 12, 1960, p. 1.
20 Cornelius Dalton, *Boston Traveler*, Aug. 31, 1960, p. 26.
21 *Boston Globe*, Sept. 11, 1960, p. 36.

want expanded welfare and education programs. Murphy was also hindered, in the opinion of his own campaign manager and his opponents, by the "fact" that he is neither physically attractive nor appealing in manner on television. Lacking "popular appeal" and a flair for public relations, Murphy was spurned by most of those who traditionally supply the bulk of campaign contributions. It is possible also that Murphy's reputation as "Mr. Integrity" discouraged some potential contributors.

In contrast to Murphy's blandness, Francis E. Kelly's political style was dynamic; he presented a plan that some voters found attractive and dramatic, purporting to offer at once pleasure and immediate tax relief. Kelly, who had relatively little money to work with, relied primarily on radio. He ignored the "issues" raised by Ward and Murphy, although he cried out night after night that he was "the only candidate with a program" designed to meet the rising cost of government. He reminded his hard core of supporters, whom he estimated at 100,000-strong (he received 98,107 votes in the primary), that the state legislature had "violated the will of the people" by refusing to pass a law establishing a sweepstakes after the people had approved it by an "overwhelming mandate" in 1958.

Endicott Peabody hoped to receive the support of different segments of the electorate. Assuming that the regulars would remain with Ward and that the Irish vote would be split among the four Irish candidates, Peabody directed his efforts to middle-class and suburban Democrats and independents, who, he believed, were disillusioned with corrupt and professional politicians. Peabody's supporters facilely assumed that these voters would readily perceive Peabody as the only "clean," nonprofessional politician in the race. However, suburban Democrats and independents fail to vote in large numbers during primaries, and thus, as Peabody warned the citizens of Massachusetts in large front-page ads, two out of every three persons eligible to vote in the Democratic primary forfeit their right to restore clean government to the Bay State. He also urged independents to go to the polls, explaining to them that although they would have to declare themselves as registered Democrats, they could easily return to the status of "independent" after the election. Assuming that potential suburban voters were more liberal than Democrats from Boston, Peabody had Professor John K. Galbraith, a key Kennedy adviser, announce that Peabody would introduce the ideas of the New Frontier to Massachusetts. In addition to appealing to liberal Democrats and independents, Peabody had to differentiate himself from "machine politicians" in order to strengthen what he thought was his "nonpolitical" image. This necessitated a break with Governor Furcolo and the other incumbents. Unlike Murphy, who openly split with the governor on the issue of a limited sales tax, Peabody failed to criticize the administration, although he knew that significant blocs of voters were disgusted and disillusioned with Furcolo. Peabody, however, was afraid that a direct and vigorous attack on the Furcolo administration might antagonize many Italo-Americans who might otherwise favor him. He decided, therefore, to attack the administration indirectly, by means of such mild and innocuous statements as: "People don't want shifty, insincere men running the state. They are fed up with wheelers and dealers. I would give the positions of responsibility to those most qualified and most eager to render 100-per-cent service to the state."[22] His billboard and newspaper advertising was undramatic, unvituperative. He campaigned on the slogan: "The People Pick Peabody." In his newspaper ads, Peabody asked the voters, "Which Democratic candidate has the honesty and responsibility needed by our next Governor?"[23]

The only original and creative bit of public relations that came from the Peabody camp was a series of five-minute "news" broadcasts on television, called "The Political Roundup." The format of the program was similar to that of any TV news summary, consisting of several "news" clips dealing with international and national as well as local events. Interspersed in these reports were movies showing Peabody surrounded by admirers. The "news" analyst, an employee of the Peabody organization, "reported" a groundswell for Peabody. Although "The Political Roundup" was preceded and followed by the legally required statement: "This broadcast is (or was) sponsored by the Peabody for Governor Committee," the format suggested that it was a regular news broadcast—that is, an objective report. The manager of the Boston television station on which this program first appeared cancelled it after a few days because he thought it was confusing to viewers.

Despite the originality of this gambit, Peabody did not have any

[22] *Boston Traveler*, Aug. 30, 1960, p. 39.
[23] Peabody advertisement, *Boston Herald*, Sept. 9, 1960, p. 4.

issue by means of which he could clearly differentiate himself from his opponents. There was some reason to believe that Peabody might receive the endorsement of John Fitzgerald Kennedy, which probably would have been a tremendous asset. One of the major issues, if not *the* major issue, of Kennedy's campaign was the Democratic nominee's religion. Would the voters of the United States elect a Roman Catholic as president? The problem with the Democratic party in Massachusetts in 1960 was precisely the reverse. Would the members of the party, who are overwhelmingly Roman Catholic, vote for a Protestant? If Peabody was nominated by the Democratic party in Massachusetts, Kennedy could appeal to voters thoughout the country to emulate the example of his own party in transcending ethnic and religious bigotry. One endorsement of Peabody, which appeared in a Lowell, Massachusetts, newspaper, argued, "The man who could really help Senator Kennedy countrywide, if nominated for Governor, would be Chub Peabody."[24]

On August 17, Peabody met with Kennedy in Washington. No report of their conversation was released to the press, but soon afterward a large number of signs were posted in various parts of the state: "Kennedy for President, Peabody for Governor." The implication of the meeting was obvious. Thomas Winship, of the *Boston Globe,* reported that "Peabody came away [from the meeting with Kennedy] with encouragement, but no endorsement"; he also pointed out that several of Kennedy's brain-trusters from Harvard were also working for Peabody.[25] Although the senator's campaign manager, Robert F. Kennedy, indicated that his brother had endorsed no one, the impression that Kennedy favored Peabody was widespread. Nevertheless, Peabody needed some dramatic issue to activate suburbanites and rally independents to his cause. Such an issue was born on August 28, 1961, when Secretary of State Joseph Ward released to the press copies of the ballots which were to be used on election day, September 13.

The "Ballot-rigging" Issue

The secretary of state of Massachusetts is responsible for the design of ballots for all statewide offices. Massachusetts law specifies

24 *Lowell Optic,* Sept. 3, 1960, p. 1.
25 Thomas Winship, *Boston Sunday Globe,* Aug. 21, 1960, Section A, p. 3.

that the names of all candidates "shall be arranged in a horizontal row or vertical column under or opposite the titles of the offices."[26] It also states that the name of the convention endorsee shall be placed at the head of the row or the top of the column, followed by that of the incumbent, if he is running. The names of all other candidates are to be listed alphabetically.[27] The law also permits each candidate to have printed under his name "not more than eight words"[28] designating his political party, the public offices which he holds or has held, and whether he is a former incumbent. If the candidate is a veteran he may also have this fact appear in his biographical data.

Approximately 400,000 citizens of Massachusetts (those who vote in 344 of the 1080 precents in the state) vote in areas where "horizontal" voting machines are used. In 1960 the Office of the Secretary of State ordered the firm that prints the ballots used in these machines to position the names of the seven gubernatorial candidates as follows:

Ward	Kelly	
Kennedy	Magaletta	
Murphy	Peabody	Piemonte

The Office of the Secretary of State also ordered the printers to use bolder type for the biographical data to appear under the names of all convention-endorsed candidates (see Fig. 1). Massachusetts law is silent on the subject of the relative type size to be used for biographical data for endorsed as opposed to non-endorsed candidates. Massachusetts law is also silent on the subject of blank spaces. The law neither prohibits nor permits the secretary of state to place blank spaces between the names of candidates for the same office. Nevertheless, an official of Wright & Potter, the firm that has printed ballots for the Commonwealth since the Civil War, stated to the authors that biographical data for all candidates, endorsed and non-endorsed, had always appeared in the same-size type. This official also stated that no secretary of state prior to Ward had ever ordered blank spaces to be located on a horizontal ballot in any place other than after the name of the "last" candidate for a par-

26 *Massachusetts General Laws Annotated,* Vol. 6, Chap. 54, sec. 33.
27 *Ibid.,* Chap. 53, sec. 34.
28 *Ibid.,* sec. 45.

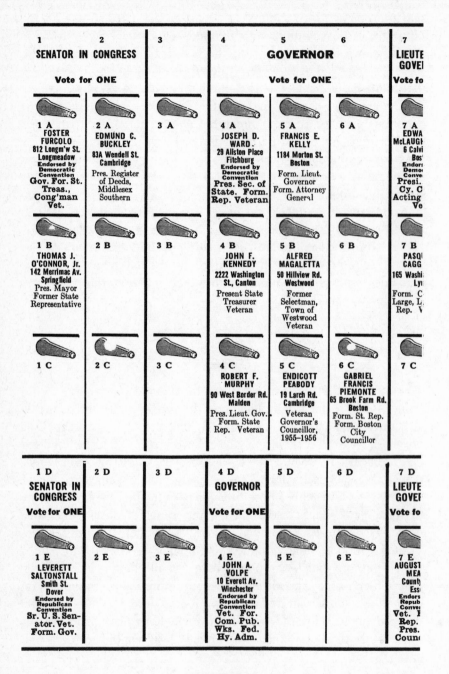

FIGURE 1

ticular office. If the ballot used in horizontal voting machines in 1960 had been designed according to custom, the names of the gubernatorial candidates would have been printed consecutively, either horizontally or vertically, with blank spaces placed only after the name of the "last" candidate. If custom had been followed, the biographical data for all candidates would have been printed in the same type size.

When Murphy and Peabody received sample copies of the ballot, they notified the press that Ward had deliberately "rigged" the ballot. Peabody accused Ward of "illegally juggling the ballot positions to further his own political ambitions." Murphy noted that some of the ballots had a "bolder, blacker faced type for some candidates and a lighter faced type for others." He informed the voters of Massachusetts that Ward not only had "rigged" the convention but had now "rigged the ballots as well."[29]

We assume that Peabody objected to the design of the ballot because he believed that the location of blank spaces made it more difficult for voters to find his name. Because the names of candidates are usually arranged consecutively in one or more horizontal or vertical lines, without blank spaces, Peabody may have assumed that voters are habituated to glance across a horizontal line or down a vertical column. If Peabody's assumption is correct, voters who used horizontal ballots would notice (first) the names of Ward and Kelly if they glanced across the top column, or the names of Ward and Kennedy if they glanced down the first column. In either case (if this assumption is correct) Peabody would be disadvantaged.

Following his statement to the press, Peabody filed a writ of mandamus in the Massachusetts Superior Court. He wished the Court to order the secretary of state to redesign the ballot and issue new ones. Peabody's request was denied, without comment, by Judge Wilfred J. Paquet on September 1, 1960. Jerome Patrick Troy, first deputy secretary of state, and a Ward supporter, testified that it would be impossible to reprint and distribute new ballots by September 13, the date scheduled for the primary.

The day after the hearing, Peabody announced that he would not appeal the decision to a higher court because, in his opinion, this would delay the date of the primary. He stated, however, that

[29] *Boston Globe,* Sept. 2, 1960, p. 5.

The ballot layout proposed by . . . Ward . . . is designed to, and will, confuse the voters of the Commonwealth when they vote in the primary on September 13. . . . The ability of the voters to register their choice freely and fairly has been compromised. . . . I am certain that in the end this shocking and scandalous trick will not help the Secretary of State. . . . [The public will vote] against the slickers and manipulators who have been involved in this scheme.[30]

Ward then issued a press release in which he referred to Peabody as the "All-American cry baby." He argued that Peabody's actions were guided by two motives:

The first, to attempt by innuendo to question the integrity of career employees of my election division and indirectly my own; and second, to bolster a sagging campaign by grasping at publicity regardless of the merits of the case. Obviously, this is a desperation move on the part of a candidate facing defeat.[31]

Ward, however, offered no explanation of why blank spaces appeared after the names of Kelly and Magaletta.

The "ballot-rigging" episode became Peabody's major issue during the last ten days of the campaign. The issue was, in a sense, made to order for him, as the "nonpolitical" candidate, for there is profound cynicism in Massachusetts toward politicians, and the episode provided disillusioned voters with some "concrete evidence" for focusing their hostility on Ward. Until the "ballot rigging" took place, his campaign manager stated, Peabody had "no major issue [on which] to campaign."

On election day, Peabody placed the following paid political advertisement in some Boston newspapers:[32]

TELL US, JOE

WHY as Secretary of State did you use three lines to list the names of seven candidates for governor while you found room for 16 candidates for state representative on the top row of horizontal voting machines?

WHY did you order the printer to set biographical data under your name in bigger, bolder type than the names of the other candidates for governor?

[30] *Christian Science Monitor*, Sept. 2, 1961, p. 2.
[31] *Ibid.*
[32] *Boston Globe*, Sept. 13, 1960, p. 1; *Boston Record*, Sept. 13, 1960, p. 1.

WHY did you leave blank spaces after the names of two candidates for governor on the horizontal machines?

WHY did you call yourself the official Democratic nominee for governor when you know THE PEOPLE will pick the official nominee on Tuesday?

TO INSURE HONEST GOVERNMENT
PEABODY
For GOVERNOR

Obviously worried by the attacks of his opponents, Ward appeared on television the evening before the election and branded them as "six selfish, self-seeking men interested in their own aggrandisement." He accused Kelly of attempting to "make Boston the Las Vegas of the East. . . . This man wants to put Massachusetts in the crime business." He stated to the people that John Francis Kennedy "sits there winding his watch and waiting for you to be misled. He has nothing but a cynical approach. I have more confidence in you." He chided Murphy for disputing the decision of the convention when in the past Murphy had said the convention decisions "were wonderful things." He castigated Peabody for branding "everyone a rogue and a knave except him[self]." Ward also urged voters, "If you feel the ballot is unfair, then vote against me." He concluded his speech with an appeal to "stay with your party." He also urged each voter "as a thinking American to go to the polls."[33]

Endicott Peabody appeared on television after Ward's speech and stated: "Ward sanctimoniously urged a code of ethics [yet] rigged the ballot to fix the election. . . ."[34] Murphy made one of his rare appearances on television the same evening, stating that Ward had "never been elected by the people," referring to himself as the "victim of a rigged convention," and charging that Ward had "taken unfair advantage [of his power to design the ballot] for himself." He concluded by referring to the "deep distrust of politics and politicians" he thought was characteristic of the Massachusetts electorate.[35]

Magaletta also appeared on television the night before the election. He stated that the people "are fed up with the pols, who care

[33] Joseph Ward, Channel 7, Boston, Sept. 12, 1960, 7:00 P.M.; Channel 4, Boston, Sept. 12, 1960, 8:00 P.M.
[34] Endicott Peabody, Channel 7, Boston, Sept. 12, 1960, 11:20 P.M.
[35] Robert Murphy, Channel 4, Boston, Sept. 12, 1960, 7:40 P.M.

for nothing except to fill their pockets." He referred to John Francis Kennedy as "the great imposter" and to Kelly as the candidate who "rides on promises of riches to the poor." He asked where Murphy had been "when the contracts were handed out." He stated that "some day the boy [Peabody] will make the grade, but we don't have time to give him on-the-job training." He concluded: "Let's get rid of the 'pols' and elect a business man."[36] In its final hours, the campaign thus took on a note of innuendo and open accusation.

Although the Democratic gubernatorial primary campaign was one of the most vicious and scurrilous in recent years, one newspaperman wrote that it was "far from spirited"[37] while another referred to it as "the most humdrum of campaigns."[38] Nevertheless, "the experts" accurately predicted that the vote would be larger than usual because of the large number of candidates. On September 13, 623,160 Democrats and 237,354 Republicans (32% of the eligible voters of the state) went to the polls. The Democrats evidently repudiated the Furcolo administration by nominating Mayor Thomas O'Connor for United States Senator (270,081 votes) in preference to Governor Furcolo (217,939 votes). Every other candidate endorsed by the Democratic pre-primary convention was nominated. Ward, who received approximately 30 per cent of the votes cast for governor, defeated Peabody by 28,086 votes. The results of the gubernatorial vote[39] were as follows:

Ward	180,848	(30.2%)
Peabody	152,762	(25.5%)
Kelly	98,107	(16.4%)
Murphy	76,577	(12.8%)
Kennedy	52,972	(8.9%)
Piemonte	28,199	(4.7%)
Magaletta	8,826	(1.5%)

A Socioeconomic Analysis of the Vote

Ward's victory was essentially a triumph of urban low- to lower-middle-income "regular" Democrats over middle-class suburban

[36] Alfred Magaletta, Channel 4, Boston, Sept. 12, 1960, 7:45 P.M. Magaletta appeared on television on two other occasions.

[37] William J. Lewis, *Boston Globe*, Sept. 12, 1960, p. 2.

[38] William J. McCarthy, *Boston Herald*, Sept. 13, 1960, p. 1.

[39] Of those people who voted for candidates for other offices, 24,826 refrained from choosing a gubernatorial candidate.

Democrats and independents. Ward received pluralities in almost every major industrial city in Massachusetts. He received more votes than Peabody, for example, in Worcester, Fall River, Springfield, Brockton, Holyoke, Lynn, New Bedford, and Lowell. Peabody, however, defeated Ward in the more well-to-do suburbs of Boston—Brookline, Newton, Arlington, Woburn, Watertown, Lexington, and Winchester.

The bulk of the Boston vote was divided fairly evenly among Ward, Kelly, and Peabody:

Kelly	36,825
Peabody	31,242
Ward	30,496
Murphy	15,450
Piemonte	11,245
Kennedy	10,751
Magaletta	2,123

Kelly received pluralities in 14 of the city's 22 wards, Peabody defeated his opponents in six wards, while Ward and Piemonte each prevailed in one ward. Kelly's strength was concentrated in the low- and lower-middle-income, predominantly Irish areas of the city. Piemonte, one of the two Italo-American candidates, received a plurality in one of the two predominantly Italian wards; the other was captured by Peabody. Peabody was victorious in ward 5, the wealthiest and most strongly Republican ward in the city; ward 14, which is predominantly Jewish; and wards 20, 21, and 22, which are basically middle- to upper-middle-income Irish (ward 21 has a substantial number of Jewish residents).

Outside of Boston, Peabody was the only candidate who seriously challenged Ward. He carried his home town of Cambridge with a plurality of 4,141 votes and defeated Ward in a few strongly Democratic working-class cities located near Boston—Somerville, Medford, Chelsea, and Revere. Three of these cities have significant numbers of Italo-American voters and two of them have large numbers of Jewish residents.[40] Although Peabody lost the city of Springfield to Ward, he carried the four middle- to upper-middle-income suburbs which surround the city. Although Ward failed to win the Italian areas of the state, he did well among the Portuguese Ameri-

---

[40] Revere and Chelsea have large numbers of Jewish voters; Somerville, Medford, and Revere have large numbers of Italo-American voters.

can sections of New Bedford and Fall River and in the heavily Polish American and Franco-American precincts of several larger cities.

Ward's victory demonstrates that the Democratic party in 1960 was still composed of ethnic and religious blocs. If Peabody represented the aspirations of alienated Democrats and reform liberals, as his close supporters claimed, he also served as a rallying point for many of those who resented the "all green" ticket. It is obvious that a significant proportion of those who voted for the only Yankee on the ballot were non-Irish Democrats and independents, although Peabody received the support of many "lace curtain" (i.e., upper-income) Irish as well. Economically, there appear to be two Democratic parties in Massachusetts. One is composed predominantly of urban lower- and lower-middle-income Irish, Portuguese, and Polish voters. The other is composed primarily of suburban middle- and upper-middle-income Irish and Jewish voters and Italo-Americans of various classes. The latter "Democratic party," in alliance with the staunch Republicans, elected John Volpe in 1960.

It may be possible to deepen our understanding of the results of the primary by examining, in addition to gross election statistics, some of the public-opinion data collected by the authors during the campaign. Between August 28 and September 11, the authors interviewed a sample of 320 registered voters in Massachusetts. The sample, which was selected at random from voting lists, was designed to explore the political attitudes of various subgroups in the population that were eligible to vote in the Democratic gubernatorial primary—i.e., registered Democrats and unenrolled citizens. The sample included no registered Republicans (although 26 respondents stated that they preferred the Republican party) and was not designed to be a microcosm of the state's voting population. Of the 320 persons who were interviewed at their place of residence, 160 were registered Democrats, 160 were unenrolled citizens. Half of each group was male and half female. Three fifths of the sample was drawn from Boston, and the Boston sample was selected equally from upper-income precincts, middle-income precincts, and lower-income precincts. One fifth of the sample was drawn from Arlington, which can be regarded as a typical Massachusetts suburb, and one fifth was drawn from Stow, which can be regarded as a typical rural town. Within the Arlington and Stow samples, half of the respondents were registered Democrats and half unenrolled citizens. Among the Democrats and unenrolled citizens in Arlington and Stow, half of the respondents were male and half female.

These respondents were asked 33 questions, including: "Which candidate for Governor is your choice to be the Democratic candidate for Governor in November?" Each respondent was then presented with a card which listed the seven gubernatorial candidates in a vertical column, with Ward's name at the top and the names of the other candidates in alphabetical order. A breakdown of the preferences of respondents according to their level of education, occupation, and religion is presented in Tables 6, 7, and 8.

TABLE 6

"Which Candidate for Governor Is Your Choice to Be the Democratic Candidate for Governor in November?" (Responses Classified by Education; N = 317)*

	No Response	Some Grammar School	Some High School	Some College or Graduate School
Ward	10%	10%	21%	15%
Kelly	40	20	11	7
Kennedy	15	12	13	3
Magaletta	0	0	1	0
Murphy	10	8	7	3
Peabody	0	0	8	18
Piemonte	0	10	5	5
Undecided	0	8	6	3
No response	15	28	23	27
Non-applicable (Republican)	10	4	6	19
	100%	100%	100%	100%
	(N = 20)	(N = 50)	(N = 174)	(N = 73)

* Three respondents stated that they had never attended school. One of these preferred Kelly, one preferred Kennedy, and one refused to state a preference. Their responses are not included in the table.

Table 6 shows that Kelly was preferred by the highest proportion of respondents who refused to indicate their educational history. We believe it likely that the overwhelming majority of respondents in studies of voting behavior who refuse to reveal the level of their education are relatively unschooled. Kelly was also preferred by more respondents who had not gone beyond grammar school. Not one respondent in either of these groups preferred Peabody. Ward was preferred by the largest proportion of respondents who had attended some high school (the largest subgroup in the sample and probably

TABLE 7

"Which Candidate for Governor Is Your Choice to Be the Democratic Candidate for Governor in November?" (Responses Classified by Occupation; N = 308)*

	Professional	Semi-professional and Managerial	Clerical, Skilled Trades	Semi-skilled, Minor Clerical	Slightly Skilled	Day Labor
Ward	23%	21%	15%	14%	17%	24%
Kelly	5	3	10	22	3	26
Kennedy	9	3	10	11	21	9
Magaletta	0	0	2	0	0	0
Murphy	9	7	6	7	0	12
Peabody	9	17	12	7	7	0
Piemonte	5	7	1	8	17	3
Undecided	5	7	8	1	7	0
No response	23	21	25	26	17	24
Non-applicable (Republican)	14	14	11	4	11	2
	100%	100%	100%	100%	100%	100%
	(N=22)	(N=29)	(N=101)	(N=93)	(N=29)	(N=34)

* Ten respondents refused to state their occupation and two described themselves as "rural owners." Their responses have not been included in the table.

in the Commonwealth), while Peabody was preferred by the largest proportion of respondents who had had some college training.

Table 7 shows that Kelly was preferred by the largest proportion of day laborers, with Ward a close second. Peabody was not preferred by a single respondent in this category. Ward was preferred by the largest proportion of "professional," "semi-professional and managerial," and "clerical, skilled trades" respondents. Except for the "professional" group, which overwhelmingly preferred Ward, the proportion of Peabody preferences steadily decreased as the occupation became less skilled.

In our sample (those eligible to vote in the Democratic primary) Catholics outnumbered Protestants almost four to one, while the proportion of Protestants who stated a Republican preference outnumbered their Catholic counterparts more than four to one. The preference of Protestant respondents was divided fairly evenly among

TABLE 8

"Which Candidate for Governor Is Your Choice to Be the Democratic Candidate for Governor in November?" (Responses Classified by Religion; N = 306)*

	Protestant	Catholic
Ward	8%	20%
Kelly	9	18
Kennedy	9	11
Magaletta	0	1
Murphy	6	7
Peabody	9	8
Piemonte	2	6
Undecided	3	6
No response	32	18
Non-applicable (Republican)	22	5
	100%	100%
	(N = 65)	(N = 241)

* Two respondents refused to state their religious preference; three respondents were Jewish; three claimed membership in "other" religious groups; and six respondents stated that they had no religion. The responses of these 14 persons have not been included in the table.

Ward, Kelly, Kennedy, and Peabody. Two and a half times as many Catholics preferred Ward as preferred Peabody, and almost twice as many Catholics chose Kelly over Peabody.

The Gubernatorial Campaign

The internecine warfare that characterized the Democratic gubernatorial primary and the scandals that had occurred during the Furcolo administration determined, to a large extent, the strategic boundaries within which Joseph Ward and John Volpe could operate during the general election campaign. The "ballot rigging" issue had obviously hurt Ward's reputation. Peabody, Murphy, and Piemonte had unequivocally informed the voters that Ward had first rigged the pre-primary convention and then the primary ballot. Ward's opponents had obviously succeeded in focusing upon him much of the political cynicism existing in Massachusetts. Ward knew this. Having originally blundered by permitting the ballot to be designed in a manner that left him open to criticism, Ward was forced to "prove" during the general election that he had more integrity than Volpe, or that Volpe had less integrity than he. Both he and Volpe assumed, accurately, that by the middle of September most voters were preoccupied with the problem of corruption in government and that they would vote primarily on some estimate of the candidates' relative integrity or venality. Ward therefore attempted to prove that John Volpe had been involved in several conflicts of interest while Commissioner of Public Works.

"Vote the Man, Vote Volpe"

Volpe, as the candidate of the "minority" party, faced a slightly different problem. Assuming that John Fitzgerald Kennedy would sweep Massachusetts, Volpe attempted to draw the attention of the electorate away from the Republican-Democratic axis of the state and fix it on a contest of individual men: John Volpe versus Joseph Ward. He therefore ran on the slogan: "Vote the Man, Vote Volpe." The fact that Volpe was not a member of the Furcolo administration was undoubtedly an advantage for him. When Furcolo was repudiated in the Democratic senatorial primary, Volpe knew that he had much to gain by suggesting to voters that Ward was Furcolo's protegé and therefore not in a position to clean house. Thus, Volpe's second slogan was: "End the Scandals—Restore Honor to Our State." The campaign centered on the issue of corruption.

Regardless of the "issue," the execution of political strategy in a state as large as Massachusetts requires considerable financial support. Volpe, whose candidacy was not contested in the primary, had the enormous advantage of being able to conserve his funds for the general election, whereas Ward was forced to spend sizable sums during the primary campaign. Furthermore, the Democratic state committee, which had raised more than $1,000,000 for Senator Kennedy, had evidently collected nothing for Ward. After the general election, Ward's chief campaign coordinator appealed to the loyal for funds to pay off the campaign deficit. "Most of you know," he wrote, "that the Ward-for-Governor Committee received no financial assistance from either the State or National Democratic Committees."[41] Unlike Ward, who was forced to curtail part of his advertising campaign during the general election, Volpe was in a position to execute his plan with no anxiety about funds. His public-relations chief informed the authors, "I never have been deprived of any money that I thought was necessary."

In addition to his financial advantage, Volpe had good relations with the Massachusetts press, which is overwhelmingly Republican. With the exception of the *Haverhill Journal,* which supported Ward, every major newspaper in Massachusetts either supported Volpe in its editorials or remained neutral. The *Springfield Daily News,* which had not supported a Republican for eighty years, endorsed Volpe. Even the *Fitchburg Sentinel,* Ward's home-town newspaper, supported the Republican candidate. In an editorial that was typical of those in the newspapers that supported Volpe, the *Sentinel* suggested to voters:

When you go into the polling booth to cast your ballot, you should take with you memories of what has gone on at Beacon Hill under the domination of a Democratic governor and legislature. . . . Think also of the heritage of low politicking which has downgraded our commonwealth to the bottom of the list of states on a basis of political and governmental standards.[42]

When asked by the authors about his press coverage, Ward replied, "I get none, I get none."

During the first three weeks of the campaign, Volpe and Ward received very little publicity. Their efforts were overshadowed by the presidential campaign and by the investigation of the Metropolitan District Commission, which was reported on the front pages of most Massachusetts newspapers for several weeks.

[41] Letter from Paul H. King concerning a testimonial dinner for Joseph D. Ward (undated, but apparently written in February or March 1961).

[42] *Fitchburg Sentinel,* Nov. 9, 1960, p. 4.

"The People vs. *Political Contractor Volpe"*

Five weeks before election day, Joseph Ward began to attack John Volpe in his campaign. Ward, who is an articulate and forceful orator with considerable courtroom experience, decided to attack Volpe by conducting a series of television trials, which he called "The People *vs.* Political Contractor Volpe." Ward acted as both judge and prosecutor "in the public interest," thus violating the sense of fair play of some voters. He was assisted by four attorneys who presented "evidence" that Volpe, as Commissioner of Public Works, had participated in several "deals" for "self-enrichment at public expense." This "distinguished panel of attorneys," as Ward referred to them, was composed of Jackson Holtz, a Jew, Paul Counihan, a member of a well-known Irish-American family, Joseph De Guglielmo, former mayor of Cambridge and a prominent Italo-American, and William Homans, a Yankee. After the first session of the trial, Homans returned to "private" practice. He evidently preferred the courtroom to the television studio.

The case had obviously been prepared with considerable care. The "evidence" was shown to the television audience in closeup shots of large cards, which consisted primarily of photostatic copies of parts of "public" files obtained from the Department of Public Works and of letters that Volpe had evidently left in the Department archives. In a series of four "trials," beginning on October 12, 1960, and ending on October 25, 1960, Ward "charged" Volpe with four major breaches of public trust and private morality, to wit:

1. Volpe, he said, had "paid off" an employee of the Department of Public Works by making him chief engineer of the Department in return for a favor performed for the Volpe Construction Company. The favor consisted of a vote by the employee, who was also a member of the Beverly, Massachusetts, School Building Committee, to award a contract for the construction of a junior high school to the Volpe Construction Company, "despite the fact that another firm submitted a lower bid."

2. Volpe, said Ward, had approved, in violation of state law, a contract for $343,000 for the construction of a ramp from a state highway (the Southeast Expressway) without requesting competitive bids.

3. Volpe had given special consideration to the firm of Cabot,

Cabot, and Forbes, which develops land for industrial use. For this purpose, the firm had purchased 200 acres in Waltham, Massachusetts, "gambling on being able to convince Volpe to give them access to Route 128 [a major highway]." Such access would have enormously increased the value of the land. Ward and his associates argued that Cabot, Cabot, and Forbes originally agreed to pay for the access road but that Volpe, ignoring the opposition of the DPW's engineers, agreed that the Commonwealth would pay for the road. The road, Ward argued, cost the state $305,000. Volpe's action was described by Ward as "contrary to long-established policy and good engineering practices."

4. The Volpe Construction Company had received a "10-million-dollar sweetheart" contract to build the North Shore Shopping Center at Peabody, Massachusetts. Ward and his colleagues argued that Volpe had received the contract in return for thwarting the attempt of others to build what would have been a competing shopping center. As Commissioner of Public Works, he had refused to grant access to Route 128 to the potential competitor. According to Ward, Volpe then gave Jordan Marsh, one of the largest department stores in Massachusetts, permission to build the center at Peabody, and a tunnel was constructed from Route 128 to this property, at state expense. The Jordan Marsh Company, Ward alleged, rewarded Volpe with the construction contract.

The last charge was clearly the most serious and potentially damaging to Volpe. Ward did not present it until October 25, the concluding day of the "trial." He argued that the taxpayers had been cheated of two million dollars, the cost to the state of the access road from the Waltham property to Route 128 and the tunnel to the North Shore Shopping Center. One reporter wrote that Ward "shocked a statewide television audience with the demand that Volpe withdraw as the G.O.P. candidate."[43] Ward concluded each session of the trial with a summary of Volpe's "violation of the public trust, give-away program of public funds, and conflict of interest." These charges were repeated on television and given wide coverage by the press. In a press release on October 18, 1960, Ward asserted that never in history "has a candidate for governor acted in such a manner as Mr. Volpe is doing today. The time has come to show some

43 *Boston Globe*, Oct. 26, 1960, p. 28.

maturity and responsibility and to stop dodging and running away from the truth—truth documented by legal papers and photostatic copies of letters."[44]

The Democrats also raked Volpe in newspaper advertisements. One typical advertisement featured the caption "Do YOU Recognize This Man?" Underneath the caption there appeared two photographs of Volpe, a full-face portrait showing the Republican candidate with an attractive smile, and a profile shot showing Volpe, teeth fully exposed, with an idiotic grin. The format was not unlike that which appears in F.B.I. handbills of the "ten most wanted criminals." A list of statements allegedly made by Volpe appeared under the full-face shot. A list of statements or actions by Volpe which "contradicted" those in the first column was printed under the profile shot:

THIS MAN appeared before the state Legislature as a spokesman and strong supporter for a sales tax.

THIS MAN as a political candidate says he is against a sales tax and for the people.

THIS MAN in a statement which appeared in all Boston newspapers, proposed that we close Boston City Hospital, haven for the sick and the poor people.

THIS MAN as a political candidate wants the people to believe he is for the poor and sick, so he denies having suggested that we close the hospital.

THIS MAN says he is a businessman, who will bring honest and efficient government to Massachusetts.

THIS MAN is a political contractor who has used political influence to secure millions of dollars in contracts.

THIS MAN proposed a $10 use tax for the owners of all automobiles in the area served by the MTA.

THIS MAN as a political candidate says that he will not propose any new taxes in Massachusetts.

THIS MAN claims he is not a politician, that he has never run for office before and that he has no connection with political bosses.

THIS MAN was a candidate for Lt. Governor in 1952 and withdrew as part of a deal. He has also been Vice Chairman of the Republican State Committee.

[44] Ward press release, Oct. 18, 1960.

THIS MAN as Public Works Commissioner gave away billions of dollars in contracts without competitive bidding.

THIS MAN as a political candidate says the awarding of contracts without competitive bidding is evil, wrong, and irresponsible.

Both these men are John A. Volpe, Republican Candidate for Governor. Can we believe this man? Can we trust this man?[45]

Several members of the Volpe inner circle were convinced that the trial of "The People *vs.* Political Contractor Volpe" had severely damaged Volpe's public reputation. Volpe's public-relations chief reported to the authors:

. . . the more outrageous they [Ward's charges] are, the more difficult they become to answer. I am also concerned with the difficulty in catching up with Ward's relentless allegations and charges. You start to explain something and the people are not interested in your explanation. They are much more interested in the naked charge and the assumption that evil has been done. I think Ward has been extremely clever, extremely clever in handling this thing. It has affected the Volpe vote to some extent because you can never catch up with the lies of this kind of accusation.

The basic strategic problem faced by the Volpe organization therefore was how Volpe should "answer" Ward's charges.

The suggestion that Volpe should answer the charges one by one, as Ward presented them, was rejected on the theory that this would have put Volpe permanently on the defensive. The suggestion that Volpe accept Ward's challenge to a face-to-face television debate was rejected because Volpe's advisers believed that Volpe did not have the kind of background (Ward· is a trial lawyer) that would have made him an effective debator. Volpe's manager stated to the authors that after four weeks Ward's charges would be perceived by voters as "repetitious and boring." The Volpe forces finally decided to wait until Ward had completed his charges and then have Volpe "answer" them in general, once, and on television.

While the "trial" was still in session, some newspapers favorable to Volpe "answered" some of the charges. The *Lynn Daily Item* featured a front-page story presenting "the facts in the case" and censuring Ward for making "inaccurate statements, innuendos and

45 *Arlington Advocate*, Oct. 27, 1960, p. 5.

accusations." The author of the story, discussing the construction of the Beverly School, pointed out that a Massachusetts court had declared the Volpe Construction Company to have been the "lowest bidder"—six months before Volpe was appointed commissioner of the Public Works Department.[46] Three days after this story was published, Ward went to the office of the *Lynn Daily Item* and insisted that the newspaper had not answered the specific charge he had made. The same evening, he told an organization of Franco-Americans in Lynn that the Volpe supporters were conducting an insidious "whispering campaign," urging Italo-Americans to "vote for one of your own."[47]

Other newspapers—the *New Bedford Standard Times,* for example —rallied to Volpe's defense. Before the Republican state convention, this paper had criticized Volpe on the grounds that a flagrant conflict of interest was unavoidable when the president of a major construction firm ran for public office. When Ward cited this editorial on television, the newspaper retorted with a very strong endorsement for Volpe on the ground that he had promised that his firm would refrain from bidding on state contracts.[48]

After the final session of the "trial," the Volpe forces proceeded to rebut Ward. Volpe, who was angered by the charges, announced that he might sue Ward for libel. He demanded an investigation by the Massachusetts Bar Association (it never took place). The president of Jordan Marsh also requested that the Association examine "the action of the lawyers who participated in the scandalous proceedings." He also stated publicly that Volpe's company had submitted the lowest bid of four firms for the construction of the North Shore Shopping Center, contrary to Ward's allegation that the award was made without competitive bidding. Next, Volpe's campaign manager, James Gaffney, appeared on television on October 21, 1960, and stated that Ward's second charge was false. He referred to Ward's attack as "scurrilous and irresponsible," and stated that the High Street ramp, which was a subject of contention, directly adjoined a stretch of the Central Artery that was already under construction. According to Gaffney, the award of a no-bid contract to a firm for the purpose of completing a related and adjacent project

[46] *Lynn Daily Item,* Oct. 17, 1960, p. 1.
[47] *Boston Globe,* Oct. 20, 1960, p. 5.
[48] *New Bedford Standard Times,* Oct. 31, 1960, p. 4.

was "sound engineering practice."[49] Gaffney ended his speech with the statement: "There were no scandals during Volpe's public career, either as commissioner of Public Works or as the federal highway administrator. He is not now involved in a scandal. He is merely victimized by the unscrupulous use of distortion." The firm of Cabot, Cabot, and Forbes answered the third charge in a news release stating that Volpe's decision that the Commonwealth should pay for the access route was made on the grounds that several companies, the city of Waltham, and the state as a whole would benefit from the new access road. The land developers pointed out that they had had no dealings with the Volpe Construction Company and that the land involved had been so well developed that 40 companies were now using it.

Seventeen days before the election, John Volpe appeared on television in a taped speech to defend his integrity. He began: "I appear before you tonight alone with my conscience and with the truth. It has not been easy for me and my loyal associates to listen to the evil attacks. . . ." Volpe denied every charge made by Ward and repeated the "arguments" offered by Gaffney, the president of Jordan Marsh, and the firm of Cabot, Cabot, and Forbes. He scored Ward as the "hand-picked successor of a corrupt administration," and indicated that he had waited to answer the attack on his character, reputation, and, "by implication, even my ancestry" until "Joseph Ward succeeded in enmeshing himself beyond retreat in a web of fabrication, distortion, and outright lies."[50] Immediately after Volpe's taped presentation, the secretary of state appeared "live" on television. He reiterated and elaborated the charges, waving aside Volpe's denials. Ward accused Volpe of "taking the low road" by alleging that he (Ward) and the Democratic party were involved in the Metropolitan District Commission scandals.

Except for this "defense" on television, Volpe pursued a predetermined strategy, campaigning on such issues as corruption in mass transportation, the need for urban development, and the desirability of "streamlining" state government with a "businesslike approach." He promised to eliminate corruption in the Department of Public Works, the Metropolitan District Commission, and the Metropolitan Transit Authority.

49 James Gaffney, Channel 4, Oct. 21, 1960, 6:45 P.M.
50 *Boston Herald*, Oct. 28, 1960, p. 1.

A few days before the election, he summarized what he thought was the key issue: "The one issue in this campaign is corruption, corruption, and corruption, which I am not only fighting against but will eliminate."[51] In support of this contention that his opponent was corrupt, he cited Murphy's charge that Ward had rigged the convention and Peabody's charge that he had rigged the primary ballot.

While Volpe was relying on the issue of corruption to put him into office, Ward stressed the need for party loyalty. The more astute members of the Ward entourage sensed that Ward's attacks on Volpe had backfired and placed their last hope on a tremendous Kennedy plurality.[52] Ward did everything he could to persuade Senator Kennedy to tour Massachusetts during the last day of the campaign. The *Wall Street Journal* quoted a Massachusetts Democratic leader who put the matter quite simply: "If Jack could make a whistle-stop swing across Massachusetts our problems would disappear in the dust."[53] Kennedy, whose coolness toward Ward was noticed by many professionals in both parties, saw no need for a statewide tour. He appeared in Massachusetts only once, on the final day of the campaign. On the evening before the elections an enormous and enthusiastic crowd greeted the senator in the Boston Garden. Theodore White noted that Kennedy's speech that night

. . . was a bad performance. The candidate for President was surrounded on the dais by a covey of the puffy, pink-faced, predatory-lipped politicians who had so dominated Massachusetts politics before he had taken

[51] *Boston Globe,* Nov. 1, 1961, p. 1.
[52] John Harris, political columnist for the *Boston Globe,* conducted a "public-opinion poll" in Worcester, Massachusetts, toward the end of October. Although his respondents predicted that Ward would not run far behind Kennedy, "three out of five" stated that the chief issue of the state campaign was "the Beacon Hill scandals: "In picking the scandals as No. 1 issue, the voters phrased it in many different ways: 'Cleanliness in government . . . corruption, graft, larceny . . . graft and corruption . . . investigation . . . good government . . . that M.D.C. thing . . . clean government.'
"Some mentioned scandals but took a different viewpoint. These were few in number. Some of their views: 'Scandals happen at all times regardless of who's in. . . . Scandals shouldn't have been built as a main issue. They have to do with a past administration; neither Ward nor Volpe had anything to do with them. . . . What's the use of talking scandal; they always come up and after the election they're forgotten' " (*Boston Globe,* October 27, 1960, p. 1).
Harris also noted, "Many felt that Ward's attack on Volpe has been hurting his prospects. This indicated some cutting of Ward in favor of Volpe" (*Boston Globe,* October 28, 1960, p. 13).
[53] *Wall Street Journal,* Oct. 27, 1960, p. 1.

over. The candidate for President was exhausted beyond the margin of normal exhaustion. . . . What he said that night before his election is not at all memorable. I remember only the remark of Richard Donahue, one of the candidate's Praetorian Guard, who listened to him and then pointed out to me the envious faces of the local politicians watching the candidate as he spoke. "You know," said Donahue, "they can't understand this. They think he has a trick. They're listening to him because they think if they learn the trick they can be President too."[54]

Kennedy did mention every member of the Democratic state ticket, beginning with the candidate for treasurer. He stated, to the amusement of the audience, that State Auditor Thomas Buckley, whose audits had led to several investigations, would probably receive more votes in Massachusetts than he himself. (Buckley did, in fact, receive more votes in Massachusetts than Kennedy.) Kennedy heartily endorsed Kevin White, the Democratic candidate for secretary of state, Edward McCormack, the candidate for attorney general, and Edward McLaughlin, the candidate for lieutenant governor. Of the Democratic candidate for governor, Kennedy remarked, with notable reserve, "It is my hope that Joseph Ward will be elected governor." He then praised Thomas O'Connor, the Democratic candidate for the United States Senate. One month before election day, a Boston journalist noted that Kennedy had informed some friends that he favored Peabody in the primary but did not feel he could openly support him.[55]

The Election Results:
The Interpretation of the Press

The nomination of Senator Kennedy in Los Angeles in July 1960 seemed to ensure the election of the Democratic candidate for governor of Massachusetts, along with the entire state ticket. Registered Democrats outnumbered registered Republicans in Massachusetts, and Kennedy's drawing power in the Bay State promised to get them all to the polls. Four months later, John Volpe's pollsters predicted

[54] White, *op. cit.,* pp. 343-44.
[55] Thomas Winship, *Boston Globe,* Oct. 7, 1960, p. 3.

—accurately, as it turned out—that Volpe, a Republican, would be elected by a plurality in excess of 85,000 votes. By November, the Boston City Hall "regulars," the inside dopesters, and a few of the more astute political "pros" knew that Joseph Ward was in serious trouble. Ward's opponents in the primary did not forget or forgive the "rigged convention" and "rigged ballot." Most of them remained silent during the final campaign, and one, Piemonte, publicly endorsed Volpe. Some of those who had supported the six losing primary candidates actively campaigned for Volpe. David Farrell, a political analyst of the *Boston Herald,* reported that in southeastern Massachusetts many former Murphy supporters worked for Volpe. The Americans for Democratic Action enthusiastically endorsed Kennedy, O'Connor, and McCormack but pointedly ignored Ward. Many members of this liberal Democratic group indicated privately that they were going to cast a reluctant vote for Volpe. Professor Mark De Wolfe Howe, of the Harvard University Law School, who spoke in behalf of Senator Kennedy at a rally in Cambridge, stated that he was going to vote for Volpe.

The liberal and intellectual element in the Massachusetts Democratic party, however, is small. It is doubtful that Ward was disturbed by Professor Howe's remarks. However, Ward was very much concerned about the Italo-American vote. During the final days of the campaign, he met with several leaders of the Italo-American community and urged them to remain loyal to the party. "It matters not," he said, "whether a descendant of Cicero or of Patrick sits in the governor's chair next January. What counts is that he is one who can do the job."[56]

November 8 was a clear, cool day in Massachusetts—an ideal day for a large turnout, and hence a large Democratic vote. The "experts" who predicted a turnout of more than 90 per cent in parts of the state were not wrong. The election returns from Boston, where voting machines are used, began to flow into party headquarters shortly after the polls closed at 8:00 P.M. It became obvious that Senator Kennedy would amass a tremendous plurality and that Leverett Saltonstall would defeat Thomas O'Connor. Shortly after 9:15 P.M., Volpe's pollsters reported, on the basis of a projection of the Boston vote, that he would win the election by at least 100,000

[56] *Boston Globe,* Oct. 31, 1960, p. 24.

votes. A few minutes later (while the returns showed Ward to be far ahead), Volpe announced on television that he was the next governor of Massachusetts. The final election results in Massachusetts were as follows:

President:	Kennedy	1,487,174
	Nixon	976,750
United States Senator:	Saltonstall	1,358,556
	O'Connor	1,050,725
Governor:	Volpe	1,269,295
	Ward	1,130,810

Democratic candidates for all other statewide offices were elected. Auditor Buckley received more votes than Senator Kennedy; McCormack defeated his rival for attorney general by 432,316 votes; and the Democratic candidate for treasurer, John Driscoll, won by 396,298 votes. McLaughlin, the Democratic candidate for lieutenant governor, was elected by a margin of 208,565, while his running-mate for secretary of state, Kevin White, defeated Edward Brooke, the first Negro ever to run for statewide office, by 111,790 votes. Every Democratic candidate for the governor's council was elected, and the Democratic party increased its margin in both branches of the state legislature.

Most of the newspapers in Massachusetts attributed Ward's defeat to the alleged corruption in the Democratic party. The analysis of the *Berkshire Eagle* was typical:

Obviously Ward's defeat was largely a reaction against Democratic shenanigans of the sort that came to light in the MDC and public works investigations. But the fact that the voters didn't give the same treatment to the other five Democratic candidates for consitutional offices indicates more than merely a turn-the-rascals-out mood. Mr. Ward was singled out, presumably, not only because he was head of the state Democratic ticket, but also because large numbers of voters were displeased with his destructive and excessively personal style of campaigning.[57]

Volpe's brain trust had sensed the preoccupation of voters with the scandals on Beacon Hill and they also understood that cynicism about politics and feelings of political powerlessness were important

[57] *Berkshire Eagle*, Nov. 9, 1960, p. 22.

factors in Massachusetts. This is why they stressed the theme that Volpe's aim was to "Restore Honor to Our State."

Three weeks before the election, a reporter for the *Boston Herald* interviewed several students at Waltham High School concerning their political attitudes.[58] He was startled by the results of his interviews:

Massachusetts is one of the most corrupt states in the United States. I know of a great deal of graft that goes on that you never see in the newspapers. I have friends who are connected with the government and some of the things they tell me I'm really shocked at.

No, I wasn't shocked at the findings of the MDC probe. It's no different from anything else in Massachusetts. I don't think an honest man would dare run now with the mess they're in. An honest man wouldn't really stand a chance in politics.

The political attitudes of young people customarily reflect those of their parents.[59]

A few leaders in the Democratic party interpreted the results of the election in a different way. The Democratic president of the Senate, John Powers, denied that the results of the MDC and the DPW investigations had anything to do with Ward's defeat. The authors' post-election survey suggests that Powers' view is incorrect. Powers, however, correctly claimed that the shift of Italo-American Democrats to Volpe, particularly in Boston, was a critical factor in the election. Francis E. Kelly asserted that 70,000 Democratic voters had switched from Ward to Volpe because the latter promised, five days before the election, that he would not veto a bill establishing a Massachusetts sweepstakes if such a bill were passed by the General Court.[60] Volpe did make such a promise, although most newspapers failed to report it and those that did mention it buried the story on the back pages.[61] Prior to this announcement, Volpe had made no public statement regarding a sweepstakes for Massachusetts, and the Republican party has traditionally opposed a Massachusetts sweepstakes.

[58] *Boston Herald*, Oct. 19, 1960, p. 2.
[59] See, for example, Eleanor Maccoby *et al.*, "Youth and Political Change," *Public Opinion Quarterly*, Vol. 18 (Spring 1954).
[60] Cornelius Dalton, *Boston Traveler*, July 21, 1961, p. 20.
[61] *Dorchester Argus*, Nov. 10, 1961, p. 4; *Boston Traveller*, Nov. 3, 1961, p. 14.

A Socioeconomic Analysis of the Vote

The results of the 1960 elections suggest that a majority of voters in Massachusetts still identify with the Democratic party. The results also indicate, however, that this identification may be offset by certain short-term factors that may operate during a particular election. Such factors may include: (1) scandals in an incumbent Democratic administration, (2) a Democratic candidate who is perceived as personally repugnant, (3) a prestigious Republican candidate who is perceived as "above" politics (e.g., Saltonstall), (4) a Republican candidate whose ethnic background or religious affiliation is the same as that of a significant bloc nominally identified as Democratic. The existence of one or more of these factors may result in the victory of a Republican candidate. All of these factors were in operation during the 1960 election, although each factor affected different segments of the electorate in different ways.

The basic identification of the majority of voters in Massachusetts is evident from Table 9.

TABLE 9
Democratic Proportion of the Two-Party Vote in
Three Massachusetts Elections

Office	1956	1958	1960
President	40.5%		60.4%
U. S. Senator		73.6%	43.6
Governor	53.0	56.6	47.1
Lieutenant Governor	51.7	61.0	54.6
Secretary of State	53.9	63.0	52.5
Treasurer	53.4	62.5	56.5
Auditor	57.7	63.7	66.5
Attorney General	49.1	52.3	59.2

Undoubtedly Eisenhower's popularity in 1956 reduced the "normal" Democratic majority in Massachusetts. The combined average Democratic percentage of the vote for the six state offices (governor, lieutenant governor, secretary of state, treasurer, auditor, and attorney general) was 53.1 per cent in 1956, 59.8 per cent in 1958, and 56.1 per cent in 1960. Although Saltonstall and Volpe won in 1960, the election does not indicate a fundamental reversal of majority opinion from the Democratic to the Republican party.

Saltonstall's victory surprised very few analysts of Massachusetts politics; he has always commanded the respect of large numbers of Democratic voters, who support him for senator and Democrats for all other offices. Volpe's victory also does not represent a turning point in Massachusetts political history. He really did not "win" the election; as the saying goes, Ward lost it. The election of Volpe must be viewed as a punishment inflicted upon Ward by Democrats and independents for the scandals on Beacon Hill and for his style of campaigning, which was regarded with distaste by many voters. In fact, the overwhelming victory of the Democrats in the state legislature (see Tables 4 and 5) indicates that the voters of Massachusetts are more Democratic than ever.

Ward lost the election because of defections in Boston, in the Springfield area, and in the Boston suburbs. In general, he did well in those areas in which Kelly had shown strength in the primary and poorly in those areas in which Peabody had done well in the primary. The authors' post-election public-opinion data indicate that significant numbers of Peabody and Murphy supporters switched to Volpe in November. An analysis of the election returns indicates that Volpe did receive the support of the majority of Italo-American voters who are nominally Democrats.

Boston

Boston traditionally is a Democratic stronghold (only one ward is strongly Republican). Predominantly Irish, the Hub customarily provides a 100,000-vote plurality for the Democratic candidate, which he usually needs in order to offset Republican pluralities in the suburbs and rural areas outside Boston. Ward, however, defeated Volpe in Boston by only 51,839 votes while O'Connor defeated Saltonstall in Boston by 33,340 votes. The most serious defections from the normal Democratic vote occurred in areas of the city that are heavily Italian, Jewish, and upper-middle- to upper-income Irish—that is, primarily the areas carried by Peabody in the primary. Volpe actually won one of the two Italian wards. He also carried ward 12, which has a significant number of Jewish and Negro voters, and ward 21, which is predominantly an upper-income Jewish and Irish area. In ward 20, a relatively upper-income area which is predominantly Irish, Volpe received 38 votes more than

Ward. The total vote in this ward was 21,730. It is obvious that
many Italo-Americans, Jews, and upper-middle- to upper-income
Irish voters who usually vote Democratic were cross-pressured.
Their normal Democratic affiliation was offset by some combination
of dislike for Ward as a person, disillusionment with the incumbents,
and the attraction of an Italo-American or at least a non-Irish candidate.

Table 10, which shows the Republican proportion of the two-
party vote for governor (1950-60) in certain wards, illustrates the
attraction of non-Irish candidates in wards that are predominantly
upper-income Irish, Italo-American, or Jewish.

TABLE 10

Ethnic Voting Patterns in Selected Boston Wards, 1950-60:
Republican Percentage of the Two-Party Vote for Governor

	1950	1952	1954	1956	1958	1960
Ward 3 (Italo-American)	21%	24%	28%	20%	16%	53%
Ward 6 (Low-income Irish)	13	19	17	20	13	21
Ward 14 (Jewish)	21	24	37	21	21	38
Ward 20 (Upper-income Irish)	40	49.9	49.8	44	37	50.1

Candidate:

Republican	Coolidge	Herter*	Herter*	Whittier	Gibbons	Volpe*
Democratic	Dever*	Dever	Murphy	Furcolo*	Furcolo*	Ward

* Denotes the victor.

In the elections of 1950, 1952, and 1954, the Republican candidate was a Yankee "blue blood," the Democratic candidate an Irish
American. These elections are "typical" of many gubernatorial
contests since the 'thirties. Voters in the low-income Irish ward (6)
provided Irish Democratic candidates with their greatest pluralities
in these elections (among these selected wards).[62] Voters in the
upper-income Irish ward (20) provided Yankee Republican candidates with their largest pluralities. The Republican candidates won
proportionately more votes in the Jewish ward (14) and the Italo-
American ward (3) than in the low-income Irish ward. This is the

[62] Eisenhower's popularity may account for the increase in the Republican vote
in ward 6 in 1952.

"normal" voting pattern when a Yankee opposes an Irish American for the governorship.

In the elections of 1956 and 1958, the Democratic candidate was an Italo-American and the Republican candidates were "swamp Yankees." Furcolo did better in the Italo-American ward than Irish American Democratic candidates had done in the three previous elections, and in 1958 he also received a larger plurality in the low-income Irish ward than two of his predecessors had.[63] Furcolo also received a higher proportion of votes in the Jewish ward than Irish American candidates had received in the elections of 1952 and 1954.

Volpe received a larger share of the vote than any Republican candidate since 1950 in every ward sampled. In the five previous elections, the Republican Yankee candidate had received an average of 21.8 per cent of the vote in the Italo-American ward; Volpe received 53 per cent of the vote in this traditionally Democratic ward. The four Republican candidates in those years averaged 24.8 per cent of the vote in the Jewish ward; Volpe received 38 per cent of the vote in ward 14 in 1960. Although, as we have noted, many factors undoubtedly entered into Volpe's high showing in these areas, it is very likely that his ethnic origin was particularly attractive to Italo-American and Jewish voters. Several months after the election, Ward claimed that the ballots of "Italo-Americans who ordinarily vote Democratic . . . cost me 200,000 votes."[64]

The Boston Metropolitan Area

The voting pattern in Boston was accentuated in the suburbs surrounding the city. In the primary, Ward had lost most of the suburbs, particularly the upper-income non-Irish suburbs, to Peabody. Volpe received substantial pluralities in most of these areas, particularly in the wealthier suburbs—Brookline, Newton, Winchester, Belmont, and Lexington. Within these suburbs, the less Irish the precinct, the greater, in general, was Volpe's plurality. Although several traditionally Democratic cities that are close to Boston remained in the Democratic column, the "normal" Democratic majority was severely reduced. Democratic losses were particularly heavy

[63] The 1958 election was a special situation in which the Republican candidate, George Fingold, died shortly before election day and the new candidate, Charles Gibbons, had very little time in which to campaign.

[64] Radio station WMEX, Boston, Oct. 9, 1961.

in Revere (down 19% f :om 1956), Chelsea (down 12%), and Somerville (down 11%). In .he primary, Peabody received pluralities in these cities and in Cambridge. Substantial numbers of Italo-Americans and Jews reside in Revere, Somerville, and Chelsea. Volpe also did well in those cities and towns that are beyond the circle immediately around Boston. He received pluralities in Medford, Everett, and Waltham. Medford and Everett have large numbers of Italo-American residents. The smaller towns beyond Boston, which are traditionally Republican, gave Volpe larger pluralities than is usual for a Republican gubernatorial candidate.

On the South Shore, where the Democrats had made spectacular gains in 1956 and 1958, the Republicans recouped. Voters in Quincy, Brockton, Dedham, and Weymouth returned to the ranks of the GOP in large numbers. An analysis of the wards and precincts in these cities indicates that the switch was greatest in the middle-income Irish Catholic areas. Norwood and Hull, normally Democratic, remained with the party, although the Democratic majority was severely reduced.

The Springfield Area

The Connecticut Valley, particularly Springfield, was the only section of Massachusetts in which the Democrats lost support between 1956 and 1958. The trend toward Republican pluralities was extended in the 1960 election, when the majority of the voters in the Valley preferred Volpe to Ward, although they supported Kennedy over Nixon. The *Springfield Daily News,* a Democratic organ, was pleased by the "tremendous vote for Mr. Volpe, whom we strongly endorsed in a front-page editorial"; it went on to say:

Springfield backed Mr. Volpe by giving him a smashing 17,453 margin. He showed similar strength in Greater Springfield and topped both Senator Saltonstall and Senator Kennedy in Agawam, East Longmeadow, Southwick, West Springfield, Westfield, Hampden and Wilbraham. Mr. Volpe might have been defeated without this tremendous Greater Springfield vote.[65]

In 1956, 62 per cent of the voters in Springfield preferred the Democratic gubernatorial candidate, Foster Furcolo, who was a home-

[65] *Springfield Daily News,* Nov. 9, 1960, p. 8.

town boy. In 1960, 62 per cent of the voters favored Volpe. The Democratic party suffered its greatest losses in the Connecticut Valley. Compared with the election results in 1956, the results of the 1960 election show that the Democratic vote fell off by 29 per cent in Ludlow, 24 per cent in Springfield, 23 per cent in West Springfield, and 22 per cent in Agawam. In the heavily industrial areas of the Connecticut Valley (e.g., Holyoke and Chicopee), the traditional Democratic margin was heavily reduced.

West of Springfield, in Berkshire County, the Democrats also suffered significant losses. North Adams favored a Republican candidate for governor for the first time since 1938, and Pittsfield, the "political barometer" of the region, which had given Furcolo 51 per cent of its vote in 1956 and 56 per cent in 1958, gave Ward only 48 per cent. In the rest of the state, Ward's vote compared favorably with that received by Furcolo in 1956, particularly in the industrial centers—Fall River, New Bedford, Taunton, Lawrence, Haverhill, and Lowell. Analysis of the election returns of these cities indicates that lower-income Irish voters and other ethnic minorities in southeastern Massachusetts and the Merrimack Valley were not moved by the Republican attack on corruption. In the central part of the state (Worcester County), particularly in the city of Worcester, Ward received approximately the same proportion of the vote that Furcolo had received in 1956 and 1958.

Our understanding of the election may be deepened by an analysis of some data collected by the authors in a post-election public-opinion poll. Within ten days after the general election the authors were able to interview 244 of the 320 persons who had been interviewed before the primary. Some of these citizens were interviewed on the telephone, others returned questionnaires which had been mailed to them. The same set of questions was asked on the telephone and in the mailed questionnaires. Respondents in this post-election survey were asked whether they had voted for president, United States senator, and governor and, if they had, for whom. Respondents were also asked the following questions:

> Why did you vote for [your choice] for governor?
> What do you like best about Ward?
> What do you like least about Ward?
> What do you like best about Volpe?
> What do you like least about Volpe?

These 244 respondents (123 unenrolled citizens and 121 registered Democrats) split their vote as follows:

President:	Kennedy	74%
	Nixon	23
	No vote	3
		100% (N=244)
U. S. Senator	Saltonstall	55%
	O'Connor	42
	No vote	3
		100% (N=244)
Governor	Ward	50%
	Volpe	43
	No vote	7
		100% (N=243)[66]

Table 11 presents the distribution of the gubernatorial vote among unenrolled voters and registered Democrats.

TABLE 11

Gubernatorial Vote of a Sample of Registered Democrats and Unenrolled Voters, 1960

Candidate	Registered Democrats (N=121)	Unenrolled Voters (N=122)
Volpe	30%	53%
Ward	64	41
No vote	6	6
	100%	100%

Almost one third of the registered Democrats deserted their party's nominee and voted for Volpe, while a majority of the so-called independent (unenrolled) respondents favored Volpe. It is probably safe to assume that Volpe received the overwhelming majority of votes cast by registered Republicans (as indicated by analysis of the election returns from traditional Republican strongholds). Since registered Republicans form a minority of the voters in Massachu-

[66] One respondent voted for Nixon, Saltonstall, and Henning Blomen, the Socialist Labor candidate for governor. She stated: "Felt in either case better men could have been provided. The vote was a protest vote. The Socialist candidate at least had a record of loyalty to his party."

setts, these data suggest that Volpe was elected by Republicans in combination with registered Democrats and independents.

We have already suggested that a significant bloc of Italo-Americans, who are traditionally Democratic, voted for Volpe. By analyzing how the supporters of the various Democratic candidates in the primary cast their votes in the general election we may be able to pinpoint with greater accuracy the sources of Volpe's strength. We have pointed out that Volpe did well in those areas of the state where Peabody had shown strength and in areas that have heavy concentrations of Italo-Americans. Table 12 presents the distribution of the vote for Volpe and Ward among those who preferred various Democratic candidates in the gubernatorial primary.

TABLE 12

Gubernatorial Vote by Preference in the Primary Election (N = 224)*

| | Final Vote | |
Primary Preference	Volpe	Ward
Ward	6%	88%
Kelly	25	69
Kennedy	33	57
Murphy	44	44
Peabody	40	56
Piemonte	55	45
No response	67	28
Non-applicable (Republican)	73	24

* Magaletta was preferred by only two respondents in the pre-primary sample; since this number was not significant, he is not included in this list. The tallies for each primary candidate do not add up to 100% because we have not presented the proportion of those who voted for other candidates or failed to vote.

It is clear that Ward retained the loyalty of the overwhelming majority of those respondents who had favored him in the primary election and slightly more than two thirds of those who had supported Kelly. The significant fact shown in this table is that Volpe received at least one third of the votes of those who had preferred Kennedy, Murphy, and Peabody. The internecine warfare that characterized the primary evidently caused significant numbers of Democrats and unenrolled voters to support Volpe. The only group that preferred a Democratic candidate in the primary and Volpe in the general election consisted of former Piemonte supporters. If the bulk of those who had supported Piemonte in the primary were Italo-Americans (which is what the election returns indicated), then these data are consonant with Ward's contention that a very large number of Italo-American Democrats supported Volpe. In view of the fact that Peabody received the second largest number of votes in the primary, the data also suggest that Peabody's former supporters played an important role in Volpe's victory. Approximately two thirds of those respondents who stated no primary preference ultimately voted for Volpe. These data indicate that the general election campaign activated a large number of voters who had not voted in the primary; these voters played a significant role in Volpe's victory.

With respect to the education of respondents, Ward received a majority (53%) of the votes cast by those who had not gone beyond grammar school and a majority (56%) of the votes cast by those who had completed some years of high school but no college. Volpe received 57 per cent of the votes cast by respondents with some college or postgraduate education. Ten per cent of those in the grammar- and high-school categories failed to vote while only 2 per cent of those in the college group failed to vote. These data are consonant with the findings of several studies of voting behavior. The proportion of Democrats is customarily greater among those who have had no high-school education than among those who have attended high school. The highest proportion of Republicans is customarily found in the group with some college training.

The authors' post-election sample included 54 Protestants and 177 Catholics.[67] Among the Protestant group, 72 per cent voted for Volpe and 24 per cent for Ward; the remaining 6 per cent failed to vote or voted for some other candidate. Within the Catholic group, 57 per cent voted for Ward, 36 per cent voted for Volpe, and 7 per cent failed to vote.

In analyzing the election returns, the press assumed that Volpe's victory was, in part, an expression of resentment against the incumbents. If this view is correct, we should expect to find Volpe's greatest strength among those who were most dissatisfied with the Furcolo administration and Ward's greatest strength among those who thought that the incumbents had done a respectable or good job. This hypothesis is supported by the authors' post-election public-

---

[67] Twelve of the remaining 13 respondents were either Jewish, unchurched, or members of other religious groups. One refused to state a religious preference.

opinion data. Respondents who were interviewed prior to the primary
were asked, "How well do you think the people who have been running the state during the last four years have done the job?" The
distribution of responses was as follows:

Very bad	10%
Bad	18
I don't like Furcolo	7
Fair	41
Good	13
Very good	2
No answer	9
	100% (N = 320)

Among the 244 respondents who were interviewed after the
Ward-Volpe contest, the distribution was virtually identical:

Very bad	10%
Bad	19
I don't like Furcolo	5
Fair	41
Good	14
Very good	2
No answer	9
	100% (N = 244)

Table 13 shows the gubernatorial preference of these respondents
according to their attitude toward the performance of the previous
(Democratic) administration.

TABLE 13
Gubernatorial Preference, by Attitude Toward Incumbent
Democratic Administration (N = 243)*

Attitude	Volpe	Ward	No vote
Very bad	56%	36%	8%
Bad	53	40	7
I don't like Furcolo	45	55	0
Fair	40	52	8
Good	31	66	3
No answer	45	46	8

* One respondent voted for a candidate other than Volpe or Ward. The category
"very good" contains only four respondents and is therefore not statistically
significant.

Volpe's margin was greatest among those respondents who believed that the incumbents had done a "very bad" or "bad" job, while Ward's strength was greatest among those who believed that the Furcolo administration had done a "fair" or "good" job. These data suggest that Ward was "punished" by Democrats and independents who probably accepted Volpe's argument that Ward was the hand-picked candidate of the Furcolo administration.

Of the 122 respondents who voted for Ward, 100 answered the question "Why did you vote for Ward?" Several individuals gave more than one reason. The distribution is presented below. Percentages indicate the proportion of the 100 respondents who chose each answer.

Party identification	45%
Like Ward's personality	26
Like Ward's experience or education	21
Anti-Volpe	11
Ward is lesser of two evils	10
Like Ward's family	8
Like Ward's platform	7
Ward is honest	5

In interpreting this table the reader should keep in mind that half of this sample consisted of registered Democrats. It is not surprising, therefore, that 45 per cent of those respondents who voted for Ward mentioned as a reason for doing so the fact that Ward was the Democratic candidate or that they were Democrats. Many of these respondents were obviously disturbed by the legacy of scandal and the vituperativeness of Ward's campaign. Their comments indicate, however, that they would probably support any candidate of the Democratic party even if he happened to be Ward. Some typical responses of this group are: "He was a Democrat." "I'm a Democrat." "By voting for Ward I thought I'd be better off. . . . I figured he's a Democrat and working conditions always seem better under a Democrat. We fare better." "I tell you I had rather have Peabody than Ward but as long as it's a Democrat it's all right." "Quite frankly, I was quite disgusted with the name calling by both candidates and voted for Ward strictly on a party basis." "Always vote straight Democratic." "I'm more a Democrat than a Republican."

Nevertheless, Ward's personality (26%) and his experience and education (21%) were perceived as attractive by many Democrats.

He was seen by some as "sincere," by others as "intelligent" and "straightforward." Some typical comments follow: "I think he is more capable than anyone else." "I think he is a serious-thinking man." "I liked the way Ward talked to you as an individual on TV— he talked to you as if you were a person—right to you." "Personal integrity beyond reproach and he has a splendid character." "I thought he had more experience." "More education than Mr. Volpe."

Interspersed with such remarks were several comments indicating that some respondents were favorably impressed by Ward's family: "He is a family man." "He has a charming family." "His family and personality background is good." "He's a very good family man and a very good citizen." "I done it on principle. . . . Figured if he could raise a big family like that he must be all right."

Although some aspect of Ward's personality or experience was perceived as attractive by approximately 20 to 25 per cent of those respondents who voted for him, our data suggests that two groups of respondents cast what they regarded as a negative vote. Many voted for Ward with reluctance, simply because they did not like Volpe or disliked him more than they disliked Ward. The categories "Anti-Volpe" (11%) and "Ward is the lesser of two evils" (10%) were coded separately; only those respondents who specifically made an anti-Volpe comment ("so much controversy about Volpe and that construction business") were placed in the former category, while only those who made disparaging comments about both candidates were placed in the latter category ("I thought he was the lesser of two evils and I usually vote Democratic anyway." "I wasn't happy with either Ward or Volpe but Ward had more experience in state government and he is a Democrat." "Not much to offer between either—almost left it blank." "I might as well vote as not vote.")

Of the 106 respondents who voted for Volpe, 88 responded to the question "Why did you vote for Volpe?" The distribution of responses to this question is shown below.

Like Volpe's personality	35%
Anti-Ward	19
Volpe is the lesser of two evils	17
Party orientation	14
Like Volpe's experience or education	14
Volpe is a businessman	12
Volpe is honest	12

It is not surprising that more respondents mentioned Volpe's personality rather than his party since our sample included only registered Democrats and unenrolled voters, although a small number of the latter stated that they preferred the Republican party even though they were not registered as Republicans. Therefore most of the respondents reacted in terms of Volpe's personality. Undoubtedly if the authors had interviewed registered Republicans, the proportion of those who were party oriented would be much greater than it is in this sample. Nevertheless, this sample sheds much light on Volpe's victory because a Republican candidate in Massachusetts must receive the support of significant numbers of independents and registered Democrats if he is to win.

Some of those who liked Volpe's personality commented on his "sincerity," but most respondents simply stated: "Volpe is a better man" or "much better than Ward." Those who specifically mentioned Volpe's honesty (12%) were classified separately. Some exemplary comments from this group follow: "TV thing—honest in answering Ward's remarks on Jordan Marsh—dug into them." "Most honest of the two men in my opinion. At least I hope he is at least half honest."

It is interesting to note that the same number of respondents commented favorably on Volpe's "business experience" as on his honesty. Despite the fact that contractors are held suspect by many citizens in Massachusetts, the Horatio Alger character of Volpe's rise from poverty favorably impressed some voters, as the following typical comments suggest: "I take my hat off to any man who started work as a hod carrier and worked up the ladder to aspire to the governorship of our state." "Decided on Volpe early—a Republican and a businessman." "Thought he was better man. Had more business in him." "Lot of bad things about him but he is head of construction. In charge of a lot of men. Knows how to handle money."

Approximately one third of those respondents who voted for Volpe (as opposed to 22% of those who voted for Ward) did so for negative reasons—i.e., "lesser of two evils" or "don't like Ward." Again, this is not surprising since none of these respondents was a registered Republican. The categories "Anti-Ward" and "Volpe is the lesser of two evils" were coded separately. A typical remark of those respondents who commented unfavorably about Ward (19%) was: "Just didn't care for Mr. Ward's comments on TV—all that corruption business." Comments of those who disparaged both candidates (17%) included: "I did not like either candidate for governor, but after reviewing both their records, I decided Volpe was the lesser of two evils." "Not too much choice—contradiction in both candidates, but Volpe is from my home town." "I felt that Volpe was the lesser of two evils . . . in view of the scandals in the recent administration and Ward's smearing campaign."

* * *

The incidence of corruption in Massachusetts public life during the 1950's, the continuous round of investigations, grand-jury proceedings, indictments, convictions, and exposés of flagrant conflicts of interest, have so affected public opinion that the stereotype of the politician as a crook has become common in the Bay State. Even if they are scrupulously honest men, candidates for public office must cope with this massive suspicion. Most of the 1960 gubernatorial candidates realized that if the cynical and alienated members of the electorate voted, it would be on the basis of some estimate of the candidate's relative honesty or venality, not on the basis of his program. It requires political artistry of the highest order to win the allegiance of citizens who are preoccupied with the candidate's character and who evaluate it in terms of some highly subjective and intuitive "gut reaction."

In Part II we shall analyze the political strategy which was developed by the candidates in response to what they thought were the political, ethnic, religious, and "psychological" preferences of the voters. The analysis is based on 18 tape-recorded interviews with several of the candidates, their campaign managers, public-relations men, and fund raisers, prior to the primary election and again prior to the general election. In Chapter 3 we shall attempt to define a "rational" political strategy and suggest how "rational" candidates in Massachusetts might attempt to appeal to alienated voters.

* * *

PART II

The Political
Strategy

MURRAY B. LEVIN

* * *

3.
Political Strategy for the Alienated Voter

* * *

"Where are you going?"
"To Minsk."
*"Shame on you! You say this to make me think you are going to
Pinsk, but I happen to know you are going to Minsk."*

A JEWISH ANECDOTE

There is a traditional preoccupation in political thought with the problem of how political power may be achieved and perpetuated; it is a concern for politics devoid of moral considerations, often supported by force and always decided by expediency. The French refer to this concern as *raison d'état*, the Germans as *Realpolitik*, the Anglo Saxons as Machiavellianism. Writers in this tradition, whatever it is called, pride themselves on being realists who describe the political world as it actually operates. Assuming that the driving force behind political behavior is the desire of men for dominance and control, they contend that most political leaders often find it necessary to divorce politics from morality. In 1513, Machiavelli founded modern political realism by publishing *The Prince*, the first "practical handbook" to show how politicians can achieve and maintain power regardless of their reasons for wishing to do so. He thus developed one of the first theoretical models of political strategy.

Machiavelli's assumptions about strategy and expedience were made at a time when an electorate did not exist, except in a figurative sense: the leader in Renaissance politics who was supported militarily by the greatest number had the strongest mandate to press his fortunes. Since Machiavelli's assumptions have proved so durable (they are remarkably similar to those that are the basis for some modern theories of political strategy), we might pause to consider aspects of his theory today. There are two actors in Machiavelli's political world: politicians, who are activists and who selfishly seek power, and the masses, who are fundamentally passive and obedient if provided with minimal security. Machiavelli took it for granted that politicians wish to gain or maintain power. The question that interested him (and that interests modern theorists) is simply what means are most likely to achieve the desired end, given specific historical circumstances and limited resources. The political practitioner who desires to succeed, Machiavelli assumed, must not bind himself by the conventional ethical standards. He must not permit his moral standards to interfere with the pursuit of power:

The experience of our times shows those princes to have done great things who have little regard for good faith, and have been able by astuteness to confuse men's brains. A prudent ruler ought not to keep faith when so doing it would be against his interest.[1]

Machiavelli did not favor immorality *per se*. He, like so many modern politicians, merely advocated it when it was politically expedient.

The politician, however, does not operate unobserved. In order to maintain political power, Machiavelli shrewdly observed, he must ultimately receive the confidence and consent of the masses. This consent may be manufactured by skillful manipulation on the part of the prince, it may be the product of the masses' habitual indifference, it may be a response to satisfactory rule; but it must be present if the existing reign is to sustain itself for long periods of time. To gain or create this confidence, the prince must be cognizant of the nature and needs of the masses, since they are the other actor in the political system. Although Machiavelli assumed that "men in general . . . are ungrateful, voluble dissemblers, anxious to avoid danger, and

[1] Niccolo Machiavelli, *The Prince,* in *The Prince and The Discourses* (New York: Modern Library, 1940), p. 65. I am indebted to the interesting treatment of Machiavelli by Andrew Hacker, *Political Theory* (New York: Macmillan, 1960), Chap. 5.

covetous of gain,"[2] he realized that the masses have some elemental needs that must be satisfied by the political system before they will show confidence in the ruler. A sophisticated ruler who knows that the needs and hopes of the masses are simple (they prefer security to liberty)[3] can easily predict their reaction to his policies. This is precisely what makes political strategy a "science" for the prince. Although it may be wise (expedient) for the prince to satisfy the needs of the masses, he may be able to win and maintain public approval by skillfully manipulating images and appearances. This is possible, according to Machiavelli, because "the great majority of mankind are satisfied with appearances as though they were realities and are often more influenced by things that seem than by those that are."[4] The basic elements of many modern theoretical models of political strategy (or, indeed, public relations) are contained in Machiavelli's system. Like "the moderns," he is interested in determining how to get maximal results from one's resources, how to achieve power observing only the expedient minimum of moral concern.

We are interested in the problems faced by political strategists in a democratic society in which politicians must seek votes in periodic elections. Although Machiavelli did, at times, discuss political strategy within the context of "democracy," we may find it useful to examine a more recent theory of strategy specifically designed to analyze problems of modern democratic politics. We do this in the hope of discovering some analytic framework into which we may fit the strategic problems of politicians in Massachusetts, where a significant proportion of the electorate is hostile to politicians, disheartened by the quality of candidates, and alert to scandal.

Rational Political Strategy

Since the eighteenth century, economic theorists have written about the artificial "economic man" (*homo economicus*), who makes decisions that are rational and selfish—rational in the sense that he selects

---

[2] *Ibid.*, p. 61.
[3] *Discourses on the First Ten Books of Titus Livius,* in *The Prince and the Discourses, op. cit.,* p. 163.
[4] *Ibid.*, p. 182.

the most efficient means to reach a chosen end (profit), selfish in the sense that the ends selected serve his own interest. Certainly the concept of "economic man" is an abstraction, and in many cases a false one, since at least some men act irrationally or unselfishly at least some of the time. But the concept is necessary and useful because it permits economists to develop theoretical models on the basis of which they can analyze economic relations and predict behavior in a manner not possible were they to assume that all economic decisions are simply taken at random. It is also possible, using the model world (in which men are expected to act rationally) as a standard, to discover those aspects of the real world that cause men to act rationally, those aspects that cause men to act irrationally, and the manner in which men deviate from rationality when they do.

In the eighteenth century, Jeremy Bentham, a founder of English Utilitarianism, developed a theoretical model of democracy based on the hypothetical "political man," who is both rational and self-interested. Assuming that man is a computer machine programmed to seek pleasure and avoid pain in the pursuit of self-interest, Bentham argued that the problem of democratic politics centered on the fact that the pleasure of the governing elite would not necessarily coincide with that of the greatest number of citizens. He argued, therefore, that democracy depended upon the development of a technique that would permit the pleasure-seeking and self-interested majority to force the self-interested governing elite to pursue policies conducive to the greatest happiness of the greatest number rather than to the pleasure of the governors. The appropriate technique, he argued, was the election, which would permit the citizens to reject an elite that did not please the majority.

Recently, Anthony Downs[5] has constructed a more sophisticated theoretical model of democratic politics by amplifying and refining several insights of Bentham and others. Downs's model is useful to us because it contains a theoretical framework for analyzing problems of rational decision-making by politicians and voters. Rational decision-making is, of course, the object of the political strategist, who wishes to select from a number of alternative strategies those which will result in his receiving the greatest possible number of votes for the time, money, and manpower that he has at his disposal.

[5] Anthony Downs, *An Economic Theory of Democracy* (New York: Harper & Bros., 1957).

A model that will permit us to differentiate rational from irrational political strategies and to explore the consequences of both may prove interesting.

Downs assumes that the democratic political stage contains two actors: politicians and voters, both of whom behave rationally and selfishly. The politician in Downs's model is interested only in himself; he is concerned only with the rewards that victory at the polls makes possible, be they power, graft, prestige, creative leadership, or reform. If he is rational, the politician formulates platforms and campaign programs only because he believes that they will gain more votes than they will lose. "Politicians," Downs assumes,

. . . never seek office as a means of carrying out particular policies; their only goal is to reap the rewards of office *per se*. They treat policies purely as a means to the attainment of their private ends, which they can reach only by being elected. . . . [P]arties formulate policies in order to win elections, rather than win elections to formulate policies.[6]

To win elections the politician must formulate the "right" policies —i.e., those that please voters. It is obvious, therefore, that a major problem of political strategy is to determine voter preferences and the intensity with which these preferences are held. The rational strategist must attempt to discover what programs and policies are preferred by significant blocs of voters and then proceed to advocate these policies, regardless of his own inner convictions. When the "will of the people" changes, so must the platform of the rational strategist. If a significant number of voters move to the "left" or the "right," so must the rational politician. This rule may produce candidates who are "hollow men," pale and empty reflections of the majority will. Nevertheless, democracy is based on the sovereignty of the popular will, and politicians (according to the classical democratic theory) are supposed to execute the will of the people rather than their own wills. If democratic communities require strong and vigorous leadership and if the will of the people is incoherent, poorly informed, or contradictory, then, in all likelihood, rational candidates (who follow the lead of the electorate) will not provide a way out of the morass. This, we contend, is a paradox inherent in democratic societies.

The rational strategist is the strategist who uses his resources most

[6] *Ibid.*, p. 28.

efficiently. His object is to get the greatest possible return (votes) for a given expenditure (time, money, and manpower), or to make the minimal expenditure for a given return.[7] The term "rational," therefore, applies to the means selected by the politician, the strategic alternatives, not to his ends, which are assumed to be selfish. One must assume for the sake of model clarity that the most noble and the most degraded goals, *in that they are desired by an individual of the political process,* are equally "selfish." Efficient utilization of resources, not success, is the criterion of a rationally determined strategy. The strategist who wins an election, therefore, is not necessarily the one who has behaved most rationally; the man who loses it has not necessarily behaved irrationally. It is possible for a candidate to have a tremendous plurality several months before the election, pursue a less rational strategy than his opponent during the campaign, and still win by a small margin. A candidate may allocate his resources in the most efficient manner and yet face obstacles that prevent him from winning.

Downs defines the rational decision-maker as one who behaves as follows:

. . . (1) he can always make a decision when confronted with a range of alternatives; (2) he ranks all the alternatives facing him in order of his preference in such a way that each is either preferred to, indifferent to, or inferior to each other; (3) his preference ranking is transitive; (4) he always chooses from among the possible alternatives that which ranks highest in his preference ordering; and (5) he always makes the same decision each time he is confronted with the same alternatives.[8]

In addition to following these rules, the rational political strategist who is "systematically making mistakes will cease to do so if (1) he discovers what the mistake is and if (2) the cost of eliminating it is smaller than the benefits therefrom."[9]

At first glance the problem of developing a rational political strategy in a democratic system appears to be quite simple—at least theoretically. Since the rational candidate wishes to get the greatest possible number of votes and since he can do this only if he stands for what the majority prefers, he ought to subject "each decision to a hypothetical poll and always choose the alternative which the

[7] *Ibid.,* p. 5.
[8] *Ibid.,* p. 6.
[9] *Ibid.,* p. 9.

majority of voters prefers. . . . [He] must do so because if he adopts any other course, the opposition party can defeat [him]."[10] For example, if the candidate of the incumbent party proposes a platform that the majority prefers except for issue x, then the candidate of the opposition should propose a platform identical to his rival's except for issue x, on which he assumes a position that is in agreement with the majority. In a political world composed of rational citizens, who, according to Downs's definition, vote in terms of party actions and platforms and select the party that offers them the better chance of achieving political and economic goals, the election narrows down to issue x, since the voters will be indifferent to all other issues (the parties' positions on them being identical). In this situation, the opposition will win. To avoid defeat, therefore, the candidate of the incumbents must support the majority on every issue. In practice, the crucial point is not so much how the majority feels on all the issues but how many votes would be lost on controversial issues. In a community where most people are politically middle of the road—fundamentally in agreement on most issues—it is probably much more rational for the candidate to stand firmly on all sides of all questions and avoid controversy.

Downs points out that the most efficient policy for the incumbents to follow is that which will please the majority, although it does not always guarantee victory. The opposition can sometimes defeat a majority-pleasing strategy by adopting a "complete matching of policies" or a "coalition of minorities" plan. In the first strategy, the opposition adopts a program which is identical with that of the incumbents. In a political world in which citizens vote only in terms of platforms and past party actions (Downs's model world), this strategy forces voters to decide how to vote by comparing how well they fared under the incumbents with how well they fared under previous governments. If the record of the incumbents is "poor" and if the previous record of the "outs" when they were in power was "good," then the party out of power may be wise to match the platform offered to the voters by the party in power.

A second strategy—the "coalition of minorities"—is available to the opposition if the incumbents follow the majority principle. This strategy requires that the opposition support the position of various minorities on various key issues. This strategy will work only if no

[10] *Ibid.*, p. 54.

majority exhibits perfect consensus on all issues.[11] In most elections, many voters are concerned with several issues, to which they attach different degrees of importance. A majority of voters may prefer a particular policy, to which they are not strongly committed, while at the same time some of those in the majority may also be part of a minority that feels more strongly about a different issue. This condition favors a coalition-of-minorities strategy for the opposition. Volpe, for example, followed a strategy which resembles the coalition of minorities in appealing to certain groups that customarily vote Democratic. For example, he delivered a speech solely concerned with the problems of the Metropolitan Transit Authority which, according to one of his advisers, evoked a tremendous response from strongly Democratic areas in which the MTA is widely used:

No speech that John has given has brought such a public response by telephone calls and letters. I would guess it meant 30,000 votes for him right in the metropolitan area. Of course he forthrightly assailed the political pay-offs in the MTA organization, pointed out . . . the one thing you have to do is to clean house in the upper level and restore morale among the employees by making them feel that they're working for a road that's being properly and efficiently run. The most amazing response you ever saw. . . .

Telephone calls! All day long they had three people on the telephone. People called to say: "I'm a Democrat. My name is so-and-so. After that speech I'm voting for John Volpe and I'm getting my wife and my family to vote for him."

The minority candidate may therefore be wise to direct a specific appeal to subgroups in the electorate that customarily vote with the majority party but have a strong concern about some issue. Actually, in a pluralistic society like America, any majority is inevitably composed of a coalition of minorities. Except on patriotic issues (almost everyone supports "Americanism" and is opposed to "Communism"), American candidates must create temporary coalitions of minorities in order to win elections. The fact that citizens in a pluralistic society are often concerned with several issues, to which they attach differing degrees of importance, may well be crucial to the preservation of a nonviolent, constitutional order, since a citizen who loses on one significant issue may still win on another.

11 *Ibid.*

The problem confronting the strategist, therefore, is not merely one of identifying the preferences of the majority, if a majority exists, but also of evaluating the intensity of voters' preferences on particular issues. This is obviously a most difficult undertaking. The object of the undertaking—on one level, at least—is to please the voters. It is necessary, therefore, to examine the basic logic of voting.

Rational Voters

The only criterion used by the rational strategist when planning his platform and the issues upon which he will campaign is whether or not a particular position will gain him more votes than it will cost him. While planning, he must assume that some relationship exists between what he says and does and how citizens vote; that is, he must assume that citizens will react to him in some predictable fashion. If he does not make such an assumption, or if he assumes that no logical principle of any kind governs voting behavior, he has no reason except personal preference to select one program rather than any other. The concept of rational strategy is meaningless without the assumption that the reaction of voters is also rational. In Downs's model world of democracy, the rational strategist can assume that citizens, like strategists, behave selfishly and rationally:

. . . Each citizen casts his vote for the party he believes will provide him with more benefits than any other. . . . The benefits voters consider in making their decisions are streams of utility derived from governmental activity. . . . Given several mutually exclusive alternatives, a rational man always takes the one which yields him the highest utility, *ceteris paribus;* i.e., he acts to his own greatest benefit. . . . No matter how diverse, all benefits must be reduced to some denominator. . . . The common denominator used in this process we call utility.[12]

Each rational citizen defines benefits in purely subjective terms and votes for the party that he believes will provide him with more benefits.

The rational citizen in Downs's model world, like the rational strategist, acts in politics with reference only to his economic or political goals, and he measures benefits exclusively in terms of them. Thus the citizen

> . . . votes for the party which he believes will provide him with a higher utility income [more benefits] than any other party during the coming election period. To discover which party this is, he compares the utility incomes he believes he would receive were each party in office. . . . The difference between these two expected utility incomes is the citizen's expected party differential.[13]

If the rational citizen believes that the incumbents will provide him with more benefits than the opposition (a positive expected "party differential") he will vote, and will vote for the candidate of the incumbent party. If the rational citizen believes that the opposition will provide him with more benefits than the incumbents (a negative expected "party differential") he will vote, and will vote for the opposition candidate. If the rational citizen believes that he will not benefit differentially from the election of either party (zero expected "party differential") he will abstain from voting because it is irrational for him to expend scarce resources (time and energy in going to the polls) when there is no anticipated reward. According to Downs, therefore, the size of a rational citizen's expected party differential is the critical factor determining the degree of his interest in the outcome of the election. His interest will in turn determine whether or not he votes or becomes actively involved in a campaign.

If a rational citizen believes that he will receive many benefits if x is elected and few benefits if y is elected (a large expected party differential), he will not only vote but probably campaign actively. If, on the other hand, a rational citizen believes that he will receive just a few more benefits from the election of one candidate rather than the other (a small expected party differential), he is likely to have little interest in the election and to enter the voting booth with much uncertainty. It is this voter who is most available for conversion and who should therefore be a major target of the rational political strategist.

Downs's predictions concerning the voting behavior of citizens with different expected party differentials are supported by empirical data collected by students of political behavior. For example, high interest *does* correlate with high voting turnout and low interest with

[13] *Ibid.*, p. 39.

low voting turnout; those who are most concerned with the outcome of an election *are* the most likely to vote, to try to persuade others, to contribute money, etc.[14]

It may appear that the process by which a rational citizen in this imaginary world determines his expected party differential is simple and straightforward, but such is not the case. Since the rational citizen knows that no party will be able to do everything that it says it will do, he must estimate in his own mind what each party would do if it were elected; this is no easy task. Given the fact that one of the parties is now in power, the rational citizen can use its performance (assuming some continuity) to form some idea of what it will do in the future. But what about the party that is not in power? The rational citizen must estimate what it would have done if it had been in power—a very hypothetical estimate at best. In estimating future benefits, the citizen is most rational if he proceeds to compare what he has received from the incumbents with what he thinks he would have received from the party out of power. This calculation, based primarily on current events, will give him his current party differential.[15] The rational man may add another calculation—a trend factor—when determining his current party differential. The incumbents may be steadily improving or getting worse. The rational citizen may make some projection of this trend when predicting the future behavior of the parties.

Downs is, of course, postulating a political world in which candidates behave without reference to their own moral views or personal integrity and in which citizens vote only in terms of their economic and political goals and the records of the competing parties and are not affected by the personality, physical appearance, religion, or ethnicity of the candidates. Obviously, these conditions are seldom found. Some members of the electorate pay no attention to party programs, voting for the candidate who has the "right" ethnic or religious background or who looks more honest or sincere. Some men vote to please their wives despite a belief that they would profit economically or politically from the election of the other candidate; and wives often vote as their husbands tell them to or by some arcane

[14] For a summary of the findings and generalizations of several voting studies, see Bernard R. Berelson, Paul F. Lazarsfeld, and William N. McPhee, *Voting: A Study of Opinion Formation in a Presidential Campaign* (Chicago: University of Chicago Press, 1954), pp. 337-38.
[15] See Downs, *op. cit.,* p. 39.

system of feminine preference. The voter is not simply a seeker of political or economic satisfactions. He has psychological drives and needs that may be unrelated or even antagonistic to his political or economic goals. He may vote for a particular candidate because his characterological needs (moralistic, aggressive, etc.) are "satisfied" by the personality of the candidate.[16] Thus his vote may be rational psychologically but not politically. The candidates are aware of this tendency and attempt to exploit it when formulating strategy. They talk in terms of "the Irish vote, the Jewish vote, the Negro vote," not the "rational" or "irrational" vote. They also know that voters are affected by the candidate's height, weight, posture, and style. As we shall see, many Massachusetts citizens calculate their current party differential precisely in terms of these factors. This is one of the reasons that the formulation of political strategy is so difficult in Massachusetts.

Downs is himself aware of the limited application of his model world to reality:

We do not take into consideration the whole personality of each individual when we discuss what behavior is rational for him. We do not allow for the rich diversity of ends served by each of his acts, the complexity of his motives, the way in which every part of his life is intimately related to his emotional needs. . . . He [the rational citizen] remains an abstraction from the real fullness of human personality. We assume that he approaches every situation with one eye on the gains to be had, the other eye on the costs, a delicate ability to balance them, and a strong desire to follow them wherever rationality leads him.[17]

The fact that Downs's model world is hypothetical does not mean that we can gain no understanding of the "real" political world by comparing it to the model world. For example, assuming that politicians in the "real" world wish to get maximal results for their limited campaign funds, time, and manpower, we can determine the degree to which they behave rationally by comparing their decisions with those that would have been made under similar circumstances by an imaginary rational strategist. We may even be able to discover by means of such a comparison why and how politicians behave irrationally and what conditions hamper rational decision-making. Downs pleads his case quite succinctly:

[16] See Robert Lane, *Political Life* (Glencoe, Ill.: Free Press, 1959), p. 25.
[17] Downs, *op. cit.*, p. 8.

The relevance of the model in this study to descriptive science is two-fold. First it proposes a single hypothesis to explain government decision-making and party behavior in general. Since this hypothesis leads to testable corollaries it can be submitted to empirical proof. If verified it may lead to non-obvious conclusions about the actions and development of parties, thus adding to our knowledge of reality.

Second, the model tells us what behavior we can expect if men act rationally in politics. Therefore it can perhaps be used to discover (1) in what phases of politics in the real world men are rational, (2) in what phases they are irrational, and (3) how they deviate from rationality in the latter.[18]

Even though most of Downs's assumptions are "unrealistic," it is nevertheless a fact that many candidates assume that citizens vote in terms of some definition of rational self-interest, some estimate of what will give them maximal utility income. Candidates do make estimates of what programs voters prefer, and they do attempt to assume positions that they think will be popular. Indeed, their estimate of voting behavior bears more than a passing resemblance to Downs's analysis of the logic of rational voting. For example, the incumbent candidates emphasize their party's accomplishments, knowing that many citizens take into account the utility income they have received from the party in power, while the "outs" attempt to point out the low utility income provided by the "ins." The candidates assume that the performance of the incumbents is used by many citizens as the most reliable indicator of their future performance. This is precisely why the incumbent candidates stress the party's achievements if they think their regime has provided high utility incomes and "break" with the party if they believe it has provided low utility incomes. Conversely, this is the basis on which opposition candidates decide to focus their attack on the incumbent party or on its candidate. Volpe, for example, correctly assumed that many Democrats were disillusioned with the Furcolo administration (believing that they had received a low utility income from the incumbents) and would therefore vote against Ward if they identified him closely with his party. He therefore adopted the slogan "Vote for the Man, Vote Volpe," which, among other things, implied that Ward, unlike Volpe, was the representative of a machine.

Some candidates even assume that citizens use "trend factors" to

18 *Ibid.,* p. 33.

adjust current party differentials. As a matter of fact, it was obvious to all the candidates that the trend factor for the Democrats was bad in Massachusetts, because of the scandals, and that many regulars would desert the party for this reason. The Ward brain trust even feared than many Democrats would conclude that there was no difference between the candidates (zero expected party differentials) and would therefore not vote. Indeed, one of the objects of Ward's television trial of Volpe was to create this condition for independents and Republicans, so that they would not vote.

Despite these views of the candidates, it would be absurd to argue that the model world of Downs is a completely accurate representation of the real political world. The number of citizens whose basic logic of voting is irrational, as Downs defines the term, is undoubtedly great. The utility of a theoretical model, however, lies not in the accuracy of its description of the real world but, rather, in the opportunity it provides for making predictions on the basis of the assumptions of the model. We shall utilize some of Downs's concepts in attempting to evaluate the rationality of some decisions taken by Massachusetts gubernatorial candidates in 1960 and to predict the behavior of certain types of voter.

Rational Strategy and Uncertainty

That part of Downs's theoretical model of democracy that we have summarized thus far is based on the assumption that both voters and politicians operate with full information—i.e., with certainty. The strategists know the preferences of citizens, and the citizens know the programs and the past actions of the parties. In a "certain" universe, in which candidates know the distribution of voter preferences and the intensity with which these preferences are held, the problem of political strategy, we have seen, would be a simple one. The candidates, if they were not hampered by tradition or morality (i.e., if they were completely flexible and completely rational), would simply advocate the policies desired by a majority of the citizens (assuming that a majoritarian consensus existed) or those desired by a coalition of minorities. All rational candidates would then adopt exactly the same policies, and the parties would assume identical positions.

Although candidates often do assume similar positions when the preferences of the electorate are similar and obvious, a condition of perfect certainty is impossible. Uncertainty, which Downs defines as "any lack of sure knowledge about the course of past, present, future, or hypothetical events,"[19] is intrinsic to free elections because voters can change their minds at any moment prior to casting a ballot. Because uncertainty exists (strategists do not know exactly what effect a particular tactic will have since they do not know the complete index of voters' utility incomes), parties will differentiate their programs in accordance with their definition of the uncertain situation. Uncertainty makes changing political strategy "necessary."

The greater the degree of uncertainty, the more difficult it is to determinate a rational strategy. This is precisely why strategists wish to remove uncertainty, by acquiring information concerning voters' tastes or by convincing voters that a particular decision is "right" (i.e., certain). The possibility of a varied and creative strategy naturally increases with uncertainty. So does the possibility of strategic blunders.

There was a large degree of uncertainty in both the primary and the general election with which we are concerned. In the first place, the large number of candidates in the primary created an extremely confusing situation for the candidates and the electorate. The four great unknowns of the primary election were the appeal of John Francis Kennedy's "magic name," the votes that could be attracted by Kelly's lottery proposal, the effect of Peabody's charge that Ward had rigged the ballot, and the degree to which disillusionment with the incumbents would cause Democrats and independents to vote against Ward as the representative of the "machine"—the officially endorsed candidate of the Democratic convention. The key unknowns of the general election in November were the strength of Senator John Fitzgerald Kennedy's coattails, the divisive effect of the bitter Democratic primary, the attractiveness of a Republican Italo-American candidate to the large Italo-American population which normally votes Democratic, and the degree to which voter cynicism, hostility, and disgust with the incumbents would cause regular Democrats to desert Ward.

Some of the strategists we interviewed displayed a low level of confidence in some of their own basic strategic decisions. Peabody, for

19 *Ibid.*, p. 77.

example, was not sure that he should not have appealed his "case" against Ward during the primary; Ward wondered whether his attack on Volpe in the general election had gone too far; while the Volpe forces were not confident that their candidate's rebuttal of Ward's charges had been adequate. (In Chapter 6, we shall evaluate these and other strategic decisions on the basis of their rationality.)

The candidates' relative lack of confidence in these key decisions followed mainly from their assumption—a correct one—that the traditional division of the Massachusetts electorate into a "majority" of loyal Democrats, a "minority" of loyal Republicans, and a large bloc of "independents" who could swing the balance of power was no longer valid. The disintegration of this arrangement, some of them believed, was due principally to the fragmentation of the Democratic leadership into a number of selfish feudal chieftains, each with a loyal band of retainers. This meant that Ward could count neither on the support of those who were traditionally loyal to the convention endorsee nor on the party organization, since it was virtually nonexistent. Some of the candidates sensed, however, that the shattering of the traditional alignments and loyalties was the result of a more profound development in the electorate; namely, the appearance of large blocs of voters who feel that they are wrongfully excluded from political power and who assume that elections are meaningless because the candidates and parties are corrupt, incompetent, self-interested, and power-hungry. The candidates were well aware that the continuous exposés of corruption and conflict of interest in the state government had created a mood of extreme cynicism and anger among the electorate. The strategists then faced the extremely difficult task of predicting the response of a hostile and incredulous public which was likely to vote in terms of some highly subjective estimate of the candidates' character and integrity.

Since the alienated and cynical voter assumes that all political candidates are to some extent untrustworthy or dishonest, he is likely to estimate his current party differential in terms of relative losses rather than relative benefits. He may even come to believe that his current party differential is zero or very close to zero (i.e., that it is of little or no difference to him who wins), which makes for a highly unstable and unpredictable political situation. It is necessary, therefore, to examine the impact of political alienation on pre-election uncertainty and, consequently, on the problem of political strategy.

The Alienated Voter

In his book on politics in Philadelphia, Reichley writes that "the organization . . . is practically universally regarded not only by the intellectuals but by almost all people who are not themselves in politics as a bunch of political bums bent on personal enrichment at the expense of the general welfare."[20] This cynical attitude toward local politicians is particularly strong in Massachusetts, where it has assumed the nature of *a priori* truth for large numbers of voters. The belief of the electorate that politicians are corrupt and self-interested and that voters are politically powerless affects the outcome of elections in the Bay State and the formation of political strategy, at least for those candidates who are sophisticated enough to perceive it.

The significance of political alienation as a force in Massachusetts politics was first brought to the authors' attention as a result of a public-opinion poll of 500 voters conducted immediately after the Boston mayoralty election of 1959. In that election, John Collins, a relatively unknown candidate who had little financial and political support and who had been conceded little or no chance of winning, badly defeated John Powers, the president of the Massachusetts Senate. Powers was one of the most powerful, heavily endorsed, and well-financed candidates in Boston history. The *Boston Herald* described Collins' victory as "the most staggering upset in the recent history of the city."[21] Nevertheless, Collins' victory was regarded by many of his "supporters" as a dubious triumph. Fifty per cent of those respondents who had voted for Collins stated that they had supported him because they did not like his opponent, and 13 per cent reported that they had voted for Collins because he was "the lesser of two evils."

Large numbers of respondents also reported their belief that the candidates were obligated to and dominated by a small group of men who, by contributing to the campaign coffers, were purchasing future political favors: "I felt he made deals with backers of the campaign." "He spent too much money campaigning. I thought of where all those funds came from." "[He]" was spending so much

---

[20] James Reichley, *The Art of Government: Reform and Organization Politics in Philadelphia* (New York: The Fund for the Republic, 1959), p. 94.

[21] *Boston Herald*, Nov. 4, 1959, p. 1.

money and had so much political backing I began to wonder what everybody was expecting to gain from his election."

Many respondents complained that the candidates had not presented a sincere, serious, or meaningful discussion of the issues and that the campaign had been reduced to a mudslinging contest: "In his campaign all he did was attack ——— and hardly ever talked about the issues." "He didn't say anything and I heard him speak for 45 minutes." "Both men were talking in circles about Boston's needs and how to meet them."

These remarks indicate more than resentment toward the particular candidates in this election; they indicate a profound disgust and disillusionment with the political process and politicians in general, a belief that reform is impossible and that it makes little or no difference who wins elections. Of those respondents who voted for Powers, 43 per cent thought that he would be "no better than" Collins, while 57 per cent of those who voted for Collins thought that he would be no better than his opponent. Under these conditions, politics, as it is characterized in American political folklore, tends to lose its meaning. The alienated voter believes that he has been cheated of his political birthright and stripped of his political power by corrupt and self-seeking politicians. He assumes that platforms are mere verbiage; if he votes at all, he chooses what he believes is the lesser of two evils in an attempt to minimize graft and corruption. He therefore tends to evaluate the character, personality, and integrity of the candidates rather than their platforms. This he does in terms of highly subjective "gut reactions." He may just "feel in his bones" that a candidate is not honest. In elections in which cynicism and alienation are widespread, estimates of this kind are critical. This was the case in the Collins-Powers election.

The following responses to the question "What did you like least about ———?" illustrate this type of reaction:

> his voice
> something about his eyes
> don't like his looks—tough, ugly looking
> his personal appearance
> he is fat and pudgy, that's a psychological factor against him
> smug—looks crooked
> too polished
> type with cigars

instinctively dislike him
looked icy, talked funny—the sound of his voice
stubborn and selfish
biggest stuffed shirt I've ever seen
too cocky
little Napoleon
just another Irishman
ran a dirty campaign
ladies' man
cry baby
milk sop—strictly from nowhere

Responses of this "gut reaction" type were not restricted to those who had a negative image of the candidate. They played a prominent role in determining what voters liked about candidates:

simple private life
good man to his family
he spoke to you with his heart, not his mouth
he was kind
nice quiet manner
he always had a smile and a handshake
he always had time to say hello
clean fighter
looks like he'll try
a real gentleman
just the way he spoke, I feel he is honest

The political strategist who wishes to appeal to the alienated voter must therefore have a candidate with the "right" voice, manner, and appearance. Gut reactions may, of course, also play a significant role in the calculations of non-alienated voters; however, since the non-alienated voter assumes that at least one of the candidates has some integrity, he may also regard platforms as relevant criteria for voting. The candidate's "image," as opposed to his program, is thus crucial to alienated voters and possibly relevant to non-alienated voters.

This interest in the temperament and personality of the candidate, classical democratic theory notwithstanding, is "legitimate," according to some writers. Listing the "legitimate" interests of voters in the personality of the candidates, Pendleton Herring includes the following: "Is the candidate sincere? Does he seem honest and well mean-

ing? Will he keep his promises? Who are his friends? Are they
trustworthy people?"[22] The personality of the candidate is particularly relevant for voters in the United States, in view of the decentral-
ized and undisciplined character of American political parties and
the "similarity" of the major parties. The candidate's personality is
an even more "legitimate" concern of voters in state elections, in
which ideological conflict is usually minimal.

We have emphasized the significance of political alienation for
practicing political strategists because the attitudes of voters in the
Powers-Collins election are not unique for that contest or that time.
They represent a profound, fundamental, and perhaps permanent
orientation to politics and politicians in Massachusetts, as indicated
by the results of the public-opinion poll taken by the authors prior
to the primary election of September 1960. Forty-eight per cent of
those interviewed, for example, agreed with the statement: "Public
officials in Massachusetts do not care what people like me think."
Some of them voluntarily offered the following remarks in response
to the question: "Give you the gold brick before they're elected,
afterwards give themselves the gold brick." "They care only to win
elections." "After they are elected they wouldn't look at you any
more." "Politics is all bagged. They do what they want." "Don't
think they care a hoot."

Fifty-four per cent disagreed with the statement: "The way people
vote is the main thing that decides how things are run in this state."
Again, some examples: "Anyone who believes this is crazy."
"Things always turn out the same no matter who wins." "Well, voting only decides between the politicians." "It makes no difference
who wins, Massachusetts is just a crappy state. You can't do anything with it. There is something wrong here." "Whoever you vote
for, they're going to get in and line their pockets—hooray for me and
the hell with you." None of these comments was solicited; the respondents were merely asked to indicate their agreement or disagreement with the statement.[23] If it is "political knowledge" that informs
the judgment of the rational voter and qualifies his estimates of polit-

[22] Quoted in Stanley Kelley, Jr., *Political Campaigning* (Washington, D.C.: The
Brookings Institution, 1960), p. 13.

[23] This statement and others used in this survey are slightly altered versions of
standard questions used by the Survey Research Center, of the University of Mich-
igan, to test for political efficacy. See Angus Campbell, Gerald Gurin, and Warren
Miller, *The Voter Decides* (Evanston, Ill.: Row, Peterson & Co.. 1954), Appendix A.

ical realities, it is "political worldliness" that identifies the alienated voter—expressed, as here, in suspicion and contempt for politics and politicians.

Seventy-five per cent of those interviewed before the September primary agreed that a code of ethics for public officials was needed in Massachusetts. Of these, however, only 32 per cent believed that such a code would be effective.

Needed, but would do no good. Well, my God, every time you pick up a paper you see some new scandals or another. I mean this MDC business, this handing out contracts without bids—on the other hand, you know as well as I do that getting a bill of ethics or code of conduct or whatever *could* do some good . . . but it won't because nobody's going to go by it too much even after they sign it. My God, for taxicab licenses, to get 'em they say you gotta know somebody in this city;—it's awful.

Needed. Well, certainly with all the chance and temptations that a man in public office is confronted with, I can say that I think a code of ethics is needed. But a code isn't something that you sign, it's something that you live by—that's why they call it a code. I think if they asked all the thieves in prison to sign an oath not to steal, they'd have no trouble getting signatures. I don't mean that all politicians are thieves, I just don't see how they are going to make this work.

One might notice the difference between these two statements. The latter is more literate and analytical, the respondent perhaps more likely to be able to follow and evaluate a sustained, precise presentation of political issues. But one must also notice the similarity— the burden of worldly knowledge appears to be lack of expectation, disbelief. Another echoes this:

You can't do it. I don't think it can be done. You can't call them crooks —you don't catch them. When a politician gets through, he gets a job— handing out favors. You get the runaround, though, if you don't know the politicians—you can go up to the State House and plead for all you're worth. What you need is to know the guy and have money.

From these and other remarks, one can construct the alienated voter's image of politicians and the political process in Massachusetts:

1. Politicians in general are corrupt, incompetent, or self-interested.

2. The candidates involved in these elections are politicians and there-fore are corrupt, etc.
3. The community is controlled by a tightly knit power elite composed of politicians, contractors, "the rich," bookies, elements of the un-derworld, and political "influentials" who have the "means" to secure favored treatment.
4. The members of this power elite engage in a mutually satisfactory exchange of favors for which the public at large ultimately pays and from which it is excluded.
5. Candidates who spend large sums of money electioneering are be-holden to those who contribute to them.
6. It makes little or no difference which candidate wins because (a) the so-called reform candidate is tied up with and indebted to those who support him—the nucleus of a new power elite—or (b) the newly elected candidate cannot govern without working with the old power elite, which has entrenched itself in the city government; or (c) the newly elected candidate desires the rewards of office—i.e., graft—which he can receive only by selling favors; or (d) even if the man who wins is honest he cannot remain so, because contact with politicians or the attainment of power will corrupt him.
7. Public life in Massachusetts is characterized by widespread evasion of the law. Bribes, political payoffs, and graft have replaced due process of law as the principle for conducting public business.
8. The electoral process under these conditions is a mockery of democ-racy, since the voter has no control over the political process.

It is clear that citizens who hold these opinions believe that there is a sharp dichotomy between the power elite, which uses public office for personal gain, and the voters, who are powerless outsiders, unable to affect the decision-making process. They believe that their political destiny is beyond their control—that they are manipulated and exploited by forces that they cannot uproot or even influence.

As we have observed, the feeling of being wrongfully excluded, powerless, and cheated of one's political birthright is the essential component of political alienation.[24] In a democratic society, it arises in part from the disjunction between democratic values and per-ceived political realities—between the role that democratic man be-lieves he has a right to play and the role that he perceives he is forced

[24] For further analysis of the nature and causes of political alienation, see Mur-ray B. Levin, *The Alienated Voter: Politics in Boston* (New York: Holt, Rinehart and Winston, Inc., 1960), Chap. 4.

to play. The Lockian version of democratic theory, which has dominated American political thought,[25] holds that government should be based on the will of the majority, executed by elected officials acting as passive agents. According to this theory, the citizen is interested in and informed about political affairs. He is expected to act on the basis of certain self-evident principles (natural law) that refer not only to his personal interest but also to the common good.

This theory leads its adherents to believe that they have a "right" to be politically powerful—that is, to select, influence, and remove public officials. It also leads them to expect that they will have enough information to make a meaningful choice between alternatives, and that they will be able to do this through existing institutions without violating their standards of political ethics. Classical democratic theory also leads democratic man to expect rational and honest behavior on the part of public officials. In a political system in which many individuals believe that corruption is widespread and political power is concentrated and abused, these expectations of the citizens are not met. Citizens come to believe that they are foreigners (aliens) in their own political world. For them the political structure, as a system of prescribed performances, has ceased to exist.

The foregoing description of the origins of political alienation implies that the average citizen actually expects to live in a world in which he has political power and is able to play the roles assigned to him by Lockian theory. However, we know virtually nothing about the political values and expectations of the average citizen. Almost all the studies of political behavior conducted in the United States concentrate on voting *behavior*. They tell us little about what the voter or non-voter thinks the system ought to be like.[26] An examination of grammar- and high-school civics texts indicates that

25 For a brilliant analysis of the hegemony of Locke in America, see Louis Hartz, *The Liberal Tradition in America* (New York: Harcourt, Brace & Co., 1955).

26 It is instructive to note that studies of why certain people fail to vote reveal far more about voter expectations than studies of why people vote. See, for example, Morris Rosenberg, "Some Determinants of Political Apathy," *Public Opinion Quarterly*, Vol. 18 (Winter 1954), p. 360: "Some people may sincerely embrace the social values of democracy, honesty in government, etc. We might thus expect them to be politically active in behalf of these principles. However, these values may be so high and pure, and the fact of political life so low and base, that they abandon any hope of bridging the gap between the normative and factual orders. Indeed, it is often precisely the people who embrace the value of democracy most fervently who suffer the greatest disillusionment."

American schools teach children that voting is important, that the outcome of elections makes a difference, that parties and candidates are influenced by majority rule, and that the "will of the people" is supposed to be supreme. These are in part Lockian values. The alienated voter is alienated precisely because he holds these values to some degree but has come to believe that in fact voting is unimportant, the outcome of elections makes no difference, the community is governed by a self-interested minority, and the will of the people is ineffectual. One may argue that classical democratic theory is utopian and unrealistic[27]—that is, that majority rule in any immediate sense is impossible, that voters must play the passive role while politicians play the active role. One may also argue that the values transmitted to children by grammar-school civics teachers are crude simplifications of the precepts of Locke. But the fact remains that many citizens expect to play a political role which makes them the ultimate reference point of the politicians. Their expectations, realistic or not, influence their political attitudes and behavior and affect the outcome of elections.

The voter may, of course, become alienated without having any actual contact with public officials. He may just read about "corruption" in the newspaper or hear rumors to the effect that the state government is dishonest. Alienation may develop experientially. For example, Bostonians, who live in urban centers that are predominantly slums and have to pay the highest automobile insurance rates of any city in the country, have cause to contrast the public service they receive with some subjective concept of what they ought to receive from a "legitimate" government. The alienated voter may contrast his political experience as well as his values with some ideal standard.

Political Strategy for Alienated Voters

The candidate who must campaign in communities where the alienated vote is critical—and Massachusetts is one of these—ought to be interested in the causes of political alienation, particularly if he antic-

[27] For a sophisticated statement of this position, see Joseph Schumpeter, *Capitalism, Socialism and Democracy* (3d. ed.; New York: Harper & Bros., 1950), Chap. 21.

ipates a permanent political career. However, a knowledge of the various ways in which political alienation may be experienced may be more valuable as a guide to practical political strategy. The strategist wants to know how to take advantage of the anger and frustration that lead to political alienation. To do this, he ought to speculate about the voting criteria that the alienated voter is likely to use.

Political alienation is generally experienced as either powerlessness, meaningless, or a lowering of one's political ethics. The alienated voter who feels powerless believes that his vote or any other political action he may take has no influence on the course of political events. He sees himself as excluded from the seats of power by a group of selfish and dishonest "insiders," who monopolize control. The strategist may be able to take advantage of the voter's feeling of powerlessness by identifying his opponent as the usurper, while at the same time offering the voter a way of regaining his lost power, by voting for the strategist's candidate.

Political alienation may also be experienced as meaninglessness. An individual may believe that an election is without meaning because there are no real differences between the candidates, or because he lacks the information without which he thinks an intelligent and rational decision is impossible. The degree of meaninglessness depends upon the disparity between the amount of information the voter considers necessary and that which is available. If the candidates and platforms are very similar or identical, it will be difficult to find "meaningful" information on which to base a voting decision. The political strategist may take advantage of feelings of meaninglessness by differentiating his candidate from his opponent or providing the alienated voter with information that he will consider meaningful.

An individual may also experience feelings of political alienation in the sense of lowered political ethics. This occurs when standards of political behavior are violated in order to achieve some goal, when the present political reality prevents the attainment of political objectives through institutionally prescribed means. An example of this would be the case of an individual who believes that paying a bribe to a public official is morally wrong but does so nevertheless, in order to achieve some personal benefit. When people come to believe that corrupt practices are the only ways of achieving political goals, corruption will become widespread, regardless of the reluctance of individuals to engage in it. If corruption becomes the generally accepted method of dealing with public officials, the stigma attached to it will tend to disappear and the political community will become normless (anomic). The political strategist may take advantage of the alienated voter's sense that he has violated his ethical standards by promising that his candidate can and will alter the political structure so that political objectives can be obtained through lawfully prescribed means. He might, for example, initiate unofficial exposés or propose specific investigations. The authors' public-opinion polls taken before the primary and after the general election of 1960 indicate that the proportion of alienated voters was large enough to affect significantly the outcome of these elections. The fact that the Democratic candidate for governor could lose in the state of Massachusetts in 1960 is itself dramatic testimony to the existence of large numbers of alienated voters. The fact that so many of the so-called independents who voted for Volpe perceived him as the lesser of two evils lends further credence to this view. Candidates in these elections should have been aware of the large numbers of voters who distrusted them and who were therefore likely to interpret their platforms and speeches in a most cynical manner. In other words, the number of alienated voters was large enough to warrant strategies designed specifically for them. Some of the candidates understood this and developed strategies accordingly, but most of these strategies were crude and ineffectual.

Before we turn to an examination of political strategy as it was actually practiced in these elections (Chapters 4, 5, 6), we shall present a theoretical model of political strategy as it might have been developed for the alienated voters of Massachusetts. We do this to illustrate the problems that confront political strategists in dealing with such voters. Of course, many voters in Massachusetts are either quite indifferent to politics or identify strongly with one of the parties or one of the candidates; our model is not designed for them. We do not mean to suggest by implication that candidates in Massachusetts should ignore the non-alienated and the indifferent; we merely wish to illuminate one aspect of the problem of political strategy, a very important one in Massachusetts. We shall also have to examine the question of whether political strategies designed for the alienated voter may be self-defeating—that is, whether they may repel the non-alienated segment of the electorate.

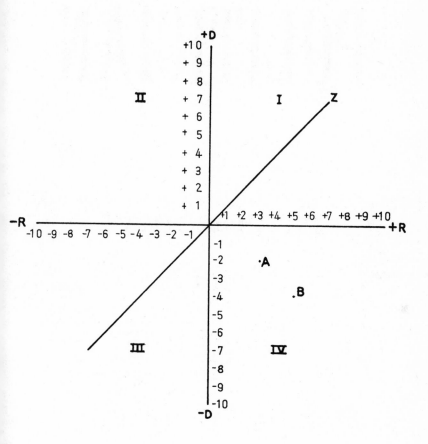

FIGURE 2

THE COMPLEAT
POLITICIAN

Errata Sheet

for

Diagrams

on Pages 159 and 165

It is customary for the political strategist in Massachusetts to plan a campaign on the basis of its potential appeal to Democrats, Republicans, independents, Protestants, Catholics, Jews, Greeks, Italians, Irish, etc. Instead of this coalition-of-minorities approach, we suggest that the strategist might find it more profitable to plan the campaign in terms of its appeal to alienated and non-alienated voters.[28] Figure 2 divides the electorate into these two groups:

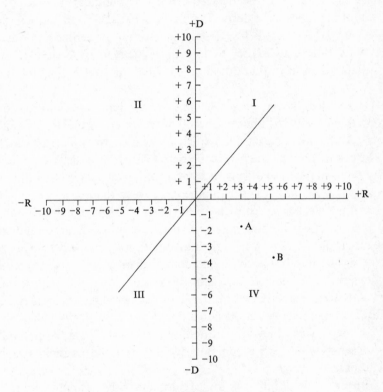

FIGURE 2

In Figure 2, D and R represent the candidates in a two-party election. A plus sign denotes a positive expectation—that is, a belief that one will benefit if the candidate is elected. A minus sign denotes a negative expectation—that is, a belief that one will suffer if the

28 The remainder of this chapter was written in collaboration with Professor Murray Eden, of the Department of Electrical Engineering, Massachusetts Institute of Technology.

candidate is elected. Like Downs, we use the terms "benefit" and "suffer" with reference only to the economic or political goals of citizens or parties.

Citizens who fall into quadrant II expect that they will benefit from the election of D and lose from the election of R. Conversely, citizens in quadrant IV expect to benefit from the election of R and lose from the election of D. Citizens who fall into quadrant I expect to benefit from the election of either candidate, although they may assess the benefits to be derived from one candidate's success as greater than those to be derived from the other's. Citizens falling into quadrant III expect to lose from the election of either candidate, although they may expect to lose more from the election of one candidate than from that of the other. Quadrant III is the quadrant of alienation.

Democratic theory suggests that citizens may expect to be confronted with political alternatives all of which are perceived as beneficial. If this were the case in reality, citizens in every election would be forced to decide which was the better of two "goods." Undoubtedly there are some citizens in some elections who see the political alternatives in these terms[29] (quadrant I). Nevertheless, a citizen who regards the election of only one of the parties as a source of economic or political gain to him may still feel that the existing system is meaningful. Citizens who fall into quadrants I, II, or IV can be assumed, therefore, to have some commitment to the system. They believe that it is possible for them to exercise some political power, since at least one candidate, in their view, represents their interests, They may not believe that it is possible to receive all the benefits to which they believe they are entitled, but they anticipate the possibility of a net gain. This is precisely what makes the political system meaningful to them.

Citizens who fall into quadrant III structure the available political alternatives in terms of the "lesser of two evils." They expect to lose in any case. They believe that they are denied representation of their interests. They therefore feel alienated, powerless, cynical, cheated, and potentially disloyal. Our studies suggest that perhaps 30 to 40 per cent of the electorate feels this way about state elections in Massachusetts.

In order to represent the party differential in Figure 2, we intro-

[29] "They're all good men. Good luck to them," said one respondent.

duce the main diagonal Z. A citizen who falls on the main diagonal has an expected party differential of zero. That is, he expects to benefit or lose to the same degree from the election of either candidate. It is rational for a citizen in this situation to abstain from voting, since the expenditure of scarce resources will result in no significant gain for him. The closer a citizen is to the main diagonal, the smaller is his expected party differential. For example, citizen A believes that he will gain three units of benefits from the election of candidate R and lose two units from the election of candidate D. His expected party differential is $+3 - (-2) = +5$. Citizen B believes that he will gain five units of benefit from the election of R and lose four units of benefit from the election of D. His expected party differential is $+5 -- (-4) = +9$. Any point to the left of the diagonal Z represents a citizen whose expected party differential is favorable to D, while any point to the right of the diagonal represents a citizen whose expected party differential is favorable to R. It should be noted also that we have extended the definition of expected party differential proposed by Downs to include differences between expected losses as well as expected benefits.

Since the distribution of citizens among the various quadrants will be a basic factor determining the outcome of the elections, some conjecture concerning the probable distribution in any democratic political system is in order. We suggest that a relatively small proportion of the electorate will be found in quadrant I, because a commitment to a particular party leads the citizen to find reasons for disliking the opposition. Several studies of political behavior indicate that citizens tend to find more and more reasons for liking the candidate they prefer and for disliking the opposition. That is, they tend to increase the distance that separates the candidates by remembering statements made by the one of their choice agreeing with their own views and statements of his opponent disagreeing with their own views.[30] This process obviously makes the citizen feel more comfortable in his political choice. We suggest, therefore, that locations in quadrant I are essentially unstable and that most citizens who initially find themselves in such a location will ultimately move either to quadrant II or to quadrant IV. The tendency to dislike at least one of the candidates is strengthened by the fact that in democratic societies politicians are one of the few culturally "legiti-

[30] Berelson *et al., op. cit.,* Chap. 10.

mate" objects of public scorn. According to the American ideology, one must love or at least respect one's neighbors, regardless of race, color, or national origin, but it is perfectly acceptable to denigrate— even slander—the political opposition. The freedom to release one's aggressions in the political realm is precisely what makes politics such an enjoyable spectator sport for so many citizens.[31]

Figure 2, which represents the potential orientations of voters, may serve as a starting point for an analysis of problems of political strategy. Citizens who fall into quadrants I, II, and IV make their vote decision on the basis of achieving maximal benefits. The rational political strategist will attempt to discover the distribution of voters among these quadrants and the intensity of their preferences (admittedly, an exceedingly difficult computation); he will then advise his candidate to adopt those positions that will bring the greatest number of votes. It is doubtful, however, that such an approach can be politically effective in dealing with citizens who fall into quadrant III. Citizens who feel that candidates are self-interested, corrupt, incompetent, venal, and boss-controlled will not base their vote decision on programmatic considerations, simply because they do not believe that the statements of the candidates have any relevance to the real world. The standard clichés and the traditional vote-getting techniques will not work with alienated voters, as we shall show. Citizens who fall into quadrants I, II, and IV have identified their well-being with at least one of the candidates. They assume, in other words, that at least some of the statements of their candidate are relevant. Since they interpret the political system in terms of benefits, they may regard the platforms of one or both of the candidates as pertinent data, as a relatively reliable indication of what they would do if elected. Citizens in quadrant III, if they vote at all, do so in terms of some calculation that has relevance to their expected *losses*. The rational strategist is obliged to discover what their criteria are and to make the most of their values for the alienated voter.

Before turning to the question of what these criteria may be, let us examine the alternatives available to such voters. The difference

---

[31] Lane points out, "Aggression can almost always find an appropriate political target, and so become rationalized in socially and personally acceptable terms. . . . For the bulk of the electorate intense political interests are certainly facilitated by a capacity to externalize aggression" (Lane, *op. cit.,* p. 122).

between citizens in quadrant III and all others, we have said, is that the former question the meaningfulness of the political alternatives with which they are confronted and ultimately of what is called democracy in the existing situation. A citizen who believes that he stands to gain from the election of one of the candidates will feel ideological pressure to vote, since he believes in the utility of democracy. A citizen who is alienated believes that whatever the political system is, it is not democracy, or, perhaps more cynically, that democracy is only what the current political reality shows it to be. Therefore, he tends not to feel ideological pressure to vote. We suggest that the proportion of non-voters in quadrant III will exceed that in any other quadrant. This does not mean that all citizens in quadrant III will not vote. It may be that the expected loss from one candidate's election is so much greater than the expected loss from the other's that it is rational for the alienated voter to vote against the greater evil simply to "win" minimal losses. However, even if an alienated voter at first differentiates between the "evils," he may feel that the loss in either case will be so great that he comes to dislike both candidates with equal vigor. The alienated voters we have interviewed tend to lump *all* candidates together as "bums," "crooks," "chiselers," and the like.

In summary, we suggest that citizens who originally regard the candidates as equally commendable will tend to like one and dislike the other by election day, whereas those who originally dislike one candidate a little more than the other will tend ultimately to dislike both equally. Rational citizens wish to reduce the expenditure of their scarce resources.[32] One of the most "efficient" ways of doing this is to reduce the complexities and refinements of party stands on issues to simple and gross stereotypes. For example, a Republican who accepts the standard cliché that the Democratic party is the party of war need not spend time or energy investigating the party's record or examining its platforms through the years. Similarly, the rhetoric of alienation—"They're all crooks," "It doesn't make any difference who wins"—is a remarkably effective time-saving device. By lumping all candidates together as equally bad, the alienated voter need not invest scarce resources evaluating relative "evils."

[32] "Rational citizens in an uncertain world are under great pressure to cut down the quantity of scarce resources they use to obtain political information" (Downs, *op. cit.*, p. 220).

There are several possible ways of handling the feelings of anger and frustration that comprise alienation. The individual may seek out and identify with a charismatic leader; he may join or attempt to create a new party; he may try to destroy the existing set of political institutions by means of revolution.[33] However, in the context of an election, only two alternatives are available to alienated voters: abstention, and voting for the lesser of two evils, both of which may be rational in the sense in which Downs uses the term. In taking the rational approach toward the lesser of two evils, the voter may derive gratification from the simple fact that his action is directed against the threat of greater economic or political losses. We suspect that another source of gratification may be the reduction of anger that comes when one "punishes" the "more evil" candidate by voting for his opponent.

Having considered the alternatives available to citizens in quadrant III, we must now examine the criteria they can use to arrive at a political decision. The alienated voter, we have said, discounts the progammatic statements of both candidates. If he votes at all, it is because in his judgment one candidate is less crooked than the other. Judgments of relative dishonesty are notoriously difficult to make on an objective basis. Essentially, such judgments turn on a subjective evaluation of the personality or character of the candidate. The alienated voter is therefore likely to depend upon intuitive feelings or "gut reactions."

It is obvious that this approach to voting is not restricted to citizens in quadrant III. Others may believe that the honesty and character of the candidate are relevant and may resort to intuitive judgments to estimate these factors. Such judgments, however, will be decisive for them only if their prior calculation of expected party differentials (in terms of programmatic statements and estimates of past performances) is small enough to leave them in doubt. Since citizens who fall into quadrants I, II, and IV identify their welfare with at least one of the candidates, they obviously assume that some of what their candidates says is to be believed; honesty is therefore not the crucial variable for them. Alienated voters who maintain interest in a campaign are preoccupied with it.

How can the rational candidate use our model and what we have

---

[33] See Levin, *op. cit.*, p. 68.

165

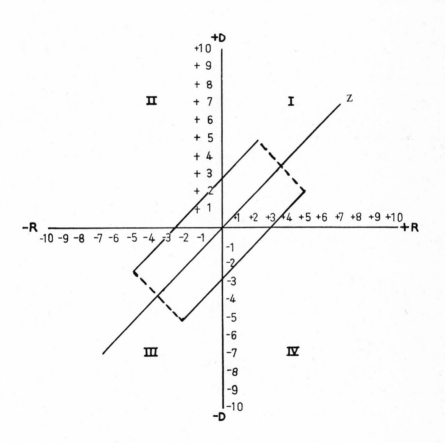

FIGURE 3

said about voting criteria in determining his political strategy? The rational candidate wishes to use his scarce resources most efficiently, to garner the greatest possible number of votes for the time, money, and manpower at his disposal. It is a commonplace of political practice not to spend time and money in areas that have been traditionally committed to a particular party when there is no reason to believe that the situation is changing. At the beginning of the campaign, therefore, every candidate seeks information on the "safety" of various wards. Delimiting the boundaries of one's potential effectiveness is the first step toward using scarce resources wisely. Precinct cap-

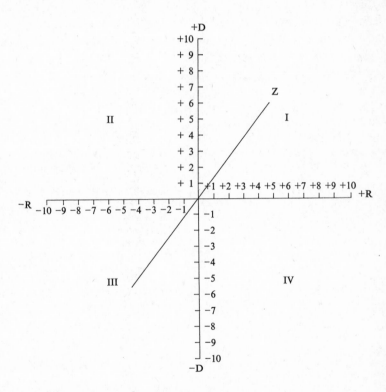

FIGURE 3

tains and ward leaders who know their business provide a cheap means of identifying areas that are "safe" or "hopeless," a far less expensive means than reliable public-opinion polls.

We can use our model to illustrate the nature of this problem by dividing the population into two groups, the committed and the un-committed. We introduce a rectangle into Figure 3 to represent the "bound of utility"—the area within which it may be worthwhile to campaign.

In Figure 3 there are four segments of the population outside the bound of utility: (1) citizens whose party differential is large enough to ensure a vote for D; (2) citizens whose party differential is large enough to ensure a vote for R; (3) a very few citizens of small party differential and great expectation of gain; and (4) citizens whose alienation is so extreme that they will not vote in any case. (Because these last two categories are impossible to pinpoint, the northern and southern limits of the "bound" rectangle cannot be specified precisely.) All citizens who fall within the bound have an expected party differential that is small enough to make them available to persuasion. The rational strategist will concentrate his resources on attempts to convert those citizens who fall within the bound.[34] However, his approach to these citizens must vary according to whether he is attempting to convert those who fall into quadrants I, II, or IV—in which case he stresses programmatic considerations—

[34] Although the bound of utility is easy to locate in theory, it is not so in practice. A public-opinion poll that attempted to locate clusters of uncommitted voters geographically would be far too expensive for any candidate involved in these elections. The candidates locate the bound in practice according to criteria of voting turnout, party strength, and ethnic concentrations. For example, Volpe concentrated his efforts in areas where the turnout in elections was traditionally large, where the party balance was not overwhelmingly Democratic, and where large numbers of voters were of Italian ancestry. Ward, who is from the western part of the state, concentrated his efforts in greater Boston. Peabody campaigned vigorously in the suburbs, where, he believed, large blocs of alienated Democrats and independents were located. In other words, the candidates campaigned in populous areas where they were little known or had reason to believe that they might attract supporters. This seems reasonable; however, such an approach may be self-defeating. Political-behavior studies indicate that the most important effect of the campaign is to reinforce the original predispositions of voters. Without the reinforcement provided by party workers and candidates, large numbers of voters may reverse their original intention or abstain. Volpe may therefore have been wise in spending some time at Republican rallies, even though most of those who attend party rallies are already strongly committed.

In a state that is nominally Democratic, the Democratic nominee should probably concentrate his efforts on the faithful. The Republican candidate, however, is forced to campaign in many Democratic areas. If the number of alienated voters is large, time spent in "opposition territory" may pay off for the "minority" candidate, for party identification is weakened by feelings of alienation. It is obvious that any effort to locate the bound of utility in practice is fraught with difficulties.

or those who fall into quadrant III—in which case he must prove his integrity or, rather, disprove their assumption that he is corrupt.

Assuming that any candidate who is well known and who has held public office for some time must be corrupt, the alienated voter tends to favor the less well-known and experienced candidate, simply on the ground that as an unknown quantity he may not be so bad as a known evil, at least at first. For the same reason, the alienated voter tends to favor the outs, on the assumption that it may take them some time to become fully corrupt. He also tends to vote against candidates who conduct opulent campaigns, because he is convinced that the opulence of a campaign indicates the degree to which the campaigner is obligated to contributors, rather than the public. For the alienated voter the ideal candidate is honest, sincere, nonpolitical, not heavily financed, "inexperienced," "nonprofessional," and not too well known. Thus, except for honesty and sincerity, the alienated voter has inverted the traditional standards that govern the selection of candidates in a healthy democratic community. Therefore, the standard political clichés and vote-getting strategies will not work for him.[35]

These "new" criteria of availability may be taken into account by political parties during the nomination process. However, politics is by and large the province of professional politicians. They may be reluctant to put in nomination a "clean" amateur whose loyalty to them is untested. From the point of view of the "organization," there

[35] Traditional vote-getting techniques may even backfire because they make the candidate who uses them appear to fit the stereotype of the typical politician even more closely. Our post-election survey provided a dramatic example of the failure of "standard practices."

Ward has seven daughters. It seemed obvious that a candidate so blessed should appear on television with his children as often as possible, not only because Massachusetts has a large Catholic population, but also because it is traditional for a candidate to be seen as a family man. Ward accordingly played up his image as a family man to a fulsome extent, as we have noted. No member of the Ward entourage doubted the rationality of this approach. In fact, however, it annoyed many voters. When respondents were asked what they liked most and least about Ward, those who mentioned his family favorably outnumbered those who objected to his use of it by approximately four to one; the significant fact is that many voters reacted negatively to this technique. We suggest that the profound cynicism of alienated voters makes them particularly hostile to the traditionally acceptable image of the "good candidate." We may assume that those who were predisposed to vote for Ward for other reasons were pleased by the evidence that he was a family man and that those who were unwilling to be impressed were indifferent to or offended by his exploitation of his family on television.

may be less risk in nominating one of their own and remaking his image (if this is necessary) to suit the criteria of a disillusioned electorate.

However, as we pointed out earlier, the strategist is likely to be more effective if he pays attention to the ways in which alienation is experienced rather than to the political stereotypes of the alienated. The response of the electorate to the "style" of a candidate is not easy to predict. Although one can estimate the proportion of voters who might be swayed by an appeal to abolish rent control, a programmatic issue, we can suggest no method of determining whether a reserved demeanor on television will be interpreted as "statesmanlike" or vacuous. Modern technology can provide the means of "changing" the color of a candidate's eyes, but the question still remains: "What color should they be?" The determinants of this question and other strategic issues are to be found in the feelings of powerlessness and meaninglessness of the alienated.

Two strategies are available to the rational candidate who wishes to exploit feelings of powerlessness in the electorate. The first is advantageous to the party that is out of power; it attempts to intensify feelings of powerlessness by emphasizing the unchecked tyranny of the incumbents and intimating that their hegemony is the cause of the citizen's powerlessness. During the Ward-Volpe contest, for example, an advertising executive who had been advising candidates in Massachusetts for thirty years suggested to an influential Republican that his party could take advantage of feelings of political powerlessness among the electorate by placing the following advertisement in newspapers throughout the state:

Negroes

Jews

Protestants

excluded from participation

in

the Democratic Party

The executive was perfectly aware of the explosive character of such an advertisement, and he was concerned with the possibility of an adverse reaction. However, he argued that it would gain many more votes for the Republicans than it would lose because it was, in his opinion, essentially true, since the Democratic party has traditionally nominated an all-Catholic, all-white ticket. What is more important, he insisted, is that most voters know it to be true. Such an advertisement, he argued, would therefore confirm or bring to the surface the feelings of powerlessness among alienated Jews, Protestants, and Negroes and would identify the Democratic party as the cause of their alienation. The effectiveness of this approach, in his opinion, would be heightened by the fact that the Republican slate included a Protestant, a Jew, and a Negro, as well as an Italian Catholic and a Polish Catholic.

The Republican to whom this strategy had been suggested rejected the proposal, first, because it might boomerang. (The Democrats could point to a small number of non-Catholics whom they had nominated or stress the "un-Americanism" of the advertisement.) Secondly, the proposed ad violated his sense of "the rules of the game." The first reason is rational in Downs's terms; the second is not, unless voters believe in the same rules.

Nevertheless, the proposal is instructive. The advertising executive stressed his conviction that Massachusetts voters, particularly the alienated, were far more sophisticated than most politicians would admit. He insisted that their feelings of powerlessness were well founded and that their image of the political system was essentially accurate. This was for him the basic consideration while formulating strategy. Although he was not averse to playing upon latent ethnic or religious prejudices, he argued that the truth embodied in a particular strategic gambit was the ultimate criterion determining its acceptance or rejection by most voters.[36] He insisted that voters sooner or later test a candidate's arguments in terms of their own experience.

The object of the proposed strategy is to suggest to the alienated

[36] This man believed that Ward had been seriously and unjustly injured by Peabody's charges during the primary campaign that Ward had "rigged" the ballot. He suggested to the authors that Ward should have campaigned during the general election with the slogan: "I have suffered because of this man's lie." The key to the slogan is the word "suffer," which, he pointed out, is a particularly connotative word for Catholics because they associate the concept of suffering with Christ's tribulation on the cross. In his opinion, this unconscious association would create a strong current of pity for Ward. Despite his contention that truth determines the effectiveness of political strategy, it seems apparent that the "suffer" gambit, at least, was designed to elicit an emotional rather than a logical or reasoned response from voters, not only because of the religious overtones of the word but also because of its implication that Ward was the cruelly wronged underdog, the traditional object of the voter's sympathy.

voter that the incumbents are the cause of his powerlessness and are deliberately excluding him. A second strategy, which is available to the incumbents as well as to the "outs," offers the alienated voter a way out of his powerless situation. In this strategy the candidate attempts to identify himself with the alienated voter by stressing his own powerlessness. He imputes power to the opposition or perhaps to some power elite (contractors, bookies, big business men, labor racketeers). This is the classical "underdog" gambit. He suggests that by combining their small amounts of power, he and the other little people may overthrow the powerful by their joint efforts. It is this appeal to collaboration that offers them a promise of power and a feeling of participation.

In the Boston mayoralty campaign, Collins, for example, pictured the contest between himself and Powers as a struggle between David and Goliath—between the little people and the professional power politician. He used the slogan "Stop *power* politics, elect a hands-free mayor" (with what the advertising executive would approve, the suggestive sinister pun on his opponent's name). Whenever possible he referred to his organization as a "small group of enthusiastic amateurs" at war with an army of mercenaries. He sponsored an essay contest for the best work defining "power politics." The winning essay, submitted by a 14-year-old girl, defined power politician as "a man who is surrounded by political bigwigs and who administers to his and their gains first, and to the people last or not at all." One Bostonian who voted against Powers stated: "I don't like the idea that since all the big guys are for him, the little people like us should be for him too."

The strategies we have described are designed to appeal primarily to feelings of powerlessness. Another aspect of alienation is the feeling of meaninglessness. As we have stated, a citizen may feel that an election is without meaning because he believes that there are no real differences between the candidates, or he may feel that he cannot make an intelligent and rational decision because he lacks the information upon which he thinks such a decision must be made. Candidates with any degree of sophistication, who believe that the alienated voter may be a decisive factor, are aware that programs mean nothing to him. Many Massachusetts politicians believe, with reason, that style rather than content is the significant variable for alienated voters. However, the difficulty of predicting what will be attractive to the voter often leaves the candidate in a quandary. For example, many newspapers reported that Nixon perspired heavily during his first television debate with Senator Kennedy and that the cameras were diverted from him while he used his handkerchief. It may be that Nixon should have loosened his tie, opened his collar, mopped his brow, and told the audience that debating in front of a television camera was hot work. This straightforward and natural approach might have convinced many voters that Nixon was "a regular guy."

A strategy that takes advantage of the voter's feeling of meaninglessness by offering him information that he did not expect to receive may also be effective. Treasurer J. F. Kennedy made explicit use of such a strategy. The alienated voter regards as meaningful information concerning the size and sources of campaign funds. Kennedy notified political reporters that he would not pay for television or radio time, newspaper ads, billboards, bumper stickers, or any other form of campaigning that requires money. He did not in fact appear on television or advertise in any other medium. Thus, with one stroke, he satisfied the syllogism of the alienated voter: Opulent campaigning indicates the candidate's indebtedness to his contributors. Kennedy's campaign is anything but opulent. Therefore, Kennedy is not indebted. Kennedy's strategy, however, may have been self-defeating, as we have mentioned, for many voters were unaware of his candidacy.

During the primary election, Endicott Peabody developed a strategic gambit intended to exploit feelings of "meaninglessness." The alienated voter tends to regard messages emanating from a candidate as meaningless because he assumes that the source is unreliable. If a candidate can communicate a message to the alienated voter without the voter's being aware of its origin, there is a chance that the message will be believed. This is why politicians often seek the public endorsement of prominent and respected non-politicians in the community. Peabody's television program, "The Political Roundup," was designed to convey the impression that it was a regular ("objective") television news report. It appeared to be unsponsored and nonpolitical and may therefore have been more credible to alienated voters. One Boston television station, as we have noted, discontinued "The Political Roundup" because it "confused" many voters.

Another strategy for taking advantage of feelings of meaninglessness is "the appeal to frankness." This consists in the candidate's
telling the voter certain "facts of political life" that are usually cen-
sored but that the alienated voter is probably aware of anyway. In
this case the alienated voter *knows* that the candidate has told the
truth. This is the strongest evidence possible to establish the integrity
of the candidate. For example, the candidate might boldly state that
campaigns cost money and that many large contributors expect special favors. He might state openly that campaigns require organization and that party workers demand patronage in return for services.
He might point out that these are the facts of political life for *all*
candidates. In other words, he could analyze the distribution of
power and the nature of influence in state and local government as
they are often analyzed in classical studies[37] and as they are understood by many alienated voters. Having established the truthfulness
of his approach, he might then proceed to differentiate himself from
his opponent. Whether the remainder of his argument is "true" or
not will depend upon the purposes and ethics of the candidate; in any
case, the voter may be more likely to believe what he has to say in
view of his "frank admissions."

Another strategy is available to the candidate who wishes to take
advantage of feelings of meaninglessness. The alienated voter believes that candidates take care of themselves and their entourage
rather than the public. Any information indicating that the candidate cares about the voter would be meaningful. A simple statement
by the candidate to this effect would clearly be worthless. During
the elections we have studied, candidates spent large sums of money
on stickers, billboards, etc., proclaiming their virtues. Perhaps a
more rational allocation of resources would have been to use a more
indirect and imaginative approach. For example, a candidate might
send large numbers of workers into areas defined by the bound of
utility in order to conduct "opinion polls." Since this poll is not
intended to serve the usual academic objectives, the criteria of sample choice would be political rather than statistical. The poll would
be conducted in conformity with standard practices except that the
pollster would inform the respondent that the purpose of the poll

[37] See, for example, V. O. Key, Jr., *Politics, Parties, and Pressure Groups* (4th
ed.; New York: Thomas Y. Crowell Co., 1958), Chap. 13.

was to furnish a particular candidate with information concerning the desires of the electorate. The questions, however, would be designed to furnish the respondent rather than the pollster with information; namely, that the candidate is interested in the respondent's welfare. The incontrovertible evidence that the candidate has spent time and money attempting to find out how the voter feels is precisely the type of information that is meaningful to the assessment of the candidate's character. Reading the voters' comments may furnish the candidate with useful information. However, the principal purpose of the poll has been accomplished the moment the poll is completed.[38]

It is plain that the sophisticated strategist must identify himself with the alienated voter and review his own strategy critically, with what might be called creative cynicism, attempting to anticipate and provide for all the obvious and as many of the subtler responses as possible. He conceives and discards strategies until he has developed the best one for his purposes.

Political Strategy for Non-Alienated Voters

Although the strategies described above were designed with the alienated voter in mind, they may have value as vote-getting devices for the non-alienated voter as well. The fact that a non-alienated citizen may regard platforms as relevant data because he assumes that at least one of the candidates is honest, sincere, and interested in the public does not mean that the candidate's image is unimportant to the voter or that information bearing on the candidate's integrity is irrelevant.

The relevance of strategies designed to communicate information regarding the candidate's "feeling"—his honesty, sincerity, etc., rather than his program—is obvious for another reason. Many voters who are not alienated vote with little or no reference to platforms or programs. Campbell and his associates discovered that 17.5 per cent of those respondents who voted in the 1956 presidential election

[38] During the campaign Volpe's pollsters conducted a public-opinion survey that was designed not only to elicit "accurate" data but also to influence the respondent. While questioning the respondent, the interviewer attempted to convert him to Volpe by presenting arguments favorable to Volpe's candidacy.

reported no interest in or knowledge of "issues."[39] "To the degree that [this 17.5 per cent] have perceptions of parties at all," they write, "they are bound up in moralistic themes like mudslinging and chicanery. More often the parties are poorly discriminated, and comment is almost entirely limited to the personal characteristics of the candidates—their personality, their sincerity, their religious practice or home life."[40] Although many of these voters may not feel powerless, they are, like alienated voters, preoccupied with "mudslinging and chicanery," and they make a voting decision partly in terms of the candidate's sincerity and integrity. The search for sincerity and honesty was not unique in the 1956 election. In his study of the 1952 presidential election, Campbell found that 23 per cent of the respondents who voted for Eisenhower made a favorable reference to his "integrity," "principles," and "honesty." This is more than twice the proportion of respondents who commended his "intelligence," "education," and "understanding." Only two other favorable perceptions of Eisenhower were mentioned more frequently than his "sincerity" and "honesty"; namely, his "leadership" (25 per cent) and his "ability to handle foreign situations" (35 per cent).[41]

There is no doubt that vast numbers of citizens are very much concerned with the candidate's integrity and sincerity (non-alienated as well as alienated voters). Whether this concern is due to the generally skeptical attitude toward politicians that exists in America or whether it is a reflection of a period in which scandals and frauds have been common we do not know; but it is obviously a critical factor in many American elections. It is even possible that some of those citizens who report a knowledge of and interest in party platforms and candidates' programs vote, not in terms of their content, but, rather, in terms of some instinctive reaction to the candidate's method of presenting his ideas—e.g., his forcefulness, or the softness of his voice, or his erect posture or bearing. Again, these are matters of style. What the candidate says may be strategically significant because it leaves the voter with the feeling that the candidate knows what he is talking about even if the voter does not understand it. Perhaps few citizens are familiar with the concept "gross national prod-

[39] Angus Campbell, Philip E. Converse, Warren E. Miller, and Donald E. Stokes, *The American Voter* (New York: John Wiley & Sons, 1960), p. 249.
[40] *Ibid.*, p. 244.
[41] *Ibid.*, p. 59.

uct," but the fact that Senator Kennedy could recite facts, figures, and percentages relating to it and to many other relatively complex and abstract concepts probably impressed many voters. With respect to this matter, a Ward adviser reported that some of Ward's supporters believed that Ward's 23-point program was too complex and should be reduced to four or five points. This adviser agreed that a 23-point program was beyond the comprehension of the average voter, but he insisted that every point be maintained because a complex program suggests to voters that the candidate has done careful research on every problem and has a lot to say. Adlai Stevenson has stated, "This idea that you can merchandise candidates for high office like cereal—that you can gather votes like boxtops—is, I think, the ultimate indignity to the democratic process."[42] However, the fact remains that the "gut reaction" induced by the manner in which the platform is presented may be as important as the content of the platform. That is, the package may be as important as the product.

Nevertheless, it is possible that strategies designed for the alienated voter may repel the non-alienated voter. If the latter wants programmatic information and the candidate merely vilifies his opponent or adopts some of the strategies we have outlined, he may antagonize the voter. A strategy designed for the alienated voter that would probably lose the non-alienated voter is the one adopted by Treasurer Kennedy—not openly campaigning. The "Negroes, Jews, and Protestants" strategy suggested to the Republican might also alienate many because it deals with a particularly sensitive subject. We do not believe, however, that Peabody's television programs, the appeal to frankness, the underdog gambit, or the public-opinion-poll strategy would offend non-alienated voters. It may well be that a mixed strategy which is focused upon feelings of powerlessness and meaninglessness and which also takes into account voters oriented toward platforms is most effective. In most cases the strategies need not be mutually exclusive. Obviously, the candidate must base his strategy on his estimate of the relative proportions of alienated and non-alienated voters and their nominal party identifications.

In a community like Massachusetts, where political alienation is a pervasive and perhaps permanent phenomenon, the "outs" are most

[42] Speech accepting the presidential nomination, Democratic National Convention, 1956.

likely to benefit from it[43] because the incumbents already have power; that is, they are politicians and therefore, from the point of view of the alienated voter, they have had the opportunity to participate in political plunder. If we are correct in analyzing the attitudes of the alienated voter and if political alienation remains an important factor, Massachusetts is likely to have a continuous turnover of political parties and candidates. The very possession of political power is a disadvantage in an alienated community. The citizen who voted for Collins because "he is a new man, no axes to grind, no big political machine behind him" probably would have voted for any candidate who was not well known or well connected. This is precisely why the incumbents may be wise to nominate a "new" man, one who is not affiliated with the inner circle and preferably one who is not even a professional politician.

The voter's attraction to a man who has not yet had the opportunity to become corrupt indicates the depth of his skepticism and disillusionment with the existing parties and candidates.[44] Although we have suggested that the political strategist may find it profitable to plan his campaign by dividing the electorate into alienated and non-alienated voters rather than into the customary categories of Democrats, Republicans, independents, Protestants, Catholics etc., we are now in a position to suggest that the alienated voter, whose disillusionment with both parties is great, is the most significant independent. His alienation has temporarily suspended his party identification. (Indeed, we can view alienation and party identification as cross-pressures.) He has abandoned his traditional party loyalties, attempting to evaluate each candidate according to his "merits," even though he calculates these by means of intensely personal and subjective criteria. The "independence" of so many voters in Massa-

---

[43] It is instructive to note that more strategies for the alienated voter are available to the "outs."

[44] Although the alienated voter is likely to vote for a new man, he casts his vote with the nagging doubt that the new man can or will remain honest once he has attained political power. One respondent stated, "Ward's mostly for the poor people and I'm in that class. But eventually *he'll end up the same way.* (Volpe?) Yes. *They all end up the same way.* (How do you mean?) They go into office as small humble men, then do what they want for their own good. I voted for a young fellow of 22 in my own ward, but he lost to ———. I say if people voted for a crook like ———, they deserve him. If ——— stole from the people, he wouldn't take such large amounts of money as ——— because he's not as experienced at being a politician."

chusetts creates a highly unstable and unpredictable political situation in which split-ticket voting becomes the norm—a tremendous majority for the Democratic presidential nominee, the election of Republicans to the Senate and the governorship, and the victory of the Democrats in both branches of the Great and General Court.

Our interviews with voters indicate that this cross-pressure of alienation and party identification results in political behavior that can be described as the politics of revenge. The fact that one's party identification, one's normal allegiance, is upset leads citizens (in this case, Democrats) to react quite violently against their own party, which has, so to speak, let them down. Many registered Democrats who supported Volpe in the final election or any candidate other than Ward in the primary were not really casting a ballot *for* anyone; they were voting against their own party's endorsee. They were interested in punishing their party.

$$* \quad * \quad *$$

In view of the hostility and anger of the alienated segment of the electorate and the intensely personal character of "gut reactions," the task that confronts political strategists in Massachusetts is extraordinarily difficult. The candidates must appeal to voters who assume that they are self-interested and deceitful. The response of the "independent" alienated voter is unpredictable. It is clear, then, that political strategies designed for the alienated voter are, at best, dangerous. We do not outline these strategies with the assurance that they will succeed. We suggest them merely to illustrate the nature of the problems faced by the candidates. We are cognizant of the high degree of uncertainty in an alienated political community. Instead of responding to the public-opinion poll by believing that the candidate who paid for it really wants to find out how he feels on the important public issues, the citizen might react by saying: "Whom does he think he's fooling with this phony poll?"

We are now in a position to examine political strategy as it was actually formulated and executed in the 1960 Massachusetts gubernatorial primary and general elections. Our tape-recorded interviews with the candidates, campaign managers, public-relations men, and fund raisers (taken before the elections) provide us with an opportunity to examine just how the insiders proceeded. By com-

paring their estimates of voter preferences and reactions with our
public-opinion polls (and some polls taken by Volpe), we may examine the problem of communication between candidates and voters.
In the following chapter, we shall analyze how the candidates gathered information and used it to develop strategy.

4.
Pollsters and Political Intuition

* * *

"I don't believe in polls. I think they are a lot of bunk. You can walk out on the street and find twenty-five people. Now, how many of those know what's going on? I think that '48 showed that polls are a lot of hooey. I really believe they are because I think the majority of the people who are asked on a poll will answer what they think you want to hear."

A MURPHY ADVISER

"We were even able to determine as the polls went along an unusual strength for Murphy and then it began to swing for Peabody and Peabody was coming very, very fast, but Ward had the edge . . . so it predicted Ward's nomination with Peabody second. . . . The polls predicted the defeat of Furcolo, which shocked me."

A VOLPE ADVISER

Despite the pollsters, the advertising agencies, and the public-relations men who would like to believe that by using the methods of social science they can analyze the voting public and adjust campaign tactics "scientifically," politics remains essentially an art. In studying the phenomena of campaign, election, and results, the political scientist does well to consider the displays of intuition that distinguish the artistry of the truly expert politician from the unimaginative techniques of the political hack. No doubt the pollsters can inform the candidate within reasonably certain limits where he is strong or weak (if he has adequate funds to sponsor a reliable poll), and the advertising men can suggest the "image" which they believe appeals to voters. Nixon's eyebrows can be trimmed to make him look less like the villain of an early western, and Kennedy's hair can be cut to give him a less boyish appearance. In every election, however, there are a number of factors that cannot be accurately reduced to figures, much less manipulated, by the new men of commercial political "science." These "unknowns" remain the province of the professional politician—the "inside dopester," if you will—whose "art" is manifest in his ability to feel or intuit the unknown factors through extrasensory political antennae.

Although even the expert politician's antennae are often insensitive and politics, as we have said, remains more an art than a science, there exists in America a stereotype of the political campaign as a carefully planned game of chess, in which every move is meticulously predetermined by experts. Like most stereotypes, this one misses the mark. This became obvious to us while interviewing the participants in the 1960 Massachusetts gubernatorial elections.

During the two weeks preceding the Democratic primary contest, the authors talked with a candidate or campaign adviser (or both) from every camp, with the exception of Kelly and Magaletta, who refused to be interviewed or to permit interviews with members of their entourages. The interviews were recorded on tape, and permission was granted to quote the contents, with the proviso that the material would be used for scholarly purposes and not published before the November election. The object of these interviews was to discover how the professionals formulated political strategy for the primary election. Three of the campaign advisers requested that copies of the transcript be sent to them for review; two of them deleted isolated statements.

During the week before the general election, Volpe's campaign manager and two other key Volpe advisers were interviewed, and on the day before the November election Ward's leading brain-truster was interviewed. The object of these interviews was to discover how strategy was formulated for the general election. All told, 18 interviews were taken, which, when typed, came to 351 pages. Some of the candidates and managers were interviewed twice, and Ward's chief adviser was interviewed three times. After the general election, Peabody provided us with a copy of an analysis of his primary campaign prepared by his campaign manager, and a member of the Volpe inner circle gave us several public-opinion polls taken for Volpe. We received permission to quote from these documents, except for certain parts marked confidential.

The interviews, which took from 45 minutes to two and one-half hours, were essentially unstructured, although an effort was made to ask a basic set of questions. Although each respondent discussed some topics to which the others did not refer, all of them commented on the following: (1) estimates of the strengths and weaknesses of all candidates; (2) the significance of political alienation; (3) the role of party organization; (4) the voters' preferences; (5) the importance of political style; (6) the reliability of various sources of information concerning voter preferences, including public-opinion polls; (7) the importance of ethnic voting; (8) the sources and significance of money in elections; (9) the utility of advertising in various mass media; (10) the importance and the corruption of the press in politics; (11) the role of ideology; (12) the significance of party identification; (13) the care and feeding of local political leaders and convention delegates; (14) disagreements among campaign advisers; and (15) the nature of political strategy itself.

The quality of the interviews varies considerably. Two respondents tended, at times, to deliver campaign speeches containing the traditional formulaic political vocabulary. One was extremely reluctant to talk; he refused on a number of occasions to respond to certain questions, stating that he knew the "answer" but preferred not to express an opinion. Questions dealing with campaign contributions and expenditures evoked strong outbursts and much resentment from some respondents. On the whole, the campaign managers were considerably more talkative, more willing to speculate, and better informed than the candidates. They also grasped more quickly than the candidates the types of problem political scientists are interested in. On several occasions some of them anticipated the interviewer's interest in a particular problem and voluntarily proceeded to talk about it at great length. The advisers often presented material that the candidates were reluctant to discuss and in some instances flatly contradicted what the candidate or some other adviser had said previously. This, of course, raises the question of whether or not the interviews give an accurate picture.

There is some evidence that parts of the interviews are not to be believed. For example, on two occasions respondents made statements immediately following the tape-recorded interview which flatly contradicted what they had first reported. Some individuals who were not interviewed during the campaign but who played a role in determining strategy reported to us months after the election that the board of strategy had strongly disagreed on some questions that the candidate or his manager had assured us were disposed of unanimously. Our knowledge of the elections one year after they took place also suggests that two respondents carefully omitted mentioning some problems that were basic to their campaigns.

The reliability of the interviews can also be evaluated in terms of the logic and internal consistency of the respondents' arguments and in terms of some facts known to all. For example, every respondent insisted that he (or his candidate) was a serious contender in the primary election, although only two candidates ran as if they thought they had any chance of winning. Some presented detailed arguments to support this contention; others merely insisted that it was true. Some claimed that they had an efficient statewide organization when everyone knew that this was not the case.

It would, of course, be naïve to expect these respondents to be completely honest and frank with an outsider. Some of the assumptions and decisions that are integral to any political campaign are, by their very nature, confidential. Nevertheless, the omissions and distortions, although important in some cases, were rare. Most of the respondents were, in our judgment, quite open and sincere most of the time. The most serious defect of the interview data consists of what was omitted rather than what was incorrectly reported. We have evaluated the statements of the respondents according to whether they checked with statements of their colleagues, with the views of the opposition, with statements made by insiders after the election was over, and with public-opinion data available to us, keeping in mind that material omitted or distorted is often most significant.

We must mention that we have not altered or rewritten the interviews quoted here. With few exceptions, the people quoted were speaking, not writing; the language is therefore the language of spoken thought—thoughts and afterthoughts often run together into faulty grammar and difficult, involuted syntax.

Intuition, "Echoes," and Information

We have pointed out that the political strategist who is rational uses his scarce resources to win the largest number of votes possible for him. To receive votes, the candidate must develop a strategy that will please the majority (or a coalition of minorities). He can do this only if he knows what is pleasing to voters. This, in turn, requires a steady flow of accurate information from the field to the board of strategy. The accuracy of the candidate's information concerning voter preferences and reactions largely determines the soundness of his strategic decisions.

Each candidate defined his problem and formulated his strategy in terms of information gathered from a variety of sources. In some cases the source was a public-opinion poll sponsored by the candidate; in others it was a report from precinct and ward workers or inside dopesters whose judgment had proved reliable in the past. Much "information," however, was merely gleaned from the currents of political gossip and rumor that circulate during every campaign. Frequently one source contradicted another. The candidate in such a situation was forced to use his intuition to judge the reliability of each bit of information and to evaluate its significance for himself and his opponents. This is where political art comes into play. It is obvious that a false bit of information (and there were many) may result in the formulation of an irrational strategy.

Although the general public may believe that candidates for major office receive a steady flow of highly detailed reports from pollsters, most office-seekers on the state level either do not have the funds necessary to pay for reliable public-opinion polls or believe that polls are worthless. Precinct captains, ward leaders, and locally influential people, the time-honored sources of political information, continue to be the most significant ones. Murphy's campaign manager, whose approach was typical, collected information, he said,

. . . largely by conversations with people in the field and in the various committees. . . . We assess it on the basis of conversations with friends of the candidate and friends of ours. Throughout this campaign we have

travelled the state, myself and other members of the staff, talking with
people, trying to get a few of them together. . . . As for assessing our
opponents' strength, we base it on what we hear when we go into the
cities and towns and talk with our friends there; usually they are brutally
frank.

A key Murphy staff member, who was assigned the task of gathering
information, described his sources as "more than reliable," although
he admitted that he always "double checks" them. He described his
method of double checking as follows: "I've travelled the circuit
five times since January. I've talked to all types of people: taxi-cab
drivers and workers, workers' meetings and people that are just—
you know, that you happen to run into, strike up a conversation."
On the basis of these "brutally frank" and "more than reliable"
random samples, the Murphy forces concluded that their candidate
had a "basic solid strength" of at least "125- or 120,000 votes" and
that he would "take the city of Worcester . . . , New Bedford, Fall
River, Salem, Somerville, Cambridge, [and] Malden." Murphy received 76,539 votes, running a dismal fourth, and carried only
Malden, his home town.

A more reasoned and skeptical approach to sources of information
was taken by Ward's key adviser, who had some idea that the
accuracy of a report depended upon, among other things, the repre-
sentativeness of the sample polled:

You have an organization of political workers, varying in caliber and
kind of their experience, but who, by the very intensity of their operation,
are daily in contact with people who are probably going to vote in the
Democratic primary, and they . . . can bring back, as they do, on pretty
much a weekly basis, what kind of problems they are facing . . . within
their own working group, which are frequently different problems than
they are faced with in the general public.

Although he believed that the reports of workers in small towns were
"reasonably accurate" because "it is possible to contact and know
practically all of the voters," he was acutely aware that such was
not the case in larger cities, where the bulk of the primary vote is
concentrated and where contacts between professionals and voters
are few.

I think it's much more difficult for them to make an estimate of the city
level with any degree of accuracy. The wards are just too large. When

you deal with a ward in Boston, you are, in effect, dealing with 10,000 potential voters. . . . Once you get a group that size it is very difficult, even on the precinct level, where you are dealing with the neighborhood of 1,000 to 1,500 voters, for your people to be that good because the precincts aren't like the town social committees very often.

Reinterpreting the reports of city workers in terms of his own feelings and intuition, he summarized the situation as follows:

Areas where you find the greatest amount of anti-Furcolo feeling . . . you have a stronger pro-Murphy feeling. . . . In sizable sections of Boston, mostly among the poorer economic units, . . . Frank Kelly has an ample amount of support. . . . I think Kelly will run strong throughout the state. Joe Ward is distinctly the frontrunner. . . . Chub [Peabody] will show strength in Brookline, Newton, ward 14, in Dorchester, in a sense the Jewish wards, where there will be an inherently strong feeling against the Irish, against the all-green ticket.

An analysis of the primary election returns indicates that these predictions were not inaccurate. On another occasion, as we will indicate, his information from the field and his intuition led him to make a colossal error in judgment.

During the general election campaign in October, information received from party workers led Ward to believe that his mock trials of Volpe on television were a great success. He proceeded, therefore, to step up the attack during the final weeks of the campaign.

My impression was that probably two weeks ago Volpe was ahead. . . . Around October 27th or 28th I had a sense that we were coming in very hard and strong. [As a result of the trials] it was no longer a one-sided situation where the Democratic candidate had horns; it was now a situation where the Republican candidate had horns, probably worse horns because they at least had involved him personally and more directly. . . . As this occurred people tended to . . . become more and more party conscious and national-ticket conscious. . . . I expect to win tomorrow by over 100,000 votes.[1]

This was, of course, pure fantasy (the trials alienated large numbers of independents), but it was congenial and it fit Ward's preconceptions. The effect of the trials was to transform the election from a party-oriented to a candidate-oriented contest, which was precisely

---

[1] A member of the Ward camp reported to us several months after the election that some members of the brain trust thought Ward would be very lucky to win by 10,000 votes.

what Volpe wanted. Although a few insiders vehemently insisted that the trials were disastrous to Ward's cause, the overwhelming majority of his advisers believed that they were an enormous success.

There are many other examples of misinformation reported from the field and of misjudgment by insiders, and not only within the Ward camp. The misinformation was almost always distorted in favor of the candidate and the current strategy. As a matter of fact, information reported by party workers, who are emotionally involved in the campaign, is often unreliable because of their intense need to perceive only what is favorable to the cause, or because of their wish to please the candidate by giving him news that he wants to hear. The very involvement of party workers makes it difficult for them to be objective. The candidate is a very special person to his followers. He is often endowed by them with charismatic qualities. When the candidate appears, a dramatic change takes place in the emotional climate at campaign headquarters. Suddenly everyone comes to life and is eager to please. The candidate prognosticates; everyone smiles and nods agreement. At critical periods during the campaign, their involvement causes many workers to lose all sense of judgment. Their reports tend to become inconsistent and contradictory and their attitudes tend to polarize at the extremes. The following statement by Ward's key adviser illustrates this tendency:

Some of our supporters . . . would say, "Well you've got to be positive, you've done enough by bringing people to realize that this [Furcolo administration] is not a *bona fide* issue, let's go on to the positive." But every time we'd shift into the positive—you'd see it in our releases, we'd have a release about education, we'd have a release about libraries, we'd have a release about housing— . . . these same people would come in: "We're slipping, we're not coming in as strong as we were." And these are the same people—I'm not talking about different people—coming in with this message.

Ward's adviser believed that the person most closely involved in the campaign—namely, the candidate—was one of the best sources of information. "In current-day political campaigning," he claimed, the candidate "must of necessity continuously expose himself to a large number of people, and it is quite possible to get some kind of inclination as to the public acceptance of the individual candidate by the way in which he is personally accepted, and his antennae are very sensitive and peculiarly valuable." There are no data to support this view. Ward's own antennae, as a matter of fact, were quite insensitive. "I have found," he stated, "as I have toured the Commonwealth, when I ask for votes, that a surprisingly large percentage of informed Democratic voters say, 'Well, aren't you the Democratic party choice?' And when I respond that I am, they say, 'Well, we are going to stay with the party.' " Our data indicate, and election results prove, that large numbers of Democratic voters not only deserted the convention endorsee in the primary but voted for Volpe in the general election. This is instructive. We cannot imagine that many citizens who talk to a candidate face to face would actually tell him that they were *not* going to vote for him. The very fact that he is a candidate immediately structures the situation. An "unpleasant" remark would probably cause too much embarrassment and discomfort to both parties. As a matter of fact, as soon as the candidate or his campaign worker reveals his identity and his preference, the response of the voter is likely to be influenced favorably, at least for the moment.

Candidates, like dictators, are therefore often victims of the "echo effect"; they are told what people think they want to hear. Thus a closed circuit of information develops which feeds on itself and continuously reinforces the original views of the candidates. The "information," however, is often unrelated to reality. Because of the "echo effect," a well-designed and well-executed public-opinion poll, conducted by objective interviewers who have no personal acquaintance or political connection with the candidate, is more likely to uncover valid data than a casual conversation between a party worker and a person on a bus.[2] What the worker learns on the bus— whether favorable or unfavorable—is likely to be transformed into what headquarters and the candidate want to hear; criticisms (that is, the most useful remarks) are often disregarded.

[2] "Judging from what is known of the participants and circumstances of political discussion, . . . the most substantial 'theme' in political discussion will be the reciprocal expression of agreed-upon political clichés and stereotypes. It is rewarding to express them both because one thereby shows that he is in the appropriate subculture and role position and because one's audience reacts with flattering expressions of agreement. It is rewarding to hear such opinions expressed because of the common bond established—through the confirmation of one's own 'opinion' or the opportunity for agreement with the spokesman. Even rumors which, through a process called 'assimilation,' are often forced to serve the communicators' prejudices and stereotypes conform to this pattern" (Robert Lane, *Political Life* [Glencoe, Ill.: Free Press], p. 87).

The attitudes of professional politicians toward public-opinion polls range from extreme cynicism and distrust to religious awe. Said a Murphy adviser, "A majority of the people who are asked on a poll will answer what they think you want to hear." This may well be true of poorly executed polls, but polls need not be poorly executed. Volpe's key adviser placed much more faith in polls, and for good reason. One of the polls conducted for Volpe predicted the outcome of the seven-man gubernatorial primary exactly as it occurred, and it also foretold Furcolo's defeat in the senatorial race.

Murphy, Piemonte, and, as far as we know, Kelly and Magaletta took no public-opinion polls, either because they did not have the money to pay for them or because they did not trust them. Volpe took a series of amazingly accurate polls, which proved on occasion to be valuable guides for the determination of strategy. Ward and Kennedy took haphazard and inaccurate polls, which told them what they wanted to hear, thus causing them to continue strategies that were costing them votes. Peabody mailed out thousands of questionnaires, of which approximately 8 to 10 per cent were returned. Although this rate of return is not large enough to ensure an accurate sampling and the mailed questionnaire is not the best method for contacting voters, some information that might have been useful was discovered, as well as some faulty information that proved to be very costly.

Ward's leading brain-truster believed that public-opinion polls could be valuable but realized that most polls are "not taken with sufficient depth . . . to gain a detailed percentage determination." This was, he claimed, "partly because you just don't have enough money to undertake that kind of poll." He did believe, however, that "if you take even small polls in given areas you can get some indication of just what you are doing and where you are, and you use these as guides more for your determination of what the election results are going to be." Ward took a few small samples before the primary, and he may have spent two or three hundred dollars on polls just before the general election in November. The latter polls, which his adviser described as "very inadequate,"

. . . indicate that we are going to do very well. . . . We may be running 10 per cent behind [Senator Kennedy][3]. . . . The thing which I think is

[3] Ward received 47.1 per cent of the popular vote. He ran 13 percentage points behind Kennedy.

most significant in the polls that were taken, and again they are small samples—you know, you take 25 here and 50 there, and you project things . . . is that Volpe is being cut by Republicans, that there are more Republicans, or at least as many Republicans, cutting Volpe . . . as there are Democrats who are voting for Volpe.

An analysis of election results indicates that Ward's polls were completely unreliable in these predictions.

Although Peabody's polls could not meet the minimal standards of excellence maintained by any scholarly study of public opinion, a poll taken on July 18 did indicate correctly that Peabody and Ward were the only important contenders. This bit of information, however, merely confirmed the original views of the Peabody camp. Responses to a second set of questionnaires, mailed during the last week in August, indicated that Peabody would win, with Ward and Kelly finishing second and third, respectively. Although Peabody did not win, this poll was correct in indicating a marked increase in Kelly's strength. This information came as a surprise to Peabody. If he had taken it seriously and acted upon it, the outcome of the election might have been altered. In a post-election analysis, Peabody's manager said: "There is no doubt in my mind that Kelly's last-minute surge in Boston and Springfield hurt Peabody." He argued, on the basis of public-opinion data, that Peabody should have "come out strongly and repeatedly against the lottery." The failure to attack Kelly was, in his opinion, a major error of judgment.

This analysis is instructive because it demonstrates that public-opinion data, if received in time, can basically alter a candidate's picture of an election. Before the August poll the Peabody forces did not believe that Kelly posed a serious threat, and therefore they ignored the lottery. The second poll provided a good lead for revising a basic strategic decision, although the fact that only 8 to 10 per cent of the questionnaires were returned made some Peabody supporters very skeptical of the results and hesitant to act on them.

In addition to information obtained from public-opinion polls, reports from field workers, and personal observation—their own and their advisers'—some candidates received unsolicited information and advice from persons unknown to them. In fact, as a Volpe adviser reported, a major problem in every campaign

. . . is pushing advisers away—well-meaning people who have the best of intentions and probably the finest of minds but because of the great number of them it only adds confusion and brings a stoppage of the campaign, instead of activity. One of my peculiar functions in the campaign has been to handle what I call the "hot-potato letters," letters from people suggesting this, complaining about that. They ranged everywhere from "If you send me $68.00 for the rent, I can get my whole family to vote for you, because I need the money for the rent and Joe Ward wouldn't send it to me and we're ready to switch to you"; to "Why is it you didn't reply to my last letter when I told you I was having trouble with the state in regard to the adoption of an 11-year-old boy who was living with me?"—a letter which we never received in the first place. . . . Then there are letters saying that your campaign stinks, you ought to do this, you ought to do that, and you have to handle that. Then you have to handle letters from people who have special interests, who say, "I read somewhere that you don't know anything about this problem. I am dismayed because I am deeply interested in this." And then you have to go on and explain that this quotation either was out of context or doesn't mean what it says and explain what John really feels.

Some of these communiqués may be "hot potatoes," but occasionally they contain a shrewd analysis of the political situation and some worthwhile suggestions for positive action. The following letter, which was written by a person not known to Volpe, is a case in point:

Dear Mr. Volpe:
   As a registered Democrat I will vote for you, but to the average voter "Volpe" is just a name. Especially your posters which say vote the man. Well—who is this man, what has he done!!! Up to now the average voter still does not know!!! The Democrats get the attention of the average voter by thunderous noise, and to beat them at their game you must do likewise, especially where Democrats predominate in the state. *Note that all late-comers in Politics are not sedate in their campaigns.* As one veteran politician once put it "A vote is a vote, and to never underestimate the ignorance of the voter."
   Therefore to the rank and file voter you must sell yourself, and for the next six weeks pull out all the stops you can, full speed ahead!!!
   To wit:
   The following repeated often with television, handbills, posters, ads, cartoons, etc., should be blown up *and repeated, and repeated.*

   1. Massachusetts is crying for a businessman in Government (A self-made man, your humble beginnings, etc.)
   2. The abuses heaped upon the State by the professional politicians

has been all out of proportion of Civil Virtue (This detail substantiated by figures and facts, to work with the *Herald-Traveler*).

3. Pictures and stories of Labor and Labor activities by you (Get the Labor vote).
4. Pictures of you with dignitaries in Washington, especially Eisenhower.
5. Pictures of you with church dignitaries (get the Catholic vote—predominantly Democratic, a Republican is going to vote for you anyway).

Being of Italian extraction, the above is the way I see it. If I can be of any help to you please be free to call on me.

If public-opinion polls are to have practical value for the determination of political strategy, they must provide information that the sophisticated professional politician could not arrive at independently through intuition or experience. The several polls taken for Volpe certainly should have provided such information, because they were thoughtfully designed, carefully executed, and quite accurate. An analysis of Volpe's public-opinion polls, therefore, may serve as a case study in the utility of polls for the determination of political strategy.

Do the Pollsters Know More than the "Pols"?

John Volpe will be elected governor of Massachusetts by a plurality of 85,000 plus.
PUBLIC-OPINION-POLL REPORT PREPARED FOR JOHN VOLPE

In contrast to the Democratic candidates, who either discounted the utility of public-opinion polls or collected information and misinformation in a haphazard, inept manner, John Volpe employed pollsters who accurately sampled the electorate and reported a voluminous amount of data indicating subtle shifts in candidate and issue orientation from August to November.[4] Compared to his opponents' sources of information, Volpe's were highly systematic and sensitive. His pollsters gathered data that indicated where he and Ward were strong and why, and what issues were uppermost in the minds

[4] Volpe received reports of different types of public-opinion polls prior to primary day and on September 16 and 19, October 3, 5, 13, 14, 17, 24, and 28, and November 7.

of voters in various parts of the state. Data relating to issues were sometimes used by his researchers in the preparation of speeches and position papers designed to appeal to that bizarre coalition of minorities that ultimately elected him to the governorship.

Although Volpe's advisers interpreted poll results in the light of their intuition (they did not slavishly follow the results of the polls in designing every strategy), they were nevertheless convinced of the value of the polls, if only as confirmation of the soundness of decisions taken before the receipt of polling data. One Volpe adviser summarized some of the poll results and evaluated their usefulness as follows:

The first group of polls were taken starting the first of August, up until about the first of September, to determine what people thought about the major issues of this campaign and who they thought would be nominated by the Democrats for governor. What the polls said were borne out by the results. We even were able to determine as the polls went along an unusual strength for Murphy and then it began to swing for Peabody and Peabody was coming very, very fast. But Ward had an edge which reflected the result of his strong organization and the work that he did throughout the Commonwealth in getting things organized. So, it predicted Ward's nomination with Peabody second. And it was right. It predicted a tremendous interest in the issue of legalized gambling or a lottery in the state. By October 1 about either party, people said that whomever they voted for president would have no effect on how they voted for governor or anybody else on the state ticket. It also showed that as far as the public was concerned the three principal issues, in this order, were corruption, inept administration, and high taxes. And so we had a guide there, if the poll was valid. . . . The poll predicted the defeat of Furcolo . . . which shocked me. . . . It showed Volpe . . . he'd gotten to 46 per cent; he'd picked up eight points in Boston. This was meaningful to me because this was the night after John Volpe made his television speech answering the charges for the first time, that Ward had made. . . . The poll [on Oct. 14] bolstered the view . . . that we were handling the thing correctly, and the results on the 28th persuaded us not to get involved in a smear contest in the last week of the campaign but to attempt to hold the line in terms of John's dignity. . . .

Public-opinion studies can provide candidates with five types of data that may have practical value: (1) a description of the perceived strengths and weaknesses of the candidate's image (if reported early in the campaign, this description may serve as a basis for altering the candidate's image); (2) a description of those areas in which the candidate may find it most worthwhile to campaign—the bound of utility; (3) a description of the issues which are of greatest concern to citizens, in terms of the location and socioeconomic status of those citizens; (4) a description of voter reactions to particular strategies; and (5) a guide to the strategies that should be followed if certain issues should become more salient in the voters' minds.[5] Although Volpe did not receive any data which predicted the future behavior of voters if the issues changed, he was provided with data that helped him to locate the bound of utility, define the most important issues in different areas of the state, and see clearly that Ward's mock-trial of him was backfiring.

Volpe's pollsters approached their assignment in scholarly fashion, by first examining past election returns in an effort to locate "barometric" wards in Boston, which could be sampled to predict the outcome of the Boston and statewide vote for governor. The validity of their polls, of course, depended upon the accuracy of their sample. Their research indicated that a sample drawn from wards 20, 21, 4, 9, 12, in that order, would provide an accurate prediction of the state vote for governor and a sample drawn from wards 17, 18, 9, 16, 22, in that order, would provide an accurate prediction of the

[5] See Thomas B. Morgan, "The People Machine," *Harpers Magazine,* Vol. 222, No. 1328 (Jan. 1961), for a description of how a simulation (an estimation of future hypothetical behavior) was made for Senator Kennedy with respect to the religious issue in the 1960 presidential election by extrapolation from available public-opinion data. The final report, excerpted below, provided the basis for a clear-cut tactical decision:

"Kennedy today has lost the bulk of the votes he would lose if the election campaign were to be embittered by the issue of anti-Catholicism. The net worst has been done. If the campaign becomes embittered he will lose a few more reluctant Protestant votes to Nixon, but will gain Catholic and minority-group votes. Bitter anti-Catholicism in the campaign would bring about a reaction against prejudice and for Kennedy from Catholics and others who would resent overt prejudice. It is in Kennedy's hands to handle the religious issue during the campaign in a way that maximizes Kennedy votes based on resentment against religious prejudice and minimizes further defections. On balance, he would not lose further from forthright and persistent attention to the religious issue, and could gain. The simulation shows that there has already been a serious defection from Kennedy by Protestant voters. Under these circumstances, it makes no sense to brush the religious issue under the rug. Kennedy has already suffered the disadvantages of the issue even though it is not embittered now—and without receiving compensating advantages inherent in it."

Boston vote. Volpe actually received 52.9 per cent of the statewide vote and 40.7 per cent of the Boston vote. In the wards that were used to predict Volpe's statewide strength he received 50 per cent of the vote, and in the wards sampled to predict his Boston vote he received 38.4 per cent. It is obvious, therefore, that the sample of wards was well chosen.

On the basis of samples in these wards and other areas, Volpe received a report before the Democratic primary that correctly predicted the defeat of Furcolo and the final ranking of the gubernatorial contenders. He "knew" in advance, therefore, that Ward would be his opponent. He also "knew" how he stood at various times and in various places before the general election. This information was used to designate areas in which he should place more or less emphasis, thus husbanding scarce resources. Some illustrations of the data Volpe received, taken from the poll of October 14, follow:

Volpe has 38 per cent of the Boston vote. The amount of votes cast in Boston will be (approximately) 308,000.[6] If Ward gets 62 per cent, he will get 191,000 votes. In order to win, Ward must get 1,200,000 minus 191,000, or 1,009,000, from the "upstate" areas. . . . Ward is a little over 3 per cent short of the "upstate" vote that is necessary to win.

On October 21 Volpe received an analysis of the poll taken on the 14th:

I have carefully studied the ward-by-ward results of the October 14th polls, which showed Volpe with 38 per cent of the Boston vote. While in some respects 38 per cent is pretty good, it is far from sufficiently encouraging to be regarded with any great optimism. I would say that Volpe's average must improve in Boston by at least 5 points before he can take anything for granted in this election. . . .[7]

I would point out that in wards 16, 17, 18, 20, 21, and 22, Volpe is averaging 34.82 per cent, whereas he should be averaging at least 42 per cent in these wards. Indeed, the history of the vote in ward 20 indicates that he should be carrying that by at least 50 to 55 per cent . . . in order to be confident of a favorable result.[8]

The conclusion must seem to be that there is plenty of work yet to be done in Boston. I repeat my prior suggestions that Volpe must make sure

[6] 277,219 votes were cast for governor in Boston.

[7] Volpe received 40.7 per cent of the Boston vote, which was more than enough to win.

[8] Volpe received 50.1 per cent of the vote in ward 20.

to do the following two things: (1) Keep Ward on the defensive so that he cannot take advantage of an expected upsurge in Kennedy's strength. (2) He should not overlook Worcester County.

A report of a poll taken on October 28 at 14 barometric points in Boston using 3,000 straw ballots indicated that between the 14th and 28th "Ward has slipped six percentage points." This suggested that Volpe's failure to debate Ward had not seriously hurt Volpe's candidacy and that Ward's television trial of Volpe either had backfired or had not been seen by many persons. The "capsule conclusion" of this poll follows:

Joe Ward should be carrying the Jewish wards by a margin of three to one in order to win.[9] Joe Ward is *not* carrying the Jewish wards at all, i.e., wards 14 and 21.

Ward 20 is the most perfect barometer point of all, in all types of elections. . . . In the last two weeks . . . John Volpe has taken a very strong and commanding lead. . . .

Joe Ward must absolutely catch on "fire"—atomic fire—in order to be able to win. This depends on what Kennedy can do in his behalf between now and election day. It should be noted that Kennedy will spend only a few hours here in Massachusetts the day before election day. Apparently the error that Joe Ward made, and he seems to be compounding it, is that he should have wrapped himself, positively, to Jack Kennedy.

It is safe to assume that John Volpe will win, but . . . in order for John Volpe to *guarantee* winning, because of the possible influence of Jack Kennedy, he must insure that he will get all the *"Old Guard"* Republican votes. . . .

It is believed that Jack Kennedy will *not* add too much to Joe Ward's vote. On October 14th, Jack Kennedy received 78 per cent of the ballots taken, and Joe Ward received 62 per cent of the ballots taken. On October 28th, Jack Kennedy stayed the same percentage-wise, while Joe Ward "slipped" by 6 per cent. This shows that public opinion at these barometer points has "crystallized" and the voting per cents for Jack Kennedy have become stable, i.e., if another poll was taken on November 4th, Jack Kennedy would still get the *same* per cent. Consequently, it can be safely assumed that Joe Ward has definitely "slipped" by 6 per cent over the last two weeks, and it appears that he *cannot* gain enough to win.

On November 7, Volpe received the report of the last survey, which

9 Ward 14: Volpe—6,667; Ward—10,992
  Ward 21: Volpe—9,120; Ward— 7,860

predicted: "John Volpe will be elected Governor of Massachusetts by a plurality of 85,000 plus."[10] The report also predicted, with a high degree of accuracy, the county-by-county vote.

Volpe therefore had a steady stream of information that pinpointed areas where he was strong or weak. The question, however, is how best to use information of this kind. It is usually a mistake, we believe, for the strategist to base his plans exclusively on poll results. For example, he might suggest that Volpe concentrate his campaigning in areas where the polls showed he had inadequate support. Such a strategy, however, would be irrational if these wards were hopelessly lost to Volpe, for then he would be wasting scarce resources by campaigning there. Once the "fact" that he is weak in these areas has been established, the question of what to do about it, or whether anything can be done, might better be answered by the local precinct captains than by the pollsters. The strategy of campaigning in weak spots might be irrational for another reason: it may be more important for the candidate to campaign in areas where he is strong, on the theory that those who supported him initially need reinforcement.[11] In fact, as we have noted, Volpe spent considerable time at Republican picnics and meetings, with the object of ensuring the loyalty of the Old Guard.

It is clear that information concerning the candidate's strength or weakness in specific areas is not very useful until it is evaluated by local campaign workers. Even then, contradictory but plausible interpretations are possible. It would be much more valuable to know where significant numbers of undecided voters are located, and this Volpe's polls did not indicate.

Polls can provide data of immense practical value if the sample is so designed as to reveal what voters of different ethnic groups believe the salient issues to be, or what they perceive as attractive or unattractive political styles or stereotypes. We mention ethnic groups specifically because in Massachusetts they form relatively solid voting blocs which are concentrated geographically and there-

[10] Volpe's actual plurality was 138,485.

[11] The most significant effect of a political campaign may well be reinforcement rather than conversion. Lazarsfeld reports that 58% of those interviewed during the 1940 presidential campaign indicated that the campaign provided them with reasons for remaining with their original choice, while only 8% were actually converted (Paul Lazarsfeld, Bernard Berelson, and Hazel Gaudet, *The People's Choice* [New York: Columbia University Press, 1944], Chap. 11).

fore are easily reached. These data can provide the starting point for the development of a "coalition of minorities" strategy. Volpe's polls were valuable precisely because they supplied this information, and early enough for him to take advantage of it.

The authors' pre-primary and post-general-election polls, we have said, indicated that a large segment of the Massachusetts electorate felt politically alienated. We suggested that the problem of the political strategist in Massachusetts is, to a large extent, the problem of appealing to such a voter. The extent and profundity of the feelings of political alienation reported to us leave no doubt that this was a crucial factor during the elections. Volpe's pollsters arrived at the same conclusions. They correctly gauged the mood of the electorate, understood the significance of style to alienated voters, and suggested several strategies designed specifically for them.

The poll report presented to Volpe on September 29 included the following remarks and suggestions:

Citizens generally are not enthused about the effect of their vote in the interest of the government they say they want. This attitude is expressed in several ways: in cynicism regarding politics, disillusionment and even hostility or alienation of interest in voting.

Practically everybody is concerned about high taxes, waste and extravagance, graft and corruption and favoritism or "cronyism," and the reputation of their state. There is a need for efficient management and integrity in government, according to the people. All the candidates all the time promise to do something about these things but nobody ever keeps his promises, they generally conclude.

Thus the Volpe campaign from here on should stress: (1) the importance of their vote ("Your Vote can do something about High Taxes and Waste and Corruption . . .") and (2) the Results they want will occur and Promises will be kept ("Here's a Man who has gotten Results in the past and who has always kept his Promises—Vote the Man, Vote Volpe for Governor").

Statements like "Yes, You can end 'machine politics,' waste and extravagance, and corruption in State Government—Vote the Man—Vote Volpe," "Yes, You can restore integrity, or Your Vote Can Restore Integrity in State Government . . . etc." "Yes, You can vote for a man who keeps his promises or Your Vote can Elect a Governor Who Can and Will Keep His Promises."

The significance of the alienated voter and the need for a strategy specifically attractive to him were noted in almost every report:

September 16: The voters don't want double talk. They want an end to what appears to be a resumption of the venal and deceptive type of lobby and dealing. They are fed up with tremendous and inexcusable waste and lax attention to conflicts of interest. They want an end to immorality in government. . . . They don't want a governor who sits on his ass visiting some sick aunt . . . while 85 cities and towns in the most important part of the state go without transportation over the Christmas holiday.

October 1: We must not bend to the temptation of talking like a politician —promising, in effect, to make everyone rich, promising that no one will have to work, while the state takes over all their problems and solves them for them. People are tired of political promises and the lust for public office by people who will offer everything as a lure for votes. They fear the cost of corruption in their taxes, the undermining of people's confidence in the Commonwealth, the injury to the security of their jobs and homes by bad management, poor business practices in government, and the running of government by officials for the private privileges of the few.

It is not surprising that Volpe's pollsters found large numbers of alienated voters, for their prevalence in Massachusetts is great. It is interesting to note that the comments of Volpe's alienated respondents were often identical, in underlying attitude and phraseology, to those reported to the authors; for example: "I don't like Ward because he is supported by the pols." "Where did he get all the money to spend?" "We need a new party and a new man to clean up the mess." "Volpe is not a politician."

Although comments of this kind are indicative of the state of mind of the electorate, Volpe did not need polls to learn that large numbers of the voters were alienated; every sophisticated politician in Massachusetts was well aware of this situation. Data concerning alienation and the relative popularity of the candidates were not, however, the only types of information provided for Volpe. An analysis of the perceived images of both candidates was also prepared for Volpe. This, too, corresponds very closely to our findings and, we believe, could have provided a solid basis for strategic decisions.

Thus Volpe's pollsters reported on Ward's strength:

Joseph Ward's initial strength comes from the fact that he is the Democratic candidate in a state where registered Democrats outnumber Republicans. . . . Those who favor Ward on the basis of his being the Democratic party's candidate usually give as their reason that the Democratic party is more sensitive to the needs of the people. Typical comments were: "A Democrat can do more for the state."[12]

Joseph Ward as a candidate is likable. . . . Certainly his family of seven daughters and an attractive wife help in this image. Coments like: "A good man with a nice personality" are indicative.

The people generally did not have anything much against Ward and by the same token did not have compelling reasons for voting in his favor. Those who were for John Volpe usually had some positive reason for their decision. The favorable reaction to Ward seemed to be basically an emotional one.

Ward's publicity campaign during the primary fight was a decided asset for his candidacy. Many spoke of his clever advertising, slogan, and publicity. As of today, the stepped-up Volpe campaign has dissipated this early advantage enjoyed by Ward.

A good deal of Ward strength in the primary came from personal contact either with Ward or with his associates. Comments like the following are typical: "I have heard people say Ward is a good man." "My friends have encouraged me to vote for Ward."

A number of voters spoke of Ward's youth and ability as reasons for favoring him. Comments went as follows: "He is young and able." "Young and full of vigor and progress." "He has good ideas."

Experience in government was another Ward asset as far as some voters were concerned. "He has experience in government." "Ward had done well as Secretary of State."

Volpe's pollsters also reported on Ward's perceived weaknesses:

The lack of really solid experience and accomplishment is a weakness in the Ward candidacy. . . . He has held no significant statewide office; even his record in the minor office of Secretary of State has been criticized by members of his own party. His sole job is to see that the elections are conducted fairly and his actions in this regard in the primary have brought forth charges of "rigging the ballot" in his favor and in that of Governor Furcolo. This is a most serious charge which should prove a serious handicap to the Ward candidacy.

In contrast to the Volpe record of solid accomplishment in business, government, military service, and community activities, the Ward record does

---

[12] Of those respondents in our post-election survey who had voted for Ward, 45 per cent gave as their reason "He is a Democrat" or "I am a Democrat."

not offer anything outstanding. "I have never heard of anything outstanding that he has done." "He has nothing to offer."

Considering the need which so many voters feel for business-management experience in the Governor's office, Ward's lack of administrative experience in contrast to Volpe's success as a business manager is a handicap. "Ward is nothing but a 'pol'; we need a businessman of integrity."

The fact that Ward is considered just another politician is a definite weakness in his candidacy. The voters are looking for a new face and something more than the usual politician with the usual gang of hangers-on. These comments are revealing: "Too much politician." "Machine man." "I don't want Ward because he is supported by the 'pols.' " "Ward has a real clique with him, he is promising everyone."

Potentially the most damaging weakness of the Ward candidacy is his tie-in with the repudiated Furcolo administration. "Ward is part of the Furcolo administration—a rotten administration." "We need a switch in state government."

This last point is significant. Volpe had a great deal to gain by associating Ward with Furcolo and attacking Furcolo. Our pre-primary poll indicated profound disillusionment, disgust, and anger with the Furcolo administration. Twenty-eight per cent of those interviewed thought that the Furcolo administration had done a "bad" or "very bad" job,[13] while only 15 per cent thought that the incumbents had done a "good" or "very good" job. Seven per cent of the respondents volunteered the comment that they "dislike Furcolo."[14] On the basis of these data it is obvious that it would have been a rational strategy for Volpe to associate Ward with Furcolo by suggesting that Ward was the hand-picked candidate of the in-

[13] These statistics, however, do not convey the depth of the feeling of resentment and disgust. Some illustrative responses follow: "Every time you pick up a paper it looks like you find something else has gone wrong. . . . I been trying to do some catching up on what goes on in state politics, but so far I haven't been able to find out. . . . I get disgusted and don't read no more." "Corrupt politics is the American way." "A bunch of money-grabbing thieves who did not care about anyone but themselves, and Furcolo was the worst of the lot. Murphy was the only decent one—at least he beat the sales tax, thank God for that or they would have wasted that money along with everything else." "Lousy, and you can quote me on that. They were a bunch of crooks and bunglers." "I don't care how honest a man is in private life, once he gets into politics he can't resist the graft. Some of the Republicans are just as bad or would be if they could ever get in there. All this stealing it just makes you sick. Every time you pick up a newspaper, every time you see where there's contracts been given out to people's friends."

[14] The remaining respondents either gave no answer (9%) or said that they thought the administration had done a "fair" job (41%).

cumbents. His pollsters knew this and urged that it "be made impossible for Ward to disassociate himself from Furcolo's collar." Ward himself feared that Volpe would adopt this tactic. Volpe, oddly enough, refused to do so, because, he said, an attack on Furcolo would anger Italo-American voters who otherwise might be persuaded to desert the Democratic camp. One of Volpe's advisers offered a further explanation: "He doesn't want to initiate an attack on anyone who hasn't attacked him . . . this isn't the way you do things in business; this isn't what he has become accustomed to."[15] Thus far, Volpe's pollsters had uncovered little that was not generally known to the insiders in his camp. They believed, before the receipt of polling data, that many voters were alienated, and they feared that the Old Guard might abstain from voting. The strategies suggested by Volpe's pollsters were therefore anything but radical.

Public-opinion data concerning the candidate's image are, of course, not necessarily restricted to his perceived weaknesses. If the candidate knows what voters find attractive about him, he may be able to enhance his style or stress aspects of his experience and record that appeal to certain subgroups in the voting population. Many suggestions relating to the "correct" political style are implied in the following excerpts from a report concerning Volpe's strengths and weaknesses:

Volpe's record and qualifications were mentioned oftener than Ward's record and qualifications. Volpe's business-management success, his record as Commissioner of the Department of Public Works, his service as Federal Highway Commissioner, his leadership in church and civic activities including his chairmanship of the Boston Chamber of Commerce, and his reputation for honesty and for getting things done were referred to repeatedly. . . .

Working for John Volpe is also the feeling of many voters of the need for change both in party and in type of candidate for governor. Revealing were such comments as "We need a new party and a new man to clean up the mess in state government." "There is less graft under Republican administrations." "Volpe is not a politician."

15 This adviser clearly recognized the rationality of attacking Ward through Furcolo: "I would say that the public-opinion-poll evidence, such as it is, suggests Furcolo is . . . not any help to Ward, to put it mildly, and therefore the closer we can tie him in and appear fair—I mean, we can't appear to be straining the thing—the better. Now, if Peabody had been the candidate, I think it would have been sort of ridiculous to try and tie him in with Furcolo; but with Ward I think there's a reasonable hope of doing it."

As already indicated in the analysis of Ward's strength as a candidate, a few voters, mostly Democrats, believed that Ward had more experience in government than Volpe. "Volpe does not know the problems of the state." Considering the quality of Volpe's experience and the importance of the D.P.W. issue, plus the greater advantage of not being just a politician, this is not a significant problem for the Volpe candidacy.

Probably potentially more serious is the confusion some voters have on his construction activities (the tendency to associate all contractors with graft), his Italian American background (Furcolo's failures have not helped Italian American candidates among other ethnic groups), and his being confused earlier in the campaign with DiNatale and with Furcolo's administration. The stepped-up Volpe campaign has done much to clear up this confusion. The challenge to the Volpe campaign now comes in the Ward charges of graft and favoritism. . . .

These comments were used by the Volpe forces as a guide to the type of image that Volpe ought to present. The fact that Volpe was a contractor was reported to be a disadvantage, but the fact that he was a successful business man was reported to be an advantage; therefore, Volpe's pollsters suggested that he try to look like the public image of a successful business man, whatever that may be. When appearing on television, therefore, Volpe wore a single-breasted suit with narrow lapels, and a folded white handkerchief cautiously peeked from his left breast pocket. He sat behind an "executive suite" type desk, which was fitted with appointments such as might be found in the office of an important corporation executive. He appeared, in other words, like the stereotype of the successful, but kindly and thoughtful, business man. More important than his appearance, however, was the problem of how Volpe should talk. Is the successful business man soft-spoken, dignified, and deliberate, or is he aggressive, raucous, and forceful? Volpe's pollsters addressed themselves to this question. In a report of the response of independents to the candidate's television presentations, the pollsters noted the voters' admiration for "Mr. Volpe's kind and gentle appearance on television, his calm and pleasant voice and general subject matter, in sharp contrast to Ward's raucousness." This is a valuable bit of information, particularly in a political community of alienated voters, who judge candidates in terms of "gut reactions" rather than platforms. Ward, of course, had no idea that his aggressiveness was repulsive to many voters, whereas Volpe's polls confirmed the "correctness" of his chosen style.

Our post-election public-opinion poll reveals that Volpe was perceived by many as "sincere," "honest," "quiet," and "nice." To some extent, we believe, this response was due to his demeanor on television. Our data indicate that the candidate who is soft-spoken, even to the point of virtual inarticulateness, does not fit the image of the Massachusetts politician, who is stereotyped as, among other things, aggressive, loud, and smooth-talking. The Volpe brain trust knew this. One adviser stated, "Style is far more important than content." The pollsters suggested the "correct" style for Volpe.

Volpe's pollsters also provided him with vital information on one of the most critical strategic problems of his campaign. The Volpe forces were obviously concerned with Ward's charge that Volpe had been involved in five major conflicts of interest. A memo of October 12 put it this way: "I believe that Ward is beginning to benefit, and Volpe to suffer too much from Ward's challenges, which have the effect of putting a question mark on Volpe in the public mind." The problem was, how should Volpe answer the charges? This problem became particularly acute when Ward challenged Volpe to a television debate. A rational response to this challenge depended upon an estimate of (1) the relative debating prowess of the two candidates, and (2) the likelihood that Ward's mock trial of Volpe would result in a "conviction." The first factor can be accurately evaluated only by submitting the candidates to an ordeal by fire; however, it was possible for Volpe to gather data with respect to the second, and this he did.

The report on television viewers quoted previously stated that "approximately 8 per cent of persons describing themselves as independent voters have actually changed their vote to Volpe as a result of seeing and hearing Volpe and Ward on television." Obviously Ward's trial was proving to be a boomerang. The report also indicated that "Mr. Volpe has already made deep inroads into the Democratic voting strength." The pollsters concluded: "Hence: Keep Mr. Volpe on TV. Keep him just the way he has been to date. Concentrate on the one, clear, simple issue (Honesty in Government). Solidifying the independent voting strength is imperative. (A bad mistake, an inaccurate declaration by or in behalf of Mr. Volpe, a mouse-trap play, or a stupid contrivance at this stage of the campaign, can prove very costly)."

The report was obviously of great value. It vividly confirmed the decision not to have Volpe debate Ward, which Volpe's brain trust had taken on the basis of their estimate of Volpe's and Ward's capabilities as public debaters, and it also confirmed Volpe's decision to speak softly and with dignity. The Volpe forces were so concerned about Ward's charges that, without the report, they might have panicked and encouraged their candidate to debate Ward. What would have happened then no one can say. They needed "objective" reassurance, and this is what the pollsters gave them. Meanwhile, Ward went about collecting "evidence" for the "trial," which he presented with vigor to "a distinguished panel of attorneys." Although one or two of his advisers suggested that the trial was a disastrous mistake, the prosecution refused to adjourn. In fact, Ward and most of his aides became even more convinced, as the trial continued, that an "indictment" was inevitable. This was because they talked only to friendly witnesses. One Ward adviser stated, "My aunt is an old-guard Republican, but she's going to vote for Joe because of these charges." The prosecution nodded in agreement.

The major findings of Volpe's public-opinion polls have been reviewed. The question at issue is, how shall these data be interpreted and used as the basis for strategic decisions? It is tempting for the armchair strategist to adopt a simplistic approach to a campaign by directly translating poll results into political action. The candidate is weak in the Negro district: step up the campaign there. The voters are concerned about high taxes: pledge no increase in the state budget. We have pointed out some of the dangers implicit in such an approach and have stressed the need to evaluate the data critically in terms of what public-relations men like to call "the big picture." In many instances, reasonable men could interpret the data and arrive at contradictory conclusions. Unless the data indicate a clear trend (in which case the politicians probably would be aware of it already), intelligent evaluation is more valuable than the information itself.

Volpe's advisers understood this and consequently used the reports on issues as guides rather than absolute commands in forming strategy. Their decision not to debate Ward and to present Volpe in a statesmanlike manner was taken prior to the analysis of television viewing and for reasons that had much more to do with Volpe's personality than with any survey data. "Mr. Volpe is not a debater," his campaign coordinator stated; "he is a business man. He is used to making responsible, documented decisions, but, frankly, he is not a quick debater. We felt that no political good could come from a debate with Mr. Ward, and that Mr. Volpe would look poorly in contrast." The poll of October 28, in the words of a Volpe brain-truster, "persuaded us not to get involved in a smear contest in the last week of the campaign but to attempt to hold the line in terms of John's dignity and his position on the thing, and this is substantially what we have done." This decision was obviously a critical one.

Throughout this analysis we have implied that, with the exception of the survey data on television viewing, which were enormously valuable, the polls reported little that was not known by the other candidates and advisers and little that was tactically useful. This, however, obscures an important point. Although the other candidates were aware that political alienation was widespread and that people were concerned with high taxes, corruption, and the like, their knowledge of these facts was "gross" while Volpe's was "refined." What they knew in general, he knew in particular. For example, although Ward had some idea of where he was strong, Volpe knew with some precision why he was strong (or weak) in various specific cities and counties. All the primary candidates knew that citizens generally were concerned with a number of issues; Volpe knew what groups in what locations were concerned with what issues. This knowledge helped in the formulation of a coalition-of-minorities strategy. Although the other candidates realized that many voters assume politicians to be corrupt, Volpe knew the specific terms and stereotypes voters were using to express their resentment and hence his advisers could suggest slogans specifically designed to appeal to feelings of powerlessness and in some cases using the phraseology of the alienated: "Your vote can do something about high taxes." "You can end 'machine politics.'" It may be that rapport was produced between Volpe and the voters by his use of this phraseology. By using their words, Volpe acted as their spokesman. This may be one of the reasons that some voters identified with him. (As a matter of fact, the phraseology used by alienated voters is so common that Volpe could have exploited it much more than he did.)

Above all, Volpe's polls were valuable because they permitted him to determine the public's response to particular strategies. If his poll of television viewers had indicated that Ward's charges were effective, Volpe could have answered them more directly or taken the offensive against Ward. An accurate poll at this juncture of the campaign could have been invaluable to Ward, who completely misjudged the effect of the trial. It is obvious, therefore, that Volpe's polls were of some value to him, particularly with respect to the most critical decision of the campaign.

There were some Ward supporters who, without benefit of public-opinion data, advised Ward that he not only should terminate the trial but should never even mention his opponent. They argued that Senator Kennedy would sweep Ward into office, that a Democratic candidate for governor, particularly one who was not well known,[16] could not possibly lose in Massachusetts in 1960. One man suggested that Ward would win "if he did nothing but recite poetry on television." This individual told a key Ward strategist that he felt the television trial of Volpe was hurting Ward. The evidence suggests that his intuition was correct. Information obtained through intuition, of course, is much less expensive than that procured by public-opinion polls. The problem is, whose intuition is correct?

The stereotype of the professional politician sees him as an "inside dopester" with antennae that help him to detect subtle shifts in public opinion. He somehow "knows" who can win elections and how. Ward's key brain-truster was sure that Ward had this quality. But political intuition is a rare quality. Certainly very little of it was exhibited by the "pros" in the elections with which we are concerned. We are skeptical, further, of the utility of blind intuition as a guide, particularly in an alienated community. One's intuition is only as good as one's experience or the extensiveness of one's contact with voters. If Ward's oracles had accurately sampled the electorate, they might have suggested that Ward ignore Volpe. Given adequate financial resources and the sophisticated techniques now available for reducing the possibility of error in public-opinion polling, we suggest that the pollsters may know more that is worthwhile to the

[16] One such individual suggested that, in the view of many leading Democrats, Ward's "greatest asset was that, as far as they knew at the time [August], nothing bad could be said about him, also . . . sure that nothing was particularly good in his record. . . . [He] was a relative blank." He stated that "the fatal error of the Volpe trial attacks and the ballot finagle created a basis for antipathy."

candidate than the "pols" do, although we do not discount the possibility of the oracular vision. However, the oracle's intuition is often based on feelings that have no basis in reality. He often merely repeats what he has heard, having been told what he wants to hear. He is often the victim of the echo effect.

In a democratic society, candidates for public office must please voters. To do so they must gather information concerning voter preferences. We have traced the process by which this was done in the primary and general elections. The rationality of political strategy depends, of course, upon the accuracy of the information at the strategists' disposal and the wisdom they display in interpreting it. On the basis of information from campaign workers, inside dopesters, pollsters, and his own intuition, each candidate in these elections gradually developed an over-all picture of the political situation, which led him to develop a grand strategy based on three major assumptions: (1) a significant proportion of the electorate is alienated; (2) ethnic voting will play a major role in the election; and (3) primary elections call for a special strategy. The strategists' problem was to appeal to the alienated voter, to exploit the ethnic base of Massachusetts politics for their candidates' purposes, and to encourage or discourage party regulars or independents from voting, depending on who their candidate was.

Assumption 1: The Alienated Voter

They give you the gold brick before they're elected; afterward, they give themselves the gold brick.

A RESPONDENT

Most of the candidates in these elections assumed that the alienated voter would play a significant role. Although the professionals were interested primarily in the immediate question of whether the alienated voter would vote and, if so, for whom, they also speculated on the causes of political alienation in Massachusetts and the nation, and discussed, with varying degrees of sophistication, strategies which they thought would be appropriate for taking advantage of it. We have already noted that Volpe received a voluminous amount of public-opinion data, from August to the eve of the election, indicating that there was a significant number of alienated voters. A Ward brain-truster commented, the day before the election, "Volpe has based his entire campaign on the concept of alienation. He's had no other issue, other than the fact that if you're alienated . . . then vote Volpe, vote the man, vote the honest man." He deplored the fact that the Democratic party was forced to attack Volpe instead of campaigning on "the bread-and-butter issues . . . the New Frontier, New Horizon, the great social reform movement." He pointed out, however, that the electorate's "innate suspicion of politics and politicians" made corruption the only significant issue and compelled Ward to attack Volpe.

Ward himself identified the fundamental problem of politics in Massachusetts as "maintaining effective government in a period when people are suspicious of politics and politicians." Piemonte agreed that "corruption or inefficiency, or lack of ethics in the administration of government" were the basic issues in the election. John Francis Kennedy, who has made it his business to exploit the alienation of the public, was certain that alienation was "widespread in Massachusetts" because "the people had been fooled for years." He continued: "They throw out a rascal, and perhaps the fellow they put in is worse than he is. That's kind of disillusioning. They don't like it, but they haven't been able to see any logical alternative to voting the way they do. I figure in this particular campaign I'll give them the alternative." A Volpe brain-truster even suggested that the prime motive behind Volpe's candidacy was his desire "to deal with what appeared to be the diminution of public confidence."

This cynicism, this lessening of public confidence, this political alienation that was assumed to be a fundamental feature of the Massachusetts electorate, was, in the opinion of many, a national phenomenon. As one candidate put it, political corruption has come to be accepted "as part of the American way of life," and alienation is the "natural" response to it. Peabody's campaign manager, who traveled widely while working for Senator Kennedy, believed that alienation "is probably nationwide. . . . I think that the . . . Powers-Collins election last year certainly indicates that the people do have some independence of thought and that any politician who attempts to underestimate the intelligence of the people is in for a shock."

Piemonte agreed with this view, adding that political alienation resulted from "breakdown of moral values, [starting] from the top." He insisted that most politicians are honest men who are "forced" to do the bidding of powerful and sinister influences in the electorate:

The average public officeholder starts off with the best of intentions, but when he is in public office he finds himself pressured by what on the surface appear to be civic groups, responsible civic groups . . . who, for example, . . . desire to bring about urban renewal programs or to protect their values on downtown properties. [They] ask, or intercede, or influence the public official into doing things that seem to set a double standard.

These "so-called civic groups," according to Piemonte, use "upper-grade influence peddlers" to put pressure on politicians. The view that an honest man cannot remain so in politics has wide currency in Massachusetts. "They all end up the same way," one voter remarked; "they go into office small humble men, then do what they want for their own good."

Some of our respondents suggested that political alienation throughout the nation resulted from an increase in the political sophistication and literacy of the average voter. Peabody's campaign manager, who agreed with this view, traced increased political awareness and sophistication to television and an improvement in "the general intellectual caliber of our society." Forty years ago, he said, "it was quite unusual for someone to go through college or even high school. As the educational standard of the country has risen, so has the intelligence, and it is only natural that people would be better informed, not only about politics, but about other facts of life." A Volpe brain-truster stated, "In the greater Boston area the average voter is quite sophisticated in his ability to see through political terminology and political strategy."

The assumptions underlying these statements are (1) that alienation is inevitable in an affluent industrial society, since it is material progress that raises the general standard of living and so makes possible improved literacy, education, and ability to understand politics; and (2) that "political terminology" is intended to deceive. As the electorate has become better informed, it has also become more skeptical of campaign promises and pronouncements.

The sophistication and alienation of the electorate, as we have pointed out, necessitate a revolution in political campaign strategy. The traditional, hackneyed, and crude political strategies of the past will no longer be effective. The development of the "soft sell" and anti-advertising advertising indicates that public-relations men are already aware of and ready to exploit the cynicism of consumers. Most of the candidates in Massachusetts, however, continue to perform political surgery crudely, with a chisel rather than a scalpel.

Predictions of the effects of political alienation in these elections were, on the whole, crude and unrealistic. In most cases, the candidate predicted that alienated voters would behave in the manner most advantageous to himself. The "pros" tended to distort reality to fit their wishes, not only when gathering information concerning voter preferences, but also when interpreting it or predicting voter reactions. Ward's manager, however, viewed the problem more realistically; he conceded that his candidate would lose some votes in the primary because some alienated voters would perceive Ward as the heir to a discredited regime or the product of a "rigged" convention. He also said that although political alienation would result in "a large number of blanks," or abstentions, in the primary, those alienated persons who voted would tend to cancel each other out by "mutual crossing over." The primary, in fact, was an extremely chaotic and vituperative contest. The seven candidates included two Italo-Americans, one Yankee Protestant, one eccentric (John F. Kennedy), and three other Irish-Americans. The complexity of this Gilbert and Sullivan situation baffled most of the alienated voters and caused them to turn their anger toward politicians in general rather than concentrate it on one man in particular. "They're all crooks" was the common refrain of those we interviewed. This diffusion of anger did result in a tendency of alienated voters to cancel out one another's vote in the primary. Ward's adviser also suggested that the alienated voter would wait for the general election, a bipartisan contest, to vote "against." This is essentially what happened in November, to Ward's detriment.

Obviously the issue of corruption in government was foremost in the minds of voters, alienated and non-alienated; and Ward had to meet this issue. Perhaps the best way for him to have done this would have been to dissociate himself from Furcolo rather than to attack Volpe. It seemed to Ward and his advisers, however, that a wiser course, in view of the prevalence of registered Democrats in the state, was to stress the social-welfare achievements of the Democratic party, thus heightening Ward's party identification. This strategy precluded an attack on Furcolo. Ward's campaign manager even claimed that the attack on Volpe made it possible for Ward to return to the dispassionate discussion of issues:

The area of controversy was this area of corruption, . . . so that there was nothing to do but to proceed with the attack to its logical conclusion and wind up as we have at this end with a reaffirmation of our ideological differences with Mr. Volpe, which are substantial. But we couldn't get people to consider the ideological differences, the program differences, until they got down below the area of newspaper hysteria about the MDC, which was a bipartisan matter existing for a multitude of years. We only got them back to thinking about junior colleges and sales taxes and gasoline taxes and better education and aid to local schools—if we have gotten them back—only after we evened off the conflict-of-interest situation by fighting at least in that area, certainly in the newspapers, to better than a draw.

As we have observed, the Ward forces miscalculated the effect of their attack on Volpe. Ward's vituperativeness apparently led many alienated voters to vote against Ward rather than abstain, as Ward's brain trust had anticipated.

Piemonte's campaign manager was considerably more insightful concerning the types and possible reactions of alienated voters:

My theory is . . . that there are different types of political alienation. The type found in the lower-income groups is of the nature of absolute disgust and disinterest with politics in general, a general throwing-up of hands and "they are all crooks." Now the political alienation of the upper-income groups and those that are better off—for example, the suburban group—tends to take a different form, and they become more involved in local issues, like town meetings, but pretty much stay away from becoming involved in urban politics. . . . They feel no kind of identification with city politics and they care less to understand it. . . . Instead they pretend a concern for politics on the very local level or on the international level. They are quite concerned about relations with Russia. They are less concerned about the relation of the city to the suburbs or the city to the state.

Much of this argument is sound. It could, in fact, have been used as the basis for a coalition-of-minorities strategy directed at different types of alienated voter. For example, the "appeal to frankness" might be rational when campaigning in lower-income areas, irrational when campaigning in the suburbs. The candidate might do well to advocate "home rule" when campaigning in the suburbs while stressing his lack of ties to Boston politicians, or perhaps emphasize the need for activity in the suburbs to clean up corruption.

Nevertheless, Piemonte's manager still argued in favor of the vigorous assault. He suggested that attacks by Piemonte directed specifically at his opponents might have been effective, implying that Piemonte's "positive" approach toward campaigns might be a disadvantage for him:

Gabe's approach has always been a pretty positive one in affairs of government. He had ample opportunity in the mayoralty campaign of last year to attack Powers, and he refused to do so on the basis that if he couldn't win on his own qualities that he did not want to win by tearing down others. You know, Aristotle once said that "vice is a virtue carried to an extreme." Gabe's great virtue is his faith in his fellow humans, and he believes that they will listen more to a positive appeal than they will to a negative one. I think that, essentially, idealistically at least, this is so, but there is no question in my mind but that Collins derived great strength from the fact that he launched a stinging personal attack on Powers.

The first assumption upon which the candidates based their strategies, although accurate, caused them, in some instances, to campaign in a manner which turned the election into a monstrous distortion of what politics in a free and healthy society ought to be. Blame for this cannot be placed exclusively on the candidates themselves, since they were responding to the prejudices and stereotypes held by voters. They did, however, reinforce the alienation of many voters: the alienated voter wants an honest man; the candidates, knowing this, proceeded to vilify one another, so that the campaign confirmed the alienated voter's contempt for politicians. The lament of the alienated voter was sounded by one woman who remarked, "I might as well vote as not vote." If she did vote, it is likely that the religious or ethnic background of the candidate played a significant role in her choice. The candidates also knew this and attempted to capture the ethnic vote. Much of their planning went into this effort. This leads us to the second major assumption made by the candidates: people tend to vote for their "own kind."

Assumption 2: Italian Catholics, Irish Catholics, WASPS, and Jews

Don't put another Italian in. Not that they're Italian, it's just the way they behave. . . . All those big contracts would continue to go out, but it wouldn't improve. Look at them—DiNatale, Perini, Volpe—they have it all sewed up. They get all their favors from Furcolo now. There are no Irishmen or good Americans in the wealthy positions any more—just these Italians. Things will go the same way if Volpe gets in.

A RESPONDENT

Massachusetts has three parties: the Democratic party, the Republican party, and the Italian party.

A POLITICIAN

Although most religious leaders, reformers, and political scientists would agree that voting for one's "own kind" is irrational, bigoted, and immature, the fact is that ethnic and religious voting is tremendously significant, not only in Massachusetts, but throughout the United States. A recent study of this subject concludes that "the ethnic factor is second only to the economic factor in influencing an American's vote."[17] Many students of the Kennedy-Nixon election have commented on the substantial correlation between Kennedy's vote and the relative concentration of Catholics from district to district throughout the United States.[18] The most thorough and scholarly study of the 1960 presidential election yet published indicates that Kennedy's religion was the fundamental issue of the campaign and that it cost him approximately 1,500,000 votes.[19] We have already noted the fact that the hostility which developed in the nineteenth century between Yankee Protestants and Irish Catholics coninues to influence voting patterns in Massachusetts today. We have

[17] Moses Rischin, *Our Own Kind: Voting by Race, Creed, or National Origin*, A Report to the Center for the Study of Democratic Institutions, 1960, p. 38.

[18] See, for example, Louis H. Bean, "Why Kennedy Won," *The Nation*, Vol. 191, No. 18 (Nov. 26, 1960), p. 409.

[19] Philip Converse, Angus Campbell, Warren E. Miller, and Donald E. Stokes, "Stability and Change in 1960: A Reinstating Election," *American Political Science Review*, Vol. 60, No. 2 (June 1961). See also V. O. Key, Jr., "Interpreting the Election Results," *The Presidential Election and Transition 1960-1961* (Washington, D.C.: The Brookings Institution, 1961). Key writes, "Probably the best guess is that Kennedy won in spite of rather than because of the fact that he was a Catholic" (p. 175).

also noted that the Democratic party in Massachusetts is a loose coalition of Catholics of Irish and Italian extraction and Jews, who often feel more loyalty to their ethnic or religious group than to the party. In 1952, for example, when the Massachusetts Republican party nominated George Fingold, a Jew, for attorney general, approximately three out of five Jewish supporters of Stevenson in Brookline "split their ticket to vote for Fingold."[20] The nomination of John Volpe by the Massachusetts Republican party was based, in part, on the theory that many Italo-Americans who strongly identify with the Democratic party would vote for Volpe because of his Italian ancestry. In Massachusetts the nomination of a Catholic by the Republican party is a rational strategy—assuming, that is, that this will not alienate the Yankees who are the core of the party.

These basic facts of Massachusetts political life, known to every politician, are rarely, if ever, referred to in the press. The politicians similarly ignore ethnic and religious factors in public, but not in their private calculations of political strategy. A man familiar with operations at campaign headquarters reported that hardly a day went by without the demand: "We need an Irishman for a meeting in South Boston! We need a Jew for a meeting in Mattapan!" Peabody's polsters gave full weight to the ethnic factor in determining their sample, as can be seen from the following description: "Seventy-five per cent [of the first mailed questionnaires] were sent to Democrats and 25 per cent to independents. Forty per cent were sent to persons with Irish names, 20 per cent to persons with Italian names, and 40 per cent to persons whose names were neither Irish nor Italian. In the second poll, Portuguese names were substituted for Italian names in Fall River." Volpe's pollsters were also careful to sample the various ethnic groups. Further, the "truth squad" for Ward's television trial of Volpe consisted of an Irish Catholic, a Jew, an Italian Catholic, and a Yankee Protestant. Thus the second major set of assumptions made by the candidates and their advisers turned on the ethnic and religious loyalties of Massachusetts voters.

Three candidates were particularly concerned with this problem: Peabody, a Yankee Protestant, and Piemonte and Volpe, Italo-American Catholics. Like Peabody himself, Peabody's opponents

[20] Rischin, *op. cit.*, p. 31.

assumed that he would get the bulk of the Jewish vote—some of them because they believed that Jews tend to be political liberals, others because they believed that Jewish voters resented the usual "all green" ticket. Ward's manager predicted:

Chub will show strength in Brookline, Newton, ward 14 . . . in a sense the Jewish wards where there will be an inherently strong feeling against the Irish, against the all-green ticket. You can see this in the [Boston City Council] fights . . . where even an Italian does better than the Irish do in Jewish wards, and a Protestant would do better than a Catholic, and a Jew, of course, would run away from both. . . .

This prediction, we have said, was basically accurate, although large numbers of Jews failed to vote in the primary. Ward himself concurred: "Peabody will be strong in ward 14 and the Brighton and Allston [Jewish] districts."

Peabody's Protestantism, however, was a handicap as well as an asset, in the opinion of at least one of his advisers. Although this strategist thought that Peabody would attract Jewish and Protestant votes, he argued:

. . . If you ask me, the fact that he's a Yankee Protestant is a great drawback in a Democratic primary . . . with the old-line voter. . . . Now, it's interesting for me to tell you that a guy out in Pittsfield . . . an old-time politician, about 75 years old, said that Norman Vincent Peale's splash in the papers [a widely quoted, apparently anti-Catholic remark] two days before the election cost Peabody five to ten thousand votes. I personally don't believe that but I have no adequate proof. . . .

Despite this possibility, a senior member of the Volpe inner circle adamantly stated that Peabody would have been Volpe's most difficult opponent, and partly because of his appeal to the members of non-Irish ethnic groups:

I think Endicott Peabody would have been our most difficult opponent. . . . I think that many Republicans would have chosen to vote for Endicott Peabody because he is a Yankee Protestant, rather than for Volpe. I think that the Democrats would have embraced him because it would give them a new look and a new approach instead of a totally "green" ticket, which some people resent. I don't happen to resent it, I happen to recognize it as a political reality in terms of the weight of Democratic vote in our Commonwealth; but some people who have a more ideological approach to this thing feel that Peabody would have had a tremendous draw from the independents—the so-called intellectual level of Democrats—and certainly among the Republicans who still look with some distaste on the adoption by the Republican party of somebody other than a Yankee Protestant as their standard bearer.

Most of Piemonte's opponents assumed that his strength would be concentrated in areas with a heavy Italo-American population. A Murphy adviser, for example, thought that Piemonte's vote would be drawn mostly from the Italo-Americans. "I don't know," he added, "how long it will take them to live here before they become integrated, but they vote along ethnic lines very heavily." He also predicted accurately that Piemonte would garner votes in the Protestant areas of Boston, for "The people in the Back Bay would more likely vote for an Italian than they would for an Irishman."

The most fascinating remarks about the Italo-American vote, however, concerned neither Piemonte nor Volpe, who were obviously going to get a large part of it. Several candidates and managers suggested that a very subtle and devious tactic had been arranged to turn the Italo-American vote to the advantage of Furcolo and Ward. This effort turned on the candidacy of Alfred Magaletta, another Italo-American. Magaletta, a complete unknown, was conceded absolutely no chance of winning by anyone. According to all of his opponents except Ward, Magaletta had been urged to run by Furcolo and Ward—by Furcolo, because he wanted a large turnout of Italo-Americans in the primary, and by Ward, because he hoped that Magaletta would cut into Piemonte's strength. John Francis Kennedy had no doubt that such a plot had been designed to stop him.

Mr. Furcolo and Mr. Ward are very happy to have him in there because he wants all of the Italians to come out to vote for him for Senator. Mr. Ward would be happy to have Mr. Magaletta in because they know that the name Kennedy is strong with the Italians. It isn't that the Italians are misled into thinking they are voting for the Senator. They don't know too much about the rest so here is a name, . . . when I was canvassing, one old Italian lady said to me, "Kennedy—that's a nice-a name."

One manager was certain that Magaletta had been nominated "to keep it Italian, to keep the Italian voter in check." He suggested, quite shrewdly, that Volpe would be the ultimate beneficiary of this gambit.

The Italo-Americans were regarded by the Volpe forces as one vital bloc in the coalition of minorities that they hoped would overwhelm the Irish Democrats. Volpe's advisers were realistic; one stated, "It is perfectly apparent that no Republican for state office could win with Republicans alone. He has to appeal to Democrats and independents. It appeared clear to us that you couldn't say 'Vote Republican.' You have to vote for the man." They, and everyone else, knew that large groups of Italo-Americans who were traditionally Democratic would vote for Volpe merely because he was Italian. "We'll get more votes from these people than most Republican candidates," remarked a political scientist who advised Volpe. "We'll do better than Del Sesto did in '56 [in Rhode Island], considerably better, in getting Italian votes for a Republican candidate, unless I'm very much mistaken. Now, whether that means 20 per cent over the normal Italian vote for a Republican or whether it means 35 per cent is hard to say. You'll find some people here who put it a lot higher than that."

The chances of a massive Italo-American shift to Volpe were especially good, not only because Volpe was of Italian descent, but also because Italo-Americans were particularly disillusioned by the scandals occurring while Democrat Foster Furcolo, an Italo-American, was governor of Massachusetts. They may have perceived a vote for Volpe as a way of punishing Furcolo. As a matter of fact, members of ethnic groups are particularly sensitive to the performance of their own political leaders. The Irish Americans whom we interviewed following the Powers-Collins election were obviously disheartened and angry toward Irish politicians who had been indicted. Our data indicate that a profound sense of shame characterizes some segments of the Irish population. The solid vote for Saltonstall among upper-income Irish voters, in addition to being economically motivated, may have been a symbolic act of purification, since Saltonstall is widely regarded as absolutely clean.

Volpe's brain trust was well aware of these attitudes and attempted to take advantage of them:

. . . Much stress should be put on the Italian-American vote which normally votes Democratic. The feeling about an Italian-American candidate for governor among other citizens and even among some Italian Americans is one predominantly either of disillusionment or "I told you so." Each Italian American has a personal stake in this campaign in point of the prestige of his ethnic group. Furcolo, unfortunately, did not reflect well; Volpe has, can, and will reflect most creditably on all Americans of Italian ancestry. A real person-to-person campaign should be engaged in here with outstanding citizens of Italian background calling on and writing to every citizen.

These suggestions were based on the findings of Volpe's pollsters, who had sampled many voters whose decision turned on ethnic or religious considerations. But, curiously enough, Volpe's ethnic and religious background cut two ways, as did that of Senator Kennedy. Volpe was expected to pick up many Italo-American votes that were normally Democratic; however, his brain trust feared that this gain would be offset by the refusal of some Protestant Republicans to vote for a Catholic. "I will hold to the view," a brain-truster remarked, "that it is the Republicans that I'm concerned about, the dyed-in-the-wool Republicans." He feared

a defection among Republicans against Volpe, leaving the ballot blank because he is the first Italo-Catholic ever nominated by the Republican party. . . . As I review the history of the Republican party in elections, I've seen a Whittier rejected, a Cahill rejected after they've been nominated by the party, and principally deserted by the Old Guard Republicans, who must insist upon a Yankee blueblood for their nominee for the position of governor.

It is obvious that the candidates and campaign managers were vitally concerned with the ethnic and religious vote and that much of their political strategy was formulated on the basis of assumptions relative to Catholics, Protestants, Jews, Irish Americans, and Italo-Americans. The theoretical and strategic implications of ethnic voting, however, go beyond the results of these elections. Ethnic voting, first of all, may weaken party identification. Many people, as we have noted, will desert their own party to support an "opponent" who has the "right" ethnic or religious credentials. Given the fact that a majority of the Massachusetts electorate identifies with the Democratic party, it is strategically rational for the Republicans to support some candidates who have the same credentials as an important ethnic group that is customarily attached to the Democratic party. This reasoning is based, of course, on the assumption that Yankee Republicans will not abstain from voting if a non-Protestant of non-Anglo Saxon origin is nominated.

From a strategic point of view, ethnic and religious variables are
easier to deal with than are feelings of political alienation. We
have already pointed out that the feelings of alienated voters are
volatile and that strategies designed to take advantage of them are
double-edged. It is very difficult to locate the "bound of utility" for
alienated voters, since they are scattered throughout the state. This
is not the case with ethnic groups, which tend to form neighborhoods
in urban centers. Politicians know where Italo-Americans, Jews,
etc., are located, and they can campaign in those wards or precincts
or appeal to them through the ethnic press. However, there is no
newspaper published specifically for alienated voters and no distinct locale in which these voters tend to cluster. Therefore strategies
directed to ethnic and religious groups are easier to construct and
execute.[21] This fact may also account in part for the prevalence of
ethnic and religious voting, since it is an easy variable to exploit.

Nevertheless, the identification suggested by the term "own kind"
may be spurious. Considering religious, ethnic, economic, ideological, and geographical factors simultaneously, there is no way of
calculating which will be the dominant factor. There is no standard
to apply here that makes the satisfaction of one need more rational
than that of another. Choosing a party program and candidate,
therefore, poses complex problems. For example, would a middle-
income Italian Catholic liberal vote for a middle- or high-income
Protestant or Jewish liberal in preference to a middle-income Italian
Catholic conservative? Would he choose an Italian conservative
rather than a low-income Irish Catholic liberal? The rural-urban
factor might be added to these alternatives to include all the basic
and traditional prejudices and antagonisms. Would the decision
taken by thinking out the implications be translated into a vote or
would a strong impulse at the voting booth interfere? During the
1960 presidential campaign, some wag said that Kennedy was the
poor man's idea of a "good" rich man and Nixon the rich man's

21 The importance of religious voting in the U. S. may diminish during the next
century. Lazarsfeld reports, for example, "Within each religious group the younger
voters show tendencies of opposition. Younger Protestants vote less Republican
than older Protestants and younger Catholics less Democratic than old Catholics"
(Lazarsfeld *et al., op. cit.,* p. 24). Berelson gives further credence to this view,
pointing out that "Young people are more likely to resolve the cross pressures of
religion and SES in favor of class" (Bernard Berelson, Paul F. Lazarsfeld, and
William N. McPhee, *Voting* [Chicago: University of Chicago Press, 1954], p.
333).

idea of a "good" poor man. This facetious explanation of the nomination of these men points to a major problem in strategic campaign (and pre-convention) decisions: having decided to exploit a man's appeal to his "own kind" and to offer him to others at the same time as a "good" something-different-from their "own kind," the strategist may find that his tactic backfires at the polls. The strength of prejudice is difficult to calculate; at the moment of its greatest pull, "good" may mean what it meant in the early-nineteenth-century definition of a "good Indian." When one considers how small a percentage of the electorate is ever persuaded to vote differently from its initial impulse, some of the complexity of the strategist's problem becomes evident.

The candidates speculated on the importance of alienated voters and of religious- and ethnic-group voting. They planned their strategies accordingly, although they believed that the political significance of these factors depended upon whether the contest was a primary or a general election.

Assumption 3: Primaries and Party Regulars

I don't think that Ward is conducting the kind of campaign that will win him a primary. . . . He is running as though he were in a final election, relying strictly on mass media . . . television, radio, signs. And I say that what wins a primary is personal contact and get-out-the-vote organization.

MURPHY'S CAMPAIGN MANAGER

We have inherited and have used the town and ward committees and the city committees in all the cities of Massachusetts . . . ; in my judgment this will be one of the more significant things in this election.

WARD'S KEY ADVISER

The Ward-Peabody-Kelly-Kennedy-Piemonte-Murphy-Magaletta contest was a primary election from which Republicans were excluded. The "pros" assume that primary elections attract largely people who are politically interested, the party regulars, and state employees (a very select group, for whom political strategy must be custom made). They further assume that independents tend not to vote in large numbers and that apathetic citizens tend not to vote at all in such elections. These assumptions lead most candidates to believe that issues are less important and campaign organization more important in primary contests than in general elections. A campaign manager put it this way: ". . . Invariably the same people turn out for primaries over and over. You can count on them. If you can concentrate on them, and if you can get a majority of them, you've got the primary." For these reasons, many insiders regarded Ward as distinctly advantaged and Peabody, who was perceived as the "anti-machine" candidate, as disadvantaged in the primary.

Since Ward had the large grass-roots organization plus the convention endorsement, his advisers were understandably confident that he would be difficult, if not impossible, to beat. No one was more concerned with Ward's initial advantages than Peabody's manager, who believed that Ward would receive the support of "the politically affiliated voter, the members of the Democratic town committees and city committees, the state employees and Turnpike employees. . . ."

I base this assumption by driving through the State House parking lot, for example. Now if the election were conducted among people who own cars in the State House parking lot Ward would win it by a substantial majority because most of the cars there have Ward stickers on them. If you drive along the Massachusetts Turnpike, most of the cars at the various exits to the Turnpike that belong to the people who are working on the toll roads, they have Ward stickers on them. This to me indicates that the state employees, the people who are politically dependent upon the state or upon the politician for jobs, will support Ward. The members of the city and town committees probably will give him some support.

Peabody's manager estimated that the party regulars plus their families totalled 100,000 voters.

Peabody's situation, according to his manager, was worsened by the fact that Ward had the endorsement of the convention. This not only made his support by the regulars likely but also "entitled him to first place on the ballot, which in a seven-man contest probably represents 5 per cent of the total vote cast, or approximately 30,000 votes." (Ward's actual margin of victory was smaller than 30,000.)

Ward's key brain-truster concurred, remarking that "The nature of the ballot forces our opponents to run against us." Given these initial advantages, Ward should probably have conducted a non-vituperative campaign, stressing his endorsement and relying upon his organization to get out the vote. He actually intended to do just this, until the "rigged ballot" charge was made. From the point of view of the Boston city-hall regulars, Ward would have had to commit a serious blunder to make the contest even close. The unusual arrangement of names on the ballot, for which Ward as secretary of state was held responsible by his opponents, turned out to be such a blunder. It became the prime issue of the campaign.

The fact that Ward, or Peabody, created a major issue was significant, because issues, as we have pointed out, are largely lacking in the usual primary. A Peabody brain-truster summarized the view of the insiders on this point:

Issues are less important in a primary than they are in an election. . . . By definition, an issue is something which people disagree about, and there are not a terrible lot of things that the various candidates are in strong disagreement about. No one has come out in favor of a sales tax, for example. No one is waging a campaign for birth control or some other issue that might be controversial. The closest thing to a real issue has been the sweepstakes, and, while I think many observers may be underestimating Kelly's appeal to the voters, not too many other candidates have come out strongly against it.

The creation of the ballot issue was therefore crucial to Peabody's effort, because he could use it to attract alienated voters and independents who might otherwise have stayed away from the polls, as they normally do in primaries. Ward, however, still believed that party organization was the key to success in primaries, despite Peabody's attempt to attract habitual nonvoters and independents. Ward had the only large-scale organization in the state, and it paid off. His manager was confident that it would do so:

I think in a primary election you have to be much more concerned with an organization because you are dealing with a smaller vote. Organization is much more important and much more significant . . . for that reason we have spent a great deal of time in building in every town and in every city in Massachusetts at least one coordinator, and in most places a committee who have been running and handling Joe's campaign for not two months but pretty close to a year and a quarter, and this will have its effect on primary day. . . . Without any question we are best organized. . . .

Ward had obviously prepared the groundwork carefully. He had cultivated large numbers of local political leaders who rang doorbells, telephoned voters, drove them to the polls, distributed leaflets, and generally spread the word. This is, an aide commented, "grubby and unglamorous work, but it wins elections." Almost every study of practical politics and political behavior confirms this view. Party organization and personal contact are essential, precisely because large numbers of voters are profoundly disinterested in politics and must be dragged to the polls by party workers. In presidential elections, about 40 per cent of the eligible electorate consistently fails to vote. The turnout for the Kennedy-Nixon election, which was "remarkably high," in the opinion of some political scientists,[22] was only 64.3 per cent.

The turnout in the average state election is considerably lower, and in state primaries an even smaller percentage votes. V. O. Key, Jr., points out, for example, that "in a sample of 15 non-southern states over the period 1926-52, in three out of four primaries not more than 35% of the potential electorate voted in primaries of one or the other of the major parties."[23] The problem is, therefore, to contact as many voters as possible. According to politicians and students of political behavior, there is no substitute for personal contact of the voter with the candidate or a party worker. There are many reasons that the candidate who has a large following of party workers and enthusiastic amateurs who are willing to go out and *talk* is likely to win. Political conversations are probably the most effective method of reaching voters who are undecided during the last few weeks of a campaign: "People," Lazarsfeld notes, "who made up their minds later in the campaign were more likely to mention personal influences in explaining how they formed their final vote decision."[24] Such personal contact is more influential than mass media, he points out, because the listener has not prepared a defense against political conversation, which often arises casually within the context of general conversation. A voter who plans to listen to a specific

[22] Converse *et al., op. cit.,* p. 269.
[23] V. O. Key, Jr., *American State Politics: An Introduction* (New York: Alfred A. Knopf, 1956), p. 34.
[24] Lazarsfeld *et al., op. cit.,* p. 151.

television program or read a particular political speech may prepare himself in advance against being influenced. Personal contact is also more influential than newspapers, radio, or television because of its inherent flexibility.

The clever campaign worker, professional or amateur, can make use of a large number of cues to achieve his end. He can choose the occasion at which to speak. . . . He can adapt his story to what he presumes to be the other's interests and his ability to understand. . . . If in the course of the discussion he discovers some pet convictions, he can try to tie up his argument with them. He can spot the moments when the other is yielding, and so time his best punches.[25]

In order to be effective, these personal contacts need not necessarily be made by professional politicians. Enthusiastic amateurs who know the voter are probably even more influential because they are trusted and familiar. Many citizens vote, not because of the candidate's appeal, but to please a friend. A major asset of professional political workers lies in their ability to enlist the aid of these enthusiastic amateurs who are willing to talk to voters face to face or on the telephone.[26] A friend, of course, is not suspected of having a material stake in the election, whereas a known professional may be. For this reason, a large organization of professionals does not guarantee success; the "pros" must know the voters personally or be able to recruit workers who do. In primaries, in which the turnout is usually small, personal contact takes on added significance, particularly in small towns. This analysis of the importance of personal contact[27] does not imply that the mass media are unimportant, particularly when many voters haven't the vaguest idea who is running. Neither Ward nor Peabody neglected to use formal means of publicity.

Other candidates, who had little or no organization and virtually no money available for the mass media, deceived themselves into thinking that because Ward advertised extensively in newspapers and

[25] *Ibid.,* p. 153.

[26] A post-election analysis prepared for Peabody cited as a significant factor in Peabody's defeat the failure to execute a massive person-to-person telephone marathon.

[27] All the politicians we have spoken to stress the significance of the candidate's shaking hands with the voter, which permits the lucky voter to say that he personally knows the candidate. During the Kennedy-Nixon campaign, James Reston reports in the *New York Times,* he heard a woman say, "You touch him [Kennedy] and I'll touch you."

over the radio and television he was neglecting the grass roots. A Murphy adviser stated:

It's amazing, all this advertising hasn't helped Ward a bit. You can go out and talk to people . . . they don't know who Ward is. A lot of people, a great number of people . . . down in Fall River, for instance, the people down there figured this "Go ForWard" bit was an advertisement for Ward Baking Company. I mean that's just to show you how effective this has been.

This man did not think that Ward was conducting "the kind of campaign that will win him a primary." The key to victory, he asserted, is "to organize as many committees as [one] can in the cities and towns to get out the vote for their candidate on primary day." His belief that the "get-out-the-vote organization" wins primaries is correct. His failure to realize that Ward was doing precisely that is another of the many self-deceptions that the politicians in these elections were given to.

$$* \quad * \quad *$$

We have examined and evaluated the sources of information used by the candidates and the key assumptions that they utilized in the formulation of political strategy. These assumptions and formulations, however, are merely theories; they are not self-executing. To make them operational, the brain-trusters must have money, grass-roots organization, newspaper coverage, platforms, and appealing candidates. These are the tools of the political trade. It is to these "tools" that we turn in Chapter 5.

5.
Money, Mass Media, and the Grass Roots

There is no doubt in my mind that if we had the money Ward is spending on the campaign, we would win this thing quite handily.
PEABODY'S CAMPAIGN MANAGER

The campaign for votes is preceded by a number of subcampaigns: the campaign for money, the campaign for convention delegates, the campaign for the support of locally influential people, and the campaign for the support or, if that is impossible, for the neutrality of the press. Each of these subcampaigns necessitates a special political strategy. Success in these campaigns goes a long way toward ensuring success at the polls. To make the ultimate strategy operational, what is needed is money, organization, access to the press, and, perhaps above all, a candidate who has personal appeal and a willingness to go along with tactics devised by "experts," even though he may perceive them as immoral or personally repugnant. We must now turn to the strategy designed for the subcampaigns. Since it has often been argued that money wins elections, we shall examine first the subcampaign for financial support.

Does Money Win Elections?

Dog-track operators do not let their ideology warp their political judgment; they can do business with either a liberal or a conservative; their chief concern is that they deal with a winner.

.V. O. KEY, JR.[1]

In his exhaustive study *The Costs of Democracy*,[2] Alexander Heard considers the question of whether or not money wins elections. His answer, in the best tradition of modern social science, is equivocal; he cites the victories of Franklin D. Roosevelt and Harry Truman, who had far less money to spend on their campaigns than their Republican adversaries, to illustrate the fact that one can win despite these disadvantages, but he also remarks:

Regardless of the fluctuating significance of financial and nonfinancial elements from one campaign to another, in virtually all campaigns, a basic amount of organizational work, communication through commercial media and getting out the vote must be accomplished if the candidate expects to compete seriously. These things require money. Unless money to meet these minimal, essential expenses is available—regardless of how large or small the amount—contestants lacking it will be decisively handicapped.[3]

Thirty years ago, Louise Overacker expounded the general rule that "expenditures are a reliable index of the outcome of the election."[4] George Lundberg demonstrated that of 156 state and local elections held before the crash of 1929, all but 11 were won by the side that reported the larger campaign expenses.[5] Some scholars have explained the close correspondence between campaign expenditures and victory at the polls during the 'twenties and 'thirties by the fact that money could enable political bosses to build up solid organizations, get dependable workers at the polls, and even buy votes. In most cities today, however, the bosses and the machines,

[1] V. O. Key, Jr., *Politics, Parties, and Pressure Groups* (4th ed.; New York: Thomas Y. Crowell Co., 1958), p. 564.

[2] Alexander Heard, *The Costs of Democracy* (Chapel Hill, N. C.: University of North Carolina Press, 1960).

[3] *Ibid.*, p. 34.

[4] Louise Overacker, "Campaign Funds in a Depression Year," *American Political Science Review*, Vol. 27 (1933), p. 770.

[5] George A. Lundberg, "Campaign Expenditures and Election Results," *Social Forces*, Vol. 6 (1928), pp. 452-57.

for a number of reasons, are pale images of their former selves. "In a day of legal safeguards and altered public attitudes," Heard writes, "the effectiveness of election-day expenditures is no longer so predictable."[6] Nevertheless, V. O. Key, Jr., writes, "A census of all races for all offices—congressional, state, local—would probably show that most, but by no means all, winners had the larger campaign purses."[7] He cautions, however, that "even so the question would remain whether money had turned the trick. Winners have a habit of attracting money."[8]

It is, of course, one thing to have adequate financial resources but quite another to spend them effectively. Although scholars and practicing politicians have argued that the mass media, direct mailings, personal contacts, and field work by party workers can influence public attitudes and alter votes, they do not agree on the relative value of these factors and others which do not cost money. Any investigation of the significance of money in elections is, therefore, clouded with uncertainties. In most elections, there are certain conditions that can affect the outcome but probably cannot be altered by the expenditure of funds—e.g., the personalities of the candidates, the number and devotion of party regulars, the need to deal with controversial issues, and the existence of profound religious or ethnic prejudice. Money cannot buy everything in politics.

Nevertheless, no serious student of politics would deny the enormous significance of money in politics. It is obvious that a perfectly designed strategy is quite useless without the funds necessary to put it into operation. As Heard points out, the need for money depends on the nature of the campaign. The closer the race, the more significant is each bit of campaigning. (The Kennedy-Nixon contest illustrates this point.) In the elections we are analyzing, money was a critical factor for Ward because he was not well known and therefore had to publicize his candidacy. Money was also a critical factor for Peabody because he was forced to appeal to independents and other voters who are usually disinterested in primaries and who therefore tend not to expose themselves to the mass media. Kelly and Kennedy, simply because of their names and the fact that they had

[6] Heard, *op. cit.*, p. 25.
[7] Key, *op. cit.*, p. 564.
[8] *Ibid.* See also below, pp. 238-40.

appeared on the ballot several times, probably needed less exposure on television and radio.

In the elections we studied, every campaign adviser pleaded poverty, with one exception. A Volpe brain-truster reported:

I have never been deprived of any money that I thought was necessary. . . . Being in charge of the public-relations picture and advertising, when I decided on a program to go on . . . I would call up the treasurer and say: "I've got to have this money and I've got to have it in such-and-such a time." Well, they either had it or they went to a bank and borrowed it, and that's the way it was.

Volpe's campaign manager reported, however, "We never in any point in our campaign have had enough money to do all of the things we wanted to." (But, he added, these "things" were "the fringe areas of public relations, special mailings, special banners, additional radio time, ads in weeklies.") Despite the apparent discrepancy between these reports, Volpe obviously had enough money to outadvertise Ward perhaps four or five to one. One of his opponents estimated that Volpe's campaign would "cost 350 to 400 thousand dollars." Other estimates by outsiders ran as high as one million dollars.[9]

It is impossible to prove but probably true that the correlation between the election results and campaign expenditures was very high, in both this primary and the general election. In the opinion of almost every politician who was interviewed, Ward had the largest supply of money of all the Democrats, with Peabody a close second and Kelly a poor third.[10] Piemonte and Murphy had so

---

[9] These estimates are probably much too high. However, the tremendous expense of these campaigns is understandable in view of the cost of television and radio time and of newspaper space. Volpe's public-relations man commented: "I don't think they [the voters] are aware of how expensive television and radio time is." He reported that a 15-minute television program on a Boston station at prime time cost $1800. "But," he said, "there's an added expense that goes with it that in fact exceeds the cost of television time, and that's the announcement in the newspapers that the candidate will be on at a certain hour." A front-page ad in the *Herald-Traveler* cost "7½ dollars a line . . . $105 an inch per column," and the newspapers "charge higher rates for political advertising . . . at least double . . . in some cases triple their normal rates."

[10] A Peabody fund raiser reported that a man "who should be qualified to know . . . says he [Ward] spent no less than $350,000 [in the primary] and I've heard estimates going up to half a million. But Ward will have to file his expenses soon, and if he files them at $200,000 you can be sure that $350,000 is a [laugh] con-

little money that, to all intents and purposes, they merely went through the motions of campaigning. Although his manager anticipated that Piemonte would appear on television "about 25 times," Piemonte actually made very few appearances. The other Democrats were unable to raise sizable sums. Although their opponents imagined that Ward and Peabody had unlimited funds, such, of course, was not the case. Both of them were forced to curtail their planned publicity efforts, particularly Peabody. His manager said after the primary that Ward's financial resources permitted him to contact voters toward the end of the campaign, at the moment that interest in the election was greatest, and that Peabody, who was gaining strength, was unable to counter because his money ran out. He analyzed this facet of the campaign in the following way:

Ward obviously spent more money . . . than any other candidate. This was an important factor in his victory. Having available such a supply of funds permitted Ward to spend freely on signs and other outdoor advertising early in the campaign, maintain a heavy radio, television, and newspaper advertising schedule, *and still put on a splurge in the final days.*

Peabody's manager contended, in an interview before the primary, that his candidate's greatest disadvantage was that

. . . he is not well known throughout the state . . . and we have difficulty raising money to make him better known through mass media. . . . There is a question now whether we will be able to give the candidate the proper amount of time. Now, to give you an example of how important this money is, last Thursday we criticized Ward on this machine-ballot business on a . . . television newscast. Ward came back that night and bought 15 minutes of television time . . . to defend himself. Now this cost a thousand dollars. We just can't throw thousand-dollar bills around

servative estimate." Peabody's manager added, "Ward will spend much more than any other candidate and possibly as much as all the other candidates combined. . . . One candidate has been on television since the first week in August. One candidate has been running ads in the papers throughout the state. One candidate has made many more television appearances than any other candidate. One candidate has many more signs. One candidate has many more bumper stickers. One candidate has many more people on his payroll. That candidate is Ward." Ward did in fact appear on television more than any other candidate. He also purchased more newspaper space and radio time than any of his opponents. One of his adversaries said, "I don't think any of the other candidates have anything approaching what Ward seems to have available to him. He even announced in the newspapers that he has unlimited funds and his words were that he was going to spend it. And I think his words were, or he intimated, that he didn't care where it came from."

like that. We don't have it, and this is the advantage of being adequately financed in the campaign. . . .

One of Peabody's fund raisers analyzed the money problem in slightly different terms:

For the three or four weeks prior to the last ten days of the campaign there never was enough money around and there was never enough potential of bringing it in; and the people started slashing down the strategy. They said, "Well, we can't have any more, we're going to have to cut down the mailings; and the mailings were delayed because the people wanted down payments, and then they didn't know what to do about the TV, and then they had to slash TV. . . . It [the election] wasn't lost because we didn't have enough money. It was lost because the money was not available when it should have been available.[11]

Whether or not Peabody could have won with more money we cannot say. There are many variables in every campaign, but adequate financial backing is obviously a critical factor—in some cases, *the* critical factor. Certainly the lack of money, among other things, eliminated Kennedy, Piemonte, Magaletta, and Murphy as serious contenders. Kelly was able to raise enough money for a modest campaign. After the election, John Francis Kennedy, the apostle of poverty, stated, "I could have demolished the issues of my opponents if I had accepted contributions and gone on TV. I was leading two months before the primary, but when I didn't go on TV and campaign, they spread the story that I couldn't win and weaned away my vote."[12]

It is necessary, however, to place the problem of money in politics within the special context of the Massachusetts electorate, a large segment of which regards opulent campaigning as a sign of the candidate's indebtedness to his contributors. The alienated voter's tendency to equate campaign expenditures with power and "obligations" led Treasurer Kennedy to adopt the slogan: "No contributions—no obligations." In view of the alienated voter's tendency to operate on the guilt-by-contribution theory, Kennedy believed that spending money was "the biggest mistake" a politician in Massachusetts could make. His opponents did not agree. A Volpe brain-

[11] Various Peabody supporters also charged that significant amounts of money had been wasted on ineffective advertising or other projects. The rational allocation of scarce funds may be as important as the size of the campaign chest itself.

[12] *Boston Traveler*, Feb. 13, 1961, p. 12.

truster, for example, taking into account both the cynicism of the electorate and his awareness that organization wins elections and costs money, insisted that he would not have held back on expenditures despite the alienated voters' attitude. "Campaign managers," according to Heard, "lacking certain knowledge, take no chances. They assume it is best to spend the most money and seem to spend the least."[13]

The view of the alienated voter that candidates are obligated to, or even "owned" by, their contributors raises the question of where funds in state elections actually come from. With respect to this question the candidates, campaign managers, public-relations men, and fund raisers were essentially agreed, although their comments have an "everybody's out of step but me" quality. According to them, campaign contributions are either political or nonpolitical, dirty or clean. Political money is money that is given in return for the promise of some future favor—e.g., a judgeship, a contract to build a tunnel. Dirty money is money contributed by elements of the underworld or bookies in return for protection. Obviously, all "dirty" money is "political," but not all "political" contributions are "dirty." The candidates argued that their own funds were nonpolitical and clean but some of them believed that some of the funds of some of their opponents were political and dirty.

Peabody's manager, for example, stated:

We have been getting most of ours from what I would consider nonpolitical sources. We have been getting contributions from old friends of the Peabody family. I'd say that probably 75 per cent of our money came from people who either never gave a contribution to a politician before or have given only to Peabody. We have very little of the so-called political money. We haven't any means of contact with the architects, the engineers, the contractors, the people who do business with the state. I don't say that it is particularly wrong to ask these people for contributions. I think what might be wrong is the manner in which some of them might be asked, the request carrying the implication that if they do not comply with a request for campaign contributions, that they will not be considered for state work, or, conversely, if they make a sizable contribution, that they should be in a favorable position. I think this is bad. We don't have any money from those sources.

He estimated that "probably 50 to 75 per cent" of all state and local

13 Heard, *op. cit.,* p. 27.

campaign funds are "political," adding, "It depends on the candidate."

According to most of the candidates and brain-trusters, contractors and real-estate operators are the major sources of funds. Treasurer Kennedy was certain that

the biggest source of contributions are the contractors; the capital-outlay program of the state lends itself to a lot of work contractors will do, then certainly they've got to give these contractors special preference. Either that or be an ingrate, and I think that if the word got around "there's an ingrate," they'd find the contributions drying up the next time.

He estimated that a "major part" of the funds contributed to gubernatorial candidates came from this source. Candidates for state representative evidently have greater difficulty in obtaining funds. "Of course," Kennedy reported,

when you're dealing with the reps, well, they have to scratch for the money and get it wherever they can, and of course every time they collect the money, then they're collecting obligations at the same time which they either honor or they're an ingrate, and in either case, if they honor them, then they're unfaithful to their duties.

In addition to contractors, Kennedy claimed, bookies play a prominent role in financing campaigns.

Bookies are quite influential and affluent and fat cats for these campaigns. I don't say specifically that any particular candidate is accepting money from the bookies, but some of them I have my suspicions of. . . . They are interested in getting their case fixed up so that they won't have to pay a fine or go to jail, or if they are going to pay a fine, they won't have to pay such a high fine . . . putting two and two together, you can come up with a pretty good opinion that the bookies have got a pretty big influence in the legislature halls and the governing halls of this state.[14]

Kennedy's opinions are apparently shared by others. On November 29, 1961, the Columbia Broadcasting System televised an hour-

---

[14] On the opening day of the Senate investigation into gambling in the United States (August 24, 1961), a headline in the *Boston Herald* read, "$50 Billion Bookie Empire Buys Police, Senators Told." Senator Henry Jackson (D. Wash.) stated, "You and I know what the problem is, they buy off the judge. They buy off the prosecutor and they buy off the law-enforcement officer." Internal-revenue agents cited Boston as one of the five major "layoff" cities in the nation.

long documentary film entitled, "Biography of a Bookie Joint." The film showed

ten Boston policemen entering or leaving an alleged Back Bay bookie joint [ostensibly a key-making shop] while it was in full operation. . . . Photographed with hidden cameras last June 1-3 were eight uniformed officers, a motorcycle officer and a detective attached to headquarters at the time. A total of 1246 persons were counted as they entered the key shop in one day. . . . Police cruisers were shown parked outside a bookie establishment on Massachusetts Avenue with an estimated weekly handle of $25,000.[15]

The film, which was not shown in Boston, was described by the *Christian Science Monitor* as follows:

A carefully documented, hour-long program, it is a story alleging flagrant illegal gambling, police inactivity and delay, threats of physical harm, attempts to bribe public officials, underworld influence on legislators and elections, all climaxing in public cynicism for law enforcement as voiced by one sidewalk citizen on Massachusetts Avenue.[16]

Tom McArdle, former chief counsel of the Massachusetts Crime Commission, was interviewed by CBS and stated that a bookie had offered to give him $250,000 if he would discontinue the commission's investigation of illegal gambling.[17] Harrison Chadwick, a Republican member of the Massachusetts House of Representatives, stated that bookies have contacts with Massachusetts legislators. "In many instances," Chadwick remarked, "bookies are able to throw organizational workers and very considerable finances into a campaign to defeat someone who they feel is hurting their operations."[18]

Kennedy asserted that the police know where bookie joints are located. He described the relation between police and bookies as one of "protection, payments, bribes. . . . It works this way. The average policeman on the beat is more or less told, 'Lay off this place.' If any unauthorized place opens up, they are soon raided and put out of business." An adviser to one of Kennedy's opponents, speaking of the supporters of yet another candidate, said, "The ma-

---

[15] *Boston Herald,* Dec. 1, 1961, p. 1.
[16] *Christian Science Monitor,* Dec. 1, 1961, p. 1.
[17] *Ibid.*
[18] *Boston Herald,* Dec. 2, 1961, p. 1. Chadwick was censured by the House of Representatives for his remarks on the show. He announced his candidacy for lieutenant governor in May 1962.

jority are all anglemen, all, more or less, to come right out and say it, racketmen. . . . You name it [the racket], they've got it."

According to these individuals, the relationship between the candidate and the contributor is mutually beneficial. The winning candidate is in a position to dispense largesse. The return on a successful political investment may be much higher than that on a blue-chip stock. However, return on capital depends upon the size of the investment. Kennedy remarked, "They'll have their agent call up people and say, 'If you give a hundred dollars you are put on the preferred list. If you give a thousand dollars, you're a bond holder."

While the contributor is regarded as an "investor," the candidate, for his part, thinks he must solicit funds from individuals who, as one informant said, "stand to gain something from having given to the governor . . . contractors, engineers, architects, insurance men, bondsmen, lawyers, judges, D.A.'s, professional people . . . large business. I would say that business interests do not come out in the primaries too heavily and I think only the endorsed candidate tends to get the reciprocal [political] money in the primary." The candidates select as potential contributors persons who can profit from political connections. As one politician remarked, "They have to put the old slug in everyone who is willing to cough up, without being too fussy where they got it from. . . ." The process by which a typical candidate raises money was described by one fund raiser as follows:

He would call up the contractor in essence and say this: "I'm running for governor, I'd like your support." And the contractor's argument would be, "I'm awful low on dough right now, you know . . . the company's receipts were not so good, but business picks up around October and it gets mighty good in November." In other words, "In October, if you make it through the primary, we will get a little bit of dough for you, and in November we'll be around to see you." It's just a hard-nosed method of going to reciprocal guys because there are many guys who will do half and more than three quarters of their business with the state. The procedure is to take a list of the people who do business, there are lists of people who do business with the state, there are lists of architects who have been hired by the state, lawyers, and you go down the list. If you're a man of experience let's say, well, I don't know if I should use the word shaking-down in approaching these people. And you tell them, look, dad, you had mighty good relations with the governor in the past two years, but you know, it's not going to be the same guy, and we would awfully like to have you have the same pleasant relationship you used to have.

It must be pointed out, however, that although each respondent attributed the bulk of his opponents' support to political or dirty contributions, each of them reported that many persons who were *not* looking for favors or protection gave *him* money. Referring to his own candidate, a campaign manager reported, "I'm surprised and pleased to find out there are so many people who want to contribute just because they like what [the candidate] stands for, and not in small chunks either, in good-sized substantial amounts."

The naïve may be shocked by these "facts," but there is much evidence to indicate that they are more or less national in application. A balanced view of campaign financing would, of course, have to recognize that political gifts do not necessarily carry influence in proportion to their size and that the motivation for giving may be complex: selfishness is not the only wellspring of human behavior. Some people give because they are concerned about government policy; some give because they feel a deep sense of personal identification with a party or candidate; some give because they feel that it is their civic duty to support the political process with money; and some give to conform to the prevailing mores of their peers or in response to pressure from their employers.[19] Nevertheless, the number of sizable gifts that are made to state and local candidates by individuals who are interested in governmental policy is probably very small because the policy differences between state and local parties are usually negligible; in the case of contested primaries, they are often nonexistent. The citizen who gives one dollar on "Dollars for Democrats Day" will probably not contend that this contribution entitles him to be appointed a U.S. Marshal. He may have given the dollar because a friend asked for it or because he ardently believes in the New Frontier.

Having satisfied, we hope, the need to recognize "clean" contributors, let us try to examine the underlayers of the picture, the parts that are painted over. Heard points out:

Historically two classes of patronage beneficiaries have been especially significant as sources of political money: government contractors and government officials. . . . The government contract has declined as an

[19] See Heard, *op. cit.,* Chap. 4.

item of barter as purchasing procedures have improved. Nineteenth-century practices by which every state government agency bought its own supplies on its own terms opened the doors to corruption. Central purchasing systems have eliminated much of the old waste and peculation and contributions resulting from the compound of bribery and extortion that prevailed here diminished correspondingly. Nevertheless, important exceptions are still found in what central purchasing agents buy—common exclusions include highway materials, educational supplies, perishable goods—and only about half the states have anything like complete centralized systems.[20]

Heard then notes the following:

(1) Officials of corporations holding high federal contracts frequently turn up among reported campaign contributors of $5,000 or more. . . .
(2) In state and local politics more direct connections are observable between contributors and the business they seek.[21]
(3) The current importance of contributions from public employees in financing the political system ought not to be minimized . . . in 1952 state employee contributions in North Carolina supplied around one-half of the $90,000 income of the Democratic state executive committee.[22]

Bearnd, writing on Georgia primaries, notes, "Figures on receipts by major candidates in recent years (1946-54) indicate that at least 50 per cent of the money handled by central headquarters and auxiliary groups comes from highway contractors and liquor dealers."[23] In their *Guide to Pennsylvania Politics,* Cooke and Janosik write, "Competition for state contracts is keen, and individual representatives of business firms vie with one another in the financial support of political parties."[24] It is obvious that contractors, government employees, and business men who have relations with the state are major sources of campaign funds, particularly on the state and local level.

This, however, does not complete the story. The head of the Department of Justice's Special Group on Organized Crime declared

20 *Ibid.*, p. 143.
21 *Ibid.*, p. 144.
22 *Ibid.*, p. 153.
23 Joseph L. Bearnd, *The Role of Campaign Funds in Georgia Primary Elections, 1935-1958* (Macon: The Georgia Journal, Inc., 1958), p. 3.
24 Edward F. Cooke and G. Edward Janosik, *Guide to Pennsylvania Politics,* (New York: Holt, 1957), pp. 89-90.

in 1960, "The underworld gets about $9 billion of the estimated $47 billion [a year] spent illegally on gambling. Fully half of the syndicate's income from gambling is earmarked for protection money paid to police and politicians."[25] The Massachusetts Crime Commission reports that campaign funds are "the most important" of the bonds between the underworld and politicians in the Bay State.[26] Heard, who believes that "the sums involved in organized crime seem to number in the neighborhood of 10 per cent of the national income,"[27] estimates contributions to state and local politics by criminals as follows: "After immersion in the literature of the subject, a guess— and that is what it is—of 15 per cent of expenditures at state and local levels seems as good as any."[28] Moynihan points out that in 1952, according to Heard's estimate, the sums contributed by criminals to state and local politicians would have been $16 million, "ten times the national contributions of organized labor."[29] He adds:

Crime has not only corrupted American government for its own purposes, it has also tended to immobilize government for many other purposes. The problems of the American city, to speak only of that level, are not going to be solved by dimwits whose campaigns are financed by the syndicate. . . . Is there any reason to suppose that the leaders of organized crime are incapable of perceiving that they will be better off if American municipal government remains fragmented, uncoordinated and in the hands, as much as possible, of incompetents?

Before we examine the implications of these facts and theories for political strategy and the political system itself, it is possible to demonstrate that many big contributors in Massachusetts are not motivated by an interest in constructive government policy, or by a deep sense of personal identification with the candidate or the party, or by any sense of civic duty to support the political process. Some of our respondents stated that contributions tended to ebb and flow according to the candidate's chances of winning. We have implied that the problem of adequate financing involves not only raising

[25] Quoted by Daniel P. Moynihan, "The Private Government of Crime," *The Reporter*, Vol. 25, No. 1 (July 6, 1961), p. 14.
[26] Report, Massachusetts Crime Commission, 1955, p. 187.
[27] Heard, *op. cit.*, p. 156.
[28] *Ibid.*, p. 163.
[29] Moynihan, *op. cit.*, p. 18.

money but also having it available at critical junctures during the campaign. For example, a Peabody fund raiser reported:

Now the money, this is an interesting point. . . . We should have been raising money . . . in a steady manner so that more and more and more and more money should have been spent as the campaign went on. In other words, . . . the largest amount of the money, 80 per cent of our money, was supposed to be spent in the last two weeks. So if you were to draw a curve it would look like a straight line on the money. Well, in actual fact, the raising of the money went something on this order, there was a sudden spurt at the start, then there was a tremendously slow period of raising money which went slowly down . . . until almost the end and then there was a tremendous spurt. . . . We actually began to raise more money about two and one half weeks before the end of the campaign. . . . In the last few days of the campaign . . . we had so much money coming in we overspent in Boston, and Ward came out in the television once [and said] on the front page of the paper there were not less than four or five Peabody ads, and he held it up in the television and said, "There's $11,000 that the Peabody organization spent today. Look, they got the dough and they got the machine."

Ward's key adviser noted, just before the November election, "A large amount of our campaign contributions have come in during the last week or ten days, when I think it became abundantly more clear to many that Jack's sweep in Massachusetts was to be very substantial and that in their thinking, if that was to be so, the state ticket very likely was going to get in." Thus money flowed into the Ward camp late in October, when it looked as though Kennedy would be able to pull Ward in. Money also flowed to Peabody near the end of the primary campaign, after a "tremendously slow period" during the middle of the campaign, which preceded Peabody's charge that Ward had rigged the ballot. During this slow period, Peabody had little reason to be optimistic; Ward, as the convention endorsee, obviously had a significant head start, which caused many contributors to rally to his cause. When Peabody began to get a favorable response to the ballot-rigging charge, potential contributors evidently sensed a change and the money started to pour in. In a gross way, it is thus possible to demonstrate that contributions fluctuate according to the contributors' estimates of who is most likely to win.

Some people like to contribute to a winner just for the personal satisfaction of being with a winner; some want political favors and therefore *must* be with the winner. If we consider the estimate of Peabody's manager that 50 to 75 per cent of all contributions to state candidates are political and Heard's "guess" that 15 per cent of the contributions come from organized crime, we have some idea of how much money comes from those who seek a "return" on their investment. Favor seekers must be associated with the winner. Therefore, for some contributors at least, the critical factor is not the candidate's ideology, personality, or even his party affiliation but his likelihood of winning. The contributor's estimate of the candidates' relative popularity determines not only who gets money but also when it is given, for the odds may change. For example, in the primary, the odds on Ward were high following his endorsement by the convention, and they remained so until Peabody made his charge that Ward had rigged the ballot. As the final campaign wore on, many insiders came to believe that Volpe would win. Ward's key adviser said on the day before the election, "I didn't think it was any secret that we in the Ward campaign have had a difficult time raising money."

It would be absurd to argue that the correlation between the odds and campaign contributions is perfect. There is, however, no doubt that for most "big givers," the major question is simply: Who is going to win? It is, of course, possible to "hedge one's bets" by contributing to more than one candidate. An informant reported that this is "standard practice, it's just insurance."

In view of these trends, political money giving may have some of the characteristics of a self-fulfilling prophecy. Many years ago the distinguished sociologist W. I. Thomas noted, "If men define situations as real, they are real in their consequences." In other words, the fact that men assign meaning to a situation itself affects the objective situation. In terms of politics, this means that the candidate who is perceived as having the best chance of winning—whether or not this perception is objectively valid—is likely to receive the bulk of the "political" money, and this in turn increases the likelihood that he will win. Candidates who appear to have little chance of winning will not receive much "political" money. This decreases their chance of winning. The odds on an election, realistic or not, may therefore be a significant factor in the outcome.

We have stressed the belief that money is often the most critical variable in elections. Although he generally disagrees with this view, Heard states that

. . . the necessity for obtaining essential election funds has its most profound importance in the choosing of candidates. The monies can usually be assured, and often can be withheld, by the relatively small corps of political specialists whose job it is to raise money. If a prospective candidate cannot get assurances of the support necessary to meet the basic costs of the campaign, he may as well abandon hope of winning.[30]

Several insiders in Massachusetts politics agree. Referring to the importance of money in the nominating process, one strategist stated: "It would seem to me that many candidates who have solid sources of funds are able to derive voting strength from uncommitted delegates by wooing them assiduously during the two days of the convention." Lieutenant Governor Murphy concurred with this view. "Votes," he said on the day after the convention, "went to the highest bidder."

The implications of this discussion for political strategy and for democracy are frightening, particularly within the context of Massachusetts public life. In view of Massachusetts' long and notorious history of corruption in politics, those who contribute to a candidate's funds are likely to assume that the opportunities for profit from their investment are considerable. As political and dirty money flows into the coffers of the campaign, potential nonpolitical and clean contributions may be driven away. And the more difficult it is to attract clean money, of course, the more candidates find it necessary to rely on dirty money. This cycle, in turn, increases the possibility that the legitimate objectives of government policy will be subverted and that government will serve the desires of venal and self-seeking individuals.[31] The potential candidate who refuses to promise a

30 Heard, *op. cit.*, p. 35.

31 A distinguished political scientist and former mayor of Middlebury, Connecticut, made the following remarks, bearing on this problem. "Upon reflection, it is my firm belief that in so far as party politics interfere with the pursuit of the public interest, it is largely a result of the necessities of campaign finance. Much venality in public life could be abolished or reduced to insignificance if the public would assume responsibility for broadly based campaign financing and would insist on the public auditing and disclosure of all campaign gifts and expenditures. This would not eliminate corruption entirely, for wherever power and money converge, some venality will be found. But our present method of financing political campaigns is, in my estimation, the single most corrupting factor in public life—local, national, and, especially, state" (Stephen K. Bailey, *Ethics and the Politician* [New York: Center for the Study of Democratic Institutions, 1960], p. 7).

payoff in return for financial support is not likely to receive that support. This means that even before the campaign begins a network of promises is likely to be established between those who have a chance of being nominated and the significant contributors. As we have pointed out, the donors of political or dirty money have nothing to gain from good government or intelligent and honest candidates. Indeed, they have a stake in government-by-special-interest, in the maintenance of venal and corrupt officeholders, party bosses, and police forces. These are the implications for democracy of the prevalence of political and dirty money in politics. What of the implications for political strategy?

Candidates who have, willingly or unwillingly, made "deals" with special interests in exchange for financial support may be the type of men who will resort to unethical or illegal tactics during the campaign. The combination of unscrupulous candidates and amoral public-relations men may bring about an age of hidden persuasion, in which the public is manipulated for the benefit of a few. Public relations and public-opinion poll-taking are businesses, and as such they make their services available to the highest bidder. There are public-relations men who have vilified a candidate in one election and worked for him in the next.

Nevertheless, there are a number of factors, some of them inherent in the campaign situation, that may make it impossible to "buy" an election. Some well-heeled candidates may be inept when it comes to planning strategy; other candidates, who may have that sixth political sense, may be hindered in executing strategy by the uneven flow of funds. Some candidates waste sums on irrational or ineffective tactics. Even though big money can buy the best public-relations men and the best pollsters, the fact remains that even the "experts" do not yet know enough about the relative effectiveness of the various mass media in politics or about the "correct" political style to anticipate and control the responses of the electorate with precision.[32] Nor have the pollsters so developed their techniques that

[32] Ward gave an example of the differences among political "pros" concerning the effective use of mass media: "The question of the utilization of television has come into play greatly. . . . My advisers seem to think that I am an effective public speaker before a group but that my effectiveness is almost completely dissipated when I speak on television. . . . [Some] suggest that I should give a fighting speech, that I should attack someone, because they feel that I might be more effective on television if I were attacking. Others feel that I should talk on television as though if I were talking to seven or eight thousand people rather than to a small

they can divine the inner mysteries that motivate many voters. Therefore, although one can say that a candidate who does not have money
is clearly not in the running, it is not so easy to translate money into
votes. Heard has suggested that money "has its greatest impact on
the choice of public officials in the shadow land of our politics where
it is decided who will be a candidate for a party's nomination and
who will not."[33] This leads us to a discussion of the political strategy
involved in obtaining the support of convention delegates and the
party organization.

Party Organization, Patronage, and The Boys

*In communities where we did have a solid organization and where
we were able to acquaint Peabody with the voters . . . our vote held
up well.*

PEABODY'S CAMPAIGN MANAGER

Every politician who has worked his way from errand boy to precinct
captain to ward leader knows that party organization and the personal contact that it makes possible pay off on election day—particularly on primary election day. This is why the candidates and
campaign managers estimated each other's strength primarily in
terms of the size and loyalty of their organizations. It is no accident
that Ward and Peabody received more votes than all their opponents
combined. They had organizations. For this reason, among others,
they feared each other and discounted the opposition.

"Perhaps we are being a bit cavalier in our dismissal of five candidates," Peabody's manager said, "but right from the very start our
opinion has been . . . that if we can beat Ward we will win the election. . . . Therefore we concentrated on beating Ward. Now, the
other five candidates we were never seriously worried about." In
support of this position, he offered a realistic analysis of Ward's
strength:

Ward started sooner. He has more money than the other candidates.
We gather this from his expenditure of money. He has a better organiza-

black eye on a camera. Others feel that I should talk conversationally as if I were
in someone's living room. . . . Everyone has a different opinion and no one knows
what the final conclusion will be."
[33] Heard, *op. cit.*, p. 35.

tion than any other candidate with the possible exception of our own.[34] He does have the endorsement of the convention, and his name is first on the ballot.

In a post-election analysis, he pointed out that Peabody's strength in various cities and towns had varied directly with the strength of his organization. Peabody's fund raisers agreed with this view, attributing his defeat to inadequate "time for the organization to be set up in a calm and effective manner" and the failure of the organization to campaign actively in certain areas. They also pinpointed areas of Peabody strength and weakness in terms of the amount of grassroots politicking that had been done.

The campaign for votes, we have stated, is preceded by two subcampaigns: a campaign for money and a campaign for organizational support. Success in these subcampaigns determines to a large degree the likelihood of success at the polls. Joseph Ward was able to pursue his particular strategy for votes in the primary only because he succeeded in the campaigns for money and the convention endorsement. Since he was relatively unknown prior to the convention, with little or no organization behind him, he had to get the endorsement of the Democratic convention, which would automatically give him a hard core of devoted party workers and make him well known, in order to have a good chance of winning the primary. Piemonte merely formulated the view of all Ward's opponents, and some of his supporters as well, when he remarked that "without the convention he [Ward] wouldn't have got off the ground." Ward's key adviser recognized that the endorsement placed the local town, ward, and city committees at Ward's disposal. "This," he argued, "will be one of the more significant things in the election."

These local committees are the backbone of a statewide organization. They are often crucial, particularly in the smaller towns, where the politically influential people are in everyday contact with the local populace. In the larger cities, local committees are less significant because their members are less likely to know large numbers of voters personally. As Ward's adviser remarked, "In towns, when you have a 35-man town committee in a town that maybe has 2000 population and 500 Democrats of whom 300 are going to

---

[34] Ward's organization was, in fact, considerably larger than Peabody's.

come out, the town committee represents a very strong bloc of voters." He stated:

There are fewer voters to be talked with and be reached by people who may have some association with them and this, of course, is the great advantage in a town. If you have 20 people on a town committee who are with you, and there are only 400 votes in the community, among the 20 people there should be someone who knows each of the . . . 400 voters and who, on a personal basis of having personal knowledge of the candidate's qualifications and programs, can affect the judgment of an individual who other than by that contact may be confused [or] . . . will have no opinion or just not be sufficiently informed. . . . You can take the same ward committee . . . in a ward perhaps going to be around 14,000 votes. Now, those 15 people on the ward committee will be lucky if they themselves know 300 voters. . . . I don't think any Boston ward can be spoken for by any group of political leaders, and I don't think that in the towns they can be spoken for, but you are far more certain that if you know you have the support of the leadership in those communities that it is more likely to represent an actuality in terms of voters that these people can reach, and persuade, and communicate, literally the totality of the vote that you have asked them to try and influence.

In his post-election analysis, Peabody's manager concurred:

While I am inclined to think that the actual work performed by these committees is overestimated, in a seven-man race the importance of the city and town committees was magnified. The committees also were particularly helpful to Ward in the smaller communities of Massachusetts where we simply did not have the time to organize. . . .

The critical campaign for Ward, therefore, was the campaign for convention delegates. His ultimate success in the primary depended upon the effectiveness of his pre-convention strategy. Two dramatically different versions of this strategy were offered, one by some of Ward's opponents, the other by Ward. We have noted that a few days after the convention, Murphy, who expected to get the endorsement, charged that "votes went to the highest bidder" and that the speaker of the Massachusetts House of Representatives had used his political power to "bully and bludgeon" delegates into supporting Ward. He also described the convention as "power politics at its worst." A Murphy brain-truster claimed that Ward built up delegate strength in the following way: "First of all he started out by rigging the ward and town committee fights. His slates were given first position on the ballot." Another campaign adviser agreed that "manipulations took place" with regard to the slates for town and ward committees and also reported that one member of a town committee

. . . abstained from voting at all because of pressures put on him from the State House. . . . They can put all kinds of pressure on a person who is a state employee or is related to a state employee. It's a threat. They can threaten and they do. Another means—where threats failed, where threats were ineffective, outright bribery took place.

Not surprisingly, Ward's description of the strategy by which he won the endorsement of the convention and the support of locally influential people is totally different. According to his brain trust, convention delegates are not won over during the two days of the convention, nor are they or locally influential people up for sale. Rather, the process of wooing support is long, tedious, and frustrating. It is, they argued, based on the potential nominee's ability to communicate to delegates his sense of public service and his interest in them. According to a Ward adviser, Ward's success in developing grass-roots strength was due to the fact that

He recognizes them. He has worked himself in the Democratic party 25 years. He has worked on his own city committee. He has been willing to devote the time and the effort to meet with these people, to give them the recognition, the attention which they have never received, or received from very few in political life. It is very typical and traditional that a month before the primary everybody loves the chairman of the town committee, but nobody talks to him the rest of the two-year period, asks his advice, seeks his support, or gives him a sense of being desired and wanted.

Ward himself supported the theory that recognition, not patronage, is what delegates and influential people chiefly want:

Everybody is interested primarily in the same thing—recognition. From the time my baby is old enough to raise her hands or open her mouth, she says "Mama" or waves. She wants to be recognized. She wants to be picked up. And when a person lies on his death bed at 90 years of age, he wants to make some dramatic exit from this life which will give him recognition, and this seems to be an extraordinarily fundamental human trait, that everybody wants recognition. . . . They are all interested in recognition. So if you give them this recognition, that's all they want, that's all they ask of anybody. Sometimes the touch of a hand, a word, a "hello," is enough for them and they want no more, they ask no more.

When the interviewer pointed out that the classic texts on political parties claim that patronage holds the party together, he retorted angrily:

That's a lot of bunk. That is typical of the cynicism that is creeping into the American scene and which will destroy democracy if it gains very much more favor. The fact is that there are far many more idealistic people who want to see something good come from government than the press or the analysts or the writers give the American public credit for. And to their everlasting credit, the American public will survive, I believe, when all of the analysts and all of the press of the present era have gone down the drain and have been replaced by some others who have equally fallacious conclusions probably.

What impresses and pleases delegates, Ward stated,

. . . is a simple thing and it is a human thing. If a person is a delegate to a convention, he has some sense of prestige and importance. He wants to make up his mind, but of course he is impressed if a candidate comes to see him and talks with him personally, discusses his candidacy, discusses the issues, discusses his program, and persuades the delegate that this particular candidate who has come to see him in his kitchen, in his law office, or his place of business, or in some labor union hall, sees him personally and talks it over with him; usually one who takes that avenue of approach to a delegate can count on having the delegate eventually support him unless his program is something that is diametrically opposed to that in which the delegate believes. . . . I saw them all. There were 1600 delegates and I saw almost every one of the 1600. I could almost call off their names now. If you name a city, I will tell you who the delegates were and how they voted.

Ward also denied vehemently the suggestion that most of the delegates require a commitment from the candidate before they are willing to pledge their vote.

No, no. There is another fallacious proposition that is completely discouraging to anyone in American politics. The fact is that most of these delegates are interested in good government. They don't want any commitments, they don't want anything except to be recognized a little bit. The fact that you can call them by name and say hello to them, the fact that you are willing to listen to what they have to say, the fact that you are willing to discuss issues with them is all that means anything to them. I would say that not more than three or four times in approximately 1200 interviews with delegates, individual interviews with individual delegates on a personalized basis, not more than three or four times did anyone adopt so venal an attitude as to suggest that I should make a commitment to them.

He branded as a "myth" the suggestion that there are key delegates who can control significant blocs of votes.

There is another one of the press creations, that this is all a controlled and dictated proposition, and it is a tragedy that so many intelligent people have succumbed to any such fallacious proposition that you can control anybody's vote. You just can't unless a person works for you, or is economically indebted to you, or unless there is some real and valid reason why he should submit his will to the will of another. It doesn't happen. The average delegate makes up his own mind.

Alienated voters and some of Ward's opponents would no doubt regard this exposition of pre-convention politicking with considerable cynicism. The fact is, however, that Ward's theory of the role of recognition, prestige, and personal contact, although it is probably overstated, has some validity. We have noted the sense of devotion and excitement that seem to erupt in campaign workers when the candidate appears. There are rewards in politics beyond the material, and one of them is recognition. Reichley's analysis of what keeps "the boys" in Philadelphia in politics is quite similar to Ward's. He argues that the politically influential local people—precinct captains, ward bosses, convention delegates—who attempt to deliver the vote claim "to love politics," not primarily because of the favors or graft that are available, but because of the prestige and excitement involved in being politically influential.

One explanation of their motivation would locate "the boys'" essential urge in the factor known as "prestige." The truth is, many intellectuals and many members of the upper class who have come in contact with politicians argue that, for the Irish, Jewish, Italian bright boys who pursue it, politics is a "status-conferring" occupation. . . . [They] could no doubt have earned wealth and even the respect of their fellow men by selling insurance, practicing law, and the like. But the one thing that they could not earn in these ways is a "place" in the community. Politics gives them that. As successful politicians, they can demand deference from the greatest capitalists, the toughest union leaders, the oldest of the old families. The Protestants, on the other hand, the argument continues, have "place" conferred upon them as their natural birthright, and many rise in society through the practice of the more normal professions; it is for this reason that so few Protestants are to be found in the dirty trade of politics. . . .

[The politicians] constitute a separate class—very nearly a governing class—in most of our large cities. They form a circle of consciously powerful men, united in their determination to hold control over the community, and in their conviction that loyalty to the organization is the way in which this control is most readily achieved.[35]

However, Reichley notes that "the boys" make money out of politics, whereas Ward says that "they don't want commitments."

It is our conclusion, after talking to local politicians in Massachusetts, state representatives, convention delegates, and business men who contribute funds to candidates, that some promises are made, that some convention delegates have been bribed at times, that some business men have received contracts in return for contributions, and that some business men who have not contributed have not received contracts. This does not mean that prestige and recognition are not extremely significant factors in motivating individuals in politics. One candidate explained:

Many run because they are lawyers and feel it would help their business. Many run because perhaps they are in some other business, like insurance or something like that, and they figure that it would help their business. But I would say that most of them run because of the honor and prestige of it and most of them I happen to know are not making much money out of it. They'd be doing better in private industry, but they feel like little kings, and it's human nature to want to be king of the hill. I think that is perhaps one of the motivating forces that make people want to run for governor. Why the other candidates will be running all around the town and knocking themselves out so that they are just physical wrecks by the time the campaign is over: the instinctive urge to be king of the hill. I guess it's in all of us.

What about Ward's theory that there are no key convention delegates or "local influentials" who demand patronage in return for their support? If this were true, each candidate would be forced to contact large numbers of delegates; this would diminish the importance, and the bargaining power, of any one delegate. If, on the other hand, a

[35] James Reichley, *The Art of Government* (New York: Fund for the Republic, 1959), pp. 103-05.

small number of delegates or local bosses had the power to sway blocs of votes at the convention, they would be in a position to demand significant rewards from the successful candidate. The fact is that the feudalization of the Democratic party in Massachusetts leaves the average delegate virtually autonomous and weakens the bosses and machines.

Some of Ward's opponents, as we have already noted, did not share his view of the role of patronage and "the organization." One candidate remarked:

Elections are won ordinarily as a result of large organizations, organizational work along strictly political lines, and too often the people who make up the organization are men who are interested in personal advantages. They are like hungry mouths that have to be fed, and the only fodder that can be gathered to feed these mouths is the money that is raised from the taxpayer.

He described the prime "fodder" that the candidate dispenses to the faithful as "negotiated contracts . . . appointments, favors."[36] This candidate declared that it is "Loot, public loot, or the promise of it," that holds the organization together. These organizations are not so strong as they once were, he said, but "there are individual personal machines who try to deliver the vote." According to this informant, these personal machines, based on the influence of one man, "haven't had too much success when the people feel it is a man that they trust running, and they don't pay too much attention to the political bosses."

The question of patronage and the machine has been examined by James MacGregor Burns, President Kennedy's biographer, who has been an observer of many national and Massachusetts state conventions. Of national conventions, Burns writes:

. . . The old-fashioned boss has relatively little influence in the modern national convention. . . . The bosses that are left will not control more than a tiny fraction of the delegates. . . . The people who really wield influence at national conventions are elected officeholders, such as Senators and Governors. Men who have risen to leadership in their states,

[36] This particular candidate said that he had lost elections because he refuses to promise favors in return for support. He explained his choice of a political career as follows: "You might say that I love politics because it keeps one close to the people. I love people and I know of no other way to serve the public or be close to the public than perhaps as a member of the ministry or in some fields of medicine."

who are in a position to dispense favors, jobs, and recognition back home, cannot help exerting influence at the convention, which is organized on the basis of state delegations. . . . But their power is not wholly transferable. They usually cannot deliver a solid delegation to another candidate unless the delegation is for the candidate anyway.[37]

Burns attributes this fact to

. . . the diffusion of power within both national and state parties [which] stems from the looseness of economic and social arrangements, the absence of tight class or ideological lines, the hodge-podge of ethnic, geographical and religious groups in every state. . . . Most of the delegates are subjected to such a profusion of political processes within their states that on important ballots they simply cannot be switched from one candidate to another by the dictates of one leader.[38]

This is, of course, Ward's view. The ethnic, religious, and geographical pluralism of Massachusetts and the fragmentation of the Democratic party in the state lend further credence to the position that a few key delegates cannot determine the convention's outcome and that local bosses cannot deliver large blocs of votes. If local bosses are to have this power, there must be a legacy of party discipline and a core of voters with a strong sense of identification with the party rather than with a particular candidate or issue. Neither of these conditions exists within the Democratic party in Massachusetts.

Burns's remarks, however, refer primarily to national conventions; Ward was talking about state conventions. For years rumors have circulated that delegates to the Democratic state convention of Massachusetts have been bribed or threatened by a candidate. After every convention, someone (usually a defeated candidate) makes such charges. No evidence has appeared in support of these charges. Burns comments that "cash laid on the barrelhead for delegate votes is . . . uncommon [in national conventions], although it may be somewhat more available in state party conventions."[39] The fact remains, however, that Ward, like Senator Kennedy, methodically sought out tremendous numbers of delegates, got to know them personally, and maintained contact with them for months before the election. Peabody did not go to this trouble. The conclusion seems

[37] James MacGregor Burns, "Inside the Big Pow-wow," *New York Times Magazine,* July 10, 1961, p. 1.
[38] *Ibid.,* p. 34.
[39] *Ibid.*

obvious that this strategy helped to win the convention endorsement
for Ward.

The Press and Politics

When they stop writing about you in politics, you are dead.

CLAUDE A. SWANSON[40]

*I think one of the areas where we had the greatest problem has been
getting news in. Now there are some newspapers which you'd hardly
know we were running in.*

A WARD ADVISER

"Visibility," as one "pro" put it, "is the primary asset of a politician." Except for personal appearances, the candidate is visible only
to the extent that the mass media choose to make him so, or to the
degree that he has the resources to pay for television, radio, or newspaper advertising. Newspapers, because of the continuity of their
publication and the "solidity" and permanence of newsprint, can play
a vital role in determining not only the candidate's visibility but also
his "image." The press, which is both feared and courted by candidates, is a significant tool in the execution of political strategy.

It is not uncommon for defeated candidates to trace their misfor-
tune to unfavorable or sparse coverage in the press, to charge that
political reporters are corrupt and editorial writers partisan, or to
emphasize the opposition's control of the press. No doubt a few
newspaper men accept bribes, most publishers are partisan, and the
press is a critical factor in some elections; but solid evidence on the
influence of the press in politics is extremely limited. Much survey
data, however, are available on the types of citizens who expose
themselves to the mass media, and some tentative hypotheses concerning the potential significance of the press in politics may be
based on these data.

Voters who tend most frequently to read, watch, or listen to political reporting are those who are most interested in the election; they

[40] Quoted in Frank R. Kent, *Political Behavior* (New York: William Morrow,
1928), pp. 252-53.

have been found to be relatively well educated, upper income, older, male, and urban.[41] However, "people with most interest were most likely to make their vote decision early and stick to it throughout the campaign . . . people who did most of the reading and listening to the campaign were most impervious to any ideas which might have led them to change their vote."[42] This finding plus two others—that the same people who tend to expose themselves to one media tend to expose themselves to the others as well and that voters tend to expose themselves to the communications of their own party and ignore those of the opposition[43]—indicate how limited the conversion effect of the mass media is likely to be. We should not ignore the fact, however, that a "small minority" do expose themselves to enemy propaganda, and some are converted.[44]

But these reports may underestimate the true significance of the mass media in politics. Most voting studies have examined their impact during a campaign, which lasts, after all, a relatively short period of time. What about the effect of television, radio, and the press during the years between campaigns? "We are also aware," Kurt and Gladys Lang write, "that most of what people know about political life comes to them secondhand—or even thirdhand—through the mass media."[45] In addition to the fact that citizens during a campaign usually select from the mass media only material that is congenial to their preconceptions, "The mass media also structure a larger, non-local reality from which it is hard to escape. The content [over a period of time] filters through, even though people are not directly exposed to it or do not claim to be paying a great deal of attention. There is something obtrusive about what the mass media present, something that makes their influence cumulative."[46] The real significance of television, radio, and the press may well be in their cumulative impact between campaigns. V. O. Key, Jr., suggests that the true effect of the press

[41] Paul Lazarsfeld, Bernard Berelson, and Hazel Gaudet, *The People's Choice* (2nd ed.; New York: Columbia University Press, 1948), Chap. 14.
[42] *Ibid.*, p. 254.
[43] Bernard Berelson, Paul Lazarsfeld, and William McPhee, *Voting* (Chicago: University of Chicago Press, 1954), p. 339.
[44] Lazarsfeld *et al., op. cit.*, p. 96.
[45] Kurt and Gladys Lang, "The Mass Media and Voting," in Eugene Burdick and Arthur J. Brodbeck, eds., *American Voting Behavior* (Glencoe, Ill.: Free Press, 1959), p. 230.
[46] *Ibid.*

. . . is not to be measured solely by its impact on the fortunes of the candidates during the course of a campaign. By steadily hammering their policy predilections, campaign or no campaign, newspapers over the long pull affect the attitudes of their readers, an influence that may be reflected in the voting when an election rolls around. The cumulative education effect of the press in individual communities may become both pervasive and durable.[47]

What about the role of the Massachusetts press, particularly the Boston press, which has a combined circulation of 1,397,000? The overwhelming majority of newspapers in Massachusetts, as in the nation as a whole, are Republican; their editorial pages reflect the standard Republican positions on the welfare state, foreign policy, etc. Only one of the major newspapers in Massachusetts supported Ward during the general election, and most of them refrained from endorsing any of the aspirants during the Democratic primary.

A study of how the Boston newspapers handled the 1956 presidential and state elections may provide background for evaluating the role of the press in the 1960 state elections. Scoble reports that "all five [Boston] newspapers devoted more coverage to the Republican than to the Democratic party"[48] on more than half the days on which he analyzed their content. The *Boston Daily Globe* and the *Boston Herald* gave the Republican party greater coverage more than twice as often as it gave greater coverage to the Democratic party. In terms of net excess of column inches, every Boston newspaper except the *Boston Evening American* favored the Republican party. A comparison with the *New York Times,* however, indicates that the Boston press was less "partisan." In terms of editorial treatment, "all five [Boston] newspapers were overwhelmingly Republican."[49] The political editorials, according to Scoble, "seemed to serve one or both of two purposes: (1) to exploit the opposition's weaknesses, or/and (2) to reassure readers that 'our side's' weaknesses—as pointed out by the opposition—are unreal, not true."[50] With respect to state and local issues and candidates, "The Boston press failed to exploit the editorial as an instrument of intelligence. Such failures . . . tended to enhance the position of the party or candidates pre-

---

[47] Key, *op. cit.,* p. 524.
[48] Harry M. Scoble, *Press and Politics, 1956* (Boston: Boston University Studies in Political Science, No. 3, Oct. 1957), p. 92.
[49] *Ibid.,* p. 96.
[50] *Ibid.,* p. 97.

ferred by the newspapers. Like any individual involved in politics, the Boston newspapers apparently prefer silence and ignorance to discussions with unfavorable implications."[51]

Scoble's criticism of the Boston press is mild compared to that of Peter Braestrup, a *New York Times* reporter who spent one year at Harvard University as a Neiman Fellow. Braestrup claims, "It would be hard to find any large American city that has been less adequately served by its daily newspapers."[52] The Boston press, he says, takes care not to offend its readers and advertisers, for "two of the papers are in debt to large financial institutions and all must compete strenuously to woo the inadequate number of advertisers." It is not surprising, therefore, that "sports and comics get more space than all Washington, international, and Boston news combined."[53]

The *Boston Herald*, whose "board of directors is closely tied to State Street," is predictably conservative and Republican. Its editorial page "reflects the publisher's interests even more than page one."[54] It plays up Republican achievements—both national and state—supports Republican candidates, and takes every opportunity to publicize the shortcomings of Democratic politicians and the corruption in public life. The *Boston Globe* pursues an inoffensive policy which is oriented toward folksy editorials and a little pap for everyone in the family. This minimizes its political effectiveness. A Boston reporter remarked that the editors of the *Globe* "tend to think twice before printing the weather report."[55] A campaign adviser remarked, "I don't think the *Globe* will take a stand on anything. They're so neutral it's ridiculous. I mean they have no opinions on anything." The *Globe* rarely endorses candidates for public office—local, state, or national. The Hearst papers—the *Daily Record* and the *Boston Sunday Advertiser*—tend to support Republican candidates in national elections and Democratic candidates in local elections. They concentrate, according to Braestrup, on the "usual Hearst fare . . . sports, dog racing, comics, lovelorn columnists, priest heroes, J. Edgar Hoover, crime, and girls."[56] The Hearst

---

[51] *Ibid.*, p. 112.
[52] Peter Braestrup, "What the Press Has Done to Boston and Vice Versa," *Harper's Magazine*, Vol. 221, No. 1325 (Oct. 1960), p. 79.
[53] *Ibid.*, p. 82.
[54] *Ibid.*, p. 84.
[55] Quoted in *ibid.*, p. 85.
[56] *Ibid.*, p. 90.

papers have the largest daily circulation in Boston.

The nonpolitical character of much of the Boston press may be somewhat offset by political reporters who are closely affiliated with individual politicians or by reporters who are willing to be bribed. On this point Braestrup writes:

The shabbiest heritage of Boston reporting is the payoff. In May 1954, the *Providence Journal* ran a series of articles telling how ten reporters covering the Massachusetts State House had been paid $60,000 over a four-year period "for services ranging from issuing publicity releases to work on politically appointed legislative committees."

All three Boston newspaper combines were represented, as well as the, State House News Service, a news-gathering pool on Beacon Hill financed by Massachusetts newspapers. The *Journal* went on to show even bigger payoffs from race tracks to Boston sports writers. ("The problem," as one reporter told me, "is that the newspaper managements would rather have the reporter earning extra money on the outside than pay him above scale.")[57]

Volpe's public-relations chief, who is editor of the *Medford Daily Mercury* and the *Malden News,* which are owned in part by Volpe, was quoted as follows in a speech to the Massachusetts Mayors Association: "Some newsmen are on the payrolls of public officials. . . . I deplore the fact that they use the confidence of their editors to plug certain angles. . . . This reaches up to high levels of state government. It is a flagrant example of conflict of interest."[58]

The Boston newspapers are, therefore, either strongly Republican or essentially nonpolitical, while some individual reporters have been, and perhaps still are, affiliated with candidates. Few newspapers, however, fail to publicize prominently the corruption and incompetence that they believe characterizes Massachusetts public life.[59] Only the *Christian Science Monitor* publishes anything resembling serious and balanced political analysis in depth, and its circulation in Boston is only 20,000.

This brief analysis may provide a framework for evaluating the views of the candidates, campaign managers, and public-relations men concerning the role of the press in the 1960 elections. The po-

[57] *Ibid.,* p. 92.

[58] *Christian Science Monitor,* Oct. 14, 1961, p. 10.

[59] Anthony Lewis writes, "A reader of the Boston press can hardly escape the impression that petty chicanery, or worse, is the norm in Massachusetts public life" (*New York Times,* June 19, 1961, p. 1).

liticos had strong ideas about which papers supported whom. None of them disagreed with the view of Volpe's campaign coordinator so far as the general election was concerned. In response to the question "Have you had any trouble getting equal publicity in the papers?" he remarked: "None whatsoever, Professor. Among the Massachusetts daily newspapers there has been only one, the *Haverhill Journal,* that has endorsed Mr. Ward. Every other principal paper either remained neutral or endorsed John Volpe, and a large number of those papers who remained neutral have always been neutral." This fact caused Ward's key adviser much anxiety:

I think one of the areas which we've had the greatest problem in has been getting news in. Now there are some newspapers which you'd hardly know we're running in. I'm told that in the Worcester paper, which is a peculiar situation, they even have pickets going up and down outside the newspaper saying the newspaper's unfair to Joe Ward because of the news coverage they have given.

Asked about his press coverage during the primary campaign, Ward said, "I get none. I get none." This remark is not quite accurate. In his post-election analysis, Peabody's campaign manager wrote: "We purchased a statewide news clipping service for Peabody, Ward, and Murphy, and the results of the clipping service clearly indicated that on a statewide basis, we had much more material [prepared material] used than the other candidates. Ward was second and Murphy a poor third." He added, however: "We shared with other candidates in the primary the difficulty of getting news releases printed in the metropolitan Boston press. I think this may have hurt us more than some of the other candidates because we did have a more efficient flow of news material and statements than the other candidates." A Murphy aide complained that "the newspapers bury Murphy's name in the middle of a group."

In the view of some of his opponents, Ward got a great deal of support in the primary from the Hearst press. How considerable the support was is questionable, but the Hearst papers did give Ward what might be called a mild endorsement. No other Boston paper openly supported any Democratic candidate. Although Ward knew this, he suggested that the press favored Treasurer Kennedy, and for insidious reasons: "I think they feel that . . . if he were to win the primary, they can expose him and destroy him as one who doesn't understand government, who has no background in government, and who stands for things that the Massachusetts electorate would not tolerate." A Murphy adviser concurred with this view so far as the *Boston Herald* was concerned. "I think," he stated, "the *Herald* is going to go for whoever they think Volpe can beat." It is true that the *Boston Herald* and other papers gave Treasurer Kennedy some coverage, but this was probably because a candidate who refuses to campaign or spend money is an oddity. It is much more significant in terms of the responsibility of the press that not one paper discussed the obligation of a candidate for public office to inform the public of his views or pointed out that Kennedy's refusal to campaign (regardless of his reasons) was an act of the highest irresponsibility. The newspapers' failure to perform these duties might have increased Kennedy's chances slightly; in this sense, Ward was correct. Kennedy, by the way, took the view that the press had been fair to him.

The failure of the press to cover certain aspects of a campaign may be as significant a factor in the outcome of an election as what the press does publicize. One example will suffice to illustrate this point. When Judge Paquet heard Peabody's request that Ward be ordered to redesign and reprint the primary ballots, Richard Wallace, a long-time employee of the firm that has printed state ballots since approximately the Civil War, testified that never before in his memory had the firm been asked to print the material under the endorsee's name in larger and bolder type. His statement could have been very damaging to Ward's candidacy. The *Christian Science Monitor* was the only Boston newspaper that gave the story prominent coverage.

We do not believe, however, that the press gave more extensive and favorable coverage to Democratic candidates in the primary who, they thought, would be sitting ducks for Volpe in the general election. We have already noted that some Volpe advisers and Democratic politicians believed that Peabody would have been a formidable opponent for Volpe, if not the most formidable opponent. Yet many papers, in both editorials and news columns, played up the Peabody charges, although, as we have noted, they failed to report in detail the hearing before Judge Paquet.

Regardless of each candidate's view of how the press treated him in the primary campaign, almost all agreed that the press slanted the news, and all the Democrats agreed that the slanting was pro-Republican because the newspapers are owned and controlled by Republicans. The following remark of a Ward aide is typical:

They see things only from their point of view, and . . . they allow themselves to write editorials in their news columns, and the editorials assume that there is only one kind of candidate who can do something wrong and that's a Democrat. . . . I think, however, that they should support them on the editorial page alone. I would further think that they should support them in a reasonably dignified fashion, . . . but I do not think they should utilize their editorial page for the kind of hatchet job which, for example, the *Boston Herald* does and has done in this campaign, to the extent probably of using language which other newspapers wouldn't even reprint for fear that it was libelous.[60]

Ward charged that not only the slanting of news but political alienation as well were due to the ownership of most newspapers by Republicans or Republican institutions. His views, although expressed with more vituperation than those of his primary opponents, are representative of Democratic opinion. When asked why Massachusetts voters were suspicious of politics and politicians (a view which Ward had expressed), he replied:

I think principally the attitude of the press. . . . The erstwhile control of Massachusetts politics by the press and control of politicians by the press, which, of course, is controlled by the great interests, has been traditional in Massachusetts. In recent years the response to the press by the politician and the political arena has not been quite so subservient. This being so, the press has sought to cast out those whom they felt they could not control. When they found that they could not cast them out by attacking their principles, when they found that . . .

---

[60] On this point, a Volpe aide made the following remarks: "I would say that the Massachusetts newspapers are probably—the newspapermen—are probably more predisposed to encourage tough statements in candidates than is typical of, say the *Louisville Courier Journal* or the *Washington Post* or even the *Baltimore Sun*. I can't imagine Charlie Watsizname—oh, Whitehead, White, whatever it is, on the *Baltimore Sun*—encouraging the kind of tough statements by candidates, or even publishing them, that the *Boston Post* used to and even the *Herald* and *Globe* go out of their way to try to get from them. And I think that it certainly is true. Now, whether they reflect the attitude of the constituency or try to create it is hard to say. I think also, however, that in this particular set of circumstances—wherever you have a bitter primary contest—a certain number of the supporters of the defeated aspirants in the opposition party will want you to say the kind of things they feel after the primary; I think this is nearly always true where there is a really bitter primary."

the people were far ahead of the press (the press was conservative and reactionary, and the people were fairly liberal and progressive), . . . the press set up the politician as being egregious, and every time there is a politician who is black, who is dishonest, they single him out and they scream across their black headlines so that the public becomes persuaded that all politicians are alike. . . . There was a time . . . when the press in America was able to control those in government by proferring them favorable publicity and by writing favorable stories to assure themselves of a vote on those matters in which they were interested. And the fact is that today as a result of the rather high caliber of public officials, they are no longer able to do this. The men in government today vote their conscience and their conviction. Moreover, they are responsive to the will of the electorate, . . . and the philosophy of the electorate is far more progressive than the philosophy of the American press.

The press is reactionary [because] the press is controlled by those who are "haves" as opposed to those who are "have nots." The "haves" traditionally want to hold on to what they have. They don't want any change. So they become champions of the status quo. Those who are "have nots," on the other hand, want something better for themselves. . . . On the other hand, the press, which represents the great industrial interests and the great moneyed interests of the Commonwealth, feel that any change may mean that those who have will have less and that . . . there may be a dissemination of wealth. And this being so, they feel that any change is bad. So they become champions of the status quo. . . . This can be cited by book and verse right through all of the sociological progress of the New Deal and the Fair Deal. . . .

Parts of this analysis are clearly valid. The opposition of the national press to the New Deal was notorious. The opposition of the Massachusetts press to many of the Massachusetts Democratic party's social-welfare programs was, and still is, vigorous. In his study of the Boston press during the 1956 presidential campaign, Scoble noted: "Every state-local issue on which . . . newspaper editorials took a stand was an economic issue involving taxation, the business community, and the real or potential advertising interests of the newspapers themselves."[61]

Ward did believe—and this is important for campaign strategy— that opportunities were available to Democratic candidates for off- setting the power of the press:

[61] Scoble, *op. cit.*, p. 109.

The fact is that there is some opposition to the press raised by organized labor on the one hand, raised by the capacity of radio and television, which is expensive but not too greatly expensive. We can meet the challenge of the press through these other media of public dissemination of information, and we certainly can meet them through the media of the great labor unions, which, of course, are interested in employment security.

The significance of television and radio for Democratic candidates who must campaign in communities dominated by a Republican press therefore appears to be very great, for these media are the chief weapons in the Democratic arsenal. However, weapons must be paid for, which fact reminds us once again of the critical importance of money in elections. Ward's remarks, which are not inaccurate within the context of Massachusetts politics, indicate that domination of the political money market (which the Republicans had in the general election) and a favorable press may be a formidable combination. "If it weren't for television, which is an open medium," a key Ward aide remarked, "we would have a very difficult time in getting across the position of the Democratic party in Massachusetts." Paradoxically, Ward's use of television, as we have indicated, contributed to his defeat.

Although some of Ward's opponents also blamed the press for the electorate's cynicism, many of them were much more concerned about the insufficient coverage given to politics by the press. Their concern is justified. Peabody's campaign manager, a professional public-relations man, remarked that "the only group that the Massachusetts newspapers have been treating unfairly has been the voters." His comments on this subject are representative of the opinion of his opponents:

. . . I picked up all three Boston morning papers last Saturday and I learned that a 16-year-old girl had been raped in Indiana. I learned who was leading in the four-ball tournament in the Myopia Country Club. I learned about a shark biting a man off the New Jersey coast, but there was not one line in any of the papers that would give you any indication that ten days hence the voters of this state were going to go to the polls and select the nominees for the United States Senate, for Governor, or other state offices. . . . I don't feel that they devote adequate time and use the best men to ferret out the facts of the campaign. . . .

I don't think newspapers have the right to criticize as vehemently as they sometimes do the caliber of the people who hold public office if they won't go out of their way with their facilities, vast facilities, to adequately report and evaluate the various candidates. Another thing, newspapers very seldom endorse candidates in primaries. Well, in a Democratic state like Massachusetts, especially in heavy Democratic districts, not endorsing a candidate in the primary is tantamount to not endorsing one at all because whoever wins the Democratic primary is going to win the election [sic]. So that I've no criticism as to the way they have been treating our candidate per se, but I do have criticism for the way they failed, let me say, they have failed to utilize their fullest potential in keeping the public as well informed as they could. Not only newspapers but all mass media.

This superficial treatment of politics, in his opinion, stemmed from partly economic causes:

Part of it is that it takes a lot of time for a reporter or a series of reporters to become familiar with the candidates and with the issues and to be knowledgeable with the various areas of the campaign. Newspapers just hesitate to give up their reporters to spend that much time on an election. It is expensive, I suppose.

The lack of reporting in depth and the scant coverage given to politics by the press have important implications for political strategy and the outcome of elections. It is obvious that literate and intelligent candidates who have seriously thought out the issues and developed programs to meet them are put at a disadvantage by an inattentive press—assuming that a receptive and literate public exists or may someday exist. The absence of press coverage is a great leveler. It conceals the inadequacies of incompetent candidates and the attributes of competent candidates. The candidate with the better public-relations men and contacts with reporters enjoys a significant advantage, if the newspapers, as Volpe's public-relations man insisted, simply reprint press releases.

I don't think that the coverage of the gubernatorial campaign has been anything remarkable. I think that it's been largely the handling of press releases from the office of the two candidates without any effort to distill their value or to follow them through to find out what is missing in them. . . . Newspapers have a peculiar responsibility in the community;

they enjoy a great deal of respect in the community. People believe what they read. . . .

Given this situation, the battle of candidates which might take place if the press reported and evaluated the activities, past records, and ideas of the two rivals is replaced by a struggle of competing ad man. A Ward aide pointed out that "the newspapers have a responsibility at least to communicate [press releases]. . . . Through the interchange between candidates, the public has a chance to evaluate." The problem, however, is that the public is evaluating the competence of public-relations men, not candidates. This suggests that a face-to-face debate between the candidates may well be the best technique by which the public can evaluate the competitors, stripped of their protective covering.[62]

Inadequate depth reporting also encourages candidates to advocate irresponsible and utopian programs merely because they may attract votes. Candidates who do this have nothing to fear from an inattentive press, which will not criticize their irresponsibility. Every candidate and campaign manager believed that Kelly would receive many votes ("the idiot vote," one manager called it) because of his position on the lottery, which they all believed was a fraudulent and dangerous proposal. Treasurer Kennedy suggested that "the newspapers are very lax when they have an obviously fraudulent proposition being presented to the voters and they don't make any comment on it." Although some of Kelly's opponents did attempt to expose the lottery, the press failed to take notice of these efforts.

Another example of the irresponsibility of the press and its political effect was provided by Peabody's manager. Although the following account is obviously partisan, it is also factually correct:

I'll give you an example of how hard it is to get a message across. It may be a minor point but, nevertheless, I think it is fairly significant. Joe Ward has got signs around that say he is the official Democrat nominee for governor. Of course, he isn't. The Democratic nominee will be named by the people. He will be elected September 13th. So we issued a press release . . . pointing out that this was not true, that Ward was not the official Democratic nominee, that he was trying to deceive the

62 It does not follow, however, that the better showman is the better statesman. For some very pertinent and thoughtful remarks on face-to-face debates in politics, see Stanley Kelley, Jr., *Political Campaigning* (Washington: The Brookings Institution, 1960), Chap. 3.

public and that this was an actual lie. . . . But none of the Boston papers
would give us a line on it. So it is difficult to get this type of information
across to the voter.

No discussion of the political significance of the Boston press is
complete without some mention of payoffs between candidates and
reporters. We have referred earlier to a series of articles in the *Providence Journal* that reported payoffs to ten reporters covering the
Massachusetts State House for various services to politicians and
"politically appointed legislative committees." These articles appeared in May 1954. Braestrup writes in 1960 that "every newspaper executive I talked to confessed that 'conflict of interest' continues to plague Boston newspapers—with resulting loss of prestige
and self-esteem (if nothing worse) for reporters and their papers."[63]
Precisely what constitutes a conflict of interest for a newspaper man
is difficult to specify. In the course of their daily work, political
reporters come to know most public officials and politicians. From
talking to some of these reporters, it is obvious that they like some
politicians and dislike others, and it is probably inevitable that their
columns will reflect their likes and dislikes. The *Providence Journal,*
however, referred to a grosser and more obvious form of conflict of
interest—the payoff. When we mentioned the series in the *Providence
Journal,* most of the candidates and their aides stated that the payoff
was a thing of the past. "We have no relationship other than the normal relationship with anybody on the Boston newspapers or out-of-
town newspapers, or the State House press corps," one adviser stated.
"There is no one on our payroll; no one receiving payment for
services rendered." One manager said, however, that many reporters
are "venal and corrupt. They want to get paid for every line they put
in and you would have to almost shoot the opposition candidate to
get a line printed in the paper. . . . There are certain political columnists in Boston who are on the payrolls of candidates." He stated that
this was a common practice and that "everybody knows about it."
     Students of the mass media agree that the political impact of tele-
vision, radio, and the press is difficult to determine, although none,
to our knowledge, denies that the media can exert a strong influence
on political attitudes over the long run. Although the candidates

[63] Braestrup, *op. cit.,* p. 92.

talked at length about the relative value of television, radio, and the press for the execution of political strategy, their comments revealed unusual hesitancy and vagueness. Ward, despite his bitter attack on the press, thought that it was a less significant force than it used to be. The higher advertising rates charged to political candidates (payable in advance) forced many of them to use radio, but, as one remarked, "I'm not sure if many people listen." One manager was certain that the mass media in general and the press in particular were unimportant in primaries because of the low level of citizen interest. Another believed that advertising in the metropolitan dailies "is not worth the enormous expense, but it's good in [local] papers . . . in growing suburban areas." He argued that local papers "are more thoroughly read, whereas metropolitan dailies are skimmed." An opponent, however, was convinced that advertisements in local and weekly papers "are not worth the amount of money they cost." Nevertheless, his organization was "forced to advertise in the local papers because [our] supporters get demoralized in local areas if no local ads appear." He also believed that "sound trucks lose more votes than they gain," while one of his rivals reported that "they are useful on primary day to get people out to vote. I don't think they should be used except at rallies and barbecues." Most of the public-relations men agreed that rallies, long radio programs, and the presentation of rallies on television were not really useful.

There was general agreement on the importance of television. Wherever possible, money was spent for brief television programs rather than on radio or newspaper advertising, although the cost greatly limited the use of this medium. There was also widespread agreement that the advertising campaign should reach its peak during the last few days before the election. We have already noted that the uneven flow of campaign contributions made planning of this kind difficult.

Despite the fact that the candidates often disagreed about the relative value of mass media and grass-roots organization, most of them spent the bulk of their funds on advertising, particularly on television. In view of the difficulty of determining which attributes of a candidate will be perceived as attractive by the alienated voter, and in view of the massive disinterest in primary elections customarily exhibited by the electorate, it might have been more rational to spend funds on an attempt to increase the number of local party workers.

The mass media were used in these elections primarily for two purposes: (1) to vilify the opposition, and (2) to advertise the candidate's platforms. This leads us to a discussion of the final tool for the execution of political strategy—the platform. The value of the platform in the struggle for votes may be greatly underestimated by practicing politicians, even though alienated voters tend, consciously at least, to discount it as mere verbiage.

Platforms and Political Style

The closest thing to a real issue has been the sweepstakes.

PEABODY'S CAMPAIGN MANAGER

I think the voters consider the most important issue is honesty in government . . . because for years we haven't had it.

JOHN FRANCIS KENNEDY

Democratic theory presupposes that citizens will vote on the basis of platforms and issues, as well as past party records, economic self-interest, and the personalities of the candidates. Political analysts very often underscore the saliency of issues by interpreting election results in terms of massive shifts in ideology. These analysts assume that a significant number of voters have some idea of a left-right continuum, that they place themselves at some point along the continuum, and that they are aware of the shifting positions of the parties along the continuum. The authors of the most thorough study of the voting behavior of Americans yet published write that the "changes in the partisan vote decision that attract these ideological descriptions rarely exceed a magnitude of 10 per cent of the electorate."[64] This is not to deny the fact that people in different classes hold different positions on political issues or that Republicans and Democrats hold different opinions on a variety of particular issues.[65]

Although few data are available on the significance of issues in state primaries and general elections, it is probably safe to assume

[64] Angus Campbell, Philip E. Converse, Warren E. Miller, and Donald E. Stokes, *The American Voter* (New York: John Wiley and Sons, 1960), p. 259.
[65] Berelson *et al., op. cit.,* pp. 341, 342.

that the ideological divisions that split national parties are much more significant to voters than those that divide state parties. This is particularly true for primary elections within one party, in which the electorate is relatively homogeneous. There are no foreign-policy issues at the state level, disputes over public control of power plants, or the like. State elections probably turn more often on the personality of the candidates or the most recent investigation into scandal than do contests for the presidency. And since American politics is relatively nonideological as compared to the politics of Europe, it is not surprising that even many presidential elections are candidate-oriented rather than party-oriented. We have already indicated that most of the candidates and campaign managers in the 1960 Massachusetts gubernatorial elections assumed that party platforms were more or less insignificant in closed primary elections, although they may be relevant in general elections.

It is clear, however, that Kelly's lottery proposal served a function in the primary. His incredible showing (98,107 votes) indicates that the combination of a "correct" name which has appeared often on the statewide ballot (13 times) and an exciting issue that has a small but significant following can be formidable, particularly in a multicandidate primary. The belief of the politicians that issues are insignificant in primaries may be incorrect. The candidate's problem in a multicandidate election is to differentiate himself from his opponents. Kelly's lottery proposal made his candidacy unique, even though his financial resources were modest in comparison to Ward's and Peabody's. Since the turnout in primary elections is almost always quite small and unrepresentative of the electorate as a whole, a candidate who can appeal strongly to even a tiny proportion of the total electorate stands a good chance of winning. Although Kelly might conceivably have won the primary on the basis of his issue (he received approximately 19% of the primary vote, which was equivalent to 4% of the vote in the general election), his voting base and his issue were so unique that he would probably have been swamped in a general election.[66]

With regard to the issues, Peabody's manager, in a post-election analysis, reversed the position he took when we interviewed him

[66] For an interesting analysis of the unrepresentativeness of those who vote in primaries and the political consequences of this fact, see V. O. Key, Jr., *American State Politics: An Introduction* (New York: Alfred A. Knopf, 1956).

before the primary. The reader will recall that Volpe, the minority-party candidate, attracted many votes by adopting a coalition-of-minorities strategy—that is, by appealing to groups which are customarily Democratic but which are vitally interested in special short-term issues that transcend parties. Peabody's manager sensed the potential value of a coalition-of-minorities platform, *after* the election. He wrote:

In retrospect, I feel it would have been advantageous for us to alter the Peabody program. Instead of having one program divided into six major areas—structure of government; responsibility in government; cities, towns, and suburbs; quality of living; industry and jobs; education—I feel we could have obtained more mileage out of the same material by presenting a variety of programs:
    The Peabody Program for Education
    The Peabody Program for the Aged
    The Peabody Program for Labor
    The Peabody Program for the Suburbs
This would have accentuated the appeal of these programs to the groups we were specifically trying to reach. This might not have made the difference between victory and defeat, but I now believe it would have given us a more effective vehicle for communicating the various facets of our program.

It is worth noting that Senator Kennedy's advance agents during the presidential primaries provided him with material on issues of special interest to voters in particular cities and towns, and that in the primaries he stressed different issues in different cities and states. Granted that the significance of issues is undoubtedly greater in bipartisan general elections than in closed primaries, the evidence indicates that the retrospective remarks of Peabody's manager were probably correct.

This problem, of course, is to determine what issues voters are concerned about. It is on this question that polls may be especially valuable. Commenting on the value of Volpe's polls, his public-relations man stated: "It predicted a tremendous interest in the issue of legalized gambling or a lottery . . . it also showed that as far as the public was concerned, the three principal issues, in this order, were corruption, inept administration, and high taxes. . . . And so we had a guide here." The Volpe forces put this guide to good use in the construction of their coalition-of-minorities strategy. They also used "research." According to Volpe's chief researcher:

[We are] concerned with the preparation of research on communities into which John goes, and that's what's called research here . . . getting information about who the candidates are in that community, what they want said about them, what the employment picture is in that community, things like that—background material for any place that John travels. . . . We've had several position papers which have eventuated in releases or partial releases—code of ethics . . . agriculture . . . highway safety.

In other words, the Volpe forces, by issuing these position papers, did exactly what Peabody's manager suggested that Peabody should have done.

Our post-election survey indicates that very few voters mentioned these issues. This does not mean, however, that Volpe's position papers were ineffective. We have suggested that the message a candidate communicates to the voters when talking about the issues goes beyond the mere content of the speech. Volpe's advisers understood this. One of them, a political scientist, asserted that "style is far more important than content in most issues, most of the time. . . ." He remarked that what was important was

. . . the kind of impression the guy makes. I think this is true of any professional man. Most people don't know, when a lawyer starts advising them, they have no way of judging whether his advice is good or bad. But he makes an impression on them as a guy who knows what he is talking about or a guy who doesn't; as a guy who's too cocksure or a guy who's too humble. In the same way when Joe Ward or John talk to people, some of them think "Well, about Ward, he's a ————," and maybe some of them think he's a patriot. Well, that's a matter of style. . . . The point is that the same style . . . will have a different effect on different people. But it's accumulation of these impressions which no doubt is an important factor in determining the votes of those persons who are swayable.

Thus Volpe's advisers were aware of the latent message that may be communicated to voters by platforms that seem remote and artificial and speeches on issues that appear to be abstract and perhaps boring. In communities where voters, particularly alienated voters, are interested in the personality of candidates, the manner in which a particular issue is presented, as well as the content of the issue, may be particularly important. This suggests that the public-opinion polls, most of which stress the small proportion of ideologues and the great importance of the candidate's personality, may enormously underestimate the significance of issues as a medium for suggesting personality.

✳ ✳ ✳

We have now analyzed the sources of information upon which candidates base their strategic decisions and the resources on which candidates draw to put these decisions into effect. It is obvious that, over and above the particular strategy or the funds or the press contacts available to any party, a vital element in every campaign is the candidate himself. In order to evaluate the role of the candidate and to arrive at some tentative hypotheses concerning the nature of political strategy, we must now turn to the decision-making process itself. In the next chapter, we shall analyze five key decisions taken during these elections: namely, Ward's decision to pursue a nonaggressive strategy in the primary; Peabody's three decisions—not to appeal the "ballot rigging" case to the Supreme Court, not to attack Kelly's lottery proposal, and not to attack Furcolo—and Volpe's decision not to debate Ward on television during the general election. The rationality of these decisions determined, to a large extent, the outcome of these elections.

6.
The
Decision-making
Process

* * *

In campaigns people don't develop a reasoned approach, and the trouble with most analyses of political behavior by political scientists is that they attribute a reasoned working out of things which are not worked out reasonably.

A VOLPE ADVISER

Contrary to the popular stereotype, campaign managers and public-relations men must often deal with voters who are not easily manipulated and with candidates who do not "project the right image," whatever that image may be. As we have observed, the candidate may lack the political style or personality to effectively carry out the optimal strategy for him. The candidate may even refuse to participate in a particular strategy even though his campaign manager argues that he must do so in order to win. His ethnic origin or his religious affiliation may determine where he may (and may not) campaign effectively and how he must present himself. Although the public-relations men often believe that they know what image appeals to the voting public, the fact remains that they often err because many voters are driven by uniquely personal, subjective, and "irrational" needs, which the pollsters are unable to discern. The ambiguous role of the politician in American society and the

difficulty of determining what is attractive to the alienated voter
compound the problems of the campaign manager, who must attempt
to influence the public's image of his candidate and his opponents.
He must often operate, in other words, in a highly uncertain situation, with candidates who refuse to do his bidding and unpredictable
voters. An examination of five critical decisions taken by the gubernatorial candidates in Massachusetts in 1960 may help us to understand the problems of the politicos.

The Strategy of a Frontrunner

*As the frontrunner [in the primary] it has been our determination
that what we had to accomplish was not so much an attack on any
of the individual candidates who are running against us but the
creation of an image of Joe Ward, who is not a state-known figure
. . . to create an image of Joe Ward as a human being, as a public
servant.*

A WARD ADVISER

Joseph Ward developed his political strategy for the primary campaign on the assumption that the endorsement of the Democratic
convention made him the frontrunner. At the beginning of the
campaign this assumption was well founded; it was shared by most
of the insiders in the Democratic party, including several of Ward's
opponents. The fact that Ward was able to raise sizable funds before
the campaign also supported this view.

The strategy of a frontrunner in a primary campaign, particularly
that of a convention endorsee, is relatively simple: He must not so
antagonize his opponents that, should he win, they will refuse to
support him in the general election. He must make himself visible
to the voter. He must develop a grass-roots organization. In the
case of someone who, like Ward, is relatively unknown, he must
stress the importance of party unity, party identification, and discipline. The only subtle calculation that the frontrunner must make
is just how far to go in attacking his opponents. This calculation
depends, of course, on an estimate of how large his lead actually is.

The Ward brain trust assumed that Ward's lead was substantial
because of three "facts": (1) the convention endorsement gave Ward

the support of the organization and first place on the ballot; (2) Ward himself was a physically attractive and articulate candidate; and (3) Ward's opponents had little or no grass-roots organization or lacked personal appeal. These advantages were slightly offset, in the view of the Ward camp, by three other "facts": (1) Ward was not well known in Boston; (2) Kelly had a very appealing issue in the lottery; and (3) as the party endorsee, Ward would probably bear the brunt of whatever political alienation existed in the primary. This appraisal, prior to the ballot-rigging charge by Peabody, was reasonable.

We have already commented on the widespread view that Ward would not have been a serious contender without the convention endorsement. Piemonte remarked that "without the convention he [Ward] wouldn't have got off the ground," although he recognized that because of the prevalent disillusionment with the Democratic party the endorsement "isn't the advantage it could have been." Every candidate and campaign manager believed that the candidate whose name is first on the ballot has a significant advantage. Peabody's manager, as we have noted, estimated that this position was worth "5 per cent of the total vote cast, or approximately 30,000 votes . . . in itself more than the margin of victory." Ward's manager pointed out that the ballot "forces our opponents to run against us." Studies by political scientists support this view.[1]

The convention endorsement also gave Ward the support of the official Democratic town and ward committees, another reason for assuming that he was the frontrunner. We have already discussed the candidates' and campaign managers' views on the importance of grass-roots organization in campaigns, particularly in primary campaigns. Although the Democratic party in Massachusetts is in a condition of incredible disorganization, there is little doubt that the support of the local politicos in most of the small towns of Massachusetts gained many thousands of votes for Ward. Peabody's manager suggested, after the election:

Although the amount of actual work performed by these committees is

[1] See, for example, Leon J. Kamin, "Ethnic and Party Affiliations of Candidates as Determinants of Voting," *Canadian Journal of Psychology*, Vol. 12 (1958), reprinted in S. Sidney Ulmer, ed., *Introductory Readings in Political Behavior* (Chicago: Rand McNally & Co., 1961), p. 69. See also Angus Campbell, Philip E. Converse, Warren E. Miller, and Donald Stokes, *The American Voter* (New York: John Wiley and Sons, 1960), p. 276.

probably overestimated, in a seven-man race the importance of city and
town committees was magnified. . . . These committees were particularly
helpful to Ward in the smaller communities when we simply did not have
time to organize and the only organized effort probably was the work of
the city and town committees.

The second reason for Ward's brain trust's belief that he was the
frontrunner was Ward's political style and ability as a public speaker.
A key adviser stressed this point:

I think the . . . quality that Joe has which makes him really a very adept
person in political life is the wide breadth of his ability to communicate.
There are many who can communicate at the academic level, and there
are many that can communicate with a business group, and many who
can communicate with a laboring group, and another group can get into
a barroom and talk. There aren't too many of them who can go through
all of these groups.

Ward is a forceful and articulate *ex tempore* speaker, with some of
the oratorical brilliance and flourish of the late James Michael Curley. Ward can and does adapt his style and vocabulary to fit his
audience.

Ward's rhetorical facility did not escape the notice of his opponents. In summarizing the reasons that Volpe did not debate Ward
on television, every Volpe adviser mentioned Ward's ability as a
public speaker. One Volpe aide remarked:

Ward has been a criminal attorney much of his life. I don't want to place
the stress on the adjective except for purposes of rhetoric. He's been a
courtroom attorney, let us say, for most of his life, most of his professional
life. He's taught courses in law . . . and clearly he'd be a better debater
than John. There's no question about it. But by the same token, and
by parallel, I'd say that Aaron Burr would be a better debater than
either Thomas Jefferson or George Washington.

The ability to communicate (particularly extemporaneously) is
an important asset in political campaigning; conversely, the inability to communicate is a serious liability. A Peabody aide, analyzing
the weaknesses of his candidate, made this point:

Peabody cannot afford the luxury of making extemporaneous speeches.
He didn't have one single planned speech in the entire campaign; not one
single speech that he had memorized and could go before a group and
really deliver in a forceful public-speaking manner; and I think this hurt

Peabody because I think that while people like his general method and atmosphere and his whole sort of personality, I don't think that his speaking was particularly effective. Now, on the TV it was delivered in a more hammering way because he had a prepared text that he read most of the time. He kept looking up and down, and he didn't really have a speech that he knew and could deliver, not only with sincerity but with great effect. Of course, he's not a person who has great affect. In his previous campaigns his speeches were terrible and in this campaign they were at least passable, so maybe in a future campaign they will be very good. He improved but he was not very effective as a speaker.

One Murphy adviser said, "Regrettably, a lot of people are going for a glamor boy." A colleague explained why Murphy would not appear on televison very often:

He is not the greatest orator and he's not the best-looking candidate and his speeches in the past have tended to be too long and rambling. He has corrected a lot of these things. . . . I don't think it's as important as a lot of people would have you believe in a primary. I think in an election you get great masses of people voting who really have only a superficial knowledge of politics; really superficial, and they would tend to be influenced by this flashy type of campaign more than the ones who vote in the primaries.

These insights are not profound. They simply indicate what every politician knows; namely, that the personality, physical appearance, and political style of a candidate are very significant factors in determining his vote-getting ability. We have already noted that *how* the candidate presents his material may very well be as significant as what he actually presents. However, this begs the question of what speaking style is appealing—and to whom. Ward was an articulate and aggressive speaker, and his opponents respected this, but Volpe's polls and ours indicate that this aggressiveness (Volpe's pollsters call it "raucousness") annoyed and alienated many voters. In a community where political cynicism is widespread, voters stereotype the typical politician as one who is slick, glib, and fast talking. Volpe's relative inarticulateness and Peabody's inability to talk extemporaneously may actually have been hidden assets. It is therefore at least questionable whether Ward's ability as a public speaker helped his candidacy. It is the unpredictability of attractiveness in political style that makes the formulation of political strategy so difficult in an alienated community.

The third "fact" adduced by Ward's brain trust for their assumption that Ward was the frontrunner was the "weaknesses" of his opponents. Here the Ward forces were on solid ground. Realizing that organization at the grass roots counts heavily in primaries, Ward's advisers immediately dismissed Magaletta, Piemonte, and Murphy as serious contenders. Compared to Ward or even to Peabody, these candidates ran mock campaigns. Despite the fact that the appeal of "the name's the same" was imponderable, a key Ward adviser dismissed Treasurer Kennedy's candidacy as well:

. . . more and more people have obviously become . . . convinced that you can't run for president and governor at the same time. I think that, in addition to this, there are many people who are perfectly willing to play a kind of political joke at a lower constitutional level and that this is a way of showing that "we are not going to follow either an endorsed candidate or we are not going to vote on qualifications"—and this is comical and this is funny. But they get kind of concerned and nervous when it gets to a position that obviously affects their lives or the education of their children, or taxes, and so on. . . .

This left Peabody and Kelly as the only other serious contenders. Oddly enough, before the ballot-rigging charges became an issue, the Ward forces also dismissed Peabody's candidacy. One advisor contended:

Chub has a following and he has an organization but it is spotty . . . not that Chub . . . can't do it but because he started so late . . . and because so many of the people whom he formerly had had were in many areas committed to Joe Ward some time ago and some areas would not have been with Chub even if Chub had been earlier. Some of them were committed previously and didn't think he belonged in this field.

Peabody's organization *was* spotty. Unlike Ward, Peabody had not spent months covering the state in order to build up local support. The Ward forces realized that Peabody would probably do well in the suburbs and among independents, and that he would pick up a substantial portion of the anti-Irish vote, but they believed that this would not be enough to win. It was only after the ballot-rigging charge that the Ward forces came to believe that Peabody was a serious threat.

Kelly, however, worried the Ward brain trust. His opponents were aware of the fact that the sweepstakes had much popular support—perhaps enough, in a seven-man contest, to give Kelly the nomination. A Ward adviser put the matter quite bluntly:

We found that in sizable sections of Boston, mostly among the poorer economic units, that Frank Kelly has an ample amount of support—first, on the name, which is a wonderful name for those communities. He is well known. And, secondly, because the issue of a lottery has a kind of false appeal. . . . It is a kind of pie-in-the-sky kind of solution. The people believe that this is a way in which taxes can be lowered and their real-estate tax on their home might be lowered, and their rent might be lowered because somebody else is going to pay for the lottery or they are going to pay for the lottery ticket that wins. And this represents, of course, with the mores we have in Boston, a very acceptable means of raising revenue for so many other charitable functions. They can't see why it isn't an appropriate way to raise funds for government.

Ward himself remarked:

Kelly has a real issue, a real issue. The fact is that a great many people believe that the sweepstakes is a good answer to the problem of government revenue in Massachusetts. They are persuaded that Mr. Kelly is right. . . . I am sure that I have lost votes to Mr. Kelly on this issue.

Several other candidates and campaign managers concurred in this view. Although Peabody's manager dismissed Kelly during the early phases of the campaign, after the election he admitted, "It became apparent in the last ten days of the campaign that Kelly was reaching large numbers of people in the city of Boston with his sweepstakes issue."[2] He believed that Peabody's failure to attack Kelly was a major strategic blunder. Another campaign manager predicted that Kelly would have his greatest strength among "the idiot vote, who are not informed," and that the size of this vote would be considerable.

Although Ward was worried about the appeal of the sweepstakes issue, he continued to pursue the inoffensive strategy that he and his advisers had agreed on for him. A key Ward aide summed up Ward's strategic problem as follows:

As the frontrunner it has been our determination that what we had to accomplish . . . has been to create an image of Joe Ward as a human being, as a public servant, as an individual with training and background and with a program for Massachusetts that can handle and meet the problems

[2] Kelly received a plurality of the votes cast in Boston.

THE POLITICAL STRATEGY

that appear to be of concern to the citizenry, as we have been able to evaluate it, rather than to try to attack and belittle each of our opponents. I think this is one of the major reasons why our campaign has been run on a positive level, why we have spent the time in discussing the issues in the campaign on television and in the newspapers and in brochures, while our other opponents have spent the time running against the convention, or against politicians, against the ballot, against the rigged convention or whatever else they happen to be thinking about; but it all has been essentially against a situation.

Ward decided to ignore Kelly, Treasurer Kennedy, and his other opponents because his brain trust assumed that he would receive "30 to 35 per cent of the vote"[3] and because "Ward had to minimize the disintegration of the Democratic party" in order to prepare for the general election. This strategy was indicated by a realistic evaluation of the situation. Of all possible strategies, that of the frontrunner is probably the easiest to formulate and execute, as long as an unexpected challenge does not arise.

Such a challenge, however, did arise with Peabody's charge that Ward had rigged the ballot. Everyone agreed that Peabody won some votes as a result of the charge, although no one knew just how many. Peabody's manager admitted that the ballot-rigging charge was the only dramatic issue that Peabody had and that it was fortuitous. Ward's aide stated, "I don't know that Peabody's suit has hurt us. I think it probably helped him. . . . It put his name into the newspapers and it may have given him the element in some people's minds as one of the candidates who is strongly opposing us." Ward handled the charge in a forthright manner by telling voters not to vote for him if they thought the ballot was out of order. A Peabody aide observed that this was a shrewd maneuver:

When the ballot issue was hot we were getting the maximum press from it and then in the last few days Ward recouped nicely and his tactic was . . . "Take a look at your ballot and if you think it's wrong, vote for somebody else. Don't vote for me"—and since only 400,000 ballots were in question out of three and one half million, this had a good effect. By that time the press was no longer covering it very much and I'm not sure it helped Peabody.

Nevertheless, during the last few days of the campaign, Ward's faith in his own lead was undoubtedly shaken. His style became more

[3] Ward received 30.2%.

aggressive and his epithets more vituperative. An aide defended this change:

In order to handle some of the backlash of this cynicism in the last few days [we have] called some of the opponents down on what obviously has been a lowering of the level of the campaign to mud-slinging and name-calling and misrepresentations. . . . We have had to take to TV with documented data to repudiate the basic charges that have been made.

On the evening before the election, as we have noted, Ward branded his opponents on television as "six selfish, self-seeking men, interested in their own aggrandizement." He accused Kelly of trying to "make Boston the Las Vegas of the East" and "exposed" the sweepstakes as an attempt "to put Massachusetts in the crime business." Kennedy, he claimed, "sits there winding his watch and waiting for you to be misled. He has nothing but a cynical approach." He castigated Peabody for branding "everyone a rogue and knave except him[self]." It was clear to Ward and his aides that much of the bitterness and resentment created during the primary would redound to Volpe's advantage in November. However, the upsurge of pro-Kelly and pro-Peabody sentiment during the last few days worried them, and they decided that a rebuttal was in order, despite the possibility that an attack would alienate many voters whose support Ward needed in November. In view of his estimate of which of the opposition were actually contenders, however, Ward's attack on "six selfish, self-seeking men" was excessive; singling out Murphy and Kennedy may even have been foolhardy.

This is instructive. The "inoffensive" and "passive" strategy designed for a frontrunner made sense for Ward at first, but the Ward forces were flexible enough to take the offensive against Kelly and Peabody when the situation seemed to require it. Obviously, what one's opponents do affects what one must do. The determination of strategy takes place continuously, in a process of multiple perceptions and responses. It should also be noted that the personality of the candidate is one of the most significant forces involved in this process. Given his assumption that he was the leading candidate, Ward should not have attacked Murphy or Kennedy. He was, however, obviously angered by Murphy's attacks. After the election, a man who is close to Ward said that Ward cannot resist taking an aggressive position even though it may be the wrong thing to do.

Ward's own advisers knew this, but they thought it was an advantage. These observations suggest that the execution of a rational strategy can be frustrated by a candidate whose personality is not compatible with the political style called for by the strategy. Ward's strategy required great restraint; Ward's belligerence made the execution of this strategy impossible.

Before turning to an analysis of three critical decisions taken by Peabody, which will also illustrate the crucial significance of the candidate's personality, it is necessary to examine why Ward did not meet Kelly's challenge by himself advocating a lottery. Ward explained his position as follows:

To meet this challenge is a rather difficult problem because when one is asked does one favor the lottery, if one answers honestly (and in my case I must say that I do not favor a state lottery), I then am placed in a position of having to explain my opposition to something which the public by and large favors. . . . I have to oppose the lottery because there is some question as to the tendency of the people of Massachusetts where gambling is concerned. I don't view gambling as being immoral, but I do view extensive gambling, which infringes on the economic security of the home or the ability of the breadwinner to support his family, as being immoral. I believe that the excesses which gambling can bring may be dangerous and detrimental to familial life, in which I am particularly interested, and for that reason I oppose the state lottery. And, last but not least, I oppose the state going into any kind of a business that it doesn't have to go into. I think it would be kind of a desecration of the Commonwealth's position that it should engage in a gambling business. So for these reasons, and a variety of them, I oppose the state lottery. But to try to explain this to a public that believes the lottery is a great thing, and they believe that maybe they will win, is a rather difficult thing. And İ am sure that I have lost votes to Mr. Kelly on this thing.

This illustrates a type of dilemma in which many candidates in a democratic society find themselves. In theory at least, a high value is placed on moral integrity, and yet in practice a high value is placed on success. The conflict between "Realpolitik" and moral responsibility in politics is, of course, an ancient one. Believing, as Ward apparently did, that the sweepstakes proposal was a popular one, a rational candidate, in Downs's terms, would have weighed the potential gains and losses, regardless of moral considerations, and might have decided that he too should support the sweepstakes.[4] Ward's strong views on the possible effects of a sweepstakes on family life and morality generally prevented him from doing so.

This analysis of Ward's strategy as a frontrunner suggests two tentative hypotheses about political strategy: (1) Strategy must be responsive to the activities and to the relative strength or weakness of the opposition. (It is therefore extremely important that the candidate have accurate information on these matters.) (2) The personality of the candidate may be inimical to the style required for the execution of a particular strategy. Because of these two factors, politicians are not free to select what may be the optimal strategy in theory. An examination of some decisions taken by Peabody, who did not assume that he was a frontrunner, may enable us to refine these hypotheses.

The Strategy of a Challenger

Peabody is the untainted candidate. He is the clean-cut, honest, All-American man. He has got no personality characteristics that are unfavorable. He is not associated with the machine, so-called. He is not affiliated in any way with the present administration. There is nothing that they can pin on him.

PEABODY'S CAMPAIGN MANAGER

Fifty-three days before primary day, Endicott Peabody, a graduate of the Groton School, Harvard College, and Harvard Law School, an All-American football player, and a former member of the governor's council, announced his candidacy for the governorship of Massachusetts. On every subsequent day but one, Peabody toured the state; shook thousands of hands at factories and railroad stations; spoke at tea parties, picnics, and rallies; and gave numerous speeches on television and radio. This frantic but brief effort netted Peabody 157,790 votes (approximately 25 per cent of the total votes cast), or 27,993 fewer than the votes received by Ward, who had been campaigning for several months. After the election, Peabody's manager

---

[4] We do not know if Ward calculated whether he would gain more votes than he would lose by supporting the lottery.

wrote: "We conducted an effective if not successful campaign. Considering the various factors we had against us and the amount of time we had to campaign, I think we did well."

Despite the impractically short period in which he campaigned,[5] Peabody had, in the opinion of his brain trust, several attributes that made it impossible for him to finish less than second: Peabody was not a member of the Democratic machine (he had always been a maverick); he was not part of the Furcolo administration; he did not fit the stereotype of the Boston politician; and he had not been involved in scandal. He was, in their opinion, clean and unassailable and would therefore be perceived as the candidate of reform, the nonpolitician, behind whom suburbanites, independents, and alienated voters could rally. (The problem for Peabody was that suburbanites and independents tend not to vote in primaries, while alienated voters tend to view *all* candidates as crooks and charlatans.) Furthermore, Peabody was a Protestant, and the only Protestant running for governor. Although his brain trust thought that this was both an advantage and a disadvantage, they and their opponents knew that if the Catholic vote was fragmented, Peabody might well be the next governor of Massachusetts. They also hoped to get the votes of Italo-Americans, who, they believed, would support Peabody rather than an Irish candidate. One Peabody adviser made this quite clear:

... The inner circle believed when they put Peabody into the race that he never could have beaten Ward all alone or any other Irish candidate. But one of the things, one of the planned strategies of the race, was that there would be at least three primary opponents and that these would be three Irishmen. Now, the way it looked right after the convention was that this was going to come true, because it seemed as if the only people in the race were going to be Kennedy, Murphy, and Ward, which to my mind would have been very good. Now then, the situation became complicated because ... Piemonte, Magaletta, and Kelly came into the race, and we tried to convince ourselves that this was good except for Piemonte.

Despite their belief that Piemonte would attract the votes of many

---

[5] In his post-mortem analysis of the campaign, Peabody's manager suggested that if Peabody runs again "[he should] make the decision ... well in advance of the actual campaign time. This does not necessarily mean a public announcement ... but Peabody's sights should be trained on the target ... and he should immediately begin activating his organization." In January 1962, Endicott Peabody formally announced his candidacy for the 1962 Democratic gubernatorial nomination.

Italo-Americans who might otherwise have supported Peabody, the Peabody brain trust was very optimistic. However, they did not understimate Ward's strength. They assumed, at the start of the campaign, that Ward was the candidate Peabody had to beat, believing that Ward's endorsement by the convention enormously enhanced his chances of winning. Peabody's manager wrote after the election: "As the campaign progressed, there was never any doubt that Ward remained the candidate to beat." A memorandum prepared for the Peabody staff three weeks before the primary said: "Ward is the man to beat. Don't be confused by any talk to the contrary. If we beat Ward, we win." Thus Peabody's sources of information were accurate enough to show that the contest was really a two-man race. This simplified his strategic problems considerably.

Despite his many assets, Ward was an ideal target for Peabody, given the prevalence of alienated voters and the widespread disgust with the Furcolo administration. As Peabody's manager pointed out, "One of Ward's weaknesses is that he is known as a politician. . . . He's the machine candidate." The Peabody forces also hoped to capitalize on certain inconsistencies between Ward's platform and his legislative record:

He has got a platform in which he advocates greater home rule for the cities and towns. When he was in the legislature he voted against home rule. When he was in the legislature he voted against four or five other measures, measures of that nature which he now advocates—a four-year term for governor, for example. It is part of his program. He was against it when he was in the legislature. These inconsistencies we intend to expose in the next few days. He has made some serious blunders, tactical blunders. I would think the calling himself the official Democratic nominee is something we can expound on in the next few days. His most recent one is probably the worst, on the ballot situation.

This appraisal of Peabody's position called for a double strategy: (1) Peabody had to make himself visible to suburbanites, independents, and alienated Democrats; and (2) he had to assume an aggressive position toward Ward. He could dissipate Ward's initial advantages only by vigorously attacking the inconsistencies in Ward's record, playing up the connection between Ward and the Furcolo administration, reiterating Murphy's version of the proceedings at the Democratic convention, and stigmatizing Ward as the typical politician. Nevertheless, Peabody did not make an all-out assault on Ward or any other candidate—partly because of his own lack of aggression, partly because of "conflict of interest" within the Peabody organization, partly because of inadequate funds, and partly because of serious misjudgment, if not stupidity, on the part of his advisers. We have noted that the rational candidate bases every strategic decision on a cool and deliberate calculation of which alternative will gain the most (and lose the fewest) votes for the minimal expenditure of time, money, and manpower. An analysis of three critical decisions taken by the Peabody camp indicates that coolness and deliberation seldom governed the decision-making process and that many criteria were used other than the rational one Downs describes. One of these decisions was clearly "rational," in our judgment; one was "irrational"; and one we describe to illustrate the difficulty of applying standards of rationality in some instances.

The Decision Not to Appeal the Ballot-Rigging Case

In view of the fact that Kelly had the sweepstakes issue on which to campaign, Ward the convention endorsement, Kennedy the confusing name, Piemonte his Italo-American heritage, and Murphy his promise of no new taxes, it was clear that Peabody needed a dramatic issue. The "rigging" of the ballot was such an issue. Peabody, in taking the case to court, claimed not only that the names on the ballot were arranged in an arbitrary and illegal fashion but also that Ward had given an unprecedented order to the printers to use bolder type for his biographical data. "Obviously," said Peabody's manager, "if type is bigger and bolder it is easier to read. That's why newspapers use headlines in bigger and bolder type." The Peabody forces realized that the form of the ballot provided them with an excellent issue for a number of reasons. Ward, as secretary of state, was legally responsible for the printing of the ballots. The alienated voter would seize on the issue almost joyfully, as confirmation of his wisdom in distrusting politicians. The secret ballot in America is a sacred thing; the charge of "tampering" with the ballot in any way has particularly odious connotations. And there is reason to believe that Americans are often more concerned with procedural regularity than with substantive liberty. McCloskey points out:

The observation was commonly heard during [McCarthy's] heyday that it was not the objectives of the Wisconsin Senator but his methods that deserved censure, and one suspects that this judgment, infuriating though it may be to some, largely accounts for the lapse in his fortunes. A related point has to do with predictable behavior of the American judiciary and the public reaction to that behavior. Can we not hazard the guess that our courts will in times of stress bow to the legislature on substantive issues, but maintain their supervisory activities in the procedural field, and that this discrimination between two kinds of rights be supported by public opinion?[6]

McCloskey's guess suggests that voters would probably be outraged by a procedural irregularity relating to the ballot, that the courts would be likely to look harshly on such an irregularity, and that public opinion would probably support the courts. For these reasons the ballot-rigging issue suited Peabody's needs.

While publicizing the irregular form of the ballot to the limit permitted by his funds, Peabody applied for a writ of mandamus in the Suffolk Superior Court. The writ was denied on September 1 by Judge Wilfred J. Paquet, who made no comment when dismissing the suit. The question then arose as to whether Peabody should appeal the case to the Massachusetts Supreme Court. This was *the* critical decision of the entire campaign for him, and it was an extremely difficult one to make, since there were cogent arguments both for and against appealing. In his election post-mortem, Peabody's campaign manager offered two reasons for not appealing:

1. If we won the case, it almost certainly would delay the primary and would put Peabody in the position of being directly and personally responsible for the primary delay.

2. If the suit were dismissed by the Supreme Court immediately prior to the primary, this could be very damaging to our campaign.

Another Peabody adviser suggested that "The appeal might be rejected on a purely legal ground that the public would not understand . . . that would have whipped Peabody completely. Or else, the Supreme Court would have said yes . . . [but] people would have said that 'Peabody is a sorehead.' You know, the average man . . . wouldn't have understood the intricacies of the law. . . ."

Nevertheless, there was reason to believe that Peabody would

6 Robert McCloskey, "American Political Thought and the Study of Politics," *American Political Science Review*, Vol. 51 (March 1957), p. 126.

have won an appeal and that this would have seriously damaged Ward's chances of winning the primary. According to his campaign manager:

Many of our people felt that there was substantial ground for appeal, that we could . . . carry the case to the Supreme Court and win. . . . It is interesting that the judge in dismissing the suit did not at any time comment on it, didn't say that we were wrong, didn't indicate that there was anything wrong with our legal position or question the soundness of our legal position. . . . The publicity value that could be obtained through an appeal would have helped make Peabody better known and further exposed Ward's tactics; and if we had won the case, although it would have put Peabody in a position for being responsible for delaying the primary, it also would have put Ward in the position of having caused the delay through illegal procedure and arrangement of names.

Although it may be easy in theory to calculate the gains and losses that are likely to result from a particular strategic gambit, in practice, reliable and meaningful information on which to base this calculation is often lacking. There was some reason to believe that Peabody would win an appeal, but his advisers had no grounds for perfect confidence that he would win. There was some reason to believe that winning the case would gain votes for Peabody; on the other hand, there was some reason to believe that he would have lost votes by delaying the primary. Peabody's manager believed that the mere act of appealing would make Peabody well known throughout the state; on the other hand, if his candidate lost the case, it could cost him the election. A vigorous appeal might have created an image of Peabody as a forceful, aggressive candidate defending peoples' rights against an infringer of the rules. This might have increased his vote because alienated voters are particularly concerned with the morality and integrity of candidates. "We felt very, very strongly," one Peabody adviser stated, "that from a—what one would call Peabody—as the spearpoint of the reform movement—that he should not let this tampering with the ballot go, even if it hurt him politically." A victory for Peabody in the Supreme Court would have confirmed the suspicions of alienated voters that Ward was another professional politician. Those who opposed an appeal, however, argued that an adverse decision would clear Ward's name and place Peabody in the position of being the manipulator. The only prediction that the Peabody forces could make with certainty was that the primary would be delayed if Peabody won the appeal. Peabody's manager knew that "the earliest we could have got into the Supreme Court, we figure, would be on Tuesday, the sixth of September, exactly one week before the primary, and it would have been physically impossible to reprint the ballots before the primary. . . ." An official of the firm that printed the ballots told the authors that new ballots could not have been printed and distributed in less than five weeks.

Even this "certainty" has uncertain implications, for a delay in the election might have been advantageous to Peabody. One of Peabody's advisers claimed that as a result of the additional time required for printing the ballot, "1700 candidates on the Democratic ticket and 400 on the Republican would have had their campaigns delayed, additional money would have been required, and the wrath of all politicians in Massachusetts would have been turned on Endicott Peabody." It is by no means certain, however, that these other candidates would have turned their wrath on Peabody. Even if they did, it is impossible to estimate with any certainty how many votes they could have diverted from Peabody. It is our belief that a delay in the election would have antagonized only those voters who were against Peabody anyway. Some of Peabody's opponents might have welcomed a delay because they thought they needed more time to consolidate their strength. Murphy's advisers believed that Murphy had profited from Peabody's suit, and so did Piemonte and Kennedy.

We have presented the pros and cons of this decision to illustrate the difficulties of reaching a rational position on this issue; reasonable men could have argued for or against an appeal because the variables involved in the decision were extremely complex and the information necessary to make a meaningful calculation was unobtainable. It is our belief, however, that this issue should have been resolved in terms of whether Peabody could have won the election without the extra push that a favorable court decision would have provided. One Peabody adviser understood that this was the real question: "I believe that it might have been dangerous to appeal," he said. "Peabody might have lost . . . but it was the one strong chance that Peabody had to knock Ward out of the race completely, and if he had knocked Ward out he would have won." A rational resolution of the problem therefore depended on information relative to whether Peabody or Ward was leading on or about the sixth of

September. If Peabody was in the lead it probably would have been rational for him not to appeal because of the risk of an adverse court decision. If Ward was in the lead, then Peabody should have appealed—regardless of the possibility of an adverse decision or a delay in the election—because Peabody's *only* chance of winning at this point in the campaign lay in a favorable court decision. If Peabody was not in the lead, he had to take this all-or-nothing chance. Many of Peabody's key advisers, however, assumed that he was leading Ward at this point, although the evidence to support this assumption was shaky.

During the first week in September, Peabody's pollsters reported the results of a poll taken the previous week. This poll, which was based on mailed questionnaires, indicated that Peabody was leading Ward, with Kelly running third, Murphy fourth, and Kennedy fifth.[7] On the basis of this poll (plus his own intuition), Peabody's campaign manager believed, according to his post-election report, that "for a day or two, perhaps around Thursday or Friday in the week preceeding the primary [September 8 or 9], we might have actually been ahead." However, the poll deserved little confidence, as we have suggested.[8] The fact of the matter is that the Peabody camp did not know with any degree of certainty whether Peabody was in the lead, but many insiders preferred to believe that he was. They

[7] Volpe's pre-primary poll, which was taken with much greater care than Peabody's polls (and at much greater expense), indicated that Peabody was rapidly gaining on Ward but that Ward was definitely in the lead and would win.

[8] This poll consisted of 4,000 questionnaires mailed to voters in six cities in Massachusetts. According to Peabody's manager, "Ballots were sent to each city approximately in the same proportion as the voting strength in the primary. . . . Seventy-five per cent were sent to Democrats and 25% to independents. Forty per cent were sent to persons with Irish names, 20% to persons with Italian names and 40% to persons whose names were neither Irish nor Italian. In the second poll, Portuguese names were substituted for Italian names in Fall River. Approximately 50% men and 50% women were polled each time." There are many things wrong with this particular sample and with this technique for gathering data. In the first place, mailing questionnaires is not the best method of gathering data since the rate of return is often too small and the returns too unrepresentative to warrant faith in the reliability of the data. A Peabody aide reported to us that "about 8 to 10 per cent" of the questionnaires were returned. This is not enough to be reliable, and the rate of return from the different cities and the different ethnic groups was also uneven. Secondly, it is unlikely that 25% of those who actually voted in the Democratic primary were independents, though it is interesting that the Peabody forces, who counted on receiving the bulk of the independent vote, may have led their pollsters to overweight the sample with independents. Thirdly, it is probable that the proportion of Irish Americans who vote in the Democratic primary is much higher than 40%.

may have accepted the result of the poll as accurate because it fit their preconceptions and needs. One adviser suggested that Peabody and many of his brain-trusters tended to accept as valid any information that permitted them to maintain the nonaggressive posture that suited them temperamentally. This insider said that "overconfidence in the Peabody camp . . . led them to believe that they should not rock the boat."

We have described the differences of opinion that existed among Peabody's advisers concerning the question of whether Peabody should appeal Judge Paquet's decision, and we have attempted to evaluate the reasoning of those who favored an appeal and those who did not. This decision, like many that must be taken during a political campaign, had to be made quickly and on the basis of intuition and guesswork rather than reliable information. Although Peabody's advisers were concerned with many of the variables upon which a rational decision depended, it appears that logic and reason played a minor role when the decision not to appeal was actually taken by the candidate himself. Since we are concerned here with the decision-making process, it might be useful to quote from the report of a Peabody adviser who was present when the decision was taken:

On Thursday morning the ruling came down from Judge Paquet that simply dismissed the petition without any reasons being given. Now, there was an immediate, what I would call upheaval in the Peabody organization . . . the ruling had been made by Paquet and of course the press closed in. They wanted a statement from Peabody immediately and Peabody had been out on the road campaigning . . . he came in and the pressure was real white hot, you know, and nobody knew exactly what we were going to do, whether we were going to appeal or not, and I was at the time raising money but I felt very strongly and I was called up by ———— who felt that we should appeal, so we went up and I said "yes" and he said, "Well, come up here and say so," and I knew that it wasn't part of my job . . . to get involved in top-rank decisions on the campaign. . . . But, on this one, . . . I said, yes, . . . he should appeal and then . . . he [Peabody] was adamant and it was a tense situation in which he did not quite know why but he'd taken his decision. It was an irrevocable decision right then because [the press] was closing in and then there were other people there who were very, very strong for him not to appeal. One of these people was a professor of law . . . I remember distinctly getting extremely mad . . . because [this man] gave me the reason why we shouldn't appeal is that the judges wouldn't come back, they were on vacation, and it just struck me at the time, I can remember it well, that a man who is teaching law . . . had no business to say that if the Supreme Court judges wouldn't come back on such an important matter as an appeal to the Supreme Judicial Court. . . .

This description should dispel any illusion that campaign decisions are taken calmly and deliberately. Key decisions often have to be made on the spot, under extreme pressure, and sometimes in the absence of certain important advisers. Perhaps Peabody let himself be unduly pressured by the press. A real "pro" might have given the newspapermen some vague and noncommital statement pending further deliberation. According to this witness, Peabody took his stand "not quite know[ing] why." Even after Peabody had made a statement to the newspapers, he could have reversed himself. He seems, however, to have regarded this statement as an irrevocable commitment.

Undoubtedly the question of appealing the case to the Supreme Court was extremely complex. Candidates cannot make decisions on the assumption that voters will grasp their significance and implications and deal with them logically. To anticipate the response of a voter to a complex issue may well be beyond the capacity of the wisest professional. However, more accurate information about the relative popularity of Peabody and Ward might have changed the decision or at least elevated it to the status of a considered judgment. In our view, Peabody himself gave a "gut reaction" and wilted when the pressure was on.

The Decision Not to Attack Furcolo

The authors' pre-primary polls and those taken for Volpe indicated that a large segment of the Massachusetts electorate was profoundly disgusted with the Furcolo administration. Furcolo's defeat in the senatorial primary confirmed the accuracy of these findings. Certainly Peabody's brain trust and every other insider knew that a sizable proportion of the electorate disliked Furcolo, who was tagged as a symbol of the degradation and corruption of the Democratic party. Since Ward was a member of the Furcolo administration, albeit an unimportant one, and since Murphy had suggested that Furcolo had been instrumental in Ward's nomination, it was obvious to all that much political capital could be made by attacking Furcolo and associating Ward with him. Oddly enough, both Peabody and Volpe (for different reasons) decided not to follow this course.

In his post-election analysis, Peabody's campaign manager, who considered this decision a tremendous tactical blunder, explained it as follows:

. . . It was not unrecognized that an all-out attack on the present administration, clearly linking Ward with the Furcolo administration, would have been an effective means of reaching the voters. An all-out attack on the Furcolo administration would have permitted us to capitalize to a greater extent than we did on the obviously very strong anti-Furcolo sentiment in Massachusetts. This was discussed and the decision was made not to go all out after the present administration. A prime reason for this decision was the candidate's personal feeling that, as a good Democrat, he should not wage an all-out attack on a Democratic administration, even though this seemed a sure method of winning the nomination.

Peabody himself reported to us that he was basically in agreement with much of Furcolo's program, particularly those aspects dealing with health, education, and welfare, and therefore could not, in good conscience, publicly criticize the governor. These are remarkable statements. If an attack on Furcolo "seemed a sure method of winning the nomination," a rational candidate would have attacked, despite his "personal feelings . . . as a good Democrat" or his attitude toward Furcolo's program. (It is possible, however, that Peabody could have made political capital out of his refusal to attack Furcolo by emphasizing the "irrationality"—i.e., nonpolitical nature—of the decision.)

Certainly there are other reasons for not attacking Furcolo. If both men had won the nominations they sought, Furcolo might have been Peabody's running mate, and an attack on him would have turned out to be embarrassing. However, the optimism inherent in this argument was unwarranted. Until the results of the second poll came in, Peabody had no reason to doubt that Ward was in the lead. The second poll, of highly questionable reliability, merely indicated what Peabody had preferred to believe all along: that he himself was the frontrunner. In view of the highly tenuous situation that existed during the primary, a realist would not have considered, much less taken for granted, the possibility that he would be sharing the ticket with Furcolo.

Some of Peabody's advisers were convinced that their candidate had a positive and nonpolitical image that would be weakened if Peabody stooped to behaving like a typical Massachusetts politician —that is, if he went on the attack. One of his fund raisers defended this position as follows:

In the Powers-Collins fight, Collins attacked Powers because . . . the whole concept there was . . . to get people to vote against him. We felt because first of all the race was a seven-way race and also because Peabody was . . . a positive entity whereas Collins was after all a sort of negativistic entity whom you could vote for only because you were against another guy, we felt rather that this didn't need to be done, . . . the entire organization felt that all we had to do was emphasize our man. We don't have to attack anybody else. We just have to emphasize this guy, he stands out among all the rest anyway, so why attack people. Why get people sore, they'll start calling us a sorehead, they'll start saying we don't play the ball game right.

This argument rests on the shaky premise that the Massachusetts electorate would perceive Peabody as he was perceived by his inner circle—fine and "nonpolitical." Alienated voters, however, as we have noted, tend to regard *all* politicians as corrupt. All candidates, even "nonpolitical" ones, must deal, in one way or another, with this popular stereotype. Furthermore, Peabody actively campaigned for only 53 days—hardly a long enough period to justify the assumption that his name, much less his character, was known to a sizable portion of the electorate.

According to Peabody's fund raiser, there were additional, non-rational factors influencing Peabody's decision not to attack Furcolo:

There were some people that said he should attack . . . the Furcolo administration. . . . Well, this was greatly resisted by an element within our organization which were friendly with Furcolo. . . . Not only were the Furcolo people . . . who were aiding Peabody against [a direct attack on Furcolo], but I think the candidate himself envisaged his campaign quite differently and was not really prepared to come out and vigorously attack anybody except possibly Ward. . . . In my opinion Chub Peabody was so intent on winning this election that he didn't dare do anything really radical. He felt, well, we got a fairly strong campaign, it looks really strong, let's not really go for broke, . . . let's not open up the engine so strong that we'd burn out the cylinders, so to speak. In other words, let's not do anything that might take the chance of boomeranging or go working against us. Let's not try to play double-or-nothing. . . .

That Peabody was surrounded by Furcolo supporters may have been inevitable, since both he and the incumbent belong to the liberal wing of the party, but he should have regarded their advice with some skepticism. Their divided loyalty was obvious to all the other members of the Peabody camp. Even more important, it is clear that Peabody is not a person who enjoys the attack. Thus he "was not really prepared to come out and vigorously attack anybody, except possibly Ward," perhaps because, in the words of an adviser, he is a "personality kid," a likable man who enjoys being liked and is reluctant to incur displeasure in others.

Although strong criticism of Furcolo might have proved embarrassing had he and Peabody been running mates, our analysis of the reasons that Peabody failed to attack this obviously unpopular governor (and through him, Ward) suggests that the decision was irrational. Peabody had much to gain and little to lose from an all-out attack. By assailing Furcolo, he could have made himself the spokesman for discontented Democrats and independents—groups whose support was essential to him. Yet he decided to ignore the governor. Peabody's probably faulty polling data, his loyalty to the party, and his choice of certain advisers who had divided personal loyalties within the party, all contributed to this decision. But, we suggest, the most salient reason lies in Peabody's own nonaggressive predisposition. His essential personality probably would lead him, in most situations, to select the alternative most likely to win friends and least likely to create enemies. He appears to have been afraid of personal embarrassment, the possible dissaproval of friends, and the wrath of rivals.

It is interesting to note, in passing, that Peabody's personal distaste for the attacker's role caused him *not* to pursue the aggressive strategy that would have been rational for him, whereas Ward's pugnacity caused him to abandon the strategy of restraint that would have been rational for him.

The Decision Not to Attack Kelly

At various times during the campaign, it was suggested to Peabody that he attack the lottery proposal as fraudulent, in an attempt to divert votes away from Kelly. Until the last ten days of the campaign, however, Peabody's advisers tended to ignore the sweepstakes issue as a factor in the election. Given their limited financial resources and their belief that Ward was the man to beat, they concentrated their attack on the convention endorsee. Their estimate of the situation changed in the first week of September, when their second poll indicated that Kelly was running a strong third.[9] With the results of the new poll available, Peabody's manager evaluated this new threat:

Kelly will probably run second to Peabody in Boston, possibly he will run first. Kelly will run better in the big cities than in the towns, better among men than among women. . . . [He will be strongest] in the lowest income groups. And this is the same income group that would be hardest hit by a lottery if it ever went through. . . . Kelly is selling a fraud, but he has got people believing it. . . .

Although Peabody's manager didn't believe Kelly's predictions for the Massachusetts sweepstakes,[10] he was shrewd enough to remark that "the closest thing to a real issue has been the sweepstakes. . . . I think many voters may be underestimating Kelly's appeal to the voters." When they received the results of the second poll, therefore, the members of Peabody's brain trust reconsidered the advisability of attacking the lottery.

The decision whether to attack Kelly really depended upon two estimates: (1) Would an attack on Kelly require so much money

[9] This information was especially valuable since no one had had any idea how popular the sweepstakes issue actually was. We believe that, since Peabody's polls were poorly constructed and quite unreliable, this bit of accurate information was turned up simply by chance.

[10] "He claims that the sweepstakes will bring in $600,000,000 a year. There are 2,000,000 wage earners in Massachusetts; that means that each wage earner would have to buy $300 worth of tickets a year, or every family would have to buy $500 worth of tickets, every family would have to spend $10 a week for lottery tickets. . . . He says that people will come from other states to buy them, but you can't send them through the mail and I can't imagine too many people coming from Iowa or Idaho to Massachusetts to buy a lottery ticket. He says that the lottery tickets will sell for three dollars apiece and will be distributed through statewide chartered banks. There are 700 of them in the state; if you break it down, every institution selling tickets would have to sell a lottery ticket every 33 seconds. This hardly seems possible."

and other scarce resources as to weaken future attacks on Ward?
(2) Would the voters whose favorable view of the sweepstakes was
changed by such an attack tend to switch their support to Peabody
rather than to some other candidate?

According to Peabody's manager, the primacy of the ballot-rigging
issue persuaded the Peabody forces to abandon any idea of attacking
Kelly:

> The only major difference of opinion we had was whether we should
> take off after Kelly and expose the lottery for being a fraud. I personally
> felt that we should have until this ballot thing came up, which gave us
> more of an issue. Our polls indicated that Kelly was picking up a lot of
> strength in Boston, and I was concerned that he would pick up more
> strength than was good from our point of view. And so we were debating
> whether we should come and expose . . . the lottery, showing that it is
> really a ridiculous thing. However, the consensus of the advisers at the
> moment was "let it lie," that Kelly really wasn't that serious a threat. And,
> as a matter of fact, before we got too much further on it that same day,
> the news broke on this situation here, the ballot, so that it became almost
> academic.

Another Peabody adviser, who toured the state after the election in
an attempt to find out why Peabody lost, contended that the decision
not to attack Kelly "was completely wrong" because many Kelly
supporters would have switched to Peabody if the sweepstakes had
been exposed. He defended this view as follows:

> . . . Ward got in Boston in 1956, when he ran against McCormack in a
> two-man fight, . . . 37,000 votes. . . . In this fight he received 30,000, so
> Ward slipped because of this multiple race, he slipped 7,000 from his
> maximum. Peabody, on the other hand, in the '58 race received 43,000
> votes in Boston against McCormack. . . . In this race he was only 31,000
> votes, so he slipped 12,000 from his maximum. . . . Those are the votes
> that Kelly stripped away . . . 7,000 from Ward but 12,000 from Peabody.
> . . . My argument is not that [Peabody] is a second choice [for voters].
> My argument is . . . that Ward had reached an absolute maximum and that
> Kelly's appeal to the voters was hurting Peabody, let's say, two votes for
> every one that was hurting Ward. . . . Maybe he [Ward] has a certain
> strength against Peabody 'cause he's an Irishman, but he's also an out-of-
> town man and this is an important thing, I think, in Boston.

There is, of course, no way of proving this argument. Ward may
have reached his maximal strength in Boston, but Kelly probably

took votes away from Murphy and Kennedy as well as Peabody. The areas in which Kelly ran strongly happen to be low-income and predominantly Irish—that is, areas in which Murphy and Kennedy had some appeal. Therefore, an attack on Kelly might have netted Peabody no more than three or four thousand votes, which would not have altered the outcome. Nevertheless, an all-out attack on the lottery might have helped to create an image of Peabody as a forthright and "responsible" candidate among suburbanites and alienated voters, who then might have turned out in the primary and voted for Peabody. After the election, Peabody's manager wrote that they "had sufficient material to explode the lottery myth," and went on to say:

It was my opinion then, and it is now, . . . that we should have been sharply critical of this lottery and exploded the issue. I do not know how a strong attack on the lottery could have cost us any votes and I think it would have gained us some. Kelly's success in the City of Boston— which we had expected to win—indicated to me that he did take votes away from Peabody.

Peabody's manager's analysis of this decision suggests that it was taken in a sober, deliberative fashion. Such, however, was not the case. Another insider described the way in which the matter was considered before the poll results were received:

Various people thought that we should campaign against the sweepstakes. . . . This was one of the decisions that was made in what I would say would be the wrong way to handle a campaign. The pressure was on at the time and we were jumping on Ward and then Kelly came in on the sweepstakes. . . . So anyway they had a meeting and it just so happened that a lot of people came to the meeting who happened to sort of be there; you know, they were walking down the corridor. And this is the sort of thing that you want to avoid in a campaign, obviously, but it was decided then and there, I guess three or four weeks before the end, that we would not hit the sweepstakes issue and that was that. . . . The arguments of course were that Kelly was strong and that we had better hit him, hit against him, and the arguments in favor of it were obvious. The ones against it were that first of all the sweepstakes issue is unimportant, that he's not going to draw very well in the election anyway, that by coming out against the sweepstakes then they would take the heat off of Ward and then put it onto Kelly, that Ward was our principal target, that more and more the election was a two-man race, that . . . what element was for the sweepstakes would then be very anti-Peabody, that there would be a sort of repercussion against Peabody. . . . Nobody really thought it was a real issue, everyone laughed at it. They said, Yah, the old sweepstakes!

This decision, like the decision not to appeal the ballot-rigging issue, was not an easy one to reach. Some of the arguments against attacking Kelly were reasonable. Ward was the leading candidate, and Peabody was running out of money. Even though Peabody probably would not have lost votes by attacking the lottery, an analysis of the areas in which Kelly had strength (lower-middle to lower class) suggests that a sober, moralistic, analytical attack on the lottery probably would have converted very few voters to Peabody's cause. The voters in these districts are probably among the least educated in Boston and the most devoted to the lottery as a panacea for the state.

What is of especial interest, however, is the description of the participants in the decision—"a lot of people . . . who happened to sort of be there; you know, they were walking down the corridor." There was no well-defined group of advisers in the Peabody camp who were aware of the latest polling data and could be held accountable for decisions. It is, of course, possible that some of the people who "happened" to be present when this decision was made were highly competent; it is also possible, however, that they had a special stake in the problem under discussion or were simply not familiar with the over-all situation. The result, according to a Peabody aide, was a haphazard collection of opinions, many of them poorly informed.

The foregoing analysis of the way in which the Peabody group resolved three critical problems suggests some refinements for the tentative hypotheses we noted earlier concerning the nature of the strategic decision-making process. We have pointed out that the rationality of a politician's strategy depends, to a large degree, upon an accurate estimate of the strengths and weaknesses of his opponents, and of himself. If he relies on information gathered by public-opinion polls, it is crucial that the samples be accurately drawn and the polls properly executed. Peabody's polls met neither of these criteria. Essentially by chance, the second poll predicted correctly who would finish third, fourth, and fifth. However, the poll also indicated that Peabody was in the lead. Volpe's pre-primary poll, which was constructed and executed with great care, did show that

Peabody was rapidly gaining, but it left no doubt that Ward was still in the lead. On the basis of their poll, the Peabody brain-trusters were overconfident; they therefore decided not to "do anything really radical," not to "go for broke." Since Peabody probably was never in the lead, his only chance was to "go for broke."

The first hypothesis suggested by the Peabody campaign, then, is simply that amateurish polls can lead to strategic blunders. If a candidate intends to rely on public-opinion polls he should hire professional pollsters and realize that such an undertaking is costly.

The second hypothesis concerns the selection of advisers. Several of Peabody's aides were obviously intensely loyal to Governor Furcolo and therefore urged Peabody not to attack the incumbents. Of all the decisions he had to make, this one should have been the most obvious, since no sound arguments could be presented against the proposition to attack, while the potential gains to be made from an attact were evident. Undivided loyalty is obviously a prerequisite for any brain trust.

The third hypothesis relates to the fact that in political campaigns brain trusts composed of shifting membership, accidentally gathered together, are quite common. Since some of those present when a particular decision is taken may not be familiar with all the pieces of the strategic puzzle, the results may be disastrous. Running a state-wide political campaign for a major office is a big business involving hundreds of thousands of dollars and thousands of workers. The efficient utilization of these resources necessitates a well-defined division of labor and clear lines of responsibility. Not one Democratic candidate had anything resembling an effiicent business organization.[11] Volpe's success, we will suggest, was due in part to the efficient organizational structure that was set up for him. The composition of the brain trust should be stabilized.

We have pointed out that the candidate's personality or convictions may hinder or prevent the execution of a particular tactic, often making the pursuit of a rational strategy impossible. Ward was

[11] Peabody did hire a professional public-relations man to run his campaign. According to two Peabody aides, the campaign manager introduced some system and order into the campaign because he had "the capacity to make the decisions, which have to be made every five minutes in a campaign, rapidly and fairly effectively. He also was able to keep his temper and move under stress without too much indication of that stress." Nevertheless, this professional was unable to run the campaign effectively, for the Peabody camp included several enthusiastic but uninformed amateurs whose views were given considerable weight.

unable to play the firm but passive role called for by his strategists. Similarly, Peabody's personality prevented him from carrying out his most rational strategy. Peabody should have pursued a strategy of attack and counterattack, but he was unable to play an appropriately aggressive part.

Vote the Man, Vote Volpe:
A Strategic Defense

I think it was Richelieu who said in the sixteenth or was it the seventeenth century, something to the effect that "give me six lines of an honest man's biography and I will destroy him."

A VOLPE ADVISER

Having won the primary election, Ward faced the problem of deciding on campaign strategy for the general election. His advisers, convinced that the Massachusetts electorate was interested in the problem of corruption in government to the exclusion of other issues, persuaded him to launch an all-out attack on Volpe's integrity. The chief form of the attack, as we have said, was a series of mock trials conducted on television. Ward also challenged Volpe to debate him on television. "Our strategy," said a Ward adviser, "was to put Mr. Volpe on the defensive, and quickly, and as hard as we could." This strategy confronted John Volpe with a critical question: What is the best way of answering Ward's charges and Ward's challenge to a public debate?

The Volpe forces believed that the outcome of the election depended primarily upon the response of the public to Ward's accusations, since the public was alert to scandal; they assumed that enormous political capital could be made by smear, accusation, and innuendo. Volpe's public-relations man expressed a common opinion when he stated that "the more outrageous they [the charges] are, the more difficult they become to answer." He summarized the fears of the Volpe camp:

I'm also concerned about the difficulty in catching up with Ward's relentless allegations and charges. It's very difficult to answer charges, espe-

cially if you are an honest and truthful man. You start to explain something and people are not interested in your explanation. They are much
more interested in the naked charge and the assumption that evil has
been done. I think that Ward has been extremely clever, extremely
clever in handling this thing. . . . I think the aura of respectability
which he has given these charges, by bringing in a number of lawyers
with him and nod "amen" as each allegation against Volpe was made,
has been partially effective. The process has at least produced a doubt
and confusion in the public mind. I realize the effort was deliberately
made to chip off whatever image of integrity John might have had in the
public mind. It has affected the Volpe vote to some extent, because you
can never catch up with the lies of this kind of accusation.

How and when should Volpe handle these accusations? With the
exception of the professional public-relations men, who favored a
point-by-point rebuttal early in the campaign, members of the brain
trust agreed that Volpe should go on the defensive only once, toward
the end of the campaign, by which time, they believed, Ward's
charges would have become stale, repetitious, and boring. This decision was defended by Volpe's campaign manager:

The major decision that had to be made by this organization was the
timing in answering the Ward distortions. Mr. Ward embarked upon a
program that was totally distorted, or his total focus was to distort and to
slander Mr. Volpe. We made the major decision to wait until Mr. Ward
had told a complete lie; that was the biggest and most important decision
we had to make. We felt that if a man were given time enough to tamper
with the truth that eventually he would tell a lie. . . . Some members of
our staff felt . . . that earlier we should have answered the Ward charges. I
personally objected to that strenuously for the simple reason that if we
had done that it lent credence to the Ward charges and we would have
been on the defensive naturally throughout the entire campaign because
once we started to answer charges then we could never stop, no matter
how ridiculous or far-fetched they may have been. If we had answered,
let's say, the first four, and didn't the fifth, sixth, seventh, or eighth, the
impression would be left in the minds of the voters, "Well, then these
must be true." We would have encouraged Ward, I think, to have gone
looking for more distortions. As it is, I believe, he will finish up the
campaign simply rehashing those that he has made. . . . He overdid it
very early in the game; I think his constant repetition has caused a certain
amount of boredom among the voters and I think that he has invited and
has received a great deal of switching off of his programs. . . . We

allowed almost four weeks of these distortions to go by without answering
them in a big public way. This was in line with my original thesis and
advice to the Volpe group, that as long as the man was repeating himself,
what we should do is wait until he had told a complete, absolute, fundamental lie and then go on the offensive again, or resume the offense and
never get on the defense again.

The results of Volpe's public-opinion poll of independents concerning their response to Ward's television appearances confirmed the
wisdom of this decision.

Having decided to wait four weeks before answering Ward's
charges, the Volpe brain trust had still to face the question of how
they should be answered. Several possibilities were discussed: a
half-hour television presentation by Volpe answering the charges
one by one; the same format with Volpe answering the charges in
general; a series of short (5 to 15 minutes) television presentations
by Volpe, alone or with two or three aides, etc. Since television is
probably the most significant mass medium in politics, since there are
now public-relations specialists who claim to know a great deal about
its proper use for politics, and since so much time during a campaign is spent planning television presentations, we quote the report
of a Volpe adviser on the manner in which the Volpe forces decided
how to present their candidate on television:

We had several different attitudes toward tactics, or strategy, and the
decision was not an easy one to reach. Nobody . . . was really very happy
and very definite that one decision was a better one than the other. Now
my feeling and several other people's feeling was that John could not
carry a speech that long [30 minutes] and retain an audience; it just
simply couldn't be interesting from a tactical standpoint, from a technical standpoint, and that some sort of introduction—hearts-and-flowers-
type introduction by some person of distinction, we thought of a number
of people of that sort as possibilities—saying what a fine guy this fellow
is, Volpe, and then some comments afterwards in which people of some
distinction would ask him questions—might serve to bring out—would
certainly make the program much more interesting, and probably easier
to follow. But this is not an easy thing to do, and practically, I think the
reason we didn't do this was logistic more than anything else: it was just
in terms of the time factor, in terms of the factor of having to brief
people pretty thoroughly who took part in such a program—we finally
didn't get around to it. I believe that John—I'm sure that John at one
time favored some approach in which he was not alone. However, [a

Volpe adviser] was the one person who had a definite, convinced view on this, partly I think because rhetorically he was in love with the line "I am alone with my conscience," which is a perfectly respectable thing. I think [this adviser] could have carried this thing away in 30 minutes. I'm not sure that John did. I'm not sure that he kept his audience. . . . However . . . I . . . expected the thing to go much worse than it did. I think we got a draw, whereas when we read the text of this speech—we didn't have much to do with writing the first version, but we revised— we made many revisions in it after it was initially written, to try to sim- plify it, to make it more interesting; but it went off much better than we thought it would. John did do better than his material there, much better than his material, while he often does worse than his material. . . . No real agreement, just as tonight there is no real agreement yet . . . what kind of people we should have with him, should we try to limit it to 15 minutes, should we have part of the defense by somebody else?

This report suggests that the "science" of public relations for tele- vision, at least as it is practiced in Massachusetts, is not highly developed. It is obvious that there was no consensus on the proper handling of this problem before the presentation; nor were the Volpe forces certain that they had made the right decision after Volpe's television appearance. A key Volpe adviser expressed many doubts concerning the effectiveness of Volpe's reply:

I think that the decision to wait until all of Ward's charges were in and to answer them at one time was a good decision. But I'm not certain that the people listened to or read the answers, or once having read or listened to them had things clarified in their own minds, because the im- pact of the allegations themselves is something to be recognized and once the impact is there, I'm not certain that the normal citizen follows things closely enough to realize that a complete and responsive answer has been made to the charges.

When Volpe's brain trust decided to put Volpe on television by himself to answer the charges, they also decided not to accept Ward's challenge to debate on television. There was obviously some danger in turning down the challenge, since Ward could then claim (and did) that a candidate who will not debate his opponent in public is not worthy of support in a democratic society that values the open and free exchange of ideas. Ward could also allege that Volpe's refusal to debate the charges was a sure indication of his guilt. The candidate himself, a few of his close friends, and some of the profes-

sional public-relations men employed by Volpe were strongly in favor
of the debate. Every other member of the inner circle felt that a
debate would have been disastrous. It is worth examining how this
conflict was resolved because it reveals the interplay between the
candidate's ego, the orientation of public-relations men toward political campaigning, and the insiders' unwillingness to permit their
anger toward the opposition to interfere with their political sixth
sense. One Volpe adviser explained Volpe's desire to debate Ward:

. . . the natural feeling, you know. He's a—pugnacious, maybe too—
not have quite the flavor I want—but he's a guy who meets challenges
on the whole, who has met challenges; that's how he is. In the kind of
industry he's in, with the kind of background, obviously he wouldn't
have got ahead unless he had met a number of challenges and I think it
took a good deal of dissuasion—I think his immediate response was to
meet the challenge, which is the natural thing in a person of his particular background and orientation. I think also he has more confidence
in himself—perhaps he has confidence in himself to the verge of a fault,
which is a fault on the right side—but still . . . I think he probably
didn't realize what most of his associates thought—that it was very
likely that Ward would put him into a "Have you stopped beating your
wife?" situation which he couldn't really answer.

Another brain-truster claimed that Ward's attack "has hurt John. I
mean it has hurt him inside."

In addition to the candidate, the public-relations council also
favored the debate. Volpe's campaign manager admitted that a
serious disagreement arose between the public-relations men and
himself on this problem:

. . . Those of our staff who were mostly concerned with publicity and its
impact on the public felt that [the debate] would have a high public-
relations value. This, obviously, is true. Where we disagreed was in the
area of its political value. Mr. Volpe is not a debater, he is a businessman. He is used to making responsible, documented decisions, but
frankly, he is not a quick debater. We felt that no political good could
come from a debate with Mr. Ward and that Mr. Volpe would look
poorly in contrast.

The public-relations men, according to another Volpe aide,

. . . are always trying to get the maximum coverage and the maximum—
you know—number of people listening, and so forth, and that may not

be what you wanted to get in all kinds of circumstances. They have their own ideas—they want to make Ward irritated. Well, that isn't the way you win campaigns, necessarily. They want some programs just to make Ward irritated, which, unless you figure out what Ward will do when he's irritated, doesn't necessarily do you any good.

It is obvious that a debate between Ward and Volpe would have had enormous publicity, but the question was whether such publicity would be favorable or adverse for Volpe. The answer depends on an estimate of the candidate's ability as a debater and on the problem inherent in answering charges (Volpe inevitably would have been on the defensive). Those in the Volpe organization with political experience had no doubt about Ward's superiority as a public debater, and they knew that the aggressor in politics usually has the advantage. This is why they urged that Ward's offer be turned down. Public-relations men evidently think primarily in terms of maximal coverage, but such coverage might not have been advantageous for Volpe in the circumstances. We know that committed voters tend to expose themselves only to the propaganda of their own party; however, Volpe's pollsters had reported that Ward's television appearances were harming him among the uncommitted, the independents. Further, the authors' public-opinion polls indicate that a significant number of voters were so disillusioned with the administration that, regardless of what Ward said, they were going to vote against the Democratic candidate. In a sense, it did not matter who the Republican candidate was, since he would probably retain the votes of Republican regulars. Volpe was gaining the votes of the independents through Ward's blunder, and he would profit from the estimated defection of Democrats from the current administration. If, then, Volpe was in fact a poor debater,[12] and if it was difficult or impossible to answer the kinds of allegation Ward made, it was rational that Volpe should have been prevented from debating Ward, despite the promise of wide publicity. In a sense, one way in which Ward's television trials of Volpe failed was in not provoking Volpe to attempt to answer the charges defensively, one by one or in debate. Thus the trial served as elaborate publicity for Volpe's ultimate

[12] We have suggested earlier that Volpe was effective on television (he looked like a sincere business man). This view appears to conflict with the view of his advisers that Volpe would not be a formidable debater. This apparent conflict is resolved if we keep in mind the considerable difference between a presentation with a prepared script and an unplanned debate.

appearance on television, three weeks before the election, to answer the charges generally and in his own best style: direct, businesslike, warm, gentle, sympathetic. Even Democrats tuned in to see the monster Ward had depicted. Volpe's winning, reassuring manner could not help but appear favorably—to Republicans, to independents antagonized by Ward, and to some Democrats who had been invited, in a sense, by Ward, to see what simply was not to be seen.

We suggest that the maximal-coverage orientation of the public-relations men may make sense for advertising soap or gum but not necessarily for advertising a candidate for public office. There is evidence, however (Volpe's public-opinion polls), to support the public-relations men's belief that Volpe should attempt to irritate Ward. Given Ward's predisposition to pursue an aggressive and vituperative political style and given Volpe's pollsters' report that Ward's "raucousness on television" was alienating independents, it might be argued that Volpe should have attempted to provoke Ward into further outbursts. However, events proved that Ward had done himself sufficient damage—without additional provocation—to elect Volpe.

The "fact" that Volpe was not a competent debater was not the only reason, according to his brain trust, for his not debating Ward. One adviser summarized the situation as follows:

We felt very strongly about three things. First of all, we felt that Ward was a wily and effective debater with long experience in this area. Second, we felt that we could not trust Ward to debate the issues of the campaign but that he would bring up allegations and charges, as he subsequently did, and that John was not prepared to rebut them without the documents at hand, because considerable research had to be done since John doesn't have the personal correspondence on what he did. He left them in the Department of Public Works files. . . . If, for example, they were going to discuss Ward's 23-point program and John's six-point program, that would have been one thing; but without any knowledge of what this fellow was going to talk about, it was a ridiculous proposal. Suppose he fired an accusation. . . . John would have to have documents to prove this wasn't true, but he would not be prepared to answer and then he'd have to rely on memory. . . . The third reason was that we felt that John had a good image in the Commonwealth and was strong in the Commonwealth, particularly at the time that the debates were being called for because of the scandals, and that it's a basic political reality that when you are strong and you have an advantage you don't give your opponent the same platform in order to make an appearance with you. This, of course, in hindsight, is the tragedy of the Nixon campaign. He provided a platform to prove: one, that Kennedy was no political amateur; two, that Kennedy was much older than anybody ever said he was, and that he could handle himself in the discussion. So all Nixon could get from this sort of thing was a negative result, and I think it played an important part in diminishing the Nixon advantage or whatever advantage Nixon had as he went into this campaign. We were guided by that, too.

Every Volpe adviser we interviewed agreed. They believed that Volpe may have lost the votes of some citizens who feel strongly about the value of face-to-face debates in a democratic society, but they were more concerned about the difficulties of answering Ward's complex charges.

Assuming that the arguments presented by the Volpe brain trust make sense, it is clear that the candidate, in urging the debate, was his own greatest enemy. He was "hurt" and angered by the charges, and he instinctively reacted by wanting to reply to them. His personality, in this instance, ran counter to what was a rational strategy for him. We have discussed other examples of this disjunction between the political style called for by a particular strategy and the personality and consequent political style of the candidate. We have also given some examples of how a rational strategy, developed by a brain trust, could not be put into effect because the candidate had moral or intellectual restraints which were in conflict with strategic needs. The implications of this conflict go beyond problems of political strategy. If a democratic society is to solve its problems peacefully, it is necessary that the political activists place restraints on their behavior, that they abide by certain tacit rules. This may be difficult for a candidate who knows that utopian programs win votes, or for a candidate who understands the political value of smears and false allegations, or for a candidate who knows that votes are to be won by exploiting ethnic, religious, or racial tensions, or for a candidate who knows that he can make political capital by making public certain official documents that legally are not available to him. "Realistic" observers of the political scene are prone to emphasize the ruthlessness of politicians, and political strategists frequently point out that "nice guys finish last." This may be so most of the time, but our examination of these elections indicates that at

least some candidates do restrain themselves, even at the risk of politically irrational behavior, and that some of them are groping toward
some standard of behavior for a responsible democratic order.

$$* \quad * \quad *$$

We have implied at various points in our analysis that the image
of a political campaign as an efficient and highly organized military-
style operation conducted by a professional general staff is inaccurate so far as Massachusetts is concerned. Admittedly, politics in the
Bay State has certain special characteristics due to the massive cynicism pervading the electorate and the cross-pressures of party, local,
religious, and ethnic loyalties. The political situation in Massachusetts, for these reasons, is probably much more unstable than in
most states. Caution should be exercised, therefore, in drawing
generalizations about the nature of political strategy from elections
in this exotic state. Nevertheless, if we are ultimately to understand
and theorize about the problems of political strategy as it is actually
practiced during a campaign, we must begin with an analysis of
individual cases. We suggest, therefore, that the reader regard our
findings simply as one such analysis. Many other studies of political
strategy must be made before we can speak with any certainty on
this subject.

Strategy for the 1960 Massachusetts gubernatorial contest was
formulated in a more or less haphazard manner. Candidates, campaign managers, and public-relations men operated, for the most
part, under a cloud of uncertainty. Many of them were fully aware
of the cynical, petulant, and unpredictable character of much of the
electorate. Some of them sensed that much of their information concerning voter preferences was at best tentative and should therefore
be interpreted with the proverbial grain of salt. Some appreciated
the significance of political style as opposed to the content of platforms or speeches and understood the difficulties of determining what
style would be perceived as attractive. Yet, as many of the candidates
and their advisers admitted, they made some strategic blunders.

What emerges from their comments is a picture of the political
situation as a highly fluid set of forces about which the candidates
had relatively little reliable information and over which they had
relatively little control. Many key decisions were taken by a hap-

hazard collection of people who were forced by circumstances to act quickly and without full information. A Volpe adviser, who is a political scientist, concluded from his experience, "The trouble with most analyses of political behavior by political scientists is that they attribute reasoned working out of things which are not worked out reasonably." Although we have pointed out the chaotic interplay of forces that went into the making of these decisions, the flow of misinformation, and the distortions of the "echo" effect, we feel that the picture of these campaigns presented here still overstructures what actually occurred. For the sake of analysis we have isolated various problems faced by the candidates (money, mass media, the alienated voter) as if they came up separately and were handled in an ordered sequence. In reality, of course, these problems overlap and impinge on one another.

Although in theory it may be easy to detect a strategic error in time to correct it, in practice it is not. In many instances a candidate played right into the hands of his adversary without knowing it. From the vantage point of time, one gets the feeling that in the general election Ward was a puppet whose every move was guided by Volpe. Yet on the day before the election, Ward's key adviser said, "I can't conceive of us losing tomorrow." Although his prediction was wrong, his comments on political strategy as it is actually developed during the heat of a campaign are interesting:

I think that political strategy is much more a makeshift proposition in which you make a general, over-all sense of direction of what has to be done and then constantly try to implement it but do it really quite chaotically, in most campaigns that I know of. I'm sure there are some very professionally run campaigns where money is in great supply and staff people are in greater availability but that isn't typically so and it certainly wasn't true of our campaign. I doubt if it was true of Mr. Volpe's campaign.

I think there were some basic determinations made. They required a strong and vigorous affirmative attack upon Mr. Volpe as Public Works Commissioner, and the conviction of . . . as many people as you can that John Volpe was not individually "the man" equipped by background and training to be a successful governor of the Commonwealth, and two, to tie the Democratic ticket together as a team, recognizing that from Kennedy on down, this was a strong, young, attractive, well-educated group of men with a considerable amount of political experience . . . and that with Kennedy running for president, with the Democratic sweep in the offing, if the Republican attack would at least be blunted, that this should be enough for a victory, and a reasonably safe victory.

I think this was the basic determination, but after having made that I'm sure you can realize that . . . its accomplishment was on a day-to-day basis. There are always, in any campaign, people who . . . tell you that all you're doing is totally wrong and if you'd only do it a different way you'd be sure of victory, and I'm sure that if we lose tomorrow it will be so here. . . . I feel very strongly that once a campaign gets under way it feeds on itself, and you really have to take it to its logical conclusion. You can't shift gears. For example, there are many who would say, maybe a week or ten days ago, that we should have been more positive in this campaign. But a week or ten days ago we couldn't have shifted gears into a positive campaign; you had been positive all during the primary; you had been positive in many of your press releases; but the area of controversy was this area of corruption, . . . and for you to step back at that time would have been in some degree to concede that perhaps these charges had been answered, so that there was nothing to do but to proceed with the attack to its logical conclusion and wind up as we have . . . with a reaffirmation of our ideological differences with Mr. Volpe, which are substantial.

This tendency of a campaign to "feed on itself," which Ward's adviser observed, was also noticeable in the campaigns of Volpe and Peabody. Their campaign strategies were also dictated by an irreversible inner logic. In some cases the directing force was an aspect of the candidate's personality; in other cases, it was a decision taken early in the campaign.

We have been examining the political campaign from the point of view of the candidate because our interest has centered on the problem of political strategy. In the final chapter we shall widen our focus and examine the political campaign as an instrument for crystallizing public opinion and as a technique of educating voters. We shall also consider some of the ways in which the electorate can bring about an improvement in campaigning and in the behavior of public officials.

7.
The Conscience
of Politicians

$*$ $*$ $*$

The great moral problem of American politicians is intellectual honesty. A free society cannot operate unless leaders tell the truth to the led, and when they cease to be honest with each other as well, the fabric of organized society tends to dissolve. For the wheels to turn, words have to be trusted. Life is too short for every statement to be put on paper before a notary and under oath. Montaigne wrote, "We are not men, nor have other tie upon one another, but by our word." Although average levels of honesty among men are higher than ever before, the public need for it from politicians has grown further than the standards of practice have risen.

STIMSON BULLITT[1]

During recent years friendly critics of American democracy have become increasingly concerned with the character of our political campaigns. These writers believe that candidates have an obligation to inform and educate the public by clarifying the "real" issues, presenting factual arguments in support of their programs, and criticizing their opponents calmly and objectively. Elections, they contend, can be meaningful only if voters are given complete, relevant, and accurate information on which to base their decisions. Evidence

[1] Stimson Bullitt, *To Be a Politician* (New York: Doubleday, 1959), p. 141.

gathered from many campaigns, however, indicates that candidates are more likely to offer evasions, distortions, oversimplifications, and appeals to prejudice and pipedreams.[2]

His obligation to the electorate aside, the rational candidate is interested only in maximizing his votes; he will not exert himself to inform and educate the public unless he believes that by so doing he will increase the number of his supporters. However, if the candidates fail to inform and educate the public and so encourage the electorate to make irrational decisions, the consequences for democracy will be serious. In democratic societies, the behavior of public officials will, sooner or later, be affected by the opinions of the more politically active and vociferous minorities in the electorate. As Kelley has pointed out, "If the members of these powerful minorities hold their opinions irrationally, if the demands they make on government are mere whims or prejudices, it is hardly reasonable to suppose that governmental decisions can have either the stability or flexibility that a rational response to the problems of government presupposes."[3]

In this chapter we shall examine this dilemma more closely. We shall then present some of the rules that must govern the behavior of politicians and populace in a truly democratic society. After re-evaluating the behavior of participants in the 1960 Massachusetts gubernatorial elections on the basis of these rules, we shall offer some suggestions for changing the campaign situation so as to compel candidates to fulfill their obligations toward the public.

The Politician and the Voter: Leader and Led

The rational candidate views the campaign solely as a means of increasing his vote. He plans his strategy and guides his behavior in terms of whether a particular move will gain more votes than it will lose. Since the nature of the electoral process in a democratic country forces the candidate to orient his behavior toward the pleasure of the majority or a coalition of minorities, he attempts to determine the preferences and prejudices of the public and to respond to

[2] A thorough review and analysis of this problem is contained in Stanley Kelley, Jr., *Political Campaigning: Problems in Creating an Informed Electorate* (Washington, D. C.: The Brookings Institution, 1960). I am indebted to Professor Kelley's provocative book for much of the argument of this chapter.

[3] *Ibid.*, p. 147.

them. We have noted that the candidate who permits his conscience to interfere with his quest for votes may risk losing the election. Some candidates have refused to exploit ethnic, religious, and racial antagonisms or to make utopian promises despite the apparent rationality of these tactics, but the evidence of many campaigns indicates that most (not all) candidates attempt to pursue a vote-maximizing strategy regardless of moral considerations.

Rational candidates who must compete in constituencies where the party balance is fairly even will spend the bulk of their scarce resources in an effort to convert voters who they believe are undecided. It would be comforting to believe that most of those available for conversion are intelligent and objective persons who expose themselves to the arguments of both parties, weigh them in the balance, consider the good of the larger community (as well as their own), and then vote in terms of the issues. But such is rarely the case. Data collected in two major studies of voting in America indicate that "the changers who moved from one party to the other during the campaign were least interested in the election; least concerned about the outcome; least attentive to campaign communications; last to decide on their vote decision; and most likely to be influenced by personal persuasion rather than political issues."[4] Although the rational candidate must also attempt to reinforce the loyalty of party regulars, who tend to be interested in and knowledgeable about politics, he must direct his main appeal to the relatively uninterested and uninformed voters who are more likely to be available for conversion. Since "from one election to the next, over three fourths of the voters in both [parties] do not change party position,"[5] and since "from two thirds to three fourths of the voters settle on their final vote by the time the political conventions are over,"[6] it is obvious that the rational candidate must devote much of his scarce resources to attempts to convert the group in the voting population that is most likely to respond to ambiguous and simplistic arguments and least likely to check on the accuracy of campaign statements.[7] There is

[4] Bernard Berelson, Paul F. Lazarsfeld, and William N. McPhee, *Voting* (Chicago: University of Chicago Press, 1954), p. 347.

[5] *Ibid.*, p. 345.

[6] *Ibid.*

[7] In those campaign situations in which the proportion of undecided voters is too small to be decisive, it is rational for the candidate of the majority party to ignore the criticism of his opponents and to expound well-worn platitudes in an effort to reinforce the loyalty of party regulars.

a strong temptation, in planning campaigns directed to these voters, not to supply complete, revelant, and accurate information.

The candidate who advances vague, ambiguous, and simplistic arguments may find this practice personally abhorrent, but he will argue, as a political realist, that he is merely giving the electorate what it expects and has become accustomed to. The candidate who slanders his opponent may contend that the electorate is so ethnically and religiously inbred that it will not be offended by the "right" kind of intolerant appeal or the "right" kind of slander and libel. Many practicing politicians thus attribute the "low level" of the campaign to the "low level" of the electorate. The politicians' argument is not very different from that of the indignant reformer who reminds the public that it gets what it deserves. These arguments, however, beg the question of how and why the expectations or deserts of the public have arrived at this "low" state.

We suggest that if a large segment of the public is uninformed, bigoted, and corrupt it is in part the fault of the political leaders themselves. Public opinion does not arise spontaneously from the bosom of the masses. It crystallizes during political campaigns (and at other critical periods) in response to the behavior of political leaders. Millions of Americans whose interest in politics is minimal or nonexistent between elections expose themselves to political propaganda during the last few weeks of the campaign. They can hardly fail to do so because the mass media are full of political messages at this time. Campaigners have a unique opportunity to modify public opinion, since they focus the attention of the public on certain issues, real or imaginary, and on the proposed "solutions" to these issues. By framing the questions, the rival campaigners determine, to a large extent, the nature of the answers. They are the opinion leaders. Although those who compete for political power in democratic countries must respond to public opinion, they may exercise considerable discretion when selecting issues and proposing alternative solutions, because the political ideas of most citizens on most issues are so vague or broad or held with so little intensity. Key writes:

Even on broad issues on which opinion becomes fairly well crystallized, room may remain for choice among a variety of specific actions. Furthermore, translation of opinion into actions of electoral punishment and reward is a tortuous and uncertain procedure. The predictability of electoral response to a particular action remains so uncertain that the avoidance of a sensible decision because it will lose votes is usually the work of a man whose anxieties outweigh his capacity for prediction.[8]

For these reasons, we believe, the low level of campaigning cannot be attributed so easily to the ignorance and prejudice of the public. The low level of controversy between the candidates sustains the illiteracy of the electorate and, in part, creates the political illiteracy of the next generation. This cycle must be broken if we are to have an informed and responsible public opinion and a viable democratic system.

The behavior of politicians during campaigns (and while in office) is obviously a critical factor in democratic regimes. It is important, therefore, to examine the rules that ought to govern the behavior of a political elite dedicated to democratic principles. This normative enterprise will provide us with some criteria for evaluating the behavior of the Massachusetts political elite during the 1960 gubernatorial campaigns.

The Rules of the Game: The Political Elite

Although we have frequently referred to the opinions, preferences, and reactions of voters in Massachusetts, the focus of our analysis has been the attitudes and actions of candidates and their campaign managers, public-relations men, and advisers. According to Key, the quality and stability of the political system depend largely on "the motives that activate this leadership echelon, the values that it holds, the rules of the political game to which it adheres, the expectations which it entertains about its own status in society, and perhaps some of the objective circumstances, both material and institutional, in which it functions."[9]

Political influentials, Key suggests, constitute a subculture with a distinctive system of values and with distinctive standards of behavior. He asserts that the beliefs and norms of these political activists tend, over time, to become strongly rooted in custom and become fundamental determinants of political life. It may therefore be

[8] V. O. Key, Jr., *Public Opinion and American Democracy* (New York: Alfred A. Knopf, 1961), p. 558.
[9] *Ibid.*, p. 538.

worthwhile to consider Key's definition of the value system that should guide the behavior of a democratic elite:

Fundamental is a regard for public opinion, a belief that in some way or another it should prevail. . . . The basic doctrine goes further to include a sense of trusteeship for the people generally and an adherence to the basic doctrine that collective efforts should be dedicated to the promotion of mass gains rather than narrow class advantage; elite elements tethered to narrow group interest have no slack for maneuver to accommodate themselves to mass aspirations. Ultimate expression of these faiths comes in the willingness to abide by the outcome of popular elections.[10]

In addition to these beliefs, the rules of the democratic game require that activists place considerable restraints upon themselves when attempting to exploit public opinion:

Dimly perceptible are the rules of etiquette that limit the kinds of appeals to public opinion that may be properly made. If it is assumed that the public is manipulable at the hands of unscrupulous leadership (and it is under some conditions), the maintenance of a democratic order requires the inculcation in leadership elements of a taboo against appeals that would endanger the existence of democratic practices. Inflammation of the sentiments of a sector of the public disposed to exert the tyranny of an intolerant majority would be a means of destruction of a democratic order. Or by the exploitation of latent differences and conflicts within the citizenry it may be at times possible to paralyze a regime as intense hatreds among classes of people come to dominate public affairs. Or by the encouragement of unrealistic expectations among the people a clique of politicians may rise to power, a position to be kept by repression as disillusionment sets in. In an experienced democracy such tactics may be "unfair" competition among members of the politically active class. In short, certain restraints on political competition help keep competition within tolerable limits.[11]

It is obvious that a long process of acculturation is necessary to produce a political elite that has internalized these values. Political leaders who are willing to place so many restraints upon themselves when their personal advantage might be better realized by violating the rules of the game must be men who have a highly developed moral sensibility. Few political elites have achieved a standard approximating the personal standards of their finest members. Cer-

10 *Ibid.*
11 *Ibid.*

tainly the shoddy state of Massachusetts politics is due in large part
not only to the fact that some members of the elite have violated the
rules of the game but also to the fact that many of them appear to
be unaware that such rules exist.

Since politicians are key opinion leaders, and since public opinion
tends to crystallize during campaigns in response to them, it is important that campaigners give the public an opportunity to make
rational choices. The belief that candidates should help citizens to
make rational voting decisions by providing them with full, accurate,
and relevant information is neither novel nor restricted to writers of
textbooks on American government. Kelley has pointed out that the
courts, the schools, and politicians in their public utterances take the
position that campaigners should inform and educate the public.[12]
He has suggested, and we agree, that "the extent to which rationality
in voting is encouraged . . . becomes the measure of the value of
discussion in campaigns."[13]

According to the theoretical model of democracy developed by
Downs, the rational citizen votes for the party which he believes
will provide him with more benefits than any other. Although Kelley
is not concerned with the process by which citizens compute benefits
and "expected party differentials," he too assumes that

> . . . full rationality in voting would require full information about the
> alternatives to be voted upon, full knowledge of all the effects that would
> attend the choice of each alternative, and a comprehensive and logically
> consistent system of preferences, within which values may be assigned to
> each of these effects. . . . The voter would have to know what it is that
> distinguishes the candidates for a particular office one from another; and
> he would need sufficient information to predict the future consequences
> of these differences for the realization of the purposes he holds to be
> most important.[14]

Although full rationality in voting may never be achieved in practice,
this definition provides a standard for evaluating the meaningfulness
of campaigns and for specifying the conditions which aid or hinder
rational voting.

In a model campaign discussion, campaigners would make clear

[12] Kelley, *op. cit.*, p. 8.
[13] *Ibid.*, p. 9.
[14] *Ibid.*, p. 10.

to voters precisely what they stand for and how and why they differ from each other. A candidate would indicate to voters which issues he considers significant and why, the "resolutions" he proposes and why, and how these "resolutions" could be effected. He would also indicate why his opponent's selection of issues and proposed "resolutions" are irrelevant, inadequate, or unrealizable. A full discussion centering on the differences between the candidates' positions is essential to voter rationality. If citizens are to make rational decisions, the programs of candidates must be offered in good faith, their arguments in support of their programs must be factually accurate, and their criticism of opponents must be made without slander. If voters are to evaluate the relevance and accuracy of campaign discussion, the sources of various bits of information must also be made clear. Kelley suggests the following criteria for evaluating campaign discussion:

Are voters exposed to the arguments of both sides? Does the discussion facilitate the identification of distortions and of false statements of fact? Are the candidates' statements of their views and intentions clear? Do candidates define their points of disagreement? Do campaigners offer evidence for their assertions and give reasons for favoring (or for having favored) particular policies? Are the sources of information clearly identified? If the answers to all these questions are "no," it is difficult to see how such a discussion could be expected to favor rational electoral action. If they are "yes" the probability that it will should be considerably increased.[15]

The Rules of the Game: The Public

We have suggested that if government responsive to public opinion is to flourish, the members of the elite must guide their behavior according to certain rules of the game. Democratic political systems also require that the public possess certain attitudes and behave in certain ways. Analyzing the rules that must regulate the behavior of the public, Key suggests that there are in fact several "publics."[16] Studies of voting behavior broadly classify these publics into two groups: a number of "attentive publics," which are organized and

[15] *Ibid.*, p. 16.
[16] Key, *op. cit.*, p. 538.

which exert pressure on the elite, and an "inattentive public," the great mass of citizens who are little concerned with politics. Although politicians in a democratic society have considerable discretion while formulating public policy, sooner or later they must respond to the more affluent, active, and better organized minorities that attempt to pressure them. If the members of these minorities hold irrational, shortsighted, or excessively selfish opinions, political leaders may be forced to adopt a public policy that is irrational and ultimately self-destructive.

A relatively small proportion of the public is politically active or attentive, although only about one fifth of the electorate is *totally* disinterested, uninformed, and inactive.[17] Although approximately 40 per cent of those eligible to vote in presidential elections and two thirds of those eligible to vote in state primary elections customarily fail to cast a ballot, individuals whose self-interest (and self-interest need not be only economic) is directly affected by a particular area of legislation tend to form a temporary (sometimes permanent) attentive public that seeks to exert pressure on law-makers. Key estimates that "the highly attentive and active public . . . constitutes normally no more than 10 to 15 per cent of the adult population, although at times of crisis far higher proportions may focus their attention on particular actions of government."[18] Because they make their views known to legislators, the attentive publics "play a critical role in assuring a degree of responsiveness of government to non-governmental opinion. For these publics to perform that function, though, an understanding and acceptance of their role must prevail among many people. The belief must exist that it is the public's business to engage in such activities of surveillance and criticism of government."[19] Since the attentive publics customarily contain the most active, knowledgeable, and affluent members of the community, they are in a unique position to compel the elite to conform to the democratic rules of the game. Thus they have the responsibility to oversee the behavior of those in power and to alert the less interested and active to abuses of their rights. In a sense they are the "policemen" of the democratic system.

If the members of the attentive publics are to play the political

[17] See Angus Campbell, Philip E. Converse, Warren E. Miller, and Donald Stokes, *The American Voter* (New York: John Wiley & Sons, 1960), Chaps. 5, 10.
[18] Key, *op. cit.*, p. 546.
[19] *Ibid.*

game according to the democratic rules, if they are to behave peacefully and legally, they must believe that their efforts can ultimately affect public policy, that public policy is responsive to their particular public opinion. If the attentive publics conclude that the elite will not respond to pressure, they may resort to extraconstitutional modes of behavior to accomplish their objectives.

If society is to operate with democratic procedures, belief in the responsiveness of the government to public opinion must also be widespread among the nonattentive segment of the public, even though its members may believe that they have less at stake. If the nonattentive public is to remain loyal to the democratic way of solving conflicts, it must believe that the outcome of elections makes a difference in the ultimate determination of public policy. A large segment of the public must have some sense of political potency, resting on a belief that voting is a significant act, that public officials care about the average man, and that voters do direct and limit the actions of those who govern them. They must also believe that candidates are men of integrity who will make a serious effort to fulfill campaign promises, and that they are interested in the community rather than in themselves alone. If members of the nonattentive public come to feel powerless and cheated, they may withdraw their allegiance from existing parties or perhaps from the system itself. It is even possible that they will resort to violence in an attempt to satisfy their needs and relieve their frustrations. Sooner or later citizens who have democratic values will judge the behavior of those who govern them against their own standard of how governors in a democracy should behave. If the discrepancy is great, they may no longer feel any attachment to the regime.

Public opinion, as we have noted, is formed, crystallized, and altered primarily in response to the perceived behavior of those who govern. If political activists, in their drive for power, exploit the latent or overt fears and hatreds of economic, ethnic, and religious groups, the sense of community that is necessary to democracy may be shattered. Key suggests:

Reckless leaders can disrupt the processes of government by diversionary appeals that weaken or destroy the foundations of national unity. Regimes with tight discipline in the ranks of political leadership—dictatorships, semidictatorships, monarchies—can restrain those who would activate the latent or not so latent divisive animosities of the mass of the people. Democratic elites ordinarily have less capacity to restrain their irresponsible elements. Hence, mass attitudes that yield readily to divisive appeals create special difficulties for democratic orders.[20]

If the leadership echelon, in an attempt to win votes, leads the masses to expect more than can ever be attained or, by a history of abusing public trust, creates in the masses a cynical lack of expectation, disillusionment and alienation result. This may destroy the operating base necessary for democratic regimes.

The Responsibility of the Candidates

The local, national—indeed, the international—image of Boston and Massachusetts politics as a cesspool of corruption, incompetence, and venality did not develop without cause. It grew in response to the behavior of some members of the Massachusetts political elite. Now that we have specified some of the rules of the democratic game, we can re-evaluate the behavior of the 1960 gubernatorial candidates in Massachusetts and assess the degree to which they obeyed the rules. Our purpose in doing so is to explore the causes and consequences of the conflict that may exist between the desire of the rational candidate to get as many votes as possible, regardless of moral considerations, and the rules of the game, which place certain restrictions on the behavior of those who compete for political power.

As we have seen, the long history of corruption among some members of the Republican and Democratic political elites in Massachusetts has alienated a significantly large bloc of the nonattentive public. The stereotype of the politician as a crook is widespread and deeply rooted in Massachusetts. The campaign atmosphere has been poisoned for so many years that corruption is now the only significant issue for many voters. All candidates must deal with it, regardless of their views on other issues. We have noted, for example, that Ward's key adviser expressed considerable anguish about the fact that the Democratic endorsee could not appeal to the electorate on the "bread and butter issues" but was forced to "fight a battle on an arena which the Democratic party never was at its strongest on, the battle of corruption." "Obviously," he added,

20 *Ibid.*

if there were not a substantial concern that people had an innate suspicion of politics and politicians, and on the Democratic side, this would not have had to be the Democratic position; they could simply have taken the New Frontier, New Horizon (Democrats continue the great social-reform movement) and hoped to have won on that.

We sympathize with Ward's expressed desire to debate the "bread and butter" issues in a meaningful and responsible manner. We have noted that he was the only Democratic candidate who presented a carefully researched, articulate, and comprehensive program that actually dealt with the critical problems confronting the Commonwealth. Ward and his opponents, however, suspected that "the issues" would be ignored by citizens who believe that party platforms are mere verbiage. Experience with incumbents has taught many citizens of Massachusetts that platforms are vote-getting devices rather than reliable indicators of the future action of officeholders. If the alienated voter believes that corruption is the only relevant issue, we cannot "blame" Ward or his opponents for attempting to deal with it. There are, however, many ways in which to handle this problem.

There is considerable evidence that the democratic rules of the game meant very little to some of the important participants during these campaigns. For example, every sophisticated politician knows that the position of the names on a ballot may significantly affect the outcome of an election. Ward, as the convention endorsee, was entitled to first place on the ballot in the Democratic primary election. As secretary of state, however, he was legally responsible for the form of the ballot, even if the ballot was designed by someone other than Ward himself, and even if Ward had not approved or even seen the design. Although Judge Paquet did not declare the ballot form to be illegal, there is no doubt that it was arbitrary and unprecedented. Further, the design clearly worked to the disadvantage of three candidates (Magaletta, Peabody, and Piemonte), at least one of whom (Peabody) was regarded by Ward as a serious contender.

In a democratic society, the rules of the game ensure competitors "equality of opportunity" on the ballot. A candidate who violates this rule contributes to the poisoning of the campaign atmosphere and reinforces the cynicism of the alienated voter. Capricious and arbitrary behavior by one candidate is likely to "force" his opponents to retaliate in kind, because campaign strategy is formulated in response to the moves and countermoves of one's opponents. It may be too much to expect self-restraint from a candidate who believes that his opponent has benefited from an infraction of the rules.

It may seem easy for one who has not participated in a political campaign to differentiate "good" and "evil," but the line that separates irresponsible campaigning from shrewd but "legitimate" politicking is often a thin one. According to a key adviser, Ward wished to campaign in a responsible manner—not because he believed "irresponsible" campaigning would lose votes for him, but because he believes in responsible campaigning. Following his victory in the primary, Ward correctly assumed that the key issue in the general election was the rectitude of the candidates. He and his advisers decided, therefore, that it was necessary to challenge Volpe's integrity. The character of candidates is a relevant concern to voters, particularly in Massachusetts, where party discipline and party programs mean little or nothing. A responsible candidate is obliged to criticize his opponent's character if he believes that there is a reasonable doubt concerning his opponent's fitness for public office. The content, manner, and timing of the criticism, however, determine whether or not the criticism is responsible. Ward's advisers insisted that the attack on Volpe had been conducted in a responsible fashion:

Now, typically, if you are going to make charges, you wait until the last week, and then you make the charges in a last-minute barrage, at a time when they are difficult for the other candidate to answer. Even if he tries to answer it he doesn't have time to reach the people to answer it. The charges aren't particularly documented, and . . . frequently those charges have little or no basis in fact . . . and the denial will never catch up with it. It was the feeling that Joe Ward had, and I subscribe to, that if these charges were to be made, especially in view of the fact that Volpe would not debate with him, so that they could be done in face-to-face confrontation, so that they would not look as if they were simply undertaken as a smear, but that they had factual backdrop to them and significance to them, that the proper time to do it, and also to give it enough time to develop an issue and be discussed, was early enough in the campaign that Volpe could answer it, if he wanted to. If he chose to. And that they were documented, sufficiently documented, so that you could answer the obvious countercharge, which was that it was simply a smear, and untruthful.

Irresponsible candidates do make their charges at the last moment, to make it difficult for the victim to answer them fully and to take advantage of the peak interest in the campaign. Irresponsible candidates do slander and libel their opponents on the theory that "the denial will never catch up with it." Ward, on the other hand, did present his charges early in the campaign so that Volpe had time to prepare an answer. He did give Volpe an opportunity to debate the questions, and he did "document" his charges (although we are not in a position to evaluate the validity of the documentation). This, however, does not necessarily mean that Ward's behavior was governed solely by some inner sense of morality or fair campaign practices. The timing of his charges may have been determined by strategic rather than moral considerations. The charges were complex and had to be developed in considerable detail if they were not to appear to the alienated voter simply as the attacks of a cheap politician. The object of the strategy was to put Volpe on the defensive as early as possible. Nevertheless, the fact remains that Ward *did* present the charges in sufficient time for them to be answered. He behaved, in this respect, in a responsible manner. But we must stress the ambiguity inherent in such a situation: if a candidate's object in making attacks early in the campaign is simply to accuse before being accused, then his apparently fair behavior is merely a cover for a basically irresponsible strategy. If the charges are made wholly for strategic reasons and are not valid, the candidate's action must be regarded as profoundly reprehensible.

Another problem in political ethics involves the question of whether or not a candidate has the "right" to advocate an unrealistic "solution" to a public problem simply because it is attractive to a significantly large bloc of voters. Kelly could and did argue that the lottery was favored by large numbers of citizens, as indicated by the response to the referendum on this question. He stated that he was simply responding to the will of the people and that this is what a candidate in a democratic society is supposed to do. Moral questions about gambling aside, meaningful campaigning would require that a candidate support his position with accurate and consistent data so that the public can make a rational choice. Much of the argument advanced by Kelly in behalf of a Massachusetts sweepstakes was, however, patently spurious, as we have seen. We have already noted that political activists who excite "unrealistic" expectations among the masses are preparing the ground for massive disenchantment.

We have also noted that both Peabody and Ward regarded the sweepstakes as an immoral or at least unsound technique for raising revenue. Both of them also realized that the proposal would nevertheless attract a significant number of votes to Kelly. Yet Peabody did not attack the sweepstakes publicly, and Ward's criticism consisted of a vague and general condemnation of Kelly personally. Apparently neither man was concerned with his obligation to inform and educate the public on this issue.[21] But can they be censured for not "raising" the level of campaign discussion when they believed that they would lose votes by doing so?

Where shall the line be drawn between responsible and irresponsible campaigning? If citizens are to make rational political decisions, candidates must publicly discuss the issues without distortion, evasion, oversimplification, or slander. It has been suggested that John Francis Kennedy made few public appearances because he did not want to give the citizens of Massachusetts an opportunity to observe that he was not John Fitzgerald Kennedy. Whatever his motive, it is clear that his failure to expose himself to the public prevented the electorate from learning what, if anything, Treasurer Kennedy stood for and thus made it impossible for them to evaluate his candidacy rationally.

Despite the evidence that most candidates attempt to pursue a vote-maximizing strategy most of the time, regardless of moral considerations, in a few instances candidates in the campaigns we have studied refused to follow a particular strategy for moral reasons, even though they or their advisers believed the strategy to be rational. The candidate who permits his morality to interfere with his drive for votes is behaving irrationally, but democracy can exist only when politicians restrain their behavior. Instances in which candidates restrained their behavior are therefore critical for an understanding of the democratic process. Before we suggest some techniques that might "force" candidates to curb their irresponsible

[21] It is interesting to note that Peabody's brain trust saw the problem in terms of whether or not to "expose" the sweepstakes, whereas Ward's camp saw it in terms of whether or not to espouse the proposal. During the last week of the final campaign, both Ward and Volpe stated publicly that they would not veto a sweepstakes bill if the Great and General Court approved it.

tendencies, it is necessary to examine the conscience of Massachusetts politicians.

The tension and hostility that exist among ethnic and religious groups in Massachusetts and the cynicism of many citizens create rich opportunities for irresponsible and demogogic campaigning. For the candidate with a great desire to win, the temptation to make political capital by exploiting the prejudices and fears of the intolerant, the bigoted, and the alienated is great. We have noted that many strategists, in their "private" calculations, consider tactics designed for this purpose, and that political parties frequently nominate ethnically balanced slates in the hope of attracting the largest possible following. Similarly, speakers at rallies are often selected on the basis of the ethnic and religious composition of the expected audience. It was hardly coincidental that Ward's "distinguished panel of attorneys" included representatives of the major religious and ethnic groups in the Commonwealth, or that Volpe spent much time campaigning in Italo-American communities. This, however, is standard campaign practice, neither surprising nor necessarily irresponsible.

A more significant aspect of these campaigns is that the candidates refrained from openly inciting ethnic and religious hostility. To our knowledge, no candidate disseminated "hate" literature of any kind. The Democratic candidates, unlike many of their predecessors (particularly James M. Curley), refrained from attempting to exploit smoldering resentment by reminding their Irish audiences of the shameful abuses heaped upon their ancestors by Yankee businessmen. Their restraint is particularly notable since Peabody, the only Yankee candidate, was recognized as a strong contender.

We have cited other examples of restrained and responsible campaigning. Ward, for example, believed that he would lose votes to Kelly on the lottery issue. Yet he refused to advocate a sweepstakes, in part because he felt it was immoral and unsound. Although Volpe's advisers were convinced that he would benefit by attacking Furcolo, he refused as a matter of moral principle to attack anyone who had not attacked him. Similarly, most of Peabody's advisers were convinced that he would benefit by making a stinging attack on Furcolo. Yet Peabody reported to the authors that he could not attack Furcolo in good conscience because he agreed with much of the governor's social-welfare program.

Raising the Level of Campaign Discussion

Although some observers believe that Massachusetts politicians tend to campaign in a particularly vicious, slanderous, and destructive manner, the facts of American political life indicate that the candidates in many state and local elections campaign without regard for the morality of their tactics or their obligation to inform and educate the public.[22] Unfair personal attacks are also not uncommon in presidential campaigns. According to the Fair Campaign Practices Committee, approximately 300 pieces of scurrilous literature were circulated during the Nixon-Kennedy contest, at a cost of about $750,000. The total distribution of these items is conservatively estimated at 15,000,000.[23] Analysis of several campaigns indicates that when candidates are unable to criticize the qualifications of their opponents on objective grounds, they will often resort to unfair personal attacks. However, the rational candidate always designs his strategy to fit the demands of the electorate. As we have seen in our analysis of two Massachusetts elections, tactics and platforms that may succeed at one time or in one constituency often backfire at another time or in another area. When voters are politically sophisticated, or when they expect and demand factual discussion of the issues, it is irrational for the candidate to attempt to exploit ethnic and religious tensions or to propound tired political clichés.

As Kelley has correctly suggested:

Strategy is strictly relative to the situation, and some of the characteristic strategies found in American campaigns are a response to conditions that are subject to change. By altering some of these conditions a brand of campaign discussion that will encourage rational voting can be made in the interest of campaigners as well as voters.[24]

Kelley's insight is an important one. Strategy is developed in response to a campaign situation that is affected by a large number of variables. Some of these can be altered by conscious public policy so that a new situation is created in which the candidate who be-

[22] See Kelley, *op. cit.,* Chaps. 5, 6, 7.
[23] Herbert E. Alexander, "Financing the Parties and Campaigns," in Paul T. David, ed., *The Presidential Election and Transition 1960-1961* (Washington, D. C.: The Brookings Institution, 1961), p. 132.
[24] Kelley, *op. cit.,* p. 5.

haves in an unethical manner or who fails to inform and educate
the electorate is likely to lose votes. This is not a matter of appealing
to the conscience, sense of public duty, or good taste of the candidate. It is a matter of "forcing" the candidate to campaign in a
particular way by making it to his interest to do so.

Before we turn to an analysis of some of the factors that are
amenable to change, we must point out that many of the conditions
that affect campaign strategy are relatively fixed. For example, it is
unlikely that America will abandon the two-party system in the
near future; yet this system sometimes "forces" candidates to avoid
discussion of controversial issues and adopt moderate and therefore
vaguely similar programs, thus making it difficult for voters to differentiate the parties and candidates on any meaningful basis. Similarly, the "electoral system, the competitive nature of campaign discussion, and the character of the electorate and of campaigners
are relatively insusceptible to change or change slowly."[25]

Kelley[26] and other scholars have identified several factors that
can more easily be acted on. Campaign discussion, for example,
is affected by the constitutional status of speech and publication.
In most cases, constitutional protection of freedom of speech and
freedom of the press in the United States is so broad that candidates
are able to discuss controversial issues and the "outs" are able to
attack the record of the incumbents in a manner not possible in
totalitarian regimes. The relatively unlimited freedom of speech
and the press, however, also makes it easier for campaigners to
engage in unfair personal attacks. The laws regarding slander and
libel in most states are so meager or vague or unenforceable that
campaigners have little substantive protection against politically injurious false statements made during the course of campaigns.[27]
These laws, however, can be altered to provide greater protection to
the "injured" party. This is one area in which legislation could lead
to a change in the quality of campaign discussion. State and federal
law, for example, could be revised, as Kelley suggests, to provide for

(1) making politically injurious false statements actionable, as well as
false statements that injure reputation; (2) withdrawing the conditional
privilege from false statements contained in reports of legislative proceed-

25 *Ibid.*, p. 155.
26 *Ibid.*, pp. 148-55.
27 *Ibid.*, Chaps. 5, 6.

ings and on other occasions of privileges; (3) making last-minute attacks on a candidate's reputation actionable; and (4) granting candidates the right of reply.[28]

Campaign discussion and political strategy are also affected by the manner in which the press reports the campaign to the public. Candidates, we have observed, are extremely sensitive to the amount and type of coverage they receive from the press. They evaluate proposed strategies partly in terms of what they believe will be the reaction of publishers. Candidates will be less likely to engage in unfair personal attacks if the press permits the "victim" the right of reply or publishes data that make it possible for citizens to evaluate the attacks objectively. Candidates may be less likely to advocate utopian (but appealing) programs if the press analyzes in depth the logic, internal consistency, and factual basis of these programs.

The press can do a great deal to elevate the quality of campaign discussion and campaign ethics, if editors and publishers so desire. Newspapers, for example, could evaluate statements and promises within the context of the candidate's voting record or previous stand on issues. This would require not editorializing but, rather, a review and collation of facts which are not difficult to assemble. Publishers could refuse to print last-minute charges which could not possibly be answered prior to election day. Candidates would probably be less likely to make such charges if they knew that newspapers would not publicize them. Perhaps the most effective technique available to the mass media for raising the level of campaign discussion would be a series of press conferences in which reporters could ask candidates to comment on issues that they have avoided or to clarify or support ambiguous remarks. Newspapers could also experiment with "battle pages" in which rival candidates and parties are given an opportunity, in adjoining columns, to present their case and criticize that of the opposition. Certainly the press can reduce distortion in campaign discussion by noting factual inaccuracies, by providing full coverage, and by supplying missing information. Massachusetts politicians are relatively free to attack their opponents irresponsibly, avoid a reasoned discussion of the issues, or promise pie in the sky because they know that very few newspapers in the Commonwealth have the resources, the courage, or the desire to report the campaign in depth.

28 *Ibid.*, pp. 113-14.

To inform and educate the public, campaigners must clarify their stands on issues, answer the challenges of the opposition, and discuss a variety of subjects, including some that they may wish to avoid. They have little reason to do so given present-day campaign practices. In most campaigns candidates do not confront each other in a formal debate. Rather, they tend to repeat the same speech to partisan campaign audiences who have little desire to raise embarrassing questions, and they talk past each other. They are quite free to distort facts, to smear the opposition, and to advocate the traditional political pieties without fear of contradiction. As Kelley points out:

When the attention of the campaign audience is discontinuous and segmented, campaigners will tend to sloganize their appeals; there will be a great deal of repetition; and ambiguity, evasion of issues, distortion, and irrelevance will be encouraged. When rival candidates address an identical audience that gives them continuing attention, they will be encouraged to clarify their respective positions, they will hesitate to give distorted accounts of events or of their opponents' positions, and campaign discussion will tend to assume a challenge-and-response form. When campaign discussion takes a dialogue form, as in the press conference or the forum, the ambiguity of appeals is reduced; when it assumes a monologue form, as in the typical campaign speech, appeals become more ambiguous. . . .[29]

Although face-to-face debate between rival candidates may degenerate into a mudslinging contest or a discussion of irrelevant and superficial issues, it is likely to force candidates to raise the level of campaign discussion. Direct confrontation gives rival campaigners a unique opportunity to criticize, question, and demand clarification. The debate situation forces rivals to address themselves to the same question, before an identical audience, under conditions in which it is difficult to distort the position of an opponent. In this situation, candidates discipline each other and force each other to discourse in a responsible manner. Perhaps the greatest argument in favor of the debate situation is that it gives each candidate an opportunity to present his cause to many voters who normally would expose themselves only to the propaganda of the opposition. Thus it both ensures the candidates equality of access to the campaign audience and permits voters to compare the merits of campaigners under stress. As Thomson has pointed out, television debates "can take

[29] *Ibid.,* p. 154.

place in full view of the electorate and electronic campaigning can go beyond the reinforcement and rallying of those who already know their preference."[30] Exposure to the propaganda of rival candidates is a prerequisite for informed and rational decision-making by voters.

Some students of politics have suggested that the level of campaign discussion would be raised if the federal and state governments required candidates for certain offices to debate each other on television at public expense. A series of publicly subsidized debates would not only relieve the candidates of tremendous financial burdens (and perhaps free them of obligations to contributors) but might also lead to shorter and more informative campaigns. The equal-time provisions of the Federal Communications Act could be amended to permit radio stations to provide free time for debates between candidates of major parties without incurring an obligation to provide equal time for candidates of minor parties. Television and radio stations could thereby stimulate voter interest and fulfill their public responsibilities at the same time.

We have listed above some of the objective factors that influence the content of campaign communications and the quality of campaign ethics, and we have suggested that many of these factors can be changed. Such forms of political manipulation as bribing voters and stuffing ballot boxes were expected by and acceptable to many voters in the nineteenth century but are now considered reprehensible practices. The public definition of fair play in campaigning is not static. It is the product of sustained cultural conditioning, and it can be altered by those institutions that transmit moral values from generation to generation.

The reforms we have suggested are not likely to be effective, however, until the cynicism of the alienated voter is displaced by a sense of confidence in his choice. Until this change of attitude occurs (it is likely to occur only when public officials are men of honor), rational candidates will conduct low-level campaigns in an attempt to take advantage of the frustration and anger that constitute political alienation.

    [30] Charles A. H. Thomson, "Mass Media Activities and Influence," in David, ed., op. cit., p. 113.

Alienation and Reform

Frequent investigations into the behavior of public officials and the mounting number of indictments and convictions in recent months testify to the displacement of responsible party government in Massachusetts by *quid pro quo* and the prevalence of corrupt practices among officeholders on various levels of state and local government. The result has been the deterioration of the democratic process in Massachusetts, starting at the top, with the elected officials, and infecting many of the most powerful attentive publics. As the elite has come to be responsive only to groups that are willing to buy favors, so that bribe and the fix have come to be regarded as "legitimate" business expenses.

Repeated violations of the rules of the democratic game by members of the elite of both parties and various attentive publics in Massachusetts have caused a large segment of the nonattentive public to become alienated, disillusioned with what they regard as the democratic myth. To some extent, alienation is synonymous with knowledgability, for the alienated voter correctly perceives that some members of the elite care little for the needs and wishes of the larger community, regardless of campaign bombastics, and that members of the powerful "interests" in the state exert an influence out of proportion to their numbers.

A knowledgeable electorate may provide a solid basis for constructive reform movements. Relatively few alienated voters, however, are affiliated with reform groups.[31] Despite their awareness of some very basic facts of political life, these voters are led by their tremendous anger, frustration, and feelings of political impotence to adopt nonrational alternatives. Some of them simply withdraw from political life. Others become prey to unscrupulous individuals or groups that seek to exploit the bitterness of the alienated voter for personal benefit. We suggest that the political expression of feelings of alienation is determined by two factors: (1) the nature of the alienated individual himself, and (2) the nature of the forces

[31] One exception to this is COD, a reform group, composed of Democrats, which has organized many chapters throughout Massachusetts, for the purpose of revitalizing the party structure. COD will support some candidates for the Great and General Court in 1962 and attempt to elect slates to town and ward committees in 1964.

that attempt to take advantage of his alienation. Thus some dis-illusioned members of the electorate characteristically respond to frustration by divorcing themselves from the cause—in this case, political life. Other, more active members seek a solution—perhaps in constructive reform, perhaps in some peripheral, demagogic movement.

Most politicians and members of the attentive publics are aware of the alienation of the masses. We have tried to show how campaign strategists attempt to profit from it by directing their strategies to the emotions rather than the intelligence or knowledge of the electorate. Thus the attacks on corruption, for example, are intended to take advantage of the voter's feeling that "they're all crooks" (except, presumably, the candidate who brings the charges). Similarly, promises of "pie-in-the-sky" are intended to appeal to those alienated voters who still believe that a solution is possible and whose disillusionment with the past performance of elected officials makes them ripe for radical or utopian suggestions. Once in office, however, officials abandon the attempt to involve the alienated voter in politics; on the contrary, they tend to be delighted by his withdrawal. As a state legislator put it:

Many of the old legislators . . . know this alienated-voter philosophy and they figure as long as the voter has this idea and isn't going to really do anything about it, what do we care whether we have a party philosophy or don't have a party philosophy. We just vote any way we want, and maybe I'll give the Speaker a vote this time because I may ask him for a favor next week and the public isn't going to know one way or the other. It isn't going to make a darn bit of difference to the public anyhow what I do.

This respondent made the significant point that cynicism and corruption persist among the elite because "the people that are doing a lot of the complaining" lack the courage or the initiative to challenge the politicians directly. Piemonte's campaign manager expressed essentially the same position when he said:

My theory is that . . . there are different types of political alienation. The type found in the lower-income groups is of the nature of absolute disgust and disinterest with politics in general, a general throwing up of hands and "they are all crooks." Now, the political alienation of the upper-income groups and those that are better off—for example, the suburban group—tends to take a different form, and they become more involved in local issues, like town meetings, but pretty much stay away from becoming involved in urban politics because, again, they are confused. They feel no kind of identification with city politics and they care less to understand it. This in itself is a form of escape because, of course, the leadership that must come for reform has moved to the suburbs. The suburbanites refuse to acknowledge the fact, at least openly, that they themselves possess the ability, the knowledge, the energy, the time, and the money to make a difference in city politics. Instead they pretend a concern for politics on the very local level or on the international level. They are quite concerned about relations with Russia. They are less concerned about the relation of the city to the suburbs, or the city to the state.

The withdrawal of many capable members of the public from the political arena not only gives the politician greater freedom to pursue his private ends without fear of retribution but further entrenches the existing elite.

Where, then, is reform to come from? Surely not from the entrenched professional politicians, who have a vested interest in preserving the present situation. And probably not from the alienated masses, which lack the necessary subtlety, organization, and initiative to bring about a change. There remain three groups which might spearhead reform. The minority party (the "outs") and those attentive publics that are excluded from the prevailing system of *quid pro quo* have powerful, albeit selfish, reasons for desiring a change. Since the two-party system in Massachusetts is not likely to be replaced in the near future, and since the minority party already has the nucleus of a statewide organization, we suggest that it has a greater potential for reform than disgruntled attentive publics. The alienation of the electorate is now focused primarily on the majority party and its professionals. The alienated may therefore be stirred by a powerful appeal to replace the majority party. Alienated voters, however, are likely to remain skeptical until the Republican party has demonstrated by deeds rather than words that it is a meaningful alternative. A Republican appeal to the alienated may stimulate the Democratic party to clean its own house.

In addition to the minority party and attentive publics, a third source of reform may be the "quality electorate"—the amorphous collection of civic-minded individuals and organizations already motivated to seek reform. The latter include, for example, various church discussion groups, Parent-Teacher Associations, nonpartisan political-action organizations such as the League of Women Voters, local taxpayers associations, and registered but dissatisfied members of both parties as well as independents. An organized coalition of these several groups, making intelligent use of the mass media, might be able to effect the re-entry into politics of the alienated public. Such a coalition might form around a particular candidate in a particular election and, if successful, could become permanent. Whatever the genesis of the coalition, it must persuade the alienated masses to abandon their passivity by convincing them that honesty and competence in government can be attained—if honest and competent people participate in politics. Further, it must strive for the institutional reforms that are likely to make elected officials more accountable for their actions. Thus an extension of the governor's term of office to four years would encourage him to develop long-range programs. Similarly, giving the governor the power to appoint his own department heads would not only clarify the line of responsibility but make for more efficient government. By actively supporting candidates who favor these reforms, the coalition might succeed in bringing them about. The reformers might also work to improve the level of campaign discussion by exerting pressure on the mass media to encourage informative campaigning by the means suggested earlier.

A coalition such as we have proposed has enormous latent power, for it consists of potential advertisers in the mass media, potential consumers of governmental services, potential contributors to campaign coffers, and, most important, potential electors of public officials. This power can be harnessed.